*Coalition Politics and
Cabinet Decision Making*

# Coalition Politics and Cabinet Decision Making

**A COMPARATIVE ANALYSIS OF FOREIGN POLICY CHOICES**

## Juliet Kaarbo

The University of Michigan Press
Ann Arbor

First paperback edition 2013
Copyright © by the University of Michigan 2012
All rights reserved

This book may not be reproduced, in whole or in part, including illustrations, in any form (beyond that copying permitted by Sections 107 and 108 of the U.S. Copyright Law and except by reviewers for the public press), without written permission from the publisher.

Published in the United States of America by
The University of Michigan Press
Manufactured in the United States of America
⊚ Printed on acid-free paper

2016  2015  2014  2013    5  4  3  2

A CIP catalog record for this book is available from the British Library.

Library of Congress Cataloging-in-Publication Data

Kaarbo, Juliet.
   Coalition politics and cabinet decision making : a comparative analysis of foreign policy choices / Juliet Kaarbo.
     p.   cm.
   Includes bibliographical references and index.
   ISBN 978-0-472-11824-3 (cloth : alk. paper) —
   ISBN 978-0-472-02834-4 (e-book)
   1. International relations—Decision making.  2. International relations—Decision making—Case studies.  3. Cabinet system—Decision making.  4. Cabinet system—Decision making—Case studies.  5. Coalition governments.  6. Coalition governments—Case studies.  I. Title.

JZ1305.K33   2012
327.1—dc23
                                        2012000980

ISBN 978-0-472-03546-5 (pbk. : alk. paper)

For Ryan, Ellie, and Quinn

# Contents

| | |
|---|---:|
| Preface | ix |
| 1. The Importance of Coalition Politics for Foreign Policy and International Relations | 1 |
| 2. Images of Coalition Politics and Foreign Policy | 13 |
| 3. Assessing Coalition Politics and Foreign Policy: Quantitative Analyses and the Need for Comparative Case Studies | 40 |
| 4. Dutch Foreign Policy: Excessive Compromise in Coalition Politics? | 67 |
| 5. Japanese Foreign Policy: Paralyzed by Coalition Conflict? | 122 |
| 6. Turkish Foreign Policy: Hijacked by Ideological Extremes? | 180 |
| 7. Challenging and Unpacking Images of Coalition Foreign Policy: Implications for International Relations and Governance | 232 |
| Appendix: Goldstein Conflict-Cooperation Scale for WEIS Event Data | 247 |
| Notes | 249 |
| Bibliography | 295 |
| Index | 329 |

# *Preface*

This book grows out of my interest in small groups, disagreement, and decision units. While in graduate school, I worked closely with the development of the decision units framework of Peg Hermann, Chuck Hermann, and Joe Hagan. The small-group unit particularly intrigued me, but I was less interested in groupthink, the better-known and -researched psychological "pathology" that can occur from processes of social influence. I wanted to know more about dissent—its psychological effects, how it was treated socially, and how it was embedded politically in many countries. This approach was partly motivated by my interest in any country except the United States. Our knowledge of foreign policy decision making was and still is myopically based on the U.S. system. When I looked around the world, I saw parliamentary systems and coalition cabinets in many important states. Theories of U.S. policy-making did not easily apply, but little theoretical development had occurred to explain coalition foreign policy.

My doctoral dissertation focused on the conditions of junior-party influence in coalition cabinet foreign policy and examined several cases of German and Israeli foreign policy. Since then, there has been little further development of our understanding of coalition decision making. Binnur Özkeçeci-Taner's book, *The Role of Ideas in Coalition Government Foreign Policymaking: The Case of Turkey between 1991 and 2002,* is the notable exception. As work on the democratic peace developed, bringing back domestic political variables to "mainstream" international relations research, studies included coalitions as a variable to unpack the category of democracy. Despite these efforts, the question of how a divided cabinet affected foreign policy and particularly decision making remained largely untouched. Yet assumptions and normative judgments about coalitions are often made in scholarly literature, in journalist accounts, and even in popular culture. In *The Girl Who Kicked the Hornet's Nest,* the final book in Stieg Larsson's trilogy, Swedish investigators are talking to the prime minister about the secret operations in a former government. One comments, "Let's remember that Fälldin was in power for two separate mandates. Each time, the coalition government collapsed. First he handed over to Ola Ullsten, who had a minority government in 1979. The government collapsed again when the moderates jumped ship, and Fälldin governed together with the People's Party. I'm guessing that the government secretariat was in turmoil during those transition periods."[1] Even in mystery novels, (largely negative) images of coalition politics prevail.

This book seeks to build a better understanding of the effects of coalition cabinets on policy—specifically, foreign policy. I owe acknowledgments and gratitude to many colleagues, institutions, and assistants who offered invaluable support over the life of this project. This book has roots in my doctoral research, and the mentoring provided to me by my dissertation committee—Chuck Hermann, Don Sylvan, and Peg Hermann—continues to inform my thinking and analysis of foreign policy. They have been tremendously supportive of me and my research. Likewise, in the 1990s, the National Science Foundation Research Training Group on Cognition and Collective Political Decision Making (based at the Ohio State University) and the Small Group Initiative created supportive networks that continue to operate informally. Numerous colleagues, discussants, fellow panelists, and students inside and outside of these now extended networks have reacted to the ideas presented in this book. I specifically thank Marijke Breuning, Adam Brown, Cristian Cantir, Esra Çuhadar-Gürkaynak, Will Delehanty, Joe Hagan, Christopher Hill, Baris Kesgin, Jeffrey Lantis, Darrah McCracken, Rachel McGuire, Binnur Özkeçeci-Taner, Brian Ripley, Brent Steele, Paul 't Hart, Bertjan Verbeek, Steve Walker, participants in research presentations at Radboud Nijmegen University and Bilkent University, and members of my foreign policy analysis seminars at the University of Kansas and the Graduate Institute of International Studies in Geneva. Mentoring from social psychologist John Levine, who helped me navigate the literature on minority influence, has been particularly influential in my thinking. Phil Schrodt's support and method advice are also deeply appreciated.

The University of Kansas supported research for this book through General Research Fund allocations, travel funds, a summer fellowship from the Institute for Policy and Social Research, and a sabbatical leave in 2006. I thank the library staff at England's Harlaxton College, who were particularly responsive to my requests for research materials during my sabbatical. The University of Kansas also supported a research leave for a visiting scientist fellowship from the Scientific and Technological Research Council of Turkey in 2009. This fellowship was only possible with the sponsorship of the Department of Political Science at Bilkent University and particularly Metin Heper and Esra Çuhadar-Gürkaynak, to whom I am deeply grateful. Support for professional indexing by Mary Brooks was provided by the Strategic Research Support Fund and the Politics and International Relations subject area of the School of Social and Political Science at the University of Edinburgh. Melody Herr, my point of first contact with the wonderful staff at the University of Michigan Press, gave me exactly what I was looking for in a publisher—professionalism, creativity, and kind support—and I thank her for that. I also want to thank the manuscript's reviewers for their insights, brilliant suggestions, and encouragement, and Kevin Rennells for overseeing the copyediting and page proof stages of production.

Some of the material in chapters 2 and 3 was previously published in Juliet Kaarbo, "Coalition Cabinet Decision Making: Institutional and Psychological Factors," *International Studies Review* 10 (2008): 57–86; and Juliet Kaarbo and Ryan Beasley, "Taking It to the Extreme: The Effect of Coalition Cabinets on Foreign Policy," *Foreign Policy Analysis* 4 (2008): 67–81.

A writer cannot be separated from what is going on with and around her. As research ideas form and are then carried out, life goes on. In this way, this book project has been through quite a bit with me, including pregnancy and childbirth, three moves with the family across the Atlantic and back, parenting, cancer and the effects of cancer treatment, joyful holidays and vacations, broken bones, friendships, marriage, and administrative roles. There is no doubt that this book (and this author) would not have made it through all of this without personal support from friends around the globe and my doctors in Lawrence and in Turkey. Particular thanks go to my good friends, to my students, and to Susan Gronbeck-Tedesco in the office of International Programs at the University of Kansas for all the daily support, inspiration, and motivation they have given me.

My kids, Ellie and Quinn Beasley, provide loving perspective and great joy and celebrated numerous milestones in the writing of this book. My life partner, Ryan Beasley, is more than the coauthor of the quantitative studies in this book. He informs my thinking, supports my research and writing in ways too numerous to count, challenges me to reach higher and do better, and makes me laugh. Ryan, Ellie, and Quinn create the best a small group has to offer, including dissent and disagreement, and I dedicate this book to them.

I

# The Importance of Coalition Politics for Foreign Policy and International Relations

In January 2006, considerable diplomatic attention was focused on the Netherlands. UN secretary-general Kofi Annan, NATO secretary-general Jaap de Hoop Scheffer, NATO supreme allied commander James Jones, and half of the cabinet of the government of Afghanistan met with Dutch leaders and appealed to public opinion in an attempt to influence Dutch foreign policy. The United States also sent numerous officials to persuade the government, and Paul Bremer, former U.S. ambassador to the Netherlands and U.S. administrator in Iraq, unofficially warned the Netherlands that it was risking economic sanctions.[1]

World leaders were asking the Dutch government to agree to NATO's request to send troops to Uruzgan, a southern Afghanistan province considered a Taliban stronghold. This mission was important to Afghanistan. Afghan foreign and defense ministers stressed that the mission was critical to the stability of the post-Taliban government.[2] It was also important to the United Nations and the international community. According to Annan, "No one can afford to see a destabilized Afghanistan," and a Dutch refusal to send troops "would mean that the international efforts in Afghanistan, after all the investment we put in, may not be successful."[3] For NATO, the Dutch decision was a matter of alliance solidarity, already in danger after divisions over Iraq. A no vote would also delay the operation, according to NATO officials.[4] To the United States, the Dutch debate over deployment became "a test of the transatlantic alliance's efforts to find new missions and credibility in the post–Cold War era, and a referendum on President Bush's war against terrorism. U.S. officials consider[ed] the vote a crucial measure of allies' willingness to share the risks and costs of stabilizing troubled nations and combating terrorism."[5] More practically, the

United States was counting on allied contributions to Afghanistan to allow troops to be shifted to Iraq, which was destabilizing.[6]

In the face of this international pressure, the Dutch government repeatedly delayed the decision, and the outcome was far from certain. This delay occurred despite support for deployment from the prime minister, the foreign minister, and the defense minister and the two governing parties that they represented, the Christian Democrats and the Liberals. The delay stemmed from the opposition to deployment from a junior party in the coalition, the D66. This party, which held six seats in Parliament, was critical to the maintenance of the governing coalition's slim legislative majority. The D66 threatened to withdraw from the cabinet over the Afghan troop decision; withdrawal would lead to new elections. The coalition partners finally agreed to defer the decision to Parliament. Parliament supported the deployment after Labour, the major opposition party, shifted from its earlier resistance. In 2010, the Dutch coalition between Labour and the Christian Democrats collapsed over the issue of keeping Dutch troops in Afghanistan.[7]

The two-month delay in the Dutch decision in 2006 and the very real possibility that the Netherlands could have rejected the NATO request stem from the nature of coalition politics. Multiple political parties sharing authority to make foreign policy is an enduring feature of the Dutch political system but is not limited to the Netherlands. Coalition cabinets make many important decisions in international politics, and the parties often disagree over the best course of action for their country. How—and if— these disagreements are resolved can have significant consequences for these countries and for international relations.

This book investigates the effects of coalition politics on foreign policy. It examines conflicting expectations and assumptions concerning foreign policies of multiparty cabinets in parliamentary democracies. Some scholars see coalition cabinets as generally peaceful, given their inherent political and institutional constraints, while others propose that the institutional and political dynamics of coalition politics generate particularly aggressive behavior. Coalition cabinets also raise questions about the quality of decision making. Are these decision units so riddled by conflict that they cannot make foreign policy effectively, or do the multiple voices represented in the cabinet create more legitimate and imaginative responses to the international system? This book unpacks the effects of coalition politics using quantitative cross-national statistical analyses and qualitative comparative case studies of foreign policy made by coalition cabinets in Japan, the Netherlands, and Turkey. I examine existing theoretical assumptions about coalition politics and uncover factors that trigger some outcomes (such as highly aggressive policies) versus others (such as inconsistent and fragmented decision making).

## WHY COALITION POLITICS MATTER FOR FOREIGN POLICY AND INTERNATIONAL RELATIONS

In parliamentary democracies, the authority to make foreign policy and to respond to international developments lies with the cabinet. Despite the diffusion of many governmental powers and the increased number of actors who seek to influence the process in modern democracies, "cabinets certainly matter for policy. . . . The cabinet is where the action is: it performs tasks no one else performs, in that it keeps this conglomerate together and steers it in the direction of a somewhat vaguely perceived national interest."[8] Cabinet government provides a different context than most other political systems.

> Practically no other national executive . . . requires that governmental decisions be taken by ministers as a group. Clearly dictatorial or even authoritarian systems do not have such a requirement, as they rely primarily on the power of one man or at most on a very small inner group. Nor does the requirement of group decision-making exist in the presidential system, which is the other main form of liberal rule besides parliamentary government; in presidential government, the "buck" can be passed, so to speak, to the chief executive, who appoints the ministers, these being in turn responsible to the president alone, who also allocates them the tasks that they will have to undertake. In cabinet government, on the other hand, both in theory and to a large extent in practice, ministers and prime ministers form part of a common enterprise in which they have a share.[9]

This common enterprise is complicated when the decision-making authority is shared by two or more political parties in coalition. Coalitions arise in parliamentary democracies in which the electoral rules, based on principles of proportional representation, and the political landscape create a fragmented legislature.[10] When no single party controls a majority of parliamentary seats, the largest party (typically) must forge a coalition with one or more smaller parties.[11] The coalition partners share the cabinet, dividing up the ministries and the responsibility for making decisions for the country. In multiparty cabinets, the parties are independent political actors—competitors with one another in the electoral process—and frequently disagree on their country's proper response to international situations. According to Lanny W. Martin and Georg Vanberg,

> parties that participate in a coalition are engaged in a "mixed motive" game. On the one hand, they have reason to cooperate with their partners to pursue successful common policies. On the other hand, each party faces strong incentives to move policy in ways that appeal to party members and to the constituencies on which the party relies for support. . . . In short, the policy and position-taking incentives of coalition parties continually put them in competition with one another.[12]

How competition and policy disagreements are resolved can be critical to countries' foreign policy choices. While disagreements within an executive are certainly not unique to coalition cabinets, the dynamics of bargaining and decision making differ since the continued existence of the executive is at stake. If the policy dispute is not settled, the coalition may dissolve.

Historically, coalition cabinets have ruled in important states at critical times in international relations. The French Third Republic in the late nineteenth and early twentieth centuries, Great Britain during the world depression of the early 1930s, the French Fourth Republic during post–World War II settlement and early decolonization, Israel during all the Arab-Israeli conflicts and peace processes, West Germany throughout the Cold War, and India when it declared itself a nuclear power were all governed by multiparty cabinets.[13] Coalition cabinets occur with great frequency in Western Europe. Indeed, coalitions are the dominant form of governance in this region. More than 60 percent of post–World War II Western European governments have been multiparty coalitions; in some states, such as the Netherlands, Germany, and Italy, cabinets almost always contain more than one party.[14] Today, many key states are parliamentary democracies, and many of them are ruled by more than one party. Not limited to Western Europe, coalition cabinets are found worldwide. Table 1.1 provides a snapshot of states that were recently governed by multiparty cabinets. The shared authority in the cabinet can be particularly important for foreign policy, as the key cabinet posts for foreign, defense, or trade policies are often split across party lines.

Although coalition partners do not always disagree on foreign policies, they frequently do, and such disagreements can affect policy-making, policy choices, and international politics. Even when these states are highly constrained by their international context and other domestic political factors, the effects of other international and domestic factors are funneled through the coalition, since cabinets have the ultimate authority to make foreign policy. The parties may even disagree on the nature of those other factors. One party may stress a threat in an international system, another

**TABLE 1.1. Coalition Cabinets in the Twenty-first Century**

| Western/Northern Europe | Central/Eastern Europe |
|---|---|
| Austria | Albania |
| Belgium | Bulgaria |
| Denmark | Croatia |
| Finland | Czech Republic |
| France | Estonia |
| Germany | Hungary |
| Iceland | Latvia |
| Ireland | Lithuania |
| Italy | Macedonia |
| Luxembourg | Moldova |
| Netherlands | Montenegro |
| Norway | Poland |
| Portugal | Romania |
| Sweden | Serbia |
| Switzerland | Slovakia |
| United Kingdom | Slovenia |
| **Asia/South Pacific** | **Middle East and Africa** |
| Australia | Cyprus |
| Bangladesh | Israel |
| India | Lebanon |
| Japan | South Africa |
| New Zealand | Turkey |
| Mongolia | |
| Sri Lanka | |

*Source:* Most information for this table was based on yearly cabinet summaries reported in the *European Journal of Political Research*. Additional data was found through searches in *Asian Survey* and Factiva.

*Note:* Coalition cabinets governed these countries at least once between 2000 and 2010.

an opportunity. One party may see constraints with little room to maneuver, while another is willing to challenge those constraints. One party may focus on the international game, to use Putnam's metaphor, another on the domestic game.[15]

I do not argue that other factors—such as the nature of security threats, economic interdependence, culture, history, and public opinion—are unimportant in explaining the foreign policies of countries governed by coalition cabinets. The full range of external and internal sources of foreign policy certainly is potentially causal in every case. Consistent with the decision-making approach to foreign policy and international politics, I argue that these other factors affect foreign policy only by how they are filtered through the decision-making authority—the coalition cabinet.[16] The cabinet in these states is the funnel through which other conditions are interpreted and evaluated (or not) and acted on (or not). I ask how the division of authority across multiple parties affects that process and its foreign policy outcome.

When political parties within a country disagree on foreign policy, it is clear that these other factors are not automatic determinants. As Rathbun notes, "Parties 'defend the national interest,' but different parties define the national interest in different ways. The national interest is not given objectively. . . . Parties contest the national interest."[17] If an ally is pressuring a state, for example, and the parties disagree about the proper response, that pressure is not a rationally determined, objective cause for the resulting foreign policy (even if the state caves in to the external pressure). If it were such an objective cause, then all parties would respond in a similar fashion with similar preferences. Likewise, if the public actively opposes a policy and the parties still disagree, then it cannot be argued that the public opposition was the sole cause of the policy (even if the state conforms to the public's desire). These other factors are often very important in the conflict between the parties—parties often cite external pressure and internal opposition as reasons to support a policy—but the conflict itself still matters and is not predetermined.[18] Furthermore, even if all other sources point to the likelihood that one side will prevail, the disagreement between parties may have other politically significant consequences (such as loss of prestige in the international community, side payments on other policies, new elections, or political instability).

Of course, not all foreign policy disagreements in cabinets occur along party lines—they may instead have individual, bureaucratic, or intraparty factional bases. But political ideology and partisanship are important and overlooked sources of policy disagreement. Schuster and Mair find this gap in the literature puzzling:

> Although the partisan hypothesis is widely examined, discussed, and usually affirmed in Comparative Politics and Comparative Economics, it is neglected in Comparative Foreign Policy Analysis and IRs [international relations]. Studies that explicitly examine whether the "color" of a state's government makes a difference for its external behavior in comparative perspective are very rare, even though disagreements between parties over foreign policy issues are quite common and often as fiercely debated as those about domestic issues.[19]

Rathbun's book is an uncommon exception that directly examines the role of partisanship in foreign policy. Specifically, Rathbun argues that "parties articulate and implement very different policies in the areas of humanitarian intervention and European defense cooperation due to their different ideological fundamentals. This proposition calls into question the assumption of consistent national approaches to international affairs that has long been the dominant tradition in the policy literature."[20] Although some observers may suggest that the end of the Cold War has increased partisan differences, parties in states that were presumably highly constrained by the international environment had key disagreements over many foreign policies, including "high politics" issues throughout the Cold War era. In West Germany, for example, the Social Democratic Party disagreed with the Christian Democratic Party regarding relations with East Germany and détente with the Soviet Union during the "Grand Coalition" in the 1960s.[21]

This book's focus on partisan and ideological conflict within coalition cabinets is consistent with the current attention to ideational factors in international relations theory.[22] Rathbun argues that little synthesis exists between those international relations theorists who focus on ideas and those who focus on domestic politics and domestic political institutes. For Rathbun, political parties bring "ideas through the front door."[23] Özkeçeci-Taner, one of the few other researchers to investigate coalition politics and foreign policy, also connects partisan disagreements and the importance of ideas.[24] Specifically, she argues that political parties are a primary medium for the expression of ideas, that the impact of ideas is most visible when there is political discord, and that "coalition governments present a potential venue for analyzing and operationalizing how the 'battle of ideas' at the decision-making level" influences foreign policy."[25]

Indeed, when the policy conflict falls along party lines in coalition cabinets, how that disagreement is resolved or left unresolved can be important for the country's foreign policy and, indeed, for the government's stability and legitimacy. Coalitions are relatively fragile forms of government. Strøm reports that single-party cabinets that hold a majority of votes in Parliament last substantially longer than coalition cabinets that control a majority. A plurality of coalition cabinets terminate because of government disunity—47 percent of the time—while single-party cabinets with a majority in Parliament resigned due to internal disunity only 5 percent of the time.[26] States ruled by coalitions make important choices in world politics—choices that affect, for example, NATO, the UN, the EU, development policy, and aid. In this book, I examine how shared authority across political parties affects these choices.

## HOW COALITION POLITICS AFFECT FOREIGN POLICY: COMPETING IMAGES

How coalition politics affect foreign policy is an important question unresolved in the field of international relations and in the study of foreign policy, despite existing and prevalent assumptions about the effects of coalition politics by policymakers, journalists, and scholars alike. Indeed, even though this topic is rarely the direct subject of investigation,[27] several alternative images about coalitions appear in the scholarly literature. These expectations concern both the type of foreign policies these governments are likely to choose and the quality of decision making that is associated with coalitions. The expectations are connected to larger theoretical debates regarding the role that institutions, accountability, and group processes play in foreign policy, policy-making processes, and effective governance.[28]

There are two prevailing images of the type of foreign policy that coalitions are expected to follow. The dominant view is that coalitions should be particularly peaceful in their foreign policies since the presence of multiple parties and more vigilant legislatures constrains leaders from taking aggressive, militant actions. This logic falls from the institutional explanation of the democratic peace—the more built-in constraints in democracies (via checks and balances, multiple viewpoints, and accountability), the more peace-loving domestic forces can constrain war-prone leaders. Indeed, some observers have argued that coalition governments are among the most constrained democracies and thus should be the most peaceful toward others.[29] Other scholars, however, propose that coalitions may be more aggressive to compensate for domestic political weakness and uncertainty. A diffusion of responsibility in coalition cabinets may also lead them into conflict, as it is difficult for the public to hold any single party accountable. Aggressive foreign policy could also come from junior coalition partners that hijack the policy-making process. By relying on smaller, often more ideologically extreme junior parties to make the coalition, moderate senior parties often find themselves vulnerable to blackmail or other strategies of influence by their coalition partners.

In addition to the question of how aggressive or peaceful coalition foreign policies are, there are competing expectations relating to conflict that occurs within coalitions, which can significantly influence the effectiveness and legitimacy of policy-making and the stability of governments. One image holds that coalitions are so immobilized by conflict between the parties that they produce fragmented action, if any action at all. Coalitions are often accused of taking too long to make decisions and of making excessive compromises that result in avoiding controversial issues to maintain the fragile government. Concerns about ineffective policy-making imply that these cabinets produce poor-quality policy outcomes and contribute to the instability of political systems. While some observers see partisan conflict within coalition cabinets as dangerous, others see the built-in multiple advocacy as ideal, contending that many coalition cabinets are quite stable and that the multiple voices in them can produce more legitimate politics and better decision-making processes. Junior partners, for example, are natural devil's advocates, thereby preventing premature closure on an alternative. Whether multiple advocacy creates excessive infighting relates to the enduring question of how government should be organized to produce effective policy-making, sound judgment, successful outcomes, and political stability. Indeed, debates about constitutional design and reform often revolve around these understudied assumptions about the effects of coalition governance.[30]

## ORGANIZATION OF THE BOOK

This book closely examines the theoretical expectations about how coalition politics affect foreign policy, investigates these images with a multi-methodological strategy, and uncovers the conditions under which these expectations prevail. The next chapter unpacks these images from the literature. I examine both political-institutional and psychological perspectives that underlie the competing expectations on the type of foreign policy that coalitions are likely to produce (peaceful or aggressive) and the associated quality of decision making (ineffective or legitimate and creative). Chapter 2 also reviews previous research that speaks to these expectations, including work on coalitions in the subfield of comparative politics, and argues that this research is limited in various ways. Although this book focuses on foreign policy, its conclusions may contribute to our understanding of cabinet policy-making more generally.

Chapter 3 presents original quantitative, statistical analyses designed to overcome the limitations of prior studies that have compared the international conflict behaviors of coalition cabinets to the conflict behaviors of single-party cabinets.[31] One analysis examines whether coalitions are generally more moderate or extreme in their foreign policies than are single-party governments. Although the distinct features of coalition politics affect foreign policy (more broadly defined than just conflict behaviors), there is no theoretical justification for coalition politics to promote either more peaceful or more aggressive policies. Rather, this analysis suggests that coalition politics promote more extreme foreign policies by coalitions—both more peaceful and more aggressive.

The findings on extremity and commitment are noteworthy, given that prior research confounded institutional and policy explanations when looking at the content of policies pursued by coalitions. However, these results do not tell us why coalitions might be more extreme in their foreign policy behavior. This project's second quantitative study examines some of the reasons why coalitions might be more moderate or extreme in their general foreign policy behavior by comparing cabinets for the junior party's ideological orientation, the number of parliamentary seats the coalition controls, and the number of cabinet parties. The findings suggest that coalitions with more parties are more extreme and more conflictual, that coalitions with more parliamentary support engage in foreign policies involving higher levels of commitment, and that coalitions with ideologically conservative junior parties engage in more cooperative foreign policy.

Chapter 3 also presents the qualitative, case study design for this book. While the quantitative studies provide an indication of general trends, are a straightforward examination of the institutional effects of coalition politics across a broad range of foreign policy, and unpack different institutional effects, they do not tell us much about exactly how aspects of coalition politics—fragile nature, junior party influence, and so forth—play out in decision making. Many of the alternative expectations about coalitions turn on key conditions that evolve during policy-making. Only with a case study approach can we examine those process variables, so I complement the quantitative analyses with in-depth comparative case studies of foreign policy decisions by coalition cabinets in the Netherlands, Japan, and Turkey. Chapter 3 discusses the case selection, sources, and structure of the case studies.

Chapters 4, 5, and 6 present the case studies by country. Each chapter begins by introducing the themes and the common explanations of the country's foreign policies, engaging the foreign policy literature for each state. Dutch foreign policy themes include principles, profits, and peace. More traditional explanations—such as size of the country and moralism in its political culture—are best complemented by domestic political explanations, particularly after the 1960s, when the domestic political landscape changed and the foreign policy consensus was challenged. Throughout this time, coalitions have been a constant feature of Dutch government.

Explanations of post–Cold War Japanese foreign policy have focused on debates between realists, who argue that Japan is very conditioned by its international environment, and constructivists, who point to the importance of culturally based notions of Japanese identity. Others argue that structural and cultural factors are either amplified or hindered by domestic political conditions, including the rise of coalition government in the 1990s.

Turkish foreign policy after the end of the Cold War has been characterized by new threats and opportunities and by significant changes in domestic politics. In addition to conventional explanations based on material interests and international structural imperatives, scholars of Turkish foreign policy have focused on the importance of history, ideology, and national identity and more recently on the role of domestic political actors. Like Japan, Turkey was governed by multiparty cabinets throughout the

1990s, and the political parties represented a range of orientations on Turkey's role in the world and its relationships with others.

Each country chapter also reviews the actors in that country's foreign policy and establishes the importance of the cabinet vis-à-vis other political players. I then review how coalition governments have been covered in the literature on the country's foreign policy. The general images of how coalition politics affect foreign policy resonate in commentaries on Dutch, Japanese, and Turkish foreign policies. Dutch foreign policy has been portrayed as excessively driven by consensus. Japanese foreign policy in the 1990s was criticized for being paralyzed by partisan differences. The dangers of ideological hijacking are applied to Turkish foreign policy. Yet few studies have directly addressed the effect of coalition politics on the foreign policies of these states.

Each country chapter includes four case studies of partisan disagreement about foreign policy. In each case, I present the background and significance of the issue, the positions of key players, the decision-making process and final decision, and an analysis of the role of coalition politics. Each country chapter concludes with a summary of how the expectations on coalition politics and foreign policy played out across the country's cases. The final chapter reviews the conclusions from the case studies, organized around the competing expectations of content (peaceful versus aggressive) and decision-making quality (poor versus effective) and the theoretical arguments underlying these expectations. It identifies the key factors associated with the different processes and outcomes. I conclude with suggestions for the study of coalition politics and foreign policy specifically and international politics more broadly. I also outline implications from this research for policy-makers—both inside and outside of coalitions—and for more general questions of governance and political diversity and dissent.

## 2

# *Images of Coalition Politics and Foreign Policy*

What effect, if any, do coalition politics have on the foreign policy choices of parliamentary democracies? International relations scholars have offered alternative images of the foreign policies pursued by multiparty cabinets. These images are typically based on a political or institutional logic, but parallel reasoning can be found in the social psychological literature on small-group decision making. The few research efforts that have examined these expectations have produced mixed results and are rather limited, both theoretically and empirically, in their scope. Images of coalition politics are not confined to the type of policies chosen by multiparty cabinets. Expectations about the quality and effectiveness of coalitions, also based on political and psychological perspectives, are commonly stated but rarely investigated. International relations scholars have largely ignored research on coalitions in the subfield of comparative politics. This literature is informative but also limited in its treatment of decision making and policy outputs.

### COALITION CABINETS IN THE STUDY OF COMPARATIVE POLITICS

Research on cabinets and coalition governments in the subfield of comparative politics is the place to begin for insights into how coalition politics affect foreign policy. Indeed, comparativists see coalitions as a separate area of study based on the differences between coalitions and single-party cabinets.[1] As Blondel and Müller-Rommel note, "Ostensibly at least, the distinction between single-party government and coalition government would seem to have a significant effect on the characteristics of cabinets: in some respects at least it is indeed the *summa divisio* among cabinets. It has been regarded as such by many observers and practitioners for a number of decades."[2] Frognier agrees: "Of the general variables that might help to account for differences in cabinet decision-making processes, the single-party/coalition distinction is the one that appears intuitively to be the most important."[3]

In response to the significance and distinctiveness of coalition governance, a vibrant field of research on coalition cabinets has arisen.[4] This scholarship has traditionally focused on the characteristics of the political system that give rise to coalitions, coalition formation (the birth of coalitions), coalition durability, and coalition termination (the death of coalitions). We know, for example, that certain electoral formulas (such as plurality systems) are less likely to produce coalitions than are others.[5] Research on coalition formation has examined party size, ideology, institutional constraints, and past coalition behavior and has revolved around the question of whether parties are generally "policy-seeking" or "party-seeking."[6] From analytical formal models and systematic empirical research that includes these explanatory variables, analysts can fairly confidently predict the number of parties, the size of the coalition, and the composition of the parties in the coalition.[7] Coalition formation research has also focused on how cabinet portfolios are distributed and on the nature of coalition agreements forged at the beginning of the cabinet's tenure.[8] Research on coalition durability tells us that oversized coalitions are the most durable of all cabinets, followed by single-party majority and minority cabinets. Minimum winning coalitions are only slightly less durable, but minority coalitions are the most short-lived of cabinets.[9] And from the work on coalition termination, we know that "governments that are seriously polarized on major issues tend to be relatively short-lived."[10] Defection by at least one party is a common occurrence in coalitions.[11]

While the research on coalition formation and termination is voluminous, considerably less is known about the life of coalitions between birth and death and the effects on government policy, topics that are central to this book's investigation.[12] Baylis notes that "there has been some interest in the conditions that facilitate the 'endurance' or maintenance of coalitions over time, but very little attention has been accorded to the precise nature of leadership and decision making within coalitions or the character of internal power relationships among the participants in a coalition."[13]

Andeweg referred to the study of cabinet decision making as "terra incognita."[14] Little attention has also been devoted to policy outputs. Warwick argues that

> the lion's share of the empirical work on parliamentary governments has focused . . . on the composition and survival of governments. This is not because composition and survival matter more; indeed, a good case could be made that their value largely depends on the implications they bear for policy. Rather the greater attention these matters have received largely relates to the fact that they are readily measurable. The tasks of determining which parties entered a government, how portfolios were distributed among them, and how long the government survived in office are minuscule compared with those of measuring its policy output.[15]

Addressing the gap in our knowledge of the decision-making processes in coalition cabinets is important because it provides the link between coalition formation and coalition termination and is the immediate input to policy outputs.[16] Not only can policies deviate from the coalition agreement that is reached at the time of formation, but coalitions often dissolve as a consequence of internal disagreements.[17] Therefore, what goes on in the life of the cabinet—how parties manage conflict and negotiate political and policy disagreements—is critical for a full understanding of coalition cabinets, their policy choices, and democratic stability and governance.

Some exceptions exist to this lack of attention to the policy-making processes and effects on coalition policy. Recent work has come in two forms: analyses of cabinet life focusing on the nature of party conflict in coalitions, and more policy-oriented studies on government agenda, economic policies, and the effects of coalition agreements on subsequent policies and policy-making. An example of the former is Müller and Strøm's edited volume on coalition governments in Western Europe.[18] In addition to coalition formation and termination, each country chapter covers coalition agreements and discipline, policies, and other features of governance. The volume offers some conclusions on coalition decision making. It finds, for example, that coalitions employ a variety of conflict management mechanisms in decision making and that variation occurs within countries and within similar institutional structures. Müller, Strøm, and Bergman followed up with another edited volume that examined these issues more topically and cross-nationally. They argue that the four phases of coalition politics—formation, governance, termination, and elections—should be conceptualized as interconnected in a "life cycle."[19]

Another research effort that examines cabinet decision making is *Governing Together*, edited by Blondel and Müller-Rommel.[20] This book explicitly compares single-party cabinets with coalition governments and includes a survey of cabinet ministers as well as a survey of newspaper coverage on cabinet life to investigate the role of structures, parties, and individuals in cabinet decision making and the limits of collective governance. This book focuses on conflict and its management. The surveys demonstrate, for example, that coalition cabinets tend to experience more internal conflict than do single-party cabinets and that conflict increases with more parties in the coalition.[21]

Recent research in comparative politics has also focused on policy effects of coalition governments. For example, Lanny W. Martin challenges the assumption that coalition policy-making is characterized by departmental jurisdictional boundaries, or ministerial government.[22] He argues that the incentives to renege on promises made in coalition agreements, especially if they require major concessions to partners, mean that parties cannot risk allowing ministers to independently set policies within their portfolios. Based on his analysis of bills introduced in Parliament by government coalitions, Martin concludes, "Initiatives dealing with issues that are more attractive to the cabinet as a whole tend to be introduced earlier on the agenda, while those dealing with relatively unattractive issues tend to be postponed. Thus, the policy agenda produced by coalition governments appears to be organized in a fashion that accepts the policy goals of coalition members."[23]

Other comparativists have examined the substantive policy effects of coalitions. Although Gallagher, Laver, and Mair state that "the politics of coalition appear to have a moderating effect on public policy outputs,"[24] specific studies have found that coalitions produce more extreme spending policies. Bawn and Rosenbluth, for example, argue that "coalitions of multiple parties in government negotiate less efficient logrolls than [do single-party cabinets] because policy decisions, which reflect the preferences of the coalition partner that cares most about the policy area, externalize more costs than would occur within single-party government. This argument implies that the greater inefficiencies of multiparty coalitions should show up as greater government spending when there are more parties in government."[25] Bawn and Rosenbluth find support for this argument: as the number of parties in government increases, so does the portion of the countries' gross domestic product for which government spending accounts.[26] Similarly, Iversen and Soskice find that in multiparty proportional representation systems, center parties are likely to ally with parties to their left and redistribute more than in two-party majority systems in which center-right parties typically control a majority of the cabinet.[27] This work builds on an earlier study of the policy effects of West German coalitions by Hofferbert and Klingemann.[28] Their analysis of party platforms, coalition agreements, and government spending finds that a junior coalition's platform, rather than the senior party's platform or the coalition agreement, best predicts government spending in most policy areas, including defense spending.

Overall, the research on coalition cabinets in comparative politics can serve as foundation for an investigation of how coalition politics affects foreign policy. Studies on coalition formation and termination provide the context for decision making, and the few studies on policy-making and policies give more direct clues about how differences between parties are negotiated. Although this book focuses on foreign policy, its conclusions may apply equally to domestic policy-making and thus address a very large gap in research on cabinet government. Existing expectations about coalition politics in international relations are largely divorced from this research in comparative politics and offer a separate set of images of coalition cabinets and foreign policy.

## COMPETING IMAGES OF COALITION FOREIGN POLICY: PEACEFUL OR AGGRESSIVE CHOICES?

The dominant image of coalition cabinets in the study of international relations is that they produce particularly peaceful foreign policies, compared to nondemocratic governments, presidential democracies, and single-party cabinets in parliamentary systems. Consistent with the logic of the democratic peace, peaceful policies stem from the constraints inherent in coalition politics. In the institutional explanation of the democratic peace, constraints are common in democracies (via checks and balances, multiple viewpoints, and accountability) and allow pro-peace domestic forces to prevent war-prone leaders from engaging in international conflict.[29] Democratic peace theorists Maoz and Russett contend that democracies governed by coalition cabinets have the highest level of domestic constraints.[30]

The institutional constraints on coalition cabinets stem in part from the high levels of conflict or even the potential for conflict that can occur among the multiple coalition partners. The risk of bringing down the government and facing new elections is ever-present if all parties do not support the policy; this risk arguably constrains decision makers. According to Ripsman, "Electoral systems based upon single-member constituencies will afford greater autonomy than those employing proportional representation, since the latter favor a multiplicity of parties and less stable, coalition governments. Coalition governments require the executive to consult more parties and avoid unpopular policies that might split the government."[31] In addition, because of their inherent weakness, coalitions may be more vulnerable to parliamentary involvement, adding more actors into the decision-making mix.[32]

All of these constraints arguably translate into more peaceful policies. According to Auerswald,

> Premiers in coalition governments will only reluctantly use force. They must pay particular attention to achieving immediate success or risk a parliamentary revolt, especially if the governing coalition is fragile. With unexpected elections always a possibility should the government coalition dissolve, the legislature will be especially vigilant of the premier's success or failure in international conflicts, hoping to capitalize domestically on the premier's international failure. The more fragile the coalition, the more frequent these unexpected or unscheduled elections, and the more incentive for premiers to contemplate armed conflict only when assured of success.[33]

Auerswald argues that coalition politics constrained the French in the 1956 Suez Crisis:

> French prime minister Mollet was accountable to a governing coalition as fragile as it was broad ideologically. For that reason, he had domestic reasons for hesitating before using force unless sure of quick success. His coalition partners would defect at the first sign of failure given the growing public discontent with French North African policy and the fact that new elections might improve their standing in a new government. . . . Should

the crisis come to blows, Mollet's coalition partners would defect at the slightest hint of stalemate or failure given public dissatisfaction.[34]

Accordingly, only when the Israelis came on board, providing aircraft and military bases and increasing the chance of success, could Mollet pursue an aggressive pro-intervention foreign policy.[35]

Elman focuses on the necessity of broad support and compromise in coalition cabinets as the underlying factor promoting peace. She argues that "self-serving imperialist groups are less likely to be successful in hijacking state policy in a coalitional parliamentary system where proportional representation requires parties to cooperate in order to form a government. In such cases, the demands of a narrow class or sectoral interest group will be diluted in favor of policies that command the support of all parties in a ruling the ruling coalition."[36] Elman sees these constraints operating in the Israeli cabinet in the late 1970s and 1980s. "Following the 1977 Israeli elections, the Likud party, and its dominant Herut faction, had to share power with more moderate minority parties in a coalition government—a development that stymied the Likud's foreign policy extremism."[37] Elman then lists specific examples of policies moderated by coalition necessities and argues that the 1982 invasion of Lebanon, an aggressive policy, was a result of changing coalition dynamics that diminished constraints.[38]

The competing image of coalition cabinets is that they are unconstrained and more aggressive. Aggressiveness purportedly comes from three sources—unaccountability, political weakness, and hijacking by extreme junior partners. In terms of accountability, Prins and Sprecher propose that because of the multiple parties in the cabinet, coalitions are fairly unaccountable: "With coalition governments, the voting public may be less able to attach responsibility to any one party for policy failures. Presumably then, coalition leaders would have greater flexibility in their handling of foreign affairs."[39] Hagan argues that coalitions can operate in "constraint-free" environments.[40] And Stinnett, in his study of Israeli foreign policy, finds evidence that prime ministers pursue oversized coalitions to increase their flexibility to respond to the external environment.[41]

Coalition governments may also engage in more aggressive behavior as a result of their inherent institutional weaknesses. This logic is consistent with diversionary theories of international conflict.[42] According to Hagan, "The literature suggests that even the most unstable coalition may try to act on major foreign policy issues in order to demonstrate its ability to cope with policy crises and thereby achieve some legitimacy at home.... In effect, because of their political fragmentation and vulnerability, these weakened actors were often compelled to deal with the most difficult issues in order to legitimize themselves."[43] Coalitions in the French Fourth Republic, for example, sought greater legitimacy through their foreign policies.[44] Moreover, "the relatively higher level of domestic uncertainty that surrounds coalition cabinets may . . . encourage greater risk-taking behavior."[45] In addition, a coalition's weakness and instability may allow a subset of the coalition to operate without constraints and control foreign policy. As Peterson argues,

> Governments under the [French] Third Republic often were very weak and dependent on elite coalition building to make domestic policy and even to remain in office. Nevertheless, the minister of foreign affairs typically enjoyed significantly greater freedom of action within his own substantive arena than his colleagues did in their respective areas of expertise. The foreign minister's independence derived in part from the governmental instability that defined the Third Republic. France had seventy different governments from 1871 to 1931, and on average a cabinet lived no more than ten months. If only by comparison, the management of the Quai d'Orsay was stable, changing hands only thirty-seven times in seventy different governments. The relative stability amidst turmoil gave the foreign minister a nearly free hand in shaping France's external relations, especially during an acute conflict.[46]

Finally, aggressive foreign policy behaviors could also come from junior coalition partners' ability to hijack the coalition and push it toward conflict. As Elman notes, "In less majoritarian democracies, such as presidential and coalitional parliamentary systems, groups in favor of war will be better situated to push the state down that road, even if the executive favors a more moderate approach."[47] Because the senior parties, which are often center-of-the-road catchall parties, might have to rely on smaller, often more ideologically extreme, junior parties to maintain a majority of seats in Parliament, they are vulnerable to blackmail by these partners; if the senior party refuses to bargain with its junior partner, the latter may defect from the coalition. Junior parties that are critical to the maintenance of a coalition's control of a parliamentary majority are in a particularly good position to use this interdependence and to have influence disproportionate to their size.[48] Junior parties, for example, tend to control more ministries in the cabinet then their size alone would predict, and their positions are a better predictor of many policy outcomes than are the positions of the senior party or the coalition agreement.[49]

Junior partners can use a variety of strategies to influence foreign policy. In addition to threatening to leave the coalition, junior parties can threaten to disrupt cabinet processes, to create outside pressure on the senior party, and to engage in whistle-blowing to discredit the senior party in a political scandal. Junior parties may also use the threat to collapse the coalition. In effect, they may argue that if they do not get influence on the issue, they will lose their electoral support or they will be consumed by intraparty factionalism. In other words, they can capitalize on their weakness if the senior party needs the junior parties to remain viable partners.[50] Junior parties can also make promises. They can, for example, trade support for an issue that is more important to the senior party in exchange for influence on a particular policy. Israel's National Religious Party, for example, gave its support for the 1979 peace treaty with Egypt in exchange for control over subsequent autonomy talks with the Palestinians.[51]

Strategies based on manipulation of the decision-making process are also available to junior parties that can manipulate procedures—how and where the decision is made—to try indirectly to affect the policy outcome. According to Maoz, "manipulation of decisions differs from persuasion or other direct attempts to influence choice outcomes. Whereas manipulation focuses on structuring the group decision-making situation in a manner that assures success, persuasion entails direct attempts to influence (or pressure) individual decision makers into changing their preferences."[52] A number of tactics can be used to this end. Junior parties might, for example, try to alter the composition of the decision-making group so that it is more favorable to their position. Doing so can involve excluding opponents (not informing them of the meeting time, holding a meeting when they are away, and the like). Junior parties can also try to move the decision group to a forum that includes allies. And junior parties can seek to shrink the decision group to balance junior party–senior party representation more than is found in the full cabinet, such as in "coalition talks" between the party leaders. The Free Democrats, a long-time junior partner in West German coalitions, frequently used this tactic.[53]

Junior parties can also work to change the explicit or implicit decision rule away from a focus on majority rule to one on consensus or unanimity, thus ensuring their input and approval. Finally, junior parties can try to get policies adopted incrementally so that in each decision their influence does not look so great but the cabinet ultimately endorses their position wholesale, an outcome the senior party might otherwise have rejected out of hand.[54] Procedural manipulation is an especially attractive and effective tool for junior parties because it takes less status and authority to initiate these changes than substantive changes.[55]

*Quantitative Research on the Peacefulness of Coalition Cabinets*

Several recent quantitative studies have investigated whether coalitions are more peaceful than other types of cabinets and governments. Given the conflicting expectations on the possible effects on foreign policy, it is not surprising that the empirical evidence is decidedly mixed. In support of the proposition that coalitions breed aggressive foreign policy, Prins and Sprecher found that coalition cabinets were more likely to reciprocate behavior in militarized interstate disputes than were single-party parliamentary governments, and Glenn Palmer, London, and Regan found that coalitions were slightly more likely to become involved in international disputes.[56] Conversely, Ireland and Gartner as well as Reiter and Tillman found no difference between single-party and coalition cabinets in dispute initiation, and Glenn Palmer, London, and Regan and a recent study by Clare found no difference between single- and multiparty cabinets in dispute escalation.[57] Leblang and Chan also found no difference between single- and multicabinets in war involvement but found that proportional representation electoral systems, which are often associated with coalitions, significantly damper a country's war involvement.[58]

The mixed results in these studies may stem from a couple of methodological and theoretical limitations. First, progress in research on the effects of coalition politics on foreign policy has been hindered by the tendency to focus too narrowly on conflict-related dependent variables rather than on more general foreign policy behavior. Because many studies follow in the tradition of the democratic peace, these research investigations into institutional influences on foreign policy have focused on conflict initiation and escalation, paying less attention to the wider variety of foreign policy behaviors in which governments typically engage. Such conflict-based dependent variables are problematic for at least two reasons. First, during times of conflict and crisis, disagreements within governments may be most likely to be suppressed or minimized.[59] Second, conflict and crisis behavior is a fairly narrow slice of the broad array of foreign policy behaviors in which states engage.

The past analyses have another limitation as well. Almost all of them hypothesize that coalitions are more peaceful than single-party cabinets, based on the democratic peace logic, and compare the aggressiveness or peacefulness of these different governments. Such analyses confound an institutional explanation with the parties' positions. In the expectation that coalitions are more peaceful, for example, the argument is that multiple parties and legislatures constrain the country from aggressive policies. This idea assumes that the constraining parties want peace and the main party wants conflict, but the reverse could be true. In other words, the same constraints that supposedly operate in coalitions could constrain a peace-prone prime minister, for example, from pursuing a more peaceful policy.

The alternative image has a similar flaw in its logic. The expectation that coalitions are more conflict-prone because they are using conflict to divert attention away from their fragile political situation or because they are being hijacked by an ideologically extreme junior partner also confounds institutional dynamics with positions. A fragile government could pursue a very high profile yet peaceful policy to divert attention. And an ideologically extreme junior partner that wants peace could hijack the cabinet in the peaceful direction. The Green Party, as a junior party in the German coalition in 2002, arguably pushed the cabinet, not just constrained it, toward a more peaceful position vis-à-vis Iraq in the lead-up to the U.S. invasion.[60]

Consequently, it is difficult to expect coalitions to be either generally peaceful or generally aggressive without knowing the preferences of the coalition actors. I agree with Elman that "structure alone does not account for war propensities—we need to specify actors' preferences before structure can tell us anything."[61] Without knowledge of the specific actors constraining policy choices and their substantive position on those policy choices, predicting specific policies will be difficult. In the only study that takes into account the ideological position of outlier parties, Clare found that coalitions with right-wing outlier parties are more likely to initiate disputes than are coalitions with far-left outlier parties.[62]

Yet institutions such as cabinet structure may still have an independent effect on foreign policy. Structure may tell us something about the nature but not the direction of coalition foreign policies. There are two possibilities based on the competing theoretical expectations. If one follows the logic that coalitions are vulnerable to hijacking by extreme junior parties, are largely unaccountable, and seek legitimacy in risky foreign policies, one would expect extreme behaviors, with coalitions choosing both more aggressive and more peaceful foreign policies than single-party governments choose. Alternatively, if one follows the logic that coalition politics constrain both dovish and hawkish prime ministers, one would expect moderate behaviors and coalitions to adopt middle-of-the-road policies.

*Parallel Psychological Perspectives on Coalition Cabinet Policy-Making*

The images of coalitions as pursuing peaceful, aggressive, or extreme foreign policy are largely based on political or institutional factors inherent in coalition cabinets and parliamentary democracies. When policy is made in parliamentary democracies, it is certainly made within the particular institutional and political context of the governmental cabinet and party system. Yet policy-making is also conditioned by a variety of social and psychological factors that influence the process. While the institutional context is significant for understanding the behaviors of coalitions, cabinets—as groups of individuals—are affected by group-level processes as well. Moreover, the institutional design of coalition cabinets can enhance certain group effects. Indeed, social psychological research on group processes offers parallel explanations for why coalition cabinets may make extreme choices—particularly peaceful, particularly aggressive, or both.[63]

Cabinet members meet and make decisions in the context of a small group. "In cabinet government . . . , both in theory and to a large extent in practice, ministers and prime ministers form part of a common enterprise in which they have a share."[64] Coalition cabinets meet the definition of small groups because they are "small-scale social units where political leaders, officials, experts, and . . . representatives from political parties. . . . meet, enact their respective roles, exchange information, argue, exert and experience influence, and somehow arrive at . . . decisions."[65] Although cabinet members are certainly affected by their outside ties to the bureaucracy, political parties, and Parliament, they also form a collective decision unit that creates its own internal dynamics.

As a small group, coalition cabinets are susceptible to the dynamics that often occur in small-group settings. One of the most researched effects of the group context is polarization. Over the years, numerous studies have found that groups are more than the sum of their parts, as they tend to make more extreme and more cautious choices than their individual members indicate that they prefer before engaging in group discussion.[66] While earlier research focused on the "risky-shift" tendency, assuming that groups are more risk-prone, later studies have demonstrated that the shift occurs in both directions, risky and cautious, leading to the more general term *group polarization*. Polarization means that "the average post-group response will tend to be more extreme in the same direction as the average of the pre-group response."[67] Evidence for group polarization comes from studies conducted in more than a dozen different countries and from a wide range of research on attitudes, jury decisions, ethical decisions, judgment, personal perception, and risk taking.[68] Polarization seems to be a general phenomenon, applicable to all types of groups. Although the research on polarization in social psychology has rarely looked at institutional characteristics that might enhance group polarization, polarization may be more likely in certain institutional settings, such as coalition cabinets. Indeed, the institutional explanations for extreme foreign policy behavior by coalitions parallel the most common psychological explanations for group polarization (see table 2.1).

Similar to the argument that coalitions take risks because the public is less able to blame one party for policy failures, group polarization can arise from the sense that responsibility is diffused in the group setting. "According to the responsibility diffusion explanation, in group decision-making contexts responsibility and accountability for consequences is diffused among group members. This reduces fear of failure, and thereby decision makers have incentives to make riskier decisions."[69] Vertzberger argues further that "foreign policy decisions are particularly susceptible to the consequences of risk sharing because they are decisions made for others (the na-

**TABLE 2.1. Parallel Explanations of Polarization in Coalitions**

| Institutional-Political Perspective | Psychological Perspective |
|---|---|
| Diffusion of accountability | Diffusion of responsibility |
| Diversion from domestic weakness and uncertainty | Stress from domestic weakness, excessive desire for cohesion |
| Blackmail by extreme parties | Persuasion by assertive members, minority influence |

tion, or a particular group within it). When choosing for others, people tend to prefer more cautious decisions than when they make decisions for themselves. . . . However, when decisions for others are made by a group, the tendency toward risk avoidance is less pronounced because failure can be shared with others so that anticipated personal responsibility would be reduced."[70]

Parallel to the notion that extreme foreign policy in coalition cabinets stems from their inherent weakness and need to divert attention with risky policies, polarization may also be explained by the psychological uncertainty and stress that politically weak coalitions face. Janis has argued that a stressful political environment can lead to groupthink, or excessive concurrence-seeking. According to Janis, provocative situational contexts that include high stress from threats external to the group and temporary low self-esteem induced by recent failures can create in the group an illusion of invulnerability, self-censorship, and pressure on dissenters, among other symptoms. These phenomena can lead to defective decision making, including poor information searches as well as failures to completely survey alternatives or to reexamine rejected alternatives. Such groupthink can involve polarization if groups initially concur on an extreme position; groupthink processes reinforce this choice.[71]

It may seem that coalition governments are not likely victims of groupthink because they promote differences of opinions and often involve disagreement. Yet Metselaar and Verbeek contend that "when the survival of the government is threatened and coalition partners estimate that the government's downfall may produce serious negative electoral consequences or may otherwise harm party interests, they may engage in feverish consensus-seeking."[72] They point out that the political pressures on the Dutch government in the early 1960s help to explain the groupthink symptoms in the cabinet's deliberations regarding the conflict with Indonesia over West New Guinea. Furthermore, the desire for cohesion, which coalitions often lack, may be most dangerous. Indeed, in a review of the experimental research on groupthink, Brown suggests that "maybe it is only when groups are desperately seeking to manufacture unity that they become prey to the concurrence-seeking defects that Janis identified; having once achieved it, the pressure for unanimity will be more than outweighed by the security it provides to allow criticism and dissent."[73] In effect, because of internal conflict and external problems with legitimacy, coalitions may be particularly vulnerable to polarization via groupthink.

Finally, the explanation that coalition foreign policy is a product of hijacking by junior parties finds parallel expression in the persuasion explanation of group polarization. According to Brown, persuasion, or informational influence, is probably the most accepted explanation of polarization.[74] This explanation suggests that "discussion generates arguments predominantly favoring the initially preferred alternative, including some persuasive arguments that the typical subject has not previously considered. Thus, a 'message effect' evokes response change resulting from new cognitive learning."[75] Persuasion also turns on characteristics of the proponent of the message.

> Group members with more radically polarized judgments and preferences invest more resources in attempts to exert influence and lead others.... The more self-confident and assertive members of the group are very often capable of communicating expectations that eventually their position will prevail.... These expectations may act as a powerful incentive for those who are undecided and are waiting for indications concerning which way the wind is blowing. Correctly or incorrectly, these members interpret assertiveness as a cue and throw in their support. This triggers a self-fulfilling prophecy resulting in majority support for the more polarized position.[76]

Junior parties, often more ideologically extreme than their senior partners, may be the source of these "radically polarized" preferences that influence others. While the political-institutional explanation of junior party influence turns on these actors' ability to threaten the coalition's viability or to logroll their preferences into policies, social psychology offers insights regarding the strategies junior parties can use by drawing from research on minority influence, which has been a vibrant and productive area of investigation for more than three decades.[77]

Until the 1970s, social psychologists assumed that influence largely traveled one way—from majorities to minorities. Minorities were considered targets but not sources of influence, whereas majorities were considered sources but not targets. The famous experiments conducted by Stanley Milgram, in which subjects were convinced to administer shocks, often in extreme amounts, showed that individuals were very obedient to authority.[78] Early and repeated studies by Solomon Asch showed that a majority could fairly easily convince a minority that a blue-colored slide, for example, was green.[79] Majorities influenced minorities to comply via societal threats, rewards, and appeals to social norms. Some social psychologists were concerned, however, about the assumption that minorities were only passive, conforming agents, acted on by powerful majorities, reasoning that a consideration of social change rather than social control led to the inescapable conclusion that minorities do influence majorities—that is, what were originally deviant views can ultimately prevail.

Serge Moscovici was one of the first to argue that social change requires minority influence.[80] Moscovici was motivated by an interest in revolutions—social, political, academic, scientific, religious, and philosophical in nature. In his 1976 book, *Social Influence and Social Change*, Moscovici wrote,

> We have evidence that non-conformity and marginality entail the harsh experiences of insult, ostracism, or even persecution in the defence of a belief, behavior, or area of knowledge. But the rewards are great. Otherwise one would not have seen so many religious, political, artistic, and scientific figures and subgroups taking the risks that they have, and braving severe pressure for such long periods—and finally succeeding in carrying through major changes.[81]

Moscovici turned Asch's studies around (sometimes referred to as the Asch-backward paradigm) to have a confederate minority declare that a blue-colored slide was green, for example. Moscovici noticed that sometimes (8 percent of the cases in the original study) the majority adopted the minority's (wrong) view, so he set out to investigate the conditions under which minorities were influential. As Brown notes, "The figure of eight percent may not be very startling . . . but it must be remembered that this was achieved by a deviant minority against a majority twice its size."[82]

Moscovici's ideas were based on the assumption that social influence inherently involves conflict and that minority influence differs from majority influence. He proposed a "dual-process" model whereby the process of social influence is qualitatively distinct depending on the target (majority/minority) and the source (majority/minority). Specifically, Moscovici and his colleagues argued that when majorities influence minorities, the conflict is social, and minorities comply, changing their position publicly but not privately. When minorities influence majorities, in contrast, the conflict is cognitive—it makes the majorities think and the majority convert (actually change their position), although the conversion is private and delayed, since aligning with a "deviant" minority in public is not desirable.

The most robust finding in Moscovici's research and the studies it has inspired is that consistent persuasion, demonstrating resolve and commitment, is one key to minority influence (though it is not as important to majority influence). According to Moscovici's conversion theory,

> When a minority expresses a deviant view using a behavioral style that expresses confidence and consistency, the majority group member wants to understand why they (dare) do this. In trying to understand what the minority apparently understands, a cognitive conflict is brought about and the group member, in trying to comprehend the deviant position, validates it. ... [T]he process of reconsidering one's own point of view, and the thoughtful consideration of alternative views, results in changing the (cognitive) basis of the original opinion: "real" change, not contingent upon the power of the group and its presence, but based on new ideas and cognitions. This "real" influence will be indirect rather than direct.[83]

Thus, the social psychological perspective would expect that a junior party in a coalition, even if it is completely lacking traditional political power sources, may be able to persuade other cabinet members of its position merely through consistent argumentation. Junior parties can also adopt other tactics to make their position look more credible and display commitment, both of which are important for psychologically based persuasion.[84] They can, for example, convey the impression that they arrived at their position autonomously—say, by taking a stand against their constituency. They can also argue that they have special expertise on an issue or frame the issue in a way that highlights their expertise and jurisdiction. They may also invoke the saliency argument—that is, that the particular issue has been more significant to them and to their party than it has been to the senior party.

Recent social psychological research has investigated the role of socially constructed representations in group settings and minority influence. According to this perspective, actors' positions are rooted "in a shared conceptual system (e.g., beliefs, values, assumptions, logic). The more widely shared a particular system is, the larger the potential pool of targets of influence who will recognize and accept the substance of a persuasive message. ... In this sense, 'correctness' is a social construction."[85] This notion of widely shared conceptual schemes, or shared task representations, may be critical to understanding minority influence.

> When a shared task representation does exist, asymmetries in the social influence patterns are expected, with factions favoring the alternative consistent with the shared representation being more influential than those arguing against it. However, these asymmetries will not necessarily follow "truth" in some absolute sense, but only truth in relation to the shared representation.[86]

One example of such asymmetry that favors minority influence comes from a study by Tindale, Sheffey, and Scott that found that minorities advocating risky alternatives were more influential when the problem was represented to the group in terms of loss, consistent with prospect theory.[87] A status quo bias may exist so that minorities blocking change may be more influential than minorities advocating change.[88] Shared representations may also extend beyond the group as minorities who advocate positions that are accepted by a majority outside the group or in line with the current zeitgeist are more likely to have influence.[89] And, finally, junior parties might try to frame the issue at a higher level in terms of constituency support, higher moral values, or policy principles that are shared by the entire coalition.[90]

Junior coalition partners, of course, are rarely completely powerless, as are the minorities in social psychological research, and a number of political-strategic techniques are available to junior parties beyond persuasion. But even when junior parties make threats, promises, or otherwise engage in "rational" bargaining and negotiation to influence the cabinet, a variety of social psychological factors can influence the effectiveness of these strategies. The personalities of the party leaders, for example, may affect cabinet negotiations, as may the degree of compatibility of the two or more personalities bargaining with one another.[91] Other individual differences such as negotiators' motivational orientations (cooperative, individualistic, or competitive) and images of self and others may also influence bargaining.[92] Perceptions of the intentions, credibility, capability, commitment, goals, and values of the other and the others' positions are also important, and a variety of cognitive, attributional, and motivational biases bound the rational processing of information and information exchange in negotiations.[93] More recent research on the social psychology of negotiation focuses on negotiators' mental models, the role of emotion, and the influence of ethical standards. Such research has also examined negotiations with more than two players and indicates that the greater complexity in multiparty settings increases the likelihood of cognitive simplification.[94] Multiple actors may also be affected by social relationships, not just interests. For example, "negotiators tend to form coalitions with those who have been allies in the past, even if better partners exist."[95] Thus, the use of threats and promises, which are often made by junior coalition partners, involves a number of social psychological factors.

This review of social psychological research suggests additional explanations of extremity that may occur in coalition cabinets. Coalitions, as small groups, are susceptible to group dynamics. A social psychological perspective is not competitive with an institutional one. Rather, it can provide clues to the underlying mechanisms linking the institutional context to policy-making and policy choices. The idea that social psychology can serve a complementary function is supported by psychological research that mirrors recent developments in foreign policy analysis. Since the psychological and the institutional perspectives focus on similar phenomena but do so from different angles, they can, in combination, enhance research in this area. For this research project, the social psychological perspective reinforces the expectations investigated in the following chapters.

## COMPETING IMAGES OF COALITION GOVERNANCE: POOR OR EFFECTIVE DECISION MAKING?

In addition to the question of how aggressive or peaceful coalition foreign policies are, prominent expectations are related to how conflict that occurs within coalitions can significantly influence the effectiveness and legitimacy of policy-making and the stability of governments. The issue here relates to the enduring question of how governments should be organized to produce effective policy-making, sound judgment, and successful outcomes. Specifically, the question of the effects of many voices in the executive on the quality of decision making dominates the normative judgments of coalition cabinets. While some see the multiple advocacy built into this form of governance as ideal, others see inherent dangers.

Although there is no consensus on the criteria for evaluating the quality of decision making in groups such as cabinets,[96] the quality of decision making by coalitions has been judged in three primary ways. The first two concern the process by which decisions are made. The rational decision-making perspective includes fairly accepted criteria for high-quality decision making: a survey of objectives and alternatives; a thorough search for information; assimilation and processing of new information; reconsideration of originally rejected alternatives; evaluation of the costs, risks, and implications of the preferred choice; and development of implementation, monitoring, and contingency plans.[97] When the decision-making process does not conform to these benchmarks, the process is seen as defective or even pathological. The Bay of Pigs invasion, for example, has been judged as a "fiasco" partly because policy-makers did not follow these rational procedures.[98] While rationality provides one normative standard for assessing decision making, processes are also judged by democratic principles. If the decision-making processes are inclusive, representative, consensual, and transparent, for example, then political values associated with democratic governance are met.[99]

The third way that quality is judged is by the outcome. Foreign policy decisions are often judged as high quality if they advance the national interest and if they avoid or decrease the chance for conflict.[100] There are problems, of course, in the objective assessment of the national interest and whether it was advanced. Easier to assess is the level of aggression in the policy, but not all observers agree that highly conflictual foreign policy necessarily implies a low-quality decision.[101] At a basic level, the outcome is seen as good if it effectively addresses the issue. If the government fails to act or acts inconsistently so that it does not deal with whatever problem it is facing, it is seen as ineffective. Government policy or the lack of a policy that creates unwanted and unintended consequences such as political instability are also judged negatively.

How do coalition cabinets fare on the various criteria for judging the quality of the decision-making process and the outputs produced? The dominant image of coalitions is quite negative: The multiple voices in the cabinet contribute to nonrational decision-making processes and produce outcomes that at best do not effectively address national problems and at worst spark political instability.[102] In terms of their policy-making processes, coalition cabinets certainly attract criticism.[103] Coalitions are often accused of taking too long to make decisions, making excessive compromises, and exhibiting excessive conflict. These poor policy-making procedures are supposedly the source of bad policy outcomes—primarily inconsistent, fragmented action or deadlock. While some scholars expect coalition cabinets to have more conflictual foreign policies than single-party cabinets (and there is some evidence to suggest that such is indeed the case), others studies have failed to find a relationship between cabinet type and the level of conflict in foreign policy.

The poor decision making associated with coalitions is usually related to the processes already discussed and to the underlying institutional conditions. Coalitions, for example, are often thought to avoid considering all alternatives and engaging in thorough information searches because they are hijacked by the narrow interests of small, junior coalition partners. In addition, because junior partners often possess veto power over policies, decisions require unanimity, which can produce a variety of poor decision-making processes. Charles F. Hermann summarizes the "pathologies" associated with unanimity: "It can produce long delays as the members struggle to settle their differences and achieve closure. If meaningful agreement remains elusive, the group produces either deadlock or vague generalizations that disguise unresolved divisions."[104] Similarly, Destler argues that the presence of multiple advocates in a policy-making group can lead to "the worst forms of bureaucratic political practices and outcomes—minimal compromises, deference to bureaucratic rivals in their fields of expertise, [and] continuation of contradictory courses of action by different agencies."[105] According to Gaenslen, norms of unanimity can also undermine democratic processes by stifling underlying conflict and political dissent.[106]

The breakdown of the decision-making process in coalitions can lead to numerous negative policy and political consequences. Indeed, one image of coalition cabinets is that they produce very little if any coordinated policy because they are so immobilized or deadlocked by their circumstances.[107] As Prins and Sprecher argue, "In a coalition no single party has the ability to unilaterally direct foreign policy decisionmaking, and there may not be enough of a shared interest between the coalition parties to generate and sustain a long-term foreign policy objective."[108] Elman agrees: "Political stalemates are characteristic of coalitional parliamentary governments in general. . . . Tough foreign policy trade-offs must be swept under the table in order to maintain fragile coalitions made up of diverse and contradictory bases of support. Since coalitional governments can be easily dismissed by legislative censure, there is an institutional incentive for cabinets to choose the foreign policy path of least resistance."[109] Indeed, coalitions are often accused of taking too long to make decisions and of making excessive compromises that avoid controversial issues to maintain the fragile government. Concerns about ineffective policy-making imply that these cabinets produce poor-quality policy outcomes and contribute to the instability of political systems.[110]

The expectation that coalition cabinets are immobilized is strongly rooted in historical examples from the French experience. Indeed, "a primary theme in studies of the foreign policy of the French Fourth Republic is the pervasive political constraints inherent in its succession of unstable, multiparty cabinets," which created incoherent and ineffective foreign policy programs.[111] Ripsman, for example, argues that French settlement policy after World War II was "paralyzed" by "the public and parliamentary pressure on the government—which government documents frequently acknowledged—and the fragile cabinet structure in a multiparty Assembly, which gave dissenting ministers the ability to withdraw their parties from the cabinet and topple the government."[112] The French Third Republic experienced similar foreign policy problems as a result of coalition politics. "In France, it was the Third Republic's coalitional parliamentary system that generated middle-of-the-road policies instead of the prompt, decisive action called for by external exigencies. Lack of agreement between the various coalition members [led] to immobilism."[113]

Case studies of Italian coalition cabinets also stress *immobilismo*, passivity, paralysis, and weak commitments in foreign policy as a consequence of the diffusion of authority in the executive, and similar conclusions have been offered to explain directionless foreign policies during the West German Grand Coalition of the 1960s, Japan in the 1990s, and several Dutch coalition cabinets.[114] Gallhofer and colleagues confirm this expectation more systematically in their study of Dutch cabinet decision making. In their content analysis of cabinet meeting records, they found that disagreement in the group was likely to result in incremental action. They concluded that "this striving for consensus and minimal action . . . seems to be a substitute for good quality decisionmaking (i.e., decisionmaking based on consequences and probabilities)."[115]

Thus, poor decision-making dynamics may produce poor policy and poor governance. Concerns about the policy implications of unstable and conflict-ridden coalition government often surface. Forecasting the emergence of the first-ever coalition in India, one observer warned, "It will . . . be foolhardy to think that we can afford to experiment with coalitions at the national level. One can easily imagine how a coalition with a slender majority would not be able to tackle problems like that of terrorists and subversion in Punjab."[116] Another critic of coalition governance writes that "such governments are often reluctant to make unpopular decisions because of the resistance of some coalition partner. The Palestinian problem in Israel will probably never be solved unless Israel's electoral law is changed or extraordinary foreign pressure is exerted."[117] For these reasons, many argue that majoritarian electoral rules and two-party systems are preferable to proportional representation rules and multiparty systems.[118]

While some observers see the partisan conflict within coalition cabinets as ineffective and even dangerous, others contend that the conflict arising from the multiple voices found in coalitions in parliamentary systems is more representative, is consistent with democratic principles, and can produce more legitimate policies and better decision making.[119] Blondel and Müller-Rommel argue that the time in which coalitions were seen as inherently unstable and ineffective has passed and that "major virtues have now been found in coalition governments. Far from being regarded as 'aberrations' or 'pathological' developments, they have started to be admired for the self-restraint that they require on the part of their members."[120] Furthermore, "it seems apparent that the cabinet system, far from being unable to provide leadership to the nation in an effective manner, seems better adapted to the requirements of modern liberal-democratic government than other systems in that it is more flexible and that it ensures better coordination among the various elements of the political chain."[121] In his discussion of Turkish politics in the early 1960s, Dodd notes some trade-offs regarding coalition government:

> Whether the coalition period was successful depends on the criteria by which it is judged. A single-party government might have governed more positively and have got more done, but would it have provided sufficient opportunity to represent, and meet, the many political demands that were made during this period of re-settlement after the revolution? The coalition system did not in fact break down, which meant that there was no successful challenge to the democratic political system itself. Looked at in the broad, the period 1961–5 was one of marked political success.[122]

Finally, Andeweg notes that partisan heterogeneity can overcome departmental heterogeneity in coalition cabinets: "In the form of coalition government, political heterogeneity may provide an incentive and a legitimation for taking an interest in the portfolios of ministers from other parties."[123]

*Psychological Perspectives on the Quality of Coalition Cabinet Policy-Making*

Research in social psychology is also relevant to the expectations of the quality decision making in coalition cabinets. This research predominantly reinforces the positive effects that multiple advocacy can have, although for psychological rather than democratic or legitimacy reasons. From the psychological perspective, the multiple voices that are present in coalitions contribute to better decision making by preventing premature closure on an alternative preferred by a majority. As Kameda and Sugimori have observed, Janis "himself emphasized the importance of a minority member's dissenting behavior as a possible remedy for groupthink, recommending that 'at every meeting devoted to evaluating policy alternatives, at least one member should be assigned the role of devil's advocate.'"[124] Junior parties that disagree with their senior partners are natural devil's advocates in coalition cabinets.

Not only can junior parties provide multiple perspectives and multiple options, they can improve the decision-making process in more subtle ways. One important outgrowth of Moscovici's theory and research on the conditions under which minorities can influence majorities has been a series of experiments on how the mere presence of a minority opinion can facilitate creativity. When groups are engaged in simple problem-solving tasks, a minority can generate divergent thinking, even when it is unable to influence the majority's opinion. Specifically, minorities can trigger the consideration of alternatives beyond the one suggested by the minority itself. This creative thought process is called divergent thinking.

The divergent thinking effect was first found in a study by Nemeth and Kwan, who asked participants to note the first three-letter word they discovered in a string of six letters, such as *tNOWap*. The most obvious answer is "NOW." The participants then were told whether a majority or minority of prior participants agreed with their answer as well as that some in the group answered "WON" instead. The experimenters were interested in how this feedback affected subsequent problem solving. Subjects who were told that a majority had said "WON" adopted the strategy of backward reading in subsequent problems (convergent thinking). If they were told that a minority had said "WON," they used a variety of strategies. The minority's way of thinking was not blindly followed but rather led to a consideration of all possible strategies (divergent thinking).[125]

Similarly, based on their studies on hypothesis testing, Butera and Mugny report that "individuals consider the majority's hypothesis as informative, since they use it more frequently to elaborate their own hypotheses; in contrast, when confronted with the minority's hypothesis, they elaborate new and original hypotheses. In hypothesis testing, confirmation is the most frequent strategy, but individuals confronted with a minority use disconfirmation more than those confronted with a majority."[126] Also, in an analogical reasoning task, Robin Martin and Hewstone found that a minority-endorsed proposal "caused more participants to generate the best solution to the problem than when the same base problem was supported by a majority. In short, the minority led to better performance, as judged by the generation of the best solution, than did the majority."[127] Subsequent research exploring some additional aspects of the impact of and mechanisms for minority dissent on creative thinking has found that the presence of a dissenter can increase others' resistance to conformity pressures, decrease attitude polarization, and promote role differentiation.[128]

Minority dissent appears to influence the thinking of members of the majority at an individual level. Gruenfeld and her colleagues have found that in both natural groups (the U.S. Supreme Court) and laboratory groups, majorities exhibit more integratively complex thinking than do minorities and groups that are unanimous in their opinion. In an experiment, Gruenfeld and her associates determined that this effect resulted from the presence of minority dissent rather than from a communication strategy adopted by the factions as a function of their status.[129] Similarly, others have found that a dissenting minority's presence leads the majority to change related opinions and attitudes, even if the minority does not have any influence on the attitude or opinion being discussed.[130] As one study reports, "Overall, results support the conclusion that majority arguments affect attitudes on focal issues more than on related issues because of convergent message processing, while minority arguments affect attitudes on related issues more than on focal issues because of divergent message processing and a desire to avoid identification with the source."[131]

This research on the positive effects of the presence of a minority on the quality of group decision making is supported by studies on the role of a devil's advocate and on dissent and diversity.[132] "Thus, like an appointed devil's advocate, authentic minority dissent appears to prevent teams from biased and defective decision making."[133] Moreover, even if minority members are not effective in the first consideration of a policy problem, they can subsequently become "agitators for change," constantly monitoring the information environment for feedback that the senior party's position is failing.[134] According to Kameda and Sugimori, group members who are outvoted "generally act in a nonconforming or uncooperative manner in the postdecision interaction, [and] their behaviors may consequently contribute to the reduction of collective entrapment in a group; even though the initially chosen course of action turns out to be faulty, these members with minority opinions may eventually help the group exit from entrapment."[135]

Future consequences of the presence of a minority also include sleeper and spillover effects. Not only do majorities show delayed changes in their attitudes on the topic of a minority's message (the sleeper effect), majorities' attitudes are vulnerable to change on topics not directly targeted by the minority's influence attempt. When faced with a minority with which they disagree, majorities apparently are forced to rethink their position and generate counterarguments that spill over to their attitudes on topics they see as unrelated. This effect occurs when majorities are targets of minority influence but not when minorities are targets of majority influence.[136]

Thus, research in social psychology suggests numerous ways in which the coalition context, with the presence of a junior party that disagrees with the senior partner, can push coalition decision making closer to rational standards. In particular, junior parties can stimulate a more thorough survey of alternatives. Because of a junior party's dissent, the government may search for an alternative to keep the coalition intact. Dissent within a coalition can also improve decision making by stimulating contingency planning.

Although a preponderance of research in social psychology stresses the positive effects of multiple voices on the quality of decision making, some psychological research suggests some dangers of the unanimity that is often required in coalitions. Specially, unanimity can foster psychological entrapment "whereby individuals escalate their commitment to a previously chosen, though failing, course of action in order to justify or 'make good on' prior investments."[137] Indeed, Kameda and Sugimori found experimental groups more likely to exhibit entrapment when they were under a unanimity rule than under a majority decision rule. This finding was most evident for groups that were of split opinion initially (as coalitions often are).[138]


CONCLUSION

Despite the prevalence of images and normative judgments about how coalition politics affects foreign policy, little research shines a direct spotlight on this relationship. Previous work has not produced clear conclusions and is limited in important theoretical ways. The study of coalition decision making can be enriched with insights from social psychology on dynamics in small-group processes. This research offers both parallel and alternative expectations and adds a social psychological perspective to complement a political-institutional view of coalition cabinets.

## 3

## *Assessing Coalition Politics and Foreign Policy: Quantitative Analyses and the Need for Comparative Case Studies*

The investigation of the various expectations about the effects of coalition politics on foreign policy requires a multimethod strategy, mixing quantitative statistical analyses with process tracing in case studies.[1] According to Levy, "Many analysts from each methodological perspective [quantitative and qualitative] have increasingly come to the conclusion that by combining both statistical and case study methods, researchers can use the advantages of each to partially offset the limitations of the other."[2] Tarrow and Levy agree that mixed-method research can bridge "the qualitative-quantitative divide" and that the use of qualitative analysis focusing on within-case processes to uncover causal mechanisms that underlie quantitative findings is particularly useful.[3] Specifically, "the strategy of combining the two approaches aims to improve the quality of conceptualization and measurement, analysis of rival explanations, and overall confidence in the central findings of a study."[4]

This chapter presents quantitative analyses designed to overcome limitations of previous statistical research and to move us closer to answering the why and how questions behind correlation-based findings. The quantitative research presented here better establishes that something about coalition politics generates policies different from those chosen by single-party cabinets. It also examines the role that cabinet characteristics play in coalition foreign policy, as a first cut to assess alternative explanations for the differences in foreign policy of multiparty versus single-party governments in parliamentary democracies. Case studies are the logical complement to the quantitative work and are designed to unpack the causal mechanisms in the context of the case. Case studies are also particularly useful

*Assessing Coalition Politics and Foreign Policy* 41

for examining the images of the effectiveness and quality of coalition decision making. This chapter justifies the use of case studies and the case selection strategy and previews the structure of the case chapters that follow.

## INVESTIGATING EXTREMITY AND CABINET CHARACTERISTICS: QUANTITATIVE STUDIES OF COALITION FOREIGN POLICY

As discussed in chapter 2, previous quantitative studies have investigated whether coalitions have more peaceful foreign policies than do single-party cabinets.[5] These studies have yielded mixed results, however, with some finding that coalitions are more aggressive, others that they are more peaceful, and still others that no difference exists between single-party and multi-party cabinets. This previous research is limited both theoretically and empirically. Theoretically, these studies have confounded institutional explanations with the policy positions of actors by assuming that the constraint that may be built in to coalitions is in the direction of peace.[6] In other words, this research hypothesizes that coalitions are more peaceful because they are constrained by peace-prone actors (in the form of coalition partners or legislatures). Yet there is no reason to believe that constraining actors might also prevent coalitions from more peaceful foreign policies. The same logic works for the expectation that coalitions might be more aggressive—junior parties, for example, can hijack the cabinet not only in the direction of aggression but also in the direction of peace. Thus, institutional factors that are inherent in coalitions may certainly affect their foreign policies, but the policy direction depends on the actors' particular policy preferences.

Empirically, previous studies are limited by their narrow focus on conflict-related dependent variables. Many have used the Militarized Interstate Dispute data set to examine the relationship between coalitions and dispute initiation, involvement, escalation, and reciprocation.[7] Others have used the Correlates of War data set and have focused on war involvement.[8] The focus on conflict-dependent variables comes from these authors' extension of research on the democratic peace by unpacking the different institutional effects of democracies. Conflict, however, is only a narrow slice of foreign policy behavior. Moreover, the effects of coalition politics on foreign policy may be less in conflict situations if the authority in the cabinet is contracted to exclude dissenting voices and if other factors, such as threats, produce a consensus in the cabinet.

To address these limitations in previous research, this chapter presents two quantitative studies on coalition cabinet foreign policy. Both studies use a subset of the World Event/Interaction Survey (WEIS) as developed by McClelland and updated by Tomlinson to look beyond conflict-oriented foreign policies. The WEIS data set catalogs the actions of all major international players in "newsworthy" events from 1966 to 1991.[9] For each event, WEIS identifies the actor (originator of the action), the type of action, the target of the action, and the arena or situational/episodic context in which the event occurred. Actions include both verbal acts (i.e., statements of policy support and threats) and nonverbal acts (i.e., grants of aid and military clashes). The WEIS data set allows us to investigate the effects of coalition politics on a wide range of foreign policy behaviors across a large number of events, a large set of parliamentary democracies, and a great length of time.

Both studies also address the theoretical problem discussed previously. Not only do they examine policy direction (peaceful or aggressive) associated with coalitions versus single-party cabinets (as past studies have), but they also assess the character of the policies that could result from institutions, regardless of policy positions. Specifically, the studies examine whether coalitions are more extreme (either more peaceful or more aggressive) or more moderate (either less peaceful or less aggressive). So, for example, junior parties could be hijacking the cabinet in both extreme directions, or constraints could be preventing the cabinet from moving toward either extreme. These analyses can examine whether an institutional effect is present without assuming a particular direction.

*Study 1: Coalition Cabinets' Extreme Foreign Policy*

This study compares the foreign policy behaviors of coalition cabinets with those of single-party cabinets.[10] The actors selected from the WEIS data set are the major parliamentary democracies, including many West European states as well as states in North America, Oceania, Southeast Asia, and the Middle East. A total of 26,848 events from 1966 through 1989 are analyzed, including 11,946 from single-party cabinets and 14,902 from multiparty coalitions and covering a range of issues.[11]

Whether each parliamentary democracy was a coalition or a single-party government serves as the independent variable. For each actor in the WEIS data set that was a parliamentary democracy, the cabinet type—

whether it was a single-party or coalition cabinet at the time of the event—was determined by consulting standard sources.[12] Cabinets that formally contained at least two independent political parties were coded as coalitions. Minority cabinets that included only one party but that relied on the support of other parties in Parliament were coded as single-party cabinets. Political parties that were in permanent electoral alliance (such as the Christian Democratic Union [CDU] and Christian Social Union [CSU] in Germany) were classified as single parties. The countries and their cabinet types are listed in table 3.1.

This study includes three dependent variables to examine the effects of coalition politics on international behavior. The first dependent variable is the level of cooperation and conflict in the actor's behavior. The level of co-

**TABLE 3.1. Countries and Cabinet Types**

| Actor | Events with Single Party Cabinets | Events with Coalition Cabinets | Total |
|---|---|---|---|
| Australia | 293 | 285 | 578 |
| Austria | 192 | 52 | 244 |
| Belgium | 0 | 298 | 298 |
| Canada | 1,187 | 0 | 1,187 |
| Denmark | 94 | 72 | 166 |
| Greece | 570 | 2 | 572 |
| Iceland | 0 | 138 | 138 |
| India | 1,918 | 5 | 1,923 |
| Ireland | 177 | 111 | 288 |
| Israel | 0 | 9,320 | 9,320 |
| Italy | 108 | 817 | 925 |
| Japan | 1,865 | 0 | 1,865 |
| Luxembourg | 0 | 40 | 40 |
| Malta | 3 | 0 | 3 |
| Netherlands | 0 | 329 | 329 |
| New Zealand | 272 | 0 | 272 |
| Norway | 101 | 104 | 205 |
| Spain | 307 | 0 | 307 |
| Sweden | 331 | 43 | 374 |
| Turkey | 409 | 334 | 743 |
| United Kingdom | 4,096 | 0 | 4,096 |
| West Germany | 17 | 2,958 | 2,975 |
| Total | 11,940 | 14,908 | 26,848 |

operation in the actor's behavior is indicated by the widely used conflict-cooperation scale developed by Goldstein.[13] This scale translates WEIS event categories into an ordinal scale that ranges from −10 (indicating the highest levels of conflict) to +10 (indicating the highest levels of cooperation).

The next two dependent variables are designed to assess the extremity of the foreign policy behaviors in which single-party and coalition cabinets engage. The first assesses extremity by taking the Goldstein conflict-cooperation scale and folding it at the midpoint, thereby giving a measure of the extremity of conflict or cooperative behavior.[14] Actions that are very cooperative or very conflictual have a higher score (more extreme) than those that are only moderately cooperative or conflictual (less extreme). Folding the scale eliminates information about the content of the behavior (cooperation or conflict), leaving only its character (more or less extreme). Finally, extremity is measured by classifying behaviors into two categories. Following Schrodt and Gerner, WEIS actions are divided into material and verbal categories.[15] The study then classified them as low and high commitment of resources, following East.[16] Low-commitment behaviors are purely verbal behaviors, while high-commitment behaviors involve some commitment of resources.[17] High-commitment behaviors can be considered more extreme than low-commitment behaviors.

The first hypothesis relates to the proposition that the institutional circumstances of coalitions translate directly into the content, either cooperative or conflictual, of foreign policy. As chapter 2 argues, whether or not coalition governments are more or less constrained, it is not possible to predict the level of cooperation or conflict of the foreign policy behavior. Constraints can equally affect peaceful or war-prone proclivities, and junior parties can hijack policies toward peace or toward conflict. Thus, this study expects to see no difference between coalition governments and single-party governments in terms of the conflict-cooperation variable.

The second hypothesis is aimed at the question of the institutional context of coalitions' independent effect on the characteristics of foreign policy behavior. If coalition governments are, in fact, more constrained than single-party governments, then less extreme (more moderate) foreign policy behaviors would come from coalitions than from single-party governments. If, however, coalitions are not constrained, are susceptible to ideologically extreme (dovish and hawkish) junior parties, or try to divert attention from their domestic political weakness through highly visible foreign policies, then we should see more extreme (less moderate) foreign policy behaviors. This result should apply equally to extremity related to level of conflict-cooperation, as well as extremity associated with level of commitment. In other words, coalitions and single-party cabinets may exhibit different levels of commitment in their foreign policy behaviors.[18]

In recognition that other factors have clear effects on foreign policy behavior, this study includes two control variables. A measure of the actor's power, using the Composite Indicator of National Capability (CINC) from the Correlates of War National Military Capabilities data set (Version 3.0), was included in the analyses to examine the independent effect of cabinet type on the dependent variables.[19] A country's level of cooperation and conflict and extremity are expected to reflect their level of national capabilities, regardless of the type of the cabinet.[20]

Given findings from numerous studies on the dyadic democratic peace, this study also includes a control variable in the analysis of the level of conflict-cooperation. This variable indicates whether the target of the action was democratic (all of the actors in the analyses are democratic). The Polity IV data set served as the basis for coding whether the target, if another state, was a democracy at the time of the event.[21] States receiving a democracy score of greater than 7 were coded as democratic. This study used multiple regression analysis to examine the effects of cabinet type on foreign policy behavior. Separate models were run for each dependent variable. Logit analyses were used for the commitment dummy variable.

Examining each individual event in the data set presents a challenge for drawing conclusions, since particular countries dominate the data set and may drive any results. Specifically, Israel (as the actor in more than 30 percent of the events), the United Kingdom (as the actor in more than 15 percent of the events), and West Germany (as the actor in more than 11 percent of the events) together constitute more than three-fifths of the data. Germany and Israel together account for 82 percent of the events with coalition cabinets, and the United Kingdom accounts for more than 34 percent of the events with single-party cabinets. Thus, these three countries would undoubtedly have a disproportionate influence on any results. Furthermore, Israel, with the highest percentage of events in the data set, engages in the most conflictual behavior of the parliamentary democracies and exhibits very high levels of extremity in terms of both conflict-cooperation and commitment.

For these reasons, this study performed two sets of analyses, each of which adjusts for the distortion associated with countries that dominate the data set.[22] The first set of analyses (see table 3.2) weights the cases so that all countries' events are equal in the analysis. This is done by weighting each country's events to the mean number of events across countries. In this way, no country is disproportionate in the data, and the total number of events is preserved. This analysis yields results consistent with the hypothesis that cabinet type is not related to the level of conflict-cooperation. The relationship is positive (coalitions are more cooperative than single-party cabinets) but is not significant. The relationships between cabinet type and extremity, however, are significant; coalitions engage in more extreme conflictual-cooperative behavior than single parties and are more likely to engage in high-commitment behaviors.

An alternative approach to aggregating the data was explored to further address the disproportionate influence of some countries. Instead of examining all events from single-party government in comparison to all events from coalition governments, events were aggregated by individual governments. For each country, the study established the beginning and end date of every government. Each individual government as a single party or coalition was identified, and the mean value for each dependent variable across all events for that government was calculated. Thus, each government has a score for level of cooperation-conflict based on that government's average cooperation-conflict score across all events coded for that government. The same was done for the Extremity variable and for the Commitment variable as well as for the control variables (Power and Democratic Target).[23] This approach results in a much smaller data set that consists of 216 governments (rather than 26,000+ events). It also creates

TABLE 3.2. Cabinet Type and Foreign Policy Behavior: Weighted Analyses

| Dependent Variable | Coefficient[a] | Standard Error | Significance |
|---|---|---|---|
| Cooperation/Conflict Cabinet Type[b] | .052 | .056 | .352 |
| Extremity of Action Cabinet Type[b] | .213 | .030 | .000 |
| Commitment Cabinet Type[b] | .137 | .032 | .000 |

[a]The coefficient is the unstandardized estimate from the regression analysis (logit analysis for the commitment variable).
[b]Cabinets were coded positive for coalitions (0 = single party, 1 = coalition).

greater equality for the number of observations across countries. The number of governments within countries ranges from four (Iceland and Spain) to twenty-five (Italy), with Israel having seventeen, the United Kingdom having nine, and Germany having twelve (see table 3.3).[24]

As with the weighted analysis, the results of this test (see table 3.4) support the expectation that cabinet type is not significantly related to conflict-cooperation. The results are also consistent with the previous analyses in that coalitions engage in more extreme conflictual-cooperative foreign policy behaviors than do single-party governments. Contrary to the previous analyses, however, the relationship between cabinet type and commitment is no longer significant, although it is in the same direction. All of the significant relationships in these results emerged after controlling for the power of the actor. The relationships between cabinet type and cooperation were also independent of whether the target was another democ-

**TABLE 3.3. Cabinets and Cabinet Types**

| Actor | Single Party Cabinets | Coalition Cabinets | Total Cabinets |
|---|---|---|---|
| Australia | 5 | 8 | 13 |
| Austria | 5 | 3 | 8 |
| Belgium | 0 | 8 | 8 |
| Canada | 10 | 0 | 10 |
| Denmark | 7 | 3 | 10 |
| Greece | 6 | 0 | 6 |
| Iceland | 0 | 4 | 4 |
| India | 9 | 1 | 10 |
| Ireland | 6 | 2 | 8 |
| Israel | 0 | 17 | 17 |
| Italy | 6 | 19 | 25 |
| Japan | 17 | 0 | 17 |
| Luxembourg | 0 | 5 | 5 |
| Netherlands | 0 | 10 | 10 |
| New Zealand | 9 | 0 | 9 |
| Norway | 6 | 4 | 10 |
| Spain | 4 | 0 | 4 |
| Sweden | 8 | 3 | 11 |
| Turkey | 7 | 4 | 11 |
| United Kingdom | 9 | 0 | 9 |
| West Germany | 1 | 11 | 12 |
| Total | 115 | 102 | 217 |

*Note:* Only cabinets with five or more events are included in this analysis so that a cabinet's foreign policy behavior would not be represented by a very small number of events.

racy. As expected, the power of the actor was a significant predictor for levels of cooperation, extremity, and commitment and the democratic nature of the target was significantly related to cooperation.

Overall, the results from Study 1 point to the conclusion that the institutional and political characteristics of coalitions lead them to extremity. The analyses showed a relationship between coalition governments and more extreme foreign policy behavior. In one of the tests, coalitions were significantly associated with more committed behaviors. With this aggregate data, however, it is difficult to investigate the reasons behind the more extreme foreign policies of coalitions. Several possible explanations arise from the literature, as discussed in chapter 2. First, since senior parties usually have to rely on more extreme, ideological junior parties to whom they are vulnerable with blackmail attempts, coalitions may be hijacked by these junior parties in either extreme direction. Second, if coalitions are inherently weak domestically, then they may need to engage in high-profile foreign policies to gain legitimacy and/or divert attention from their domestic problems. This argument is usually used to predict more conflictual policies, but highly cooperative foreign policies arguably would serve the same purposes. Finally, if coalitions are less constrained than single parties in that the multiple actors make it more difficult for others to assign responsibility to any single party, coalitions may feel more comfortable engaging in extreme endeavors. Again, this argument is usually made to justify the expectation that coalitions are more conflictual, but if both highly conflictual and highly cooperative behavior and high commitment behavior entail risks, then the diffusion of authority that comes with multiparty coalitions may underlie these risky choices.

TABLE 3.4. Cabinet Type and Foreign Policy Behavior: Cabinet Aggregates

| Dependent Variable | Coefficient[a] | Standard Error | Significance |
|---|---|---|---|
| Cooperation/Conflict | | | |
| Cabinet Type[b] | −.215 | .199 | .283 |
| Extremity of Action | | | |
| Cabinet Type[b] | .245 | .111 | .029 |
| Commitment | | | |
| Cabinet Type[b] | .012 | .017 | .475 |

[a]The coefficient is the unstandardized estimate from the regression analysis.
[b]Cabinets were coded positive for coalitions (0 = single party, 1 = coalition).

## Study 2: Unpacking the Effects of Cabinet Characteristics

The second study investigates the three possible explanations for extreme foreign policy behavior and examines the proposition that some coalitions are more likely to engage in conflictual behavior while others are more likely to be cooperative.[25] In so doing, this study unpacks the category of coalitions and investigates the effects of certain cabinet characteristics on foreign policy.

The actors selected for this study are the coalition cabinets in parliamentary democracies from the WEIS data set. Study 2 includes the same methods for determining parliamentary democracies and coalition cabinets as Study 1. The analyses include more than 14,000 events from 1966 to 1989. The countries, the years in which they were ruled by coalitions, and the total number of events in each country are listed in table 3.5. The study has the same three dependent variables to examine the effects of coalition characteristics on international behavior: (1) the level of cooperation in the actor's behavior; (2) the extremity of the actor's behavior; and (3) the level of commitment in the actor's behavior.

The three independent variables in these analyses correspond to the three explanations of extreme behavior. To assess the impact of a junior party, each cabinet was coded for the location of a junior party on the ideological spectrum compared to the senior party. A junior party is any party in the cabinet that is not the largest party in terms of seats controlled in Parliament. Only critical junior parties were used in the analysis. Critical parties are parties in minority coalitions and parties with enough parliamentary seats in a majority coalition that if they left the coalition, the cabinet would lose its parliamentary majority.

The expectation that critical junior parties can move policy toward their ideological position is based on examples of cases in which the junior party saw its position adopted as the government decision.[26] Justification for this hypotheses also comes from Hofferbert and Klingemann's study that found that in Germany, a critical junior party's electoral program was the better predictor of spending priorities (including foreign affairs and defense) in five out of eleven policy areas than was either the senior party's program or the compromise government declaration at the formation of the coalition.[27]

Leftist junior parties essential to the maintenance of the coalition may be able to propel the cabinet toward peace; essential rightist junior parties may be able to push the cabinet toward conflict. Dovish junior parties might be expected to argue for peaceful foreign policies, and hawkish junior parties might be expected to advocate conflictual policies. The dove-hawk (or accommodationist–hard-liner) dimension is perhaps the best predictor of specific positions on the effectiveness and use of conflict in the foreign policy context.[28] Dovish parties would be more likely to pursue co-

**TABLE 3.5. Countries and Coalitions**

| Actor | Time Period of Events with Coalition Cabinets | Total Events |
|---|---|---|
| Australia | 1/07/66–12/17/72 | |
| | 12/07/75–11/05/82 | 286 |
| Austria | 2/04/66–3/14/66 | |
| | 9/10/83–9/18/89 | 52 |
| Belgium | 1/24/66–1/17/77 | |
| | 6/07/77–5/22/89 | 298 |
| Denmark | 3/01/68–9/27/71 | |
| | 10/05/78–11/24/78 | |
| | 12/13/82–6/07/88 | 73 |
| Iceland | 7/09/66–7/01/89 | 138 |
| Ireland | 3/21/73–6/07/77 | |
| | 11/06/81 | |
| | 1/28/83–2/04/87 | |
| | 8/19/89–9/23/89 | 111 |
| Israel | 1/8/66–12/29/89 | 9,320 |
| Italy | 1/19/66–6/17/68 | |
| | 12/30/68–7/15/69 | |
| | 4/16/70–2/14/72 | |
| | 7/05/72–1/29/76 | |
| | 10/29/79–3/23/87 | |
| | 9/04/87–12/21/89 | 817 |
| Luxembourg | 3/09/67–4/22/86 | 40 |
| Netherlands | 1/24/66–4/21/89 | 329 |
| Norway | 3/25/66–1/16/71 | |
| | 10/25/72–8/15/73 | |
| | 6/08/83–2/14/86 | 104 |
| Sweden | 10/13/76–8/31/78 | |
| | 3/14/80–10/06/82 | 45 |
| Turkey | 1/25/74–12/27/77 | 334 |
| West Germany | 1/12/66–10/26/66 | |
| | 12/6/66–12/31/89 | 2,958 |
| | Total | 14,905 |

operative foreign policies, and hawkish parties would be more likely to pursue conflictual policies. The dove-hawk dimension is not independent of other dimensions along which policy positions and political parties can be placed. Citing several studies, Palmer, London, and Regan recently argued that "there is evidence that left and right parties in established democracies generally have systematic differences over foreign-policy and defense issues."[29] This research confirms that parties on the left are more dovish or accommodationist and parties on the right are more hawkish or hardline.[30]

Most previous quantitative research has not directly considered the ideological placement of junior coalition partners. In the Glenn Palmer, London, and Regan study, the cabinet's political orientation was measured as "the arithmetic mean of the positions of the parties in the coalition when each party is weighted by its number of seats."[31] Although the study reports that alternative measures that included only parties essential to the coalition and weighted equally made no difference in the statistical analyses,[32] their analysis did not consider that a critical junior party might be able to hijack the cabinet completely and that the political orientation of the junior party, not weighed in any way against that of the senior party, thus might best predict the cabinet's policy choices. Clare's study is a rare exception that includes the ideological position of the junior party. He found that cabinets with more far-right outlier parties are more likely to be involved in dispute initiations than cabinets with far-left outlier parties, thus confirming the hawk-dove expectation.[33]

Using sources that describe the ideological placement of the senior and junior parties, each cabinet was coded for the presence of a critical junior party that was left or right of the senior party.[34] This is a dichotomous variable. Consistent with the reasoning outlined earlier, this study hypothesizes that the presence of a critical junior party that is to the right of the senior party will correlate with higher levels of conflict. There are no clear predictions to make with regard to the relationship between the junior party's ideological placement and the levels of extremity and commitment in the countries' foreign policy.

To assess the proposition that the weakness of coalitions propels them to act in highly committed and extreme ways, the level of parliamentary support for each cabinet is included in the analysis. This number is simply the percentage of parliamentary seats controlled by all parties formally in the cabinet. The primary hypothesis is that coalitions with greater parliamentary support will act in less extreme and less committed ways, since weak cabinets will have more reason to engage in this high-profile behavior. This study also expects that coalitions with greater parliamentary support will be more cooperative, since conflictual behaviors may be seen as more effective diversions from domestic weakness and since the stress experienced by weaker coalitions may create poor decision making, which is often associated with conflictual policies. The third explanation, focusing on diffusion of authority, is assessed by coding the cabinets for the number of parties that are formally part of the coalition.[35] This study hypothesizes that coalitions with more parties will act in less cooperative, more extreme, more committed ways.

The same control variables from Study 1 are included here—actor's power for all three dependent variables and whether the target was democratic for the level of cooperation. Countries' levels of cooperation, extremity, and commitment should reflect their level of national capabilities, regardless of the characteristics of the cabinet.[36] Countries' levels of cooperation should be higher if the target was democratic, regardless of the characteristics of the cabinet.

To assess the effects of the three cabinet characteristics on foreign policy behavior, Study 2 also performed two separate sets of regression analyses. To deal with the disproportionate presence of Israeli and West German events in the coalition data set, the study included an analysis that weights the cases so that all countries' events are equal in the analysis. Each country's events are weighted to the mean number of events across countries. A second regression analysis aggregates the events by individual coalition cabinets using the mean value for each dependent variable for that coalition. This approach results in a much smaller data set of 129 coalitions. It also creates greater equality for the number of observations across countries. The number of coalitions within countries ranges from three (in Sweden) to twenty-one (in Italy).[37]

Table 3.6 reports the results from the analyses in which each country's events are weighted to the mean number of events across countries. In this analysis, the presence of a critical junior party to the right of a senior party is significantly and positively related to cooperation. The location of the junior party is also significantly related to levels of extremity and commitment, even though no predictions were made about these relationships. Specifically, junior parties to the right of the senior party were correlated with low levels of extremity and high levels of commitment.

The effects of coalition strength on foreign policy are also interesting. As predicted, stronger coalitions are associated with more cooperative behavior. Contrary to this study's predictions, stronger coalitions are associated with higher levels of commitment. The relationship between coalition strength and extremity comes close to being statistically significant at the .10 level in this analysis. The number of parties in the coalition is significant for all three of the behavior variables. More parties are associated with more conflictual, extreme, and committed behavior, all as hypothesized.

Again, all of the significant relationships in these results emerged after controlling for the power of the actor and for the effects of the other independent variables. The relationships between the cabinet characteristics and cooperation were also independent of whether the target was another democracy. As expected, the power of the actor was a significant predictor for levels of cooperation, extremity, and commitment, and the democratic nature of the target was significantly related to cooperation.

TABLE 3.6. Cabinet Characteristics and Foreign Policy Behavior: Weighted Analyses

| Dependent Variable | Coefficient[a] | Standard Error | Significance |
|---|---|---|---|
| Cooperation/Conflict | | | |
| Jr. Party Right of Sr. Party | +.305 | .076 | .000 |
| Coalition Strength | +1.011 | .337 | .003 |
| Number of Coalition Parties | −.235 | .038 | .000 |
| Extremity of Action | | | |
| Jr. Party Right of Sr. Party | −.105 | .040 | .008 |
| Coalition Strength | −.287 | .177 | .105 |
| Number of Coalition Parties | +.069 | .020 | .000 |
| Commitment | | | |
| Jr. Party Right of Sr. Party | +.120 | .040 | .003 |
| Coalition Strength | +.906 | .175 | .000 |
| Number of Coalition Parties | +.094 | .019 | .000 |

[a] The coefficient is the unstandardized estimate from the regression analysis (logit analysis for the commitment variable).

The next set of analyses, reported in table 3.7, is based on data aggregated by each coalition. These results demonstrate fewer and weaker statistically significant relationships. The ideological location of the junior party is not related to any of the three behavior variables. The strength of the coalition is significantly related only to levels of commitment. As in the weighted analyses, coalitions with more parliamentary support are associated with higher levels of commitment, contrary to the hypothesis. The number of parties in the coalition is correlated with the level of cooperation. As in the weighted analysis, more parties are associated with more conflictual behaviors, as predicted. The relationship between number of parties and extremity comes very close to statistical significance at the .10 level and is in the same direction as it is in the other analysis—more parties are associated with more extreme behaviors, as predicted.

Once again, all of the significant relationships in these results emerged after controlling for the power of the actor and for the effects of the other independent variables. The relationships between the cabinet characteristics and cooperation were also independent of whether the target was an-

TABLE 3.7. Cabinet Characteristics and Foreign Policy Behavior: Coalition Aggregates

| Dependent Variable | Coefficient[a] | Standard Error | Significance |
|---|---|---|---|
| Cooperation/Conflict | | | |
| Jr. Party Right of Sr. Party | +.244 | .310 | .432 |
| Coalition Strength | −1.068 | 1.569 | .498 |
| Number of Coalition Parties | −.279 | .150 | .066 |
| Extremity of Action | | | |
| Jr. Party Right of Sr. Party | −.200 | .187 | .289 |
| Coalition Strength | +.874 | .956 | .363 |
| Number of Coalition Parties | +.152 | .092 | .101 |
| Commitment | | | |
| Jr. Party Right of Sr. Party | +.019 | .027 | .483 |
| Coalition Strength | +.254 | .140 | .072 |
| Number of Coalition Parties | +.014 | .014 | .296 |

[a]The coefficient is the unstandardized estimate from the regression analysis.

other democracy. As expected, the power of the actor was a significant predictor for levels of cooperation, extremity, and commitment. The democratic nature of the target was not significantly related to cooperation in this analysis.

Table 3.8 presents the relationships that received support in at least one of the analyses. One result that received strong support was that coalitions with higher levels of parliamentary support are associated with higher levels of commitment.[38] This finding ran contrary to the study's prediction, as the diversionary explanation of coalition foreign policy would expect weaker governments to engage in the more high-profile behaviors associated with high commitment to divert attention from their domestic vulnerability. But perhaps weaker governments simply do not have the resources to produce foreign policies involving more deeds than words. Instead, coalitions that control more support may more easily mobilize the resources necessary to engage in high-commitment behaviors. Stronger coalitions may also be more risk prone, knowing that they can absorb criticism and that they face a weaker opposition. This explanation is consistent with Stinnett's argument that prime ministers create surplus majority coalitions to respond more boldly to the international environment.[39]

The relationship between cabinet strength and commitment may not be isolated to coalitions. It may be that all cabinets, both multiparty and single-party, that control a greater percentage of parliamentary seats engage in higher commitment behavior. Results from Glenn Palmer, London, and Regan's study suggest that such may be the case. Looking at coalitions and single-party governments together, the authors found that stronger

**TABLE 3.8. Supported Relationships across Multiple Analyses**

| Relationship | Supportive Analyses | Predicted? |
|---|---|---|
| (1) Stronger coalitions → higher levels of commitment | weighted, aggregated | no |
| (2) More parties → more conflict | weighted, aggregated | no prediction made |
| (3) More parties → more extreme behavior | weighted, aggregated (aggregated $p = .101$) | yes |
| (4) Jr. parties right of sr. party → more cooperative behavior | weighted | no |

governments are more likely to get involved in militarized disputes (generally high-commitment behaviors) than are weaker governments. Government strength was not, however, related to dispute escalation.[40]

The second result to receive support across the analyses was that more parties are associated with more conflictual behavior. Although the diffusion of responsibility and accountability explanation arguably could be equally applied to extreme levels of cooperation and extreme levels of conflict, the risk-taking dynamic may be biased in the direction of more aggressive foreign policy. As previously discussed, the fragmentation that comes with more parties may make coalitions with many parties resemble Snyder's "cartelized" political systems, in which decision making proceeds by logrolling and can lead governments into "overexpansion" and aggression.[41]

In addition, the relationship between more parties and conflict and extremity may be spurious since many large "national unity" coalitions are often formed as a reaction to crisis situations. Conflictual foreign policy may be a response to the crisis situation itself rather than result from decision-making dynamics associated with more parties. One way to assess this idea is to look at which countries tend to have higher numbers of parties in their cabinets. If countries that often faced foreign policy crises during the Cold War (the period of the data)—such as West Germany, Israel, and Turkey—have more parties in their governments, we might expect that the crises are creating the conflictual foreign policy. Table 3.9 lists the average number of parties in coalitions in each country in the data set. No clear pattern seems evident. Although some Cold War "frontline" states, such as Israel, do tend to have higher numbers of parties, other states, such as Belgium, also tend to have more parties in their coalition and are not typically and historically associated with foreign policy crises during this period. Of course, the coalitions with many parties in countries such as Belgium and Italy could have formed in response to a domestic (i.e., economic or political) crisis, but we would not expect that this crisis situation would automatically translate into the more extreme and conflictual foreign policy behavior that we see. Rather, the fragmentation of the party system and associated electoral laws seems to best explain the high number of parties in some countries, and this phenomenon appears to have an independent effect on foreign policy.

The third relationship, with support in one analysis and close to support in another, is that more parties are associated with more extreme behavior.[42] This finding is consistent with the diffusion of accountability and responsibility explanation of coalition foreign policy. Not only is accountability generally more diffused in coalitions than in single-party cabinets, but the results also indicate that more parties within the family of coalitions affect foreign policy behavior. With more parties, coalition cabinets may engage in more extreme behavior because the public and the Parliament will have more difficulty attributing failure of these riskier policies. From the psychological perspective, more political parties may reduce fear of failure given the diffusion of responsibility.

Finally, the fourth relationship that received support in one analysis is perhaps the most surprising. While this study hypothesized that the presence of critical junior parties to the right of the senior party on the ideological spectrum would be associated with more conflictual foreign policy, the results showed just the opposite. In the weighted analyses, rightist junior parties correlated with more cooperative behavior. It seems that these junior parties failed to influence or hijack the senior parties and that the cooperative behavior is a reflection of the senior party, which is, by the operational definition, on the left of the junior party.

Several additional operational and theoretical factors, however, could be important for interpreting this finding. First, while previous evidence suggests that junior parties on the right of the political spectrum are hawkish and favor more aggressive foreign policies, the rightist junior parties in

TABLE 3.9. Average Number of Parties in Coalitions (in ascending order)

| Country | Mean Number of Parties |
| --- | --- |
| Australia | 2 |
| Austria | 2 |
| West Germany | 2 |
| Ireland | 2 |
| Luxembourg | 2 |
| Iceland | 2.33 |
| Sweden | 2.67 |
| Turkey | 3 |
| Netherlands | 3.09 |
| Denmark | 3.4 |
| Norway | 3.4 |
| Italy | 3.81 |
| Israel | 3.82 |
| Belgium | 3.87 |

these events may not have taken a more hawkish view. Moreover, there is reason to believe that under some conditions (such as threats to humanitarian rights and trade agreements), leftist parties may favor more aggressive, less cooperative foreign policies. Second, the data used for most of the countries in this study allowed for an indication of the junior party's placement in comparison to the senior party but not in comparison to the center. In other words, some of the junior parties in this study that were left of the senior party have been right of center, and some of the junior parties that were to the right of the senior party may have been left of center. Thus, the operational definition of junior party placement used in this study may not clearly reflect the junior party's ideological position generally, on the most relevant dimension, or on the particular issues at hand. Finally, previous research suggests that not all junior parties that have the capacity to influence cabinet policy actually do so. The unanimity of junior parties and the manipulation of decision-making procedures are key factors affecting the success of junior parties' attempts to influence foreign policy.[43] Future research—both quantitative and qualitative—using alternative indicators of junior party position and examining the processes of influence would be useful for a better understanding of the hijacking hypothesis.

Such an understanding is especially important given that in the weighted analyses (see table 3.6), the ideological position of the junior party was significantly related to extremity and commitment. Not only did this finding run contrary to this study's predictions, but the two relationships were also in opposite directions despite positive correlations between these two variables. In other words, the presence of a critical junior party to the right of the senior party was associated with less extreme behaviors and high-commitment foreign policy even though extremity and commitment tend to go hand in hand.

This study provides us with additional information about the cabinet characteristics that distinguish the foreign policy behaviors of some coalitions from others. All three characteristics examined—ideological placement of the junior party, coalition strength, and number of parties in the cabinet—are important factors in these countries' foreign policies. Overall, this study suggests that the institutional features associated with coalition governments are important in the foreign policies of parliamentary democracies. Countries ruled by weak coalitions and small numbers of parties will behave differently than those ruled by strong governments and large numbers of coalition partners. These findings challenge some of the logic in much of the current research on institutional effects and particularly in research on the democratic peace. For example, institutional constraints that are often assumed to produce peaceful behavior, such as multiple voices in the cabinet, are actually related to more conflictual behavior in this study.

The quantitative studies presented here provide a more straightforward examination of the institutional effects of coalition politics across a broad range of foreign policy. They also unpack the different institutional effects. These cross-national analyses offer an indication of general trends and give a glimpse at the important dynamics operating in coalition cabinets, but they do not tell us much about exactly how aspects of coalition politics—fragile nature, junior party influence, and so on—play out in decision making. They do not indicate whether the underlying mechanism assumed in the explanation is actually operating. For example, although the results suggest that diffusion of accountability and responsibility may lie behind the extreme behavior of coalitions, there is no evidence that this dynamic is creating the extremity. A case study approach that traces the process of decision making in the cabinets is a necessary, complementary method to further unpack the effects of coalition politics on the content of foreign policy as well as to assess the competing expectations on the quality of decision making by multiparty cabinets.

## INVESTIGATING UNDERLYING PROCESSES AND DECISION-MAKING QUALITY: COMPARATIVE CASE STUDIES OF COALITION FOREIGN POLICY

At the heart of the findings from the quantitative analyses and the various theoretical expectations about the effects of coalition politics on foreign policy is the decision-making process. We need to know much more about how coalitions actually make decisions to understand the dynamics that various cabinet characteristics produce. We also need to know more about the decision-making process to understand the relative importance of institutional and psychological factors and to examine the claims about the effectiveness of multiparty decision making.

Given the understudied and conflicting assumptions about how the institutional setting of coalitions affects policy-making, case studies of foreign policy decisions are critical to building knowledge about the effects of coalition dynamics on foreign policy, policy-making effectiveness, and government stability. Case studies are most appropriate for tracing the process and uncovering the factors involved in decision making.[44] According to Levy, not only do case studies provide a specific historical account, but

> in doing so they can contribute to the process of theory development by helping to clarify the meaning of key variables and the validity of empirical indicators used to measure them, and by suggesting additional causal mechanisms, causal variables, and interaction effects. They can also help to identify the contextual variables that affect hypothesized causal processes and to identify the scope conditions under which particular theories are valid. These are all important steps in the theory-building process.[45]

Shively agrees: "The role of a case study . . . is to examine the internal workings of a theory in a case or cases, both to test the theory and to develop it further. It is fashionable to argue that we must seek the microfoundations of our theories. Well, that is what case studies do. . . . The powerful generalizing we all do from case studies is powerful not just or even primarily because of the persuasive analysis of the case, but because of how it addresses the broader theory in which it works."[46] Achen and Snidal go further and argue that "because they are simultaneously sensitive to data and theory, case studies are more useful for [developing analytic theory] than any other methodological tool."[47]

Process tracing is especially valuable in this regard. Process tracing involves analyzing the intervening causal mechanisms between initial conditions and outcomes by observing the sequence of events within the case.[48] Levy argues that "process tracing provides several comparative advantages for testing many kinds of intervening causal mechanisms, particularly those involving propositions about what goes on in side the 'black box' of decision making."[49] According to Bennett and Elman, case studies are particularly useful for discovering complex causal relations such as path-dependent dynamics. Case studies unpack how causal mechanisms operate in context and allow for the discovery of interaction effects and contingencies.[50]

The case studies in this book examine existing theoretical assumptions and discover the factors that trigger some outcomes (such as highly aggressive policies) versus others (such as inconsistent and fragmented decision making). A central argument of this project is that many of the alternative expectations about coalitions turn on key conditions that evolve during policy-making. Only with a case study approach can we examine those process variables.

*Case Selection*

Case studies of cabinet decision making can best address the questions about the effects of coalition politics on foreign policy if they are selected to be comparable on many dimensions to rule out competing explanations but different enough to be somewhat representative of the universe of cases.[51] This study combines the "most similar systems" strategy (in which cases that are similar on many characteristics are selected) with the "most different systems" strategy (in which cases are chosen across different categories to rule them out as explanatory factors).[52] Levy argues that "the basic logic of the two designs is the same—to identify patterns of covariation and to eliminate independent variables that do not covary with the dependent variable."[53] When researchers are interested in more than covariation, combining the most different and most similar systems strategies also allows for better causal analysis, including multiple causality. According to Ragin, "When qualitatively oriented comparativists compare, they study how different conditions or causes fit together in one setting and contrast that with how they fit together in another setting. . . . That is, they tend to analyze each observational entity as an interpretable combination of parts—as a whole. Thus, the explanations of comparative social science typically cite convergent causal conditions, causes that fit together or combine in a certain manner."[54]

For this project, cases are defined by a condition—the existence of interparty conflict with regard to foreign policy. The values of the dependent variables (peaceful versus aggressive foreign policies, good versus bad decision making) were allowed to vary, as were the possible explanatory factors. The goal is to establish congruence between the values of various possible explanatory factors and the values of the dependent variables and to assess the plausibility of causal mechanisms. The twelve cases in this book (listed in table 3.10) were also selected with some similarities and differences in mind. The cases are comparable in that all are instances of foreign policy disagreement between the coalition partners, allowing for an investigation of how and whether disagreements are resolved and the effects of these partisan differences. In all but one of the cases, the party that controls the prime ministership differs from the party that controls the foreign ministry, the defense ministry, or both.⁵⁵ The cases are also similar in that they come from states that are significant actors in international politics and that they cover critical decisions.⁵⁶ All three countries are parliamentary democracies that were considered stable at the time of the cases, and in all cases, the cabinets cases control a parliamentary majority. All three countries have considerable histories as democratic systems. The four cases within each country hold constant many cultural, institutional, and historical factors.

In addition, these countries differ enough that hypotheses can be examined across institutional and situational variations, as the focus of this research is on unpacking the general effects of coalition politics on foreign policy. Some of the cases cover more security issues, some political issues, and some economic policies. Most cases are from the post–Cold War period, although two Dutch cases are from the early 1980s. Other differences also exist. The Japanese cases involve the first coalition governments after decades of one-party rule. Turkey differs from both Japan and the Netherlands in terms of the role of the military and its history of military coups in the past thirty years. Despite these differences, there is no prima facie reason to believe that coalition politics and how parties attempt to resolve their differences operates dramatically differently across these different

### TABLE 3.10. Comparative Case Studies of Foreign Policy Disagreement in Coalition Cabinets

**The Netherlands**
Policy toward apartheid South Africa (1980–82)
Deployment of NATO cruise missiles (1979–84)
Participation in Iraq War (2003)
Deployment of troops to southern Afghanistan (2006)

**Japan**
Liberalization of rice imports (1993)
Debate over bid for permanent UNSC membership (1993–94)
Participation in Golan Heights peacekeeping (1995)
Debate over revision of the peacekeeping law (1998–99)

**Turkey**
Customs Union agreement with EU (1995)
"Islamic opening" (1996–97)
Helsinki Summit offer of EU candidacy (1999)
Death penalty abolition (1999–2002)

*Assessing Coalition Politics and Foreign Policy*  63

types of policies, time periods, political systems, and country-specific contexts. However, given the theory-exploratory nature of this study, differences in the countries and in the cases will be examined if they do indeed mediate the relationships under investigation. Again, this book examines the effects of coalition politics on foreign policy regardless of the differences in the cases.

The three countries in this project vary in terms of the images of coalition politics that they prima facie match. Dutch foreign policy has been condemned for excessive compromise as a result of coalition necessities.[57] Japanese foreign policy in the 1990s is often cited as unresponsive and directionless because of coalition politics.[58] Turkey is frequently used as an example of the dangers of fragile coalitions and hijacking by ideologically extreme parties.[59] This set of countries thus allows for an examination of the factors that contribute to these varied outcomes. Yet a within-country comparison will provide an examination of how some coalitions and some decisions may avoid the particular "pathologies" of coalition politics with which their country is associated. Japanese coalitions, for example, did make some meaningful policy decisions, and Turkish foreign policies are not always hijacked by extreme coalition actors. Cabinet crises and politicking have occurred in Dutch foreign policy despite that country's norms for consensus. Comparison of these cases will generate a better, more complex understanding of the institutional and process factors that mitigate between some outcomes and others, the primary focus of this study.

*Case Structure and Focus*

The case studies in this book follow George's method of structured, focused comparison in that they are built around a set of similar factors, assessed comparably across all cases, and focused only on those aspects of the historical case that are theoretically relevant to the research questions.[60] In the three country chapters that follow, the cases are introduced with a brief history of the most important themes of the country's foreign policy and the factors that scholars have typically used to explain the country's foreign policies. For each country, a discussion of the locus of foreign policy authority follows. These introductory elements are critical to this study, providing context for the cases, acknowledging potential alternative explanations, and establishing the importance of coalition cabinets for foreign relations. For each country, I argue that while other factors and actors may be important, their effect is funneled through the cabinet, especially when a difference of opinion arises among the coalition partners. This is another way in which the cases are comparable. The extant expectations about the effects of coalition politics are also reviewed for each country. The general images presented in chapter 2 are mirrored in writings about each specific country. For each case, I briefly present the background and significance of the policy. I discuss the individuals and actors in the coalition cabinet, their positions, and the positions of other domestic players. I then trace the process of how the disagreement between the coalition partners plays out and gets translated into a decision (or nondecision).

Evidence for the case studies comes from a variety of materials. Secondary source material (such as historical and political analysis and public opinion polls) provides information on which strategies the junior party used, what other factors were important in the decision, and the degree of public support for the parties' positions. Historical and journalistic accounts of cabinet decisions provide a wealth of information on the policy-making process. Primary source material (such as party manifestos and published interviews) provides evidence on the parties' positions and general foreign policy orientations.[61] Every attempt is made to support claims with more than one source, and any uncertainty, ambiguity, or conflicts in the information are acknowledged. With this evidence, I cannot go "inside the cabinet" or "inside the heads" of the decision makers. I can, however, make a good-faith effort to trace the decision-making process at a distance and to fully disclose the sources used to do this.

For theory-building purposes, the most important part of each case study is the analysis of how coalition politics affected the decision-making process and the resulting policy. The comparative case study method best contributes to the examination of assumptions and theory building if it is consciously theoretical and systematic in its approach.[62] In the analysis of each case, I examine the competing expectations detailed in chapter 2:

1. Was the resulting policy extreme or moderate, and was it peaceful or aggressive?
2. Was the decision-making process of high or low quality? Did the process contribute to legitimacy, creativity, or instability?

I assess the peacefulness, aggressiveness, or extremity of the policy with the same objective Goldstein-WEIS coding scale that was used in the quantitative studies. I also assess the policy in the context of the case and the country's international and historical circumstances, which provides a different picture in some cases. For example, the objective scale simply picks one target for each action. In multilateral policies, however, the action may be cooperative toward allies yet conflictual to a third party. This situation applies to several cases in this book. When the Dutch decided to send troops to Afghanistan, it was a cooperative action toward NATO and its peacekeeping mission but was also armed force mobilization against an enemy. In the Turkish case, in which one coalition partner attempted to reorient Turkish foreign policy toward the Islamic world, the result was an economic agreement with Iran (cooperation) that Turkey's traditional allies in the West viewed as very hostile (conflict). Another example of difference between an objective and contextual assessment of foreign policy behavior comes from Japan. The Japanese decision to announce its bid for a permanent seat on the United Nations Security Council is, on the Goldstein-WEIS scale, a very moderate, neutral "state policy." Yet in the context of post–World War II Japanese history, this effort was seen (inside and outside of Japan) as fairly extreme and nationalistic.

These differences between the objective and contextual assessment of foreign policy are not problematic for the research in this book—indeed, they are another advantage of combining quantitative and qualitative methodologies.[63] The theoretical expectations and past empirical work are based on both types of assessments, and both types thus should be included in this analysis. The use of the terms *peaceful, aggressive,* and *extreme* also connects the case studies to the quantitative studies presented in this chapter and with past quantitative research.

The effectiveness of the decision-making process in each case is addressed qualitatively, according to the criteria discussed in chapter 2. In addition to standard notions of rationality (e.g., thorough information search, cost/benefit considerations, contingency planning, and implementation), normative standards of democracy (e.g., representation, legitimacy, consensus) are assessed in each case. Whether the decision produced a desirable outcome is also analyzed with the use of expert judgments on how effectively the decision addressed the issue and whether it produced unintended or unwanted consequences.

In each case, I also analyze whether the hypothesized factors related to coalition politics were operating and can plausibly be related to the outcome:

3. If the policy was extreme (peaceful or aggressive), did it result from a diffusion of responsibility and accountability, diversion from weakness or uncertainty, and/or hijacking and minority influence by subsets of the coalition? If the policy was not extreme, did it result from the relative distribution of power among the coalition partners and/or the requirement of unanimity?
4. If the decision-making process was of low quality, did it result from the hijacking of the process and premature closure on an option, unanimity norms or requirements, and/or the need for excessive compromise? If the decision-making process was of high quality, did it result from the representation of diverse interests, devil's advocacy, creative/divergent thinking, and/or spillover effects from the presence of dissent?

In addressing these questions, I assess the evidence for the underlying mechanisms that translate causal factors and patterns of causal factors into outcomes. These questions and the possible answers in each analysis section seek to establish the validity of the explanations behind the findings in the quantitative studies. The questions stem directly from political and psychological theories embedded in the expectations about the effects of coalition politics on foreign policy (see chapter 2).

Because I examine each of the twelve cases in a comparable way, coding them for their outcomes, processes, and explanatory factors, I can look for patterns. These analyses are presented within each country at the end of chapters 4–6 and across all cases in chapter 7.

# 4

# *Dutch Foreign Policy: Excessive Compromise in Coalition Politics?*

## CHALLENGES AND FACTORS IN CONTEMPORARY DUTCH FOREIGN POLICY

Three themes of Dutch foreign policy were captured in the title of Joris Voorhoeve's 1979 book, *Peace, Profits, and Principles.* Voorhoeve, once minister of defense, presented these themes and the "traditions" of maritime commercialism, neutralist abstentionism, and international idealism as important constants in Dutch foreign policy over the years.[1] Despite some criticisms of Voorhoeve's thesis, Andeweg and Irwin have noted that considerable consensus exists on these themes in scholarship on Dutch foreign policy.[2]

The Dutch drive for profits has its roots in the "golden age" of Dutch maritime dominance, global trade, and empire and can be seen in its pro-European economic integration policies after World War II.[3] According to Rochon, "The objective of furthering trade has . . . been the single constant in Dutch foreign policy, and under most (but not all) circumstances the desire for expanding trade also led the Dutch to seek international peace."[4] The principles theme is demonstrated in the long-standing Dutch commitment to international law. "The development of international law through treaties has received great attention since the time of [Dutch legal scholar] Grotius."[5] More recently, moral and humanitarian concerns have characterized the principled aspect of Dutch foreign policy.

The importance of peace for the Netherlands changed in its expression after World War II. The policy of neutrality gave way to a commitment to the new Atlantic alliance, and Atlanticism became a cornerstone of Dutch foreign policy.[6] "Despite early altercations with the British, and later irritation over American pressure to decolonize, the Netherlands has continued to rely on these two extra-continental powers. This reliance is due in part to the importance of maritime trade, but also to the desire to have a countervailing power to the dominant state on the continent, be it German or French."[7] Atlanticism is manifest in staunch Dutch support for the NATO alliance and has also affected the Netherlands' orientation toward European integration.[8] According to Pijpers, the Dutch rejected the development of a politically and militarily independent European community partly because of their commitment to Atlanticism. "Each proposal for European cooperation in this regard met with strong suspicions and ran up against the policy of NATO's primacy."[9] Notwithstanding more open criticism of the United States and NATO beginning in the 1970s, the Netherlands was still considered and considered itself a faithful U.S. ally.

Post–World War II Dutch foreign policy generally was characterized by a consensus on a close connection with the United States and NATO, economic integration with Western Europe, and active participation in international institutions. Only specifics of decolonization, especially in Indonesia and New Guinea, produced much domestic division over foreign affairs.[10] This situation began to change in the 1970s. The Dutch commitment to the Western alliance came under strain as the Netherlands became more active in its development policies in the Third World. Not only did Dutch foreign aid drastically increase, time, but Dutch support to countries such as North Vietnam and Cuba often brought the Netherlands into conflict with its NATO partners.[11] The disagreements within the Netherlands and between the Netherlands and the United States over the stationing of cruise missiles in the 1980s also represented a break from the past in Dutch foreign policy:[12]

> Nothing symbolized the altered position of the Netherlands better and more dramatically than the reversal of official policy on nuclear weapons. In 1957 the Netherlands . . . was the first West European country to allow American nuclear weapons on its territory. Twenty years later the country was a leading force in Western Europe's drive against President Carter's plan to produce the so-called neutron bomb and to introduce this weapon into the European theatre.[13]

The debate over the cruise missiles "led to the diagnosis [by Walter Laqueur in 1981] of 'Hollanditis,' a supposedly contagious Dutch disease of pacificism. Laqueur and others speculated about a reemergence of neutralism in Dutch foreign policy, now that both gratitude for American aid and fear of Soviet expansionism had waned."[14] The 1970s also saw the rise of "principled" concerns for human rights.[15]

By the late 1980s, Dutch foreign policy was characterized by renewed harmony with NATO partners, more acceptance of the Europeanization of foreign and security policy, and a more market-oriented development policy.[16] The end of the Cold War "further helped to give Dutch foreign policy a more European, continental outlook (although still within a nominally Atlantic framework)."[17] The post–Cold War era also brought new challenges for Dutch foreign policy.[18] In particular, Dutch internationalism and moralism were expressed through the post–Cold War proliferation of NATO and UN humanitarian missions.[19] "The UN Agenda for Peace, with its rich menu of quasi-military options like preventive diplomacy, peacemaking, peace forcing, peacekeeping, and peace building, is strongly supported by the Dutch government. By the mid-1990s Dutch troops were involved in [several] UN operations," including those in Angola, Cambodia, South Africa, Haiti, and the former Yugoslavia.[20] The end of the Cold War also brought about a revision in Dutch defense policy and efforts to increase Dutch "soft power" resources through development aid, the promotion of international law, and peacekeeping participation.[21]

Dutch peacekeeping experienced a tragic setback in the ethnic conflict in the former Yugoslavia in the 1990s, an event that will likely be a watershed in Dutch foreign policy for years to come. In 1992, the United Nations declared Srebrenica, a predominantly Bosnian Muslim town, a "safe haven" from Bosnian Serb forces, and eight hundred Dutch soldiers were sent to protect it. The battalion was only lightly armed, however, and could not defend itself or the civilians of Srebrenica when Bosnian Serb forces attacked, massacring eight thousand Muslim refugees. A report by the Netherlands Institute for War Documentation found that the peacekeepers handed over the refugees despite knowing their fate.[22] "Since then, the mere mention of Srebrenica invokes a mixture of feelings of shame and disgust in the Netherlands."[23] When the report was issued in 2002, Prime Minister Kok's Labour-led government resigned. The Dutch publicly took some responsibility for the events in Srebrenica, but many also blamed the UN leadership for not doing more to prevent the tragedy and for failing to send in air support to aid the Dutch troops.[24] Although the memory of Srebrenica is divisive in the Netherlands, "one thing on which most Dutch can agree is that the rules of engagement for UN peacekeeping troops make such tragedies possible. The Dutch learned in Bosnia the painful lessons of the vulnerability that comes from embarking on a mission with limited forces and restrictive rules of engagement."[25]

What factors explain both the constants and the transformations in Dutch foreign policy? Geographical location, history of empire, small size, and religious and moral culture are often presented as explanations. According to Tonra, for example, "Dutch geography contributed in no small way to an international role committed to open and free trade across the seas and continents. Its low-lying fertile plains had endowed a robust and intensive agricultural tradition, the surplus of which needed foreign markets."[26] History is an especially commonly cited factor: "Analyses of postwar Dutch policy are often based on the premise that the country's history contains important clues to understanding contemporary policy directions and priorities."[27] Jonas, for example, argues that "the importance of the Atlantic criterion in Dutch policy can only be appreciated if seen as part of a particular conception of national interests which has emerged from the Dutch historical experience and post-war environment."[28] And Pijpers contends that Dutch commitments to NATO and the developing world during the Cold War were in part self-compensation for the loss of its empire.[29] Given its historical experiences as a great power, "The Netherlands is labouring under . . . 'rank disequilibrium,' caused by the combination of certain medium-range power characteristics with the resources of what is clearly only a small European country."[30] In other words, the Dutch identity as a great power, stemming from its history, lingers even after that identity is no longer accurate.[31]

Other scholars of Dutch foreign policy stress the objective small size of the Netherlands as the key determinant for its foreign policy. According to Jonas,

> The basic feature of the Netherlands has always been its small size. This has conditioned not only the objective range of options available to Dutch policy-makers, but also the subjective perspective from which they have viewed their world. Recognizing that the domain in which they could exercise power was restricted, the Dutch have attempted to preserve their freedom of action within that domain. They have judged that the most prudent policy was to avoid becoming entangled in alliances and in the quarrels of

the larger nations—that is, to remain neutral as possible,—and to uphold the principles and agencies of international law. Neutrality and international law have been, in a sense, the keys to the security of a small nation.[32]

Jonas agrees with Rochon that the smallness of the country makes it more vulnerable to international pressures, even though its historical experience and economic wealth put it in a better position than many other countries to control its own destiny and shape its interactions with the rest of the world.[33] Rochon retells the story of Prime Minister Drees's decision in the 1950s to create two foreign affairs ministers to satisfy coalition party demands: "Asked by a colleague from another country about the reason for this arrangement, Luns replied, 'Because our country is so small, abroad is very large.'"[34]

Verbeek and van der Vleuten also acknowledge the importance of state size. They situate their analysis of contemporary Dutch foreign affairs in the research on small-state foreign policy, which stresses the significance and constraining effects of the international environment. Verbeek and van der Vleuten point to international factors important in post–Cold War Dutch foreign policy, including the end of bipolarity, the growth of regional and international organizations, and globalization dynamics.[35]

According to Rochon, international imperatives rather than principled motives drive the foreign policy of a small state such as the Netherlands: "One need not look far beneath the core principles of Dutch foreign policy to find national interests."[36] Indeed, Rochon argues that the Dutch must rely on principled reason and international law because they are a small state. "The more forceful alternatives open to major powers have not been available to the Dutch since late in the seventeenth century."[37] Others see a genuine commitment to principles and attribute Dutch internationalism and idealism to its Calvinist religious culture.[38]

> If there exists anything like a typical trait that has had an impact on Dutch foreign policy, it may be what Heldring has called the "moralistic-legalistic attitude" of the Dutch. . . . [D]ecisions in the realm of foreign policy are taken or ought to be taken not in terms of power politics but on the merits of the issues at stake. This view is also held by many Dutch intellectuals, who feel that the Dutch know not only what is good for themselves but also for the whole world.[39]

Dutch moralism finds expression in many Dutch foreign policies. According to van Staden, for example, Dutch Atlanticism had moral overtones of gratitude for American aid in World War II in addition to self-interest.[40] Andeweg and Irwin argue that "the most conspicuous exponent of the moral dimension in Dutch foreign policy ... is the preoccupation with development aid. Whether out of a sense of guilt for its colonial past, or as a modern extension of the churches' missionary work, the Dutch attitude towards developing countries borders on *tiers-mondisme*."[41] Dutch participation in peacekeeping has also been explained by a moralist concern for human rights. In the Srebrenica case, there was certainly worry about human rights, but a government-ordered report concluded that in addition to moral concerns about ethnic genocide and war crimes, the Dutch government apparently viewed the mission as an opportunity to increase Dutch influence on the world stage and to demonstrate the importance of the Dutch military's newly created Rapid Deployment Force.[42]

Scholars of Dutch foreign policy have also recognized internal politics as a key explanation.[43] As Van Staden argues: "Small powers in alignment may be net consumers rather than producers of security and likewise their options may be more constrained than of major allies, it is nevertheless false to believe that their behaviour is completely determined by the parameters of international power constellations or that is fully conditioned by outside pressures."[44]

Domestic divisions over foreign policy became more important in the 1970s as a consequence of changes in the international environment and in the Dutch political landscape.[45] Until the end of the 1960s,

> the Netherlands was traditionally classified as a (democratic) corporatist state. . . . The institutional arrangement of relatively autonomous policy domains in which privileged societal groups, in cooperation with state actors such as civil servants, were involved in policy-making ran parallel to the pillarized nature of consociational Netherlands. In foreign policy, however, the political elites held the prerogative. Only in the field of development aid, societal groups—first representing the various societal pillars, later as professionalized organizations with electoral clout in crucial parts of main political parties—had made an inroad into the policy-making system. . . . Depillarization in the 1960s and the 1970s coincided with a wider involvement of Dutch citizens in foreign policy issues.[46]

Depillarization refers to the erosion of the consociational system of separate social, religious, and political blocs, or pillars, and came about through secularization of society and disintegration within the blocs themselves.[47] According to Van Staden, "It must be understood that the process of democratization in the Netherlands led to a domesticisation of foreign policy, in the sense that this policy domain became more and more the battleground of internal political strife, as it turned into a main issue-area in interparty coalition bargaining."[48] Voorhoeve agrees: "Foreign policy came to play an important role in domestic politics during these tumultuous years. . . . [F]oreign policy offered a field for struggle and new identity."[49] The salience of foreign policy issues increased in Dutch public opinion during this time. Writing in 1978, Baehr claimed, "Articulate public opinion has shown a permanent interest in developments abroad. This has made problem areas such as the Middle East, Vietnam, Angola, and Rhodesia, in which the Netherlands was not directly involved, into actual or potential issues in Dutch *internal* politics."[50]

Andeweg also argues that depillarization changed cabinet decision making as issues became increasingly partisan and polarized.[51] The end of the tenure of Foreign Minister Luns, who served from 1952 to 1971, also opened Dutch foreign policy to the influence of more ideas.[52]

By the 1980s, Dutch foreign policy had become more democratic, and more actors, including parties, parliament, and interest groups, had gained influence. Moreover, "foreign policy is no longer multi-partisan (in the sense that its main lines are supported as a matter of course by the major political parties) in theory or in practice. . . . The tenets of the established doctrines are at stake in many fields of foreign policy."[53] This situation continued into the post–Cold War era. According to Verbeek and van der Vleuten, a variety of domestic-level changes, such as the importance of the media, an increase in Dutch political actors' awareness of foreign policy issues, and electoral volatility, have been reinforced by changes in the international system and deeply affect Dutch foreign policy. The result is that "the Dutch political elite is increasingly divided over foreign policy issues, a larger number of departmental actors is involved in foreign policy-making, while the general public is more strongly concerned with foreign policy issues and has more opportunities to raise its voice."[54] Specifically, these authors argue that security and defense policy-making has become more politicized and "domesticated." They contend that the impact of international opportunities and pressures on Dutch foreign policy is mediated through political institutions, both international and domestic.[55]

## ACTORS IN DUTCH FOREIGN POLICY

The number of domestic political actors that can shape Dutch foreign policy has grown dramatically since the 1960s. In general, the foreign policy-making process remains in the cabinet, but actors inside the cabinet may be divided and can be susceptible to outside influence. In a survey of members of the Dutch elite in the 1970s, 87 percent responded that the cabinet has "much or quite a bit of influence on the making of foreign policy."[56] Only civil servants and diplomats, the second chamber of parliament, and political parties were viewed as influential by more than 45 percent of those responding. Still, other political actors may indirectly influence these more significant actors.

Included in these sources of domestic pressures is the general public. As a broad consensus on the goals of Dutch foreign policy eroded and as changes in the Dutch political landscape brought in more viewpoints by the 1970s, the public also became more polarized on and interested in issues of international relations.[57] Furthermore, "the more general urge of citizens and groups towards increased participation in public affairs and towards 'democratization' of society in all spheres of life has not left the area of foreign policy untouched."[58] Yet as in most democracies, the level of interest in foreign policy issues in the Netherlands is not particularly high compared to interest in domestic policies. And as elsewhere, the level of participation or active attempts to influence foreign policy is confined to an attentive elite.[59]

Public sentiments are often organized into pressure groups, such as labor unions, churches, or business. Everts, writing in the early 1980s, notes that "more specifically, one can point out the recent creation of a large number of special interest or 'action' groups . . . concerned with issues such as the problems of war and peace, armament, Third World issues, human rights, or problems of particular areas or countries."[60] Although interest group activity arguably increased in the Netherlands after the 1960s, most scholars of Dutch foreign policy do not see significant independent influence by these pressure groups or by the public they seek to represent.[61]

According to Voorhoeve, for example, "It appears from research that interventions by business circles and other economic interest groups are neither frequent nor very effective. There are, moreover, examples of Government policies which run counter to important economic interests."[62] Voorhoeve points out, however, that the government may often anticipate and agree with economic interests.[63]

In his comprehensive study of the role of the public in Dutch foreign policy, Cohen agrees with Voorhoeve that the way in which the public and interest groups have influence is often very indirect. He argues that "mass opinion does not 'act' in a policy-making process the way that other participants do."[64] Cohen suggests that public opinion and interest group pressures provide a context in which Dutch foreign policy elites make foreign policy and that these elites are often concerned with what the public prefers. But he points out that even in the controversy over the stationing of cruise missiles in the 1980s, in which pressure groups were vocal and large public demonstrations took place, this public opinion mattered more in terms of how it affected splits within the government. When those splits were resolved, the government stared down public opposition.[65]

Interest groups direct their attempts to influence primarily at parties and party groups in parliament.[66] The Dutch parliament is bicameral, consisting of a First Chamber of Senators appointed by provinces and a Second Chamber of directly elected representatives, but the Second Chamber, the Tweede Kamer, is the most important political and policy-making body.[67] And as foreign policy has become more salient to the public, the Second Chamber has also become more active in foreign affairs.[68] The Foreign Affairs Committee, for example, meets regularly, and the foreign minister must inform the committee of major policy decisions.[69] And since the government is formally controlled by the parliament, parliament can force the cabinet or a particular minister to resign by rejecting an important bill or by passing a motion of no confidence.[70] The parliament also has the constitutional powers of treaty ratification, war declaration, and budget approval.[71] According to Voorhoeve, the impact of parliament on foreign policy is often implicit, as the cabinet anticipates its criticisms:

> Certainly, parliamentary influence is more than cosmetic. The Foreign Minister knows that there is only a narrow band of acceptable policies. If he diverges from this band, his position will be seriously challenged by Parlia-

ment at home and by diplomatic opponents abroad, who could take advantage if the Dutch Minister's policies would not be based on domestic consensus.[72]

Yet parliament is generally not considered a very important player, by itself, in Dutch foreign policy.[73] It primarily comes into play when the government is divided. When the government is united or when it resolves its differences on its own, parliament tends to support it. Parliament's weak role stems from the general weakness of parliaments in a parliamentary system and from specific historical and institutional characteristics of the Dutch political system.[74] "Formal accounts of the foreign policy establishment in the Netherlands emphasize the power and autonomy of the government over parliament.... The nineteenth-century assertion of the parliamentary right to participate in policymaking did not extend to foreign policy, where executive privilege lasted much longer."[75] And although Dutch governments are dependent on a parliamentary majority to maintain their ruling position, there is somewhat of a separation of powers in the Dutch system in that cabinet ministers cannot be members of parliament and cabinets do not face a formal vote of investiture (they are appointed by the queen), thus taking away one form of influence that parliament might have on the cabinet's composition.[76] Dutch parliamentary committees also are consultative, without any policy-making capabilities, and have little or no staff.[77] In addition, "in practice, even Parliament's power to adopt a motion of non-confidence is limited, because the delicate balance within the Cabinet and the difficulty of forming a new Government . . . serve as practical restraints upon Parliament."[78] With relatively high levels of party discipline, the parties in the cabinet, who together control a majority of parliamentary votes, can usually rely on their representatives in the Tweede Kamer to support their positions. Thus, the basic conflicts in Dutch politics are between and within parties, not between the institutions of parliament and the government.[79] Parliamentary involvement in foreign policy is often a by-product of this partisan or intraparty conflict.

Although there is cross-party consensus on the broad themes of Dutch foreign policy, a number of ideological and policy differences across and within the political parties have produced significant debates in foreign policy-making.[80] Polarization and partisanship in foreign policy have generally increased since the 1960s.[81] Moreover, Verbeek and van der Vleuten

## Dutch Foreign Policy

contend that "the increase of electoral volatility from the mid-1990s . . . and the persistent growth of political parties of the far left and far right with strong views on foreign policy issues such as humanitarian intervention, migration and European integration contributed to a polarization of the political debate on these issues and increased the vulnerability of the political elites for perceived foreign policy failures."[82]

Partisan views are represented in parliament as well as in the cabinet, the Netherlands' primary foreign policy decision-making unit. The cabinet, known as the Council of Ministers, is characterized by traditions of collegial and collective government and strong departmental ministers.[83] Cabinet meetings are an important locus for governing: "In these meetings many matters are considered and an average of 25 decisions are taken. Moreover, these decisions are far from being simply rubber stamps: a careful reading of the minutes [of some of the available cabinet meetings] shows that approximately one in five decisions differs from the original proposal put to Cabinet."[84] The cabinet considers and debates international treaties, instructions to Dutch diplomats and other representatives, and all other important foreign policy issues.[85]

The prime minister, as head of the cabinet and (generally) leader of the largest party in the government, is certainly an important player in the Council of Ministers and in Dutch foreign policy-making. Yet Dutch prime ministers are less powerful than their counterparts in other parliamentary systems.[86] The dynamics of coalition government, the collegial political norms, the lack of a sizable staff, and the inability to appoint or remove cabinet ministers make for a fairly weak prime minister.[87] The prime minister does, however, chair the meetings of the cabinet and establishes the cabinet's agenda, and observers of Dutch politics argue that the position of the prime minister vis-à-vis the cabinet has strengthened over the years as a consequence of a variety of internal and external factors.[88] The prime ministers' power, however, chiefly resides in their ability to forge compromises across competing departments and parties.[89]

The foreign minister is another individual in the collective cabinet who is a key player in Dutch foreign policy and in the past may have been more important than the prime minister. Writing in 1978, Baehr argued that "the Foreign Minister is unquestionably *the* dominating figure in the field of Dutch external relations."[90] Baehr cited "a standing rule that all departments conduct their contacts with foreign governments through the channels of the Ministry of Foreign Affairs."[91] Foreign ministers are particularly strong vis-à-vis parliament because they do not owe their position to its investiture, because they refuse to publicly answer parliamentary questions on the grounds of national security, and because they are often the leader of the second-largest party in the coalition, so a vote of no confidence would likely cause the dissolution of the government.[92] Foreign ministers also control a disproportionately large staff, given the country's small size.[93]

The dominant influence of the foreign minister was perhaps at its peak from 1956 to 1971, when Luns served in that position regardless of the makeup of the coalition. According to Rochon, however, "the autonomy of the foreign ministry has significantly declined in recent decades."[94] Rochon argues that the changing nature of foreign policy and the necessary participation of many departments in international affairs means that international negotiations are no longer the foreign minister's exclusive domain.[95] Furthermore, the responsibilities of the foreign ministry were divided in the 1960s when the position of minister for development cooperation was established.[96] The result is that "since the mid-1960s there have been two persons with ministerial rank in the Foreign Ministry: one is the foreign minister, and the other is technically a minister without portfolio but actually the development cooperation minister," who is in charge of overseas development assistance.[97] This "second foreign minister" is often from a different political party and has challenged the minister for foreign affairs on many policies.[98]

The foreign minister has also competed with the rising importance of the prime minister, especially as Dutch decision making has become more Europeanized in the EU and the prime minister is the chief representative and coordinator for Dutch–EU relations.[99] In the post–Cold War period, Dutch prime ministers have also been more interested in European affairs, resulting in competition with the foreign minister and more politicization of foreign policy.[100] On some issues, the defense minister is another key cabinet member.[101]

Although the atmosphere in the Dutch cabinet is often described as collegial and consensus-seeking, it is not without conflict.[102] Indeed, decision making in the cabinet is characterized by both interdepartmental and partisan disagreements.[103] These two types of conflict often reinforce each other as the ministers of foreign affairs, cooperation, economics, and defense are usually from different parties.[104] At times, unofficial "inner cabinets" have developed within the Dutch cabinet, comprising the most important party leaders in the coalition as well as the most important ministries for the issue under consideration.[105]

## COALITION POLITICS IN DUTCH FOREIGN POLICY: GENERAL IMAGES AND FOUR CASES

Although there is no study devoted specifically to the question of how coalition politics affects Dutch foreign policy and policy-making, scholars have frequently commented on the important role that coalition politics play. The frequency of comments is certainly related to the ubiquitous occurrence of coalitions in the Netherlands. No single party ever enjoys a parliamentary majority, a situation that undoubtedly stems from its "pure" system of proportional representation. Furthermore, according to Andeweg and Irwin, coalitions are an "imperative" in the Netherlands. While few institutional barriers to forming a minority government exist, "the possibility of minority government has never even occurred to Dutch politicians, except as an interim solution after a cabinet crisis."[106] Thus, coalition politics are an enduring feature of Dutch foreign policy, and many of the observations about the effects of coalition politics are consistent with the expectations, detailed in chapter 2, that multiparty cabinets constrain choices and are ineffective at policy-making.

Although coalitions have long ruled the Netherlands, Andeweg notes, "Curiously, however, the political heterogeneity normally associated with coalitions did not seem to have much impact on the Dutch cabinet until the 1960s."[107] Before this time, cabinet policy-making was not particularly partisan or politicized.[108] One reason for this was the longevity of Foreign Minister Luns.[109] Since then, however, cabinet meetings have become increasingly politicized and partisan.[110]

Politicization can be seen from the outset of the coalition, including the distribution of ministries and the composition of cabinet committees. "When ministerial portfolios are being distributed during the cabinet formation, the effects of this distribution on the composition of the major Cabinet Committees are constantly kept in mind by the negotiators. When a coalition party is satisfied with the composition of the cabinet as a whole, but not with the party balance in some of its Committees, new Committee members are sometimes added."[111] The creation of the post of minister for developmental cooperation was also a result of coalition bargaining over the balance of portfolios.[112]

Policy differences among the coalition partners are also dealt with at the beginning of the cabinet's tenure in the coalition agreement. According to Timmermans, Dutch (and other) coalition agreements serve a variety of functions, including setting the policy agenda and preventing conflict between the parties. Coalition agreements are difficult to enforce but do affect subsequent policy-making.[113]

The differences between the coalition partners can generate coalition crises and the fall of governments. Herein lies a potential constraint on Dutch foreign policy. Coalition crises and dissolution are a pervasive part of Dutch political life. "Since World War II the average cabinet length has been about two and a half years, so that the possibility of a coalition being overturned prematurely is quite real. Only eight cabinets between 1917 and 1998 have survived the full four-year parliamentary term.... On nearly all other occasions, the life of a government was ended prematurely because of a partisan split in the coalition."[114] According to Andeweg, most cabinet crises before 1965 were intraparty quarrels involving backbenchers in Parliament: "Between 1945 and 1965 no cabinet fell because of internal disagreement. Since 1965 all cabinet crises but one have been caused by disagreement along party lines with the cabinet."[115] Rochon cites an analysis of Dutch coalition conflicts by Timmermans and Bakema that found that almost all of the coalition crises stemmed from interparty rather than interministerial disagreements and notes that "party-based conflicts in the ministerial council are especially dangerous to resolve by majority vote, because a party on the losing side of the vote could withdraw from the coalition and bring down government. Because of their potential for ending the life of a government, issues that cause interparty disagreements are very likely simply to be postponed until an acceptable compromise can be found."[116]

The potential for cabinets to fall over foreign policy and that potential's effects on Dutch foreign policy have been noted by several scholars in specific cases. For example, "between 1977 and 1981, for the first time since 1945 the threat of a cabinet crisis rooted in a foreign policy issued loomed in Dutch political life."[117] The issues involved were the sale of enriched uranium to Brazil, the neutron bomb, the deployment of cruise missiles, and the proposed oil embargo against South Africa. The decision about how to contribute to the U.S.-led coalition against Iraq in the first Gulf War in 1991 was a compromise between the two coalition partners.[118] And in 2010, the Dutch government collapsed over whether to keep troops in Afghanistan.[119] More generally, Rochon notes that Dutch domestic conditions, including coalition politics, constrain the government in international negotiations but that this constraint can be leveraged to their advantage, à la Putnam's two-level game framework.[120] One Dutch party member interviewed for this project stated that coalition politics also affects how cabinet members think in that they generally mute their differences because they know they must make the partnership work. At election time, however, coalition partners may sharpen their differences. This is especially true for the small parties who cater to electoral niches.[121] Another interviewee at the U.S. embassy in the Hague said that U.S. officials pay considerable attention to coalition politics in the Netherlands (even if those politics are frustrating) because they recognize the potential effects on foreign policy. This official claimed that most of the cables going to Washington from the embassy during the 2006 Dutch debate regarding troops for Afghanistan were about explaining and predicting the effects of coalition politics.[122]

The negative effects of coalition politics on Dutch decision making are often mentioned. Because of the political fragmentation and the resulting coalition governance, Dutch politics has been described as "an orchestra with no conductor."[123] According to Anderson and Kaeding, "The requirements of coalition government prevent the formulation of a strong central political direction" in Dutch relations with the European Union.[124] The need to keep the coalition together promotes excessive compromise and delay.[125] "Because of heterogeneity and fragmentation, the number of veto points is considerable: policymaking moves slowly, if at all. In the Netherlands this is known as the 'viscosity' (*'stroperigheid'* in Dutch; literally: syrupiness) of policy-making."[126] Inaction is a likely outcome when parties are divided.[127] In addition, Everts argues that coalition politics weakens the prime minister and makes coordination across cabinet ministries more difficult.[128]

A few scholars have acknowledged positive side effects of coalition politics on Dutch decision making. Andeweg and Irwin, for example, argue that the fact that the Dutch Cabinet is both a board of departmental ministers and a coalition of political parties also has its advantages. Ministers are moderated in their pursuit of narrow departmental interests by political cross-pressures. Parties are kept informed about departments headed by ministers from other parties through the fact that junior ministers from one party are sometimes appointed as "watchdog" at a department of another party's minister. Often, in the words of one former junior minister, "most watchdogs turn out to be guidedogs," providing a channel of communication between the other party's minister from their department and the ministers from their party.[129]

These authors also acknowledge the increased legitimacy that comes with having more voices involved in decision making: "One of the obvious advantages of consensus politics is the high legitimacy accorded to the decisions that emerge from all this negotiation and consultation, even if the decisions are unpopular."[130]

The Dutch cases for this project, listed in table 4.1, were chosen according to the principles discussed in chapter 3. Each case is an instance of conflict among the political parties in the coalition over a foreign policy decision. The cases come from four different coalitions—two in the 1980s and two in the early twenty-first century—and cover economic, human rights, alliance commitments, peacekeeping, and intervention issues. The cases differ somewhat from each other in terms of the international and domestic contexts in which they occurred. The cruise missile case, for example, took place during renewed tension between the superpowers in a bipolar world and during a wave of anti-Atlanticism and democratization of foreign policy in the Netherlands. In the Afghanistan case, conversely, the security threats were very different, and a more pragmatic consensus on Dutch foreign policy had developed. The case of Iraq is unique in this book in the sense that the primary disagreement was between potential coalition partners involved in coalition formation negotiations. Although one of the parties involved was not a formal member of the cabinet, the decision by the Dutch government at the beginning of the Iraqi war was a product of the coalition politics occurring in this formation stage. Despite the differences in the Dutch cases, they all afford an opportunity to assess how coalition politics affects foreign policy and foreign policy decision making in the Netherlands. There is no a priori reason to believe that the differences critically affect the relationships under investigation.

## SANCTIONS AGAINST APARTHEID SOUTH AFRICA

By the late 1970s, the white minority apartheid government in South Africa and its repressive treatment of its black population met with growing criticism and ostracism in the international community. "For The Netherlands, South Africa was an issue of abiding national interest. The extensive historical and cultural links between the Afrikaner population and The Netherlands made the issue one of great political sensitivity."[131] The Dutch had settled and founded a community of Europeans in the Cape Colony in southern Africa in 1652. Even after decolonization, in the Netherlands, "the situation in South Africa was recognized as one of direct national interest. The historical links between the 'Afrikaner volk' and the Dutch were strong. Until the early 1980s South Africa was widely seen as a *domaine réservée* in Dutch foreign policy. The Dutch voting position at the United

**Table 4.1. Dutch Cases**

| Case | Coalition Parties | (a) Prime Minister<br>(b) Foreign Minister<br>(c) Defense Minister |
|---|---|---|
| Sanctions against apartheid South Africa (1980) | Christian Democrats (CDA) + Liberals (VVD) | (a) van Agt (CDA)<br>(b) van der Klaauw (VVD)<br>(c) Scholten (CDA) |
| NATO cruise missiles (1981) | Christian Democrats (CDA) + Labour (PvdA) + Democrats '66 (D66) | (a) van Agt (CDA)<br>(b) van der Stoel (PvdA)<br>(c) van Mierlo (D66) |
| Iraq War (2003) | Caretaker government:<br>Christian Democrats (CDA) + Liberals (VVD) + List Pim Fortuyn (LPF)<br><br>Parties in coalition talks:<br>Christian Democrats (CDA) + Labour (PvdA) | (a) Balkenende (CDA)<br>(b) de Hoop Scheffer (CDA)<br>(c) Kamp (VVD) |
| Troop deployment to Uruzgan Afghanistan (2006) | Christian Democrats (CDA) + Liberals (VVD) + D66[a] | (a) Balkenende (CDA)<br>(b) Bot (CDA)<br>(c) Kamp (VVD) |

[a] By this time, the formal name of the Democrats '66 party had changed to simply D66.

Nations was often at variance with its early political co-operation partners."[132] Until the 1980s, Dutch foreign policy toward South Africa was largely driven by this historical relationship, relatively free from the Cold War context and security imperatives.[133]

Yet Dutch attitudes toward South Africa gradually evolved from those based on close historical ties to concerns about the morality of apartheid and issues of human rights.[134] "By the early 1960s opposition to the apartheid policies of the ruling Afrikaner-based National Party was the subject of vigorous debate in The Netherlands. The radicalization of Dutch–South African relations—prompted largely by the lobbying of anti-apartheid activists and in response to the development of 'Grand Apartheid' by the National Party—resulted in Dutch support of opposition groups in South Africa and comprehensive UN sanctions against South Africa."[135]

The international community first considered an oil embargo against South Africa in the early 1960s, and the idea gained strength throughout the 1970s when key oil suppliers, such as Iran, joined, leaving South Africa dependent on Western oil supplies. Western states, however, continued to veto oil embargo resolutions. For the Netherlands, the question of an oil embargo was controversial, given historical ties, domestic groups opposing apartheid, and economic relations (which included multinational business organizations such as the Anglo-Dutch Shell Oil company). Furthermore, the previous Dutch policy of criticizing the apartheid system while maintaining engagement with the South African government was viewed as unsuccessful.[136] The issue of South Africa became explosive for several Dutch governments in the 1970s.[137] "In spite of the almost total consensus on the rejection of apartheid, the question of economic sanctions [was] a hotly debated theme in Dutch foreign policy for a number of years."[138]

Following its assumption of office in 1977, the coalition between the Christian Democrats and the Liberals first attempted to resist domestic and international pressures to change its policy toward South Africa. "Complete isolation of South Africa was rejected; [the government] preferred a 'critical dialogue.'"[139] The government maintained that unilateral sanctions were not an option and that a multilateral effort, coordinated with the other states in a UN or EC framework, was the best strategy. Not all members of the governing parties agreed, however, and the division in the ruling coalition over the issue of a unilateral oil embargo against South Africa almost brought the government down in June 1980. An eleventh-hour compromise in parliament saved the government: it agreed to seek cooperation from Benelux and Scandinavian partners, instead of all EC members, but did not commit to a unilateral embargo if this cooperation did not materialize. The policy differences within the coalition prevented serious efforts to implement the compromise, and change in Dutch foreign policy toward South Africa was not forthcoming.[140]

*Players and Positions*

The coalition between the Christian Democratic Appeal (CDA) and the Liberals held a slim majority following the national elections in 1977 (see table 4.2). The Christian Democratic Party was a very recent merger of three religious parties, both Catholic and Protestant, and it was the second-largest party in the Tweede Kamer.[141] Although the Labour Party was the largest party, Prime Minister van Agt of the Christian Democrats put together the coalition.[142] The portfolios in the cabinet were divided fairly evenly (see table 4.3), with the Liberals getting more than their relative parliamentary strength in the cabinet. The relevant foreign affairs positions were also divided among the parties: the Christian Democrats controlled the defense ministry (under Scholten) and the position of development minister (under de Koning), while the Liberals controlled the critical post of foreign minister (under van der Klaauw).

**TABLE 4.2. Dutch National Election Results, 1977**

|  | Votes (%) | Seats |
|---|---|---|
| Labour | 33.8 | 53 |
| **Christian Democratic Appeal** | **31.9** | **49** |
| **Liberals** | **17.9** | **28** |
| D66 | 5.4 | 8 |
| Political Reformed Party | 2.1 | 3 |
| Radical Political Party | 1.7 | 3 |
| Netherlands Communist Party | 1.7 | 2 |
| Reformed Political Union | 1.0 | 1 |
| Pacifist Socialist Party | 0.9 | 1 |
| Farmers Party | 0.8 | 1 |
| Democratic Socialists '70 | 0.7 | 1 |

*Source:* Statistics Netherlands, 2009, www.cbs.nl, accessed April 18, 2009.
*Note:* The parties in the governing coalition are boldface; only those parties receiving seats in the parliament are included.

Experts place the Christian Democratic Appeal party just right of center on a general left-right dimension and the Liberal Party (VVD) to the right of center (and further right than the Christian Democrats) on a general left-right dimension. As with most liberal parties, the VVD's commitment to political and individual rights makes it more left-leaning, while its commitment to economic rights makes it more right-leaning.[143] The VVD had been growing in electoral and parliamentary strength since the early 1970s.[144] In foreign affairs, the Liberal Party consistently advocates free trade, is a strong supporter of the NATO alliance, "and propagates an active concern with in-

TABLE 4.3. Members of the van Agt I Cabinet of the Netherlands (1977–81)

| Ministry | Individual | Party |
| --- | --- | --- |
| Prime minister | van Agt | Christian Democrats |
| Vice minister, Internal Affairs | Wiegel | Liberals |
| External Affairs | van der Klaauw | Liberals |
| Defense | Scholten | Christian Democrats |
| Development | de Koning | Christian Democrats |
| Finance | Andriessen | Christian Democrats |
| Suriname and Netherlands-Antilles Affairs | van der Stee | Liberals |
| Economic Affairs | van Aardenne | Liberals |
| Justice | de Ruiter | Christian Democrats |
| Education and Science | Pais | Liberals |
| Netherlands-Antilles Affairs | van der Stee | Liberals |
| Housing | Beelaarts/ van Blokland | Christian Democrats/ Christian Democrats |
| Public Works | Tuijnman | Liberals |
| Agriculture and Fishing | van der Stee/ Braks | Liberals/ Christian Democrats |
| Social Affairs | Albeda | Christian Democrats |
| Culture and Recreation | Gardeniers-Berendsen | Christian Democrats |
| Health of the People and Environment | Ginjaar | Liberals |
| Science Policy | van Trier | Christian Democrats |

*Source:* Government of the Netherlands, Minister of General Affairs, "Cabinets since 1945," http://minaz.nl/Onderwerpen/Ministerraad/Kabinetten_sinds_1945, accessed April 15, 2009.

*Note:* There were some changes in personnel throughout this cabinet's tenure. The individual(s) during the later part of the coalition, at the time of the decisions on the South African case, are presented here. The table includes some changes that were made during the case. Andriessen stepped down from minister of finance in February 1980 and was replaced by van der Stee in March. At this time, Minister van der Stee left his post as Dutch-Antilles affairs minister and as agricultural and fishing minster and was replaced by Minister Braks in the latter position.

ternational law, including the observance of human rights. With other Dutch parties, it embraces an active policy of development aid . . . but it advocates a more immediate participation of private enterprise in the granting of aid."[145] Compared to other parties, the Liberal Party had few internal divisions, both in general and specifically on foreign policy issues.[146]

From the beginning, the cabinet's stated policy was to promote economic sanctions against South Africa within multilateral frameworks in the United Nations and the European Community.[147] By 1979, however, the government was under significant domestic pressure to pursue a unilateral oil embargo.[148] "At home, Dutch antiapartheid groups were dissatisfied and demanded that the Dutch Government make good its pledge to pursue tough unilateral sanctions against South Africa."[149] These groups included organizations formed specifically around the South African issue, trade unions, and churches, and they launched a campaign in the 1970s to inform the Dutch public and pressure party members to support a unilateral embargo. "A major element in the campaign was the support by hundreds of local groups . . . demanding the support of local organizations and spreading information among the public. In more than 150 places protest meetings were organized with the oil embargo against South Africa as their central theme."[150] Employers' organizations and companies such as Dutch Shell were to some extent counterinterests to the pro-embargo lobby, but their activities were less direct.[151] According to Everts, "Domestic consensus on this issue was fairly large; concern with the South African situation was widespread. It did not reach, however, beyond a declaration of principles. The domestic pressure groups wanted concrete actions, which were opposed by others (including the business community)."[152] Everts argues that the influence by outside groups moved government policy, even if it failed to get a unilateral embargo adopted. Key to this success was the presence of allies in parliament, both inside opposition parties and inside the governing coalition parties. In turn, the ability of key members inside the ruling parties to have influence was helped by pressure from outside interest groups.[153]

Most of the small parties in parliament as well as the largest opposition party, the Labour Party (PvdA), favored a unilateral Dutch oil embargo against South Africa. "The PvdA argued in favour of a [unilateral] Dutch embargo, to set an example to the other EC countries."[154] Although Labour was somewhat divided on this issue when it was in government (1973–77 and 1981–82), when the party was in opposition (1977–81), "it had more freedom to press this point. South Africa was to be a central element in its opposition strategy; this was reinforced by the fact that to stress this item would also allow it to play on the existing divisions in the Christian Democratic group."[155] The parties in opposition were particularly active on the South Africa issue, partly as a consequence of interest group pressures. Indeed, parliament considered the issue of an oil embargo three times between 1979 and 1981.[156]

Parliamentary opposition parties criticized the center-right coalition for continuing to resist a unilateral embargo. The junior coalition partner, the Liberal Party, was fairly unanimous in its opposition to an oil embargo. The party "rejected sanctions and claimed that these would hurt the wrong people. Economic growth would serve the goals of liberalization better."[157] One Liberal member of parliament, Frits Bolkestein, argued the case for economic engagement to facilitate social and political changes in South Africa.[158] The leadership and the majority of the Christian Democrats also opposed the embargo. Prime Minister "Van Agt felt that any isolated Dutch measures would have little effect and would simply result in a diversion of trade."[159] For the prime minister, sanctions were desirable only as part of a multilateral effort.[160]

The Christian Democrats, however, were not unified, as some representatives of the party supported a unilateral embargo.[161] "The Netherlands' relations with South Africa were . . . a bone of contention in the [CDA] party. The so-called loyalists ([later known as] dissidents), a group of Christian Democratic members of the Parliament who had objected to the formation of a new cabinet with the liberals in 1977 . . . , recommended tough economic sanctions to coerce South Africa to abandon its policy to 'Apartheid.'"[162] "The visibility and symbolic nature of the problem made it a very suitable item for the 'dissident' left wing of the Christian Democrats to show its lack of confidence in the policies of the cabinet in general, both domestically and internationally."[163] The dissidents, who had favored a coalition with Labour and declined to give the center-right government their formal support, pledged to "judge the behavior of the cabinet on its merits. Their disagreement with government policies became manifest on a number of occasions, including . . . four issues of foreign policy."[164] With each disagreement, the group introduced motions critical of the government.[165]

*Disagreements and Decision Making*

The November 1979 motion on South Africa came from the dissidents in the Christian Democratic Party in the context of a general debate on the budget for the Ministry of Foreign Affairs.[166] The motion was a resolution that the Netherlands should pursue support of an embargo with its EC partners, but if the government proved unable to do so by June 1980, it should unilaterally declare an oil embargo.[167] This motion passed the Second Chamber of parliament, although all members of the Liberal Party voted against it, and the government did not treat it seriously.[168] "Although the government carried out the motion, it was evident that it had not done so wholeheartedly. The government had stressed implicitly that it was merely carrying out the sense of parliament."[169] A significant force behind the government's lukewarm efforts was the strong opposition to a unilateral embargo by Foreign Minister van der Klaauw of the Liberal Party. Van der Klaauw argued that "such action would be ineffective, it would isolate the Netherlands internationally, and was forbidden under existing international regulations (Benelux, EEC, GATT). Moreover, it would have a negative impact on developments in Southern Africa in general. The appeal to the latter argument seemed to show that the government was at heart opposed to any embargo."[170]

Parliament was dissatisfied with the lack of results and took up the matter again in June 1980. The government added a new argument to the debate: A better strategy would be to support an independent Zimbabwe as pressure against South Africa. Accepting part of this line of reasoning, Parliament again passed a motion endorsing this broader policy toward southern Africa but also emphasizing the need for an oil embargo. This motion passed on June 18, although with less support, as eleven members of the Christian Democrats joined the Liberals and other rightist parties in voting against the motion. Van der Klaauw called the motion "very unwise."[171]

The government refused to carry out the motion,[172] and

> after intensive debates and consultations within the cabinet and with the leaders of the coalition parties, another debate took place, on June 26. The government showed itself willing to accept two parts of the . . . motion: a) a sharper policy on Namibia, and b) more support to the front line states. On the question of the oil embargo against South Africa it reiterated, however, its by now well-known view: common action by the European Community was not to be expected, and isolated action by the Netherlands alone, while possibly having some "signal function," was to be avoided, if the Netherlands did not wish to lose its influence on the matter in the EEC.

After Mr. Scholten [a member of parliament] had repeated his plea for an embargo, the leader of the Christian Democratic group, Mr. R. Lubbers, put oil on the fire by stating not only that there was majority in his group in favour of an embargo, but also that relations between the Christian Democrats in parliament and the cabinet were growing worse. He concluded that the government would need a parliamentary majority to survive. The threat was clear. After a long intermission the cabinet ceded on one point. It would try to seek support among the Benelux partners and the Scandinavia countries for an oil embargo against South Africa. Prime Minister Van Agt did not say however, whether he would be willing to adopt a unilateral embargo, if these consultations failed.[173]

The Labour Party demanded that the government follow the complete motion of the parliament, and this motion passed. "When the Prime Minister announced that his cabinet would not deviate from the position which the cabinet had arrived at, opposition leader Mr. Den Uyl introduced an implicit motion of censure, deploring the cabinet's unwillingness to carry out the . . . motion [on South Africa]. Now the chips were down, and when it came to a vote, all but six members of the Christian Democratic group came to the aid of the government, which consequently was saved. The margin was very narrow, however: 74 against 72 votes."[174] The members of the Christian Democrats who rescued the government were appeased by the last-minute compromise that the government would seek the cooperation from the Benelux countries and Scandinavia but that the support of all EC partners was not essential. The other dissidents, however, were unconvinced.[175]

The government did little to implement the compromise. When the issue was raised again in the spring of 1981, the government argued that the dissidents should not risk another cabinet crisis just before the elections. By this time, much of the steam had run out of the embargo campaign. Although a new center-left cabinet was formed in 1981 (including Labour, the Christian Democrats, and centrist Democrats '66), it did little on the issue of South Africa. The next government was center-right, again with the Christian Democrats and the Liberals, and continued to stress the importance of an international effort.[176] Not until 1984 did the Netherlands announced a voluntary agreement that would prevent Dutch oil companies from exporting crude oil to South Africa.[177]

## Role of Coalition Politics

This case demonstrates the potential impact that foreign policy disagreements among some coalition partners can have on foreign policy. The government almost collapsed over the matter of a unilateral oil embargo against South Africa. This process could not have occurred without the presence of "dissidents" within one coalition party, the Christian Democrats. In the end, however, the government's policy was largely unaffected by this challenge, even though the dissidents had support from opposition parties, interest groups, and the public. The final decision was not extreme but rather quite moderate. It can be characterized as conflictual, as it expressed determination to pursue sanctions against South Africa.[178]

This case is consistent with the expectation that coalitions can constrain more conflictual action. Despite the general support for sanctions, the Liberals, the junior party in the coalition, along with many in the senior party, constrained government policy from moving in this direction. Constraints in the conflictual direction[179] were attempted by the dissidents in the CDA, the senior party, but failed to move policy significantly toward their preferred option of unilateral sanctions and failed to force implementation of the compromise reached.

This case follows the expectation that coalitions often must compromise in their foreign policies, although the compromise in this case (to narrow the collaborative multilateral framework to Benelux or Scandinavian partners) was not excessive or a meaningless papering over of differences. The compromise was not, however, really implemented, dissidents in the party did not challenge this failure.

This case also does not demonstrate the type of poor decision making often associated with coalition cabinets. There was little delay or deadlock as a result of irreconcilable differences. Although the matter was pursued to the point of government crisis, the last-minute compromise can be considered an example of the divergent thinking that psychological research has found to be an outcome of dissension from a minority faction. Conversely, the slack between the policy decision and implementation deviates from model rational decision making.

One key factor that helps explain the outcome of this case is the disunity in the senior party, where most of the action took place. Without the presence of the Liberals in the coalition, however, this disunity might have played out differently, with different results. Thus, another key factor is the strong position of the Liberal Party and its control of the foreign ministry. The Liberal Party was in a key position to strongly oppose the embargo, along with the prime minister and other cabinet leaders from the Christian Democrats, and thus essentially could prevent the implementation of the compromise. The divisibility of the issue—the fact that there was a middle ground between EEC sanctions and unilateralism—also explains the compromise that developed and the quality of the decision making. Finally, the locus of authority in this case shifted from the cabinet to the parliament, allowing the dissidents in the Christian Democrats to join forces with opposition parties. In the end, however, some dissidents' commitment to the coalition led them to switch support back to the governing parties.

DELAYED DEPLOYMENT OF NATO CRUISE MISSILES

In December 1979, the NATO formalized its "dual-track decision." The first track involved arms control negotiations between the United States and the Soviet Union to build on the Strategic Arms Limitation Talks treaties negotiated in the early 1970s. The second track was the deployment of cruise missiles in Western Europe, with the Netherlands allowing forty-eight cruise missiles to be deployed on its territory. Although the second track was meant to be conditional on the outcome of the first track, deployment was also a tool to apply pressure in the first-track negotiations and was scheduled to start in 1983. NATO's decision to deploy cruise missiles in Western Europe came as a response to Soviet installation of SS-20 missiles aimed at Western Europe, as Western European governments were concerned that nuclear parity between the superpowers made the continent more vulnerable to war. Opponents of the decision charged that deployment was a dangerous solution that would only fuel the superpower arms race. Indeed, "NATO's modernization decision provoked a great deal of criticism in all countries concerned, especially in the Netherlands."[180]

The question of cruise missile deployment became one of the most important issues in Dutch foreign policy[181] and precipitated "probably the greatest political controversy over foreign policy since decolonization. Unprecedentedly large demonstrations (of around half a million participants each) against the missiles took place, in Amsterdam in 1981 and in the Hague in 1982."[182] The issue also divided the political parties.

Despite considerable efforts by the United States and other NATO partners to pressure the Netherlands, in December 1979, the Dutch government (composed of the Christian Democrats and the Liberals) deferred its decision to deploy NATO cruise missiles until 1981 (after the next election, thereby saving the cabinet).[183] Although the Liberals favored deployment, the Christian Democrats were divided, and the opposition parties that were against deployment helped pass a parliamentary motion to tie the government's hands. "The position taken by the Dutch government at the meeting of NATO ministers of December 12 enabled the conservative-liberals to claim that the Netherlands was still loyal to the Alliance, while the Christian Democrats could contend that the deployment issue was still open."[184] The *Economist* referred to this decision as "masterly inactivity."[185]

The decision isolated the Netherlands within the NATO alliance.[186] "The Dutch position was entered as a formal reservation into the annex of the official list of decisions made by NATO's ministers. This rather unique move was deplored in allied circles, since it was believed to undercut NATO's solidarity."[187] The issue remained unresolved for six years. Following new elections, a coalition between Labour, the Democrats '66, and the Christian Democrats formed in September 1981. The 1981 elections, according to Everts, were of significant international importance, given the parties' differences regarding the cruise missiles.[188] In coalition talks, the CDA and PvdA agreed to disagree on the issue; as a result of Labour's opposition to the missiles, the government officially announced in November 1981 that it would postpone the deployment decision until after U.S.-Soviet talks had taken place. The decision to deploy was not made until 1985. Gladdish argues that the Dutch cruise missile debate "stands as a singular example of foot-dragging by a faithful ally which had repercussions within Europe as well as upon United States–Netherlands relations."[189]

*Players and Positions*

The November 1981 decision is the focus of this case (although the original 1979 decision and many policies between 1982 and 1985 also involved policy disagreements among coalition partners). The differences between the two largest parties in the coalition—the Christian Democratic Appeal and the Labour Party—on the subject were stark even before the coalition was formed. Following the May 1981 elections (see table 4.4), the loss of public support for the Liberal Party (as well as for the Christian Democrats and

Labour) meant that the CDA had to look to new partners to form a majority coalition, and the resulting coalition divided the cabinet among three parties. The Labour Party is a social-democratic party that sits just left of center on a general left-right dimension.[190] Foreign policy issues had become increasingly salient for the Labour Party: "Since the early 1970s its party conferences have paid a great deal of attention to international and defence affairs, such as the Netherlands' membership of NATO."[191] The party's key man for foreign affairs, Foreign Minister van der Stoel, "took pride in the Netherlands being a critical ally rather than the faithful ally the country had been in the past."[192]

The third partner in the coalition was the Democrats '66 Party. Andeweg and Irwin classify this party as "progressive-liberal," distinct from the "conservative-liberal" VVD. The Democrats '66 generally stand for reforms to make the political system more democratic, such as the direct election of the prime minister. Experts place this party at the center on a general left-right dimension.[193] In the 1970s, the party generally supported the peace movement.[194]

This coalition was "born of necessity; no viable political alternative was available."[195] The Christian Democrats' van Agt continued as prime minister. The two other partners split the key security-related ministries, with Labour's van der Stoel becoming foreign minister and van Mierlo of the Democrats '66 becoming defense minister (see table 4.5). The remaining ministries were split fairly evenly between the two larger partners (the Christian Democrats and Labour), with three remaining (but important) portfolios going to the Democrats '66.

**TABLE 4.4. Dutch National Election Results, 1981**

|  | Votes (%) | Seats |
|---|---|---|
| **Christian Democratic Appeal** | 30.8 | 48 |
| **Labour** | 28.3 | 44 |
| Liberals | 17.3 | 26 |
| **Democrats '66** | 11.1 | 17 |
| Pacifist Socialist Party | 2.1 | 3 |
| Netherlands Communist Party | 2.1 | 3 |
| Political Reformed Party | 2.0 | 3 |
| Radical Political Party | 2.0 | 3 |
| Reforming Political Federation | 1.2 | 2 |
| Reformed Political Union | 0.8 | 1 |

*Source:* Statistics Netherlands, 2009, www.cbs.nl, accessed April 18, 2009.
*Note:* The parties in the governing coalition are boldface; only those parties receiving seats in the parliament are included.

*Dutch Foreign Policy* 95

The coalition partners had campaigned on competing positions, and the cruise missile policy was a major issue in the 1981 election.[196] The campaign positions of Labour and the Christian Democrats were "incompatible. This was mainly because the PvdA rejected deployment of cruise missiles (it was a key issue in the election manifesto)."[197] There were, however, some internal divisions about nuclear weapons in general within the Labour Party. In 1979, the party congress had passed a resolution supporting unilateral nuclear disarmament. Labour's leader, Joop Den Uyl, disagreed with this more "radical" leftist viewpoint and threatened to resign. His position was based on both electoral strategy (attempting to preclude a center-left coalition from emerging) and international concerns (recognizing the need to regain credibility and influence in NATO). "In the end the party election congress agreed by a 70% majority to continue its unconditional 'no' to deployment of the cruise missiles and to repeal—if necessary unilaterally—four or five of the 'nuclear tasks' of the Dutch armed forces, as

**TABLE 4.5. Members of the van Agt II Cabinet of the Netherlands (September 1981–May 1982)**

| Ministry | Individual | Party |
|---|---|---|
| Prime minister | van Agt | Christian Democrats |
| Vice minister; Social Affairs and Employment, Netherlands-Antilles Affairs | den Uyl | Labour |
| Vice minister, Economic Affairs | Terlouw | Democrats '66 |
| External Affairs | van der Stoel | Labour |
| Defense | van Mierlo | Democrats '66 |
| Development | van Dijk | Christian Democrats |
| Internal Affairs | van Thijn | Labour |
| Finance | van der Stee | Christian Democrats |
| Justice | de Ruiter | Christian Democrats |
| Education and Science | van Kemenade | Labour |
| Housing | van Dam | Labour |
| Public Works | Zeevalking | Democrats '66 |
| Agriculture and Fishing | de Konig | Christian Democrats |
| Culture and Recreation | van der Louw | Labour |
| Health of the People and Environment | Gardeniers-Berendsen | Christian Democrats |

*Source:* Government of the Netherlands, Minister of General Affairs, "Cabinets since 1945," http://minaz.nl/Onderwerpen/Ministerraad/Kabinetten_sinds_1945, accessed April 15, 2009.

*Note:* The individuals listed are those that occupied these ministerial positions at the time of the case.

part of a process toward denuclearization of the Netherlands, in order to bring about a denuclearized Europe. The . . . plea for direct removal of all nuclear weapons was rejected. Den Uyl accepted this policy."[198] The "nuclear tasks" assigned to the Netherlands by NATO already included surface-to-surface Lance missiles, antisubmarine aircraft, surface-to-air missiles, and atomic demolition munitions.[199]

The Christian Democratic Party disagreed with Labour's unconditional rejection of deployment but was divided. The "dissidents" within the party's parliamentary group (many of the same individuals who opposed their party leadership on the South African embargo issue) had been critical of the 1979 decision to postpone NATO deployment. At that time, the parliamentary group proposed a number of principles for the cruise missile deployment decision-making process, including postponing deployment until after further efforts in arms control negotiations with the Soviet Union.[200] They did, however, support modernization.[201] The Christian Democratic principles became the official Dutch policy in 1979. According to Rochon, this was "an extraordinary example of parliamentary activism, in effect a legislative dictation of Dutch treaty negotiations."[202] In the 1981 elections, the dissident members were punished by the party leadership and a conservative backlash in the party's constituency, but the left wing of the party remained committed to its concerns about the cruise missiles. Moreover, "many party members and potential voters were influenced by the increasingly strong condemnation of nuclear weapons which came from the churches to which they belong."[203] The party faced division and a dilemma: party leaders, including Prime Minister van Agt, "had tied their hands by agreeing to the NATO decision. The left was against this decision and wanted to do more to 'reduce the role of nuclear weapons.' In the end, the election programme included a number of vague paragraphs allowing widely divergent interpretations. A decision on what should be decided in December 1981, when the modernization problem would come up again for decision, was avoided."[204]

The cruise missile issue was less important for the third coalition partner, the Democrats '66, but it too was divided. In the 1981 elections, "the debates [over the cruise missiles] were less heated and emotional. Nevertheless strong differences existed and a compromise solution was found. . . . [M]odernization was rejected 'under the present circumstances'; the six nuclear tasks should gradually be reduced to two or three. D'66 also pleaded for steps toward nuclear-free zones and non-nuclear defense strategies."[205]

Given the existing divisions within the parties and the difficult coalition negotiations that were likely to emerge, the parties attempted to avoid making foreign policy issues a major election topic in 1981. However, the salience of nuclear weapons in public opinion and among domestic interest groups forced the issue to center stage in the election.[206] The role of domestic groups outside of parliament was very important in this case, especially in relation to the development of the Christian Democrats' division and the position of its left wing. "The discord within the Christian Democratic parliamentary group was very much the result of successful attempts of the church-affiliated peace organizations to make inroads in the . . . party organization by gaining the support of the churches and by mobilizing a large army of religious voters."[207] The Inter-Church Peace Council, with a history of activism on nuclear weapons issues, was the most important domestic group in this regard.[208] This and similar groups pressured members of parliament, informed the public, and mobilized protests. In the fall of 1981, many rallies took place in most West European capitals, including Amsterdam, where half a million people participated, and public opinion surveys consistently reported that a strong majority of the Dutch people (typically about two-thirds) opposed deployment.[209]

Yet the 1981 protest did not change the new government's policy of deferring but not rejecting deployment.[210] Domestic political opposition was, however, important in limiting government action and preventing an outright decision for deployment. This influence was channeled through and into conflict between the ruling coalition parties. Everts notes that other West European countries, including Britain and West Germany, also faced domestic opposition but proceeded with deployment. The explanation for the difference lies with coalition politics: "The hesitancy of the Dutch governments . . . to withstand vast domestic opposition was reinforced by unstable parliamentary coalitions, and related to this, slim government majorities. This also reflected the state of disarray the leading coalition party (i.e. the Christian Democratic Party) was in. . . . In conclusion, it was not only the strength of the anti-missile groups, but also the opportunities offered by the national political situation which accounted for their success."[211] Domestic political opposition and intraparty divisions also explain parliament's unusually important role in the cruise missile case.[212] Without a unified party, the positions of the coalition partners were not confined to those views represented in the cabinet. The views of party representatives in the parliament also mattered if the coalition was to be maintained.

## Disagreements and Decision Making

The differences between the parties over the cruise missiles were left unresolved after coalition negotiations, which lasted for more than three months.

> Before the final [coalition formation] arrangement on this issue was written down, many compromises had ended in the waste paper basket. These texts had contained all kinds of complicated clauses, all of them reflecting the lack of genuine agreement on this matter. . . . Eventually, the parties reached a procedural implicit compromise. The government first would consult the NATO partners, and then "determine autonomously when and on which points decision making will take place." In the parliamentary discussions following after this government decision making, no coalition discipline would be enforced. In other words, the coalition parties would have a free vote.[213]

Specifically, the coalition agreement stated, "With respect to nuclear weapons, the question of the long-range tactical nuclear forces, as well as a substantial reduction of the number of Dutch nuclear tasks, the cabinet will consult with the allies. The cabinet decides on the basis of its own judgment time and content of the decision-making. The parliamentary groups supporting the cabinet will judge the decisions or the postponement of such decisions also in the light of their programmes."[214] According to Everts, the word *also* in the last sentence allowed the Labour Party to pursue its total rejection of missile deployment.[215] "It was decided that the government would accept the double-track decision as a fact, but the PvdA ministers would be obliged to leave the cabinet as soon as factual preparations for deployment in the Netherlands began."[216]

Indeed, in the first meeting of the new coalition government in September 1981, the Labour ministers introduced a letter threatening to withdraw from the government if the other cabinet ministers supported the deployment of the cruise missiles.[217] Even though the third coalition partner, the Democrats '66, supported the peace movement and was skeptical about the missile deployment, the minister of defence, van Mierlo did not follow Labour's lead.[218] Given Labour's threat and the irreconcilable differences within and between the parties, the government announced in late 1981 that it would again postpone the decision for deployment.[219] The dissidents within the Christian Democratic Party played a key role. "By using their implicit veto power and joining hands with the parties of the Left, which rejected modernization outright, the dissidents could make it very difficult—if not impossible—for the government to secure a parliamentary majority on the issue of cruise missiles."[220] Everts argues that the delay in the start of the superpower arms control talks was a "blessing in disguise" for the Dutch government, since it could blame the postponement on this external factor.[221] In reality, the delay was the only possible option, given the agreement to disagree on the issue.

The Labour Party eventually left the cabinet over financial and economic issues in May 1982.[222] Early elections restored the center-right coalition between the Christian Democrats and the Liberals. The cruise missile case continued to divide the Christian Democrats, and further delays occurred. Not until November 1985, after the first-track negotiations had not produced a meaningful arms control agreement, did the Netherlands commit to deployment. Parliament approved this decision but needed the support of small religious opposition parties to do so as a consequence of negative votes from Christian Democrats.[223]

*Role of Coalition Politics*

The cruise missile case fits many of the conventional expectations regarding the role of coalition politics in foreign policy. The final decision was very moderate. It can be considered cooperative in the sense that it was not pursuing deployment of a military weapon but conflictual in terms of its stance against the NATO alliance.[224] The decision to delay was the result of a junior coalition party (Labour) constraining its senior coalition partner from taking an aggressive policy (deployment of an advanced military weapons).[225] Indeed, the cruise missile case led international affairs writer Walter Laqueur to his diagnosis of "Hollanditis"—a "disease" of pacifism and evasion that could spread across Western Europe and make it unwilling to defend itself.[226] By threatening to leave the coalition and force new elections, Labour prevented a decision. It could do so because it was relatively unified in its position and its coalition partners were divided over the policy. The case also illustrates the constraints that stem from the supposed inherent weakness of coalitions: "Only a far stronger government than the one that [came to power] could comfortably have accepted cruise missiles here."[227]

The case also meets the expectation for poor decision making characterized by deadlock and delay. "The basic reality was that the government could not act consistently in one direction or the other; it could not commit itself fully to either accepting the missiles or rejecting them. A single, coherent course of action was precluded. As a consequence, [the Dutch] engaged in minimalist foreign policy behavior regarding the cruise missile issue for a number of years."[228] The government's foreign policy was immobilized.[229] The compromise between the parties, seen in the coalition agreement, was excessive—an agreement to disagree but not to resolve the issue.

Despite the inaction and the damages it did to Dutch credibility with NATO, Hagan and his colleagues argue that although the cabinet was "deadlocked, the tensions within the government were contained effectively in a way that reflected an orderly and sustained 'papering over of differences,' resulting in some diplomatic activity within the NATO context."[230] Hagan and his coauthors claim that the government did not collapse over the issue as a consequence of strong norms of consensus that "enabled the deeply divided coalition governments to function with political restraint at home and abroad."[231] Andeweg and Irwin also point out a positive aspect of the delay, saying that the six years it took to make a decision on the cruise missiles was not necessarily detrimental: "By the time the Dutch agreed to accept the cruise missiles, an arms reduction agreement made them redundant."[232]

## PARTICIPATION IN THE IRAQ WAR

The issue of the U.S.-led war against Saddam Hussein's Iraq divided the Dutch government, as it divided most of the world. The debate over Iraq occurred during a period of significant domestic political challenges, culminating in early national general elections held in January 2003, two months prior to the beginning of the intervention in Iraq. The government in power during the lead-up to the war was a coalition between the Christian Democrats, the Liberals, and the List Pim Fortuyn Party (LPF). This government had only come to power in May 2002, soon after the assassination of the LPF's leader and namesake, Pim Fortuyn. Fortuyn was a controversial figure in Dutch politics. His assassination gave his party a considerable boost in the elections—they became the second-largest party in the Netherlands in one of the biggest electoral landslides in Dutch history.[233] After the elections, however, this leaderless party experienced considerable infighting and controversy. The coalition collapsed after only three months in office, and new elections were set for January 2003.[234] The cabinet continued as a caretaker government until a new coalition would be formed several months after the election.

In the midst of this domestic political turmoil, the Iraq issue arose. The question for the Netherlands was whether it would support the United States in a military intervention. Like many other European governments, the Dutch found themselves under pressure from their longtime ally, the United States, to join the "coalition of the willing" and under constraint from the public and other domestic political actors to not participate in the war.[235] The question of the Netherlands' participation in Iraq must also be put in context of the country's struggle to define its role in multilateral force operations since the tragic incidents in Srebrenica in 1995. In the aftermath of that massacre, the Dutch people and elites were very cautious about committing their troops to missions with high risks and ambiguous objectives.[236]

As early as August 2002, the opposition Labour Party called for a parliamentary debate about a possible attack on Iraq. The foreign ministry replied that the Netherlands had not responded to the United States because the government hoped for a joint European response.[237] By September 2002, the government's position was clearer and supportive of the United States.[238] Foreign Minister De Hoop Scheffer communicated that although the Netherlands would prefer to have a UN Security Council resolution, such a resolution was not essential for Dutch backing of U.S. military action against Iraq.[239] This supportive policy remained consistent throughout the rest of 2002. In December, Prime Minister Balkenende stated that the government was willing to back the United States and wanted to participate in prewar military preparations.[240]

As was predicted, the LPF lost much of its popular support in the January 2003 elections. As a result, the outgoing governing coalition no longer enjoyed a parliamentary majority (see table 4.6). The most obvious alternative coalition possibility was between the Christian Democrats and Labour under the leadership of Wouter Bos.[241] But those two parties disagreed on many issues, not least of which was the looming intervention in Iraq.[242] Indeed, Iraq became a central issue in the parties' coalition talks, and the Dutch government's decision to offer political but not military support to the United States at the beginning of the Iraq War was a direct result of these coalition negotiations. Since the key locus of policy-making was the coalition talks in this case, the distribution of ministries (see table 4.7) is less relevant. In this outgoing government, the ministries were divided equitably among the three parties relative to their strengths in Parliament. The Christian Democrats controlled the key posts of prime minister (Balkendende) and foreign minister (de Hoop Scheffer), and the Liberals controlled the ministry of defense (Kamp).

*Players and Positions*

The Dutch public generally opposed the war, and the issue became a salient one in public opinion. In mid-February 2003, seventy thousand protesters assembled in Amsterdam under the slogan "Not in my name." Observers commented that it was the largest demonstration since the protests against the cruise missiles in the 1980s.[243] A majority of those surveyed in a January 2003 public opinion poll opposed U.S. military intervention in Iraq.[244] By late February, 80 percent of the Dutch public opposed the war without a UN mandate.[245] Public pressure was aimed at the parties, but they split along party lines.

The two parties in coalition talks, the Christian Democrats and Labour, were far apart on their position on Iraq. The CDA favored military cooperation with the United States. As head of the outgoing government, the

TABLE 4.6. Dutch National Election Results, 2003

|  | Votes (%) | Seats |
|---|---|---|
| **Christian Democrats** | 28.6 | 44 |
| *Labour* | 27.3 | 42 |
| **Liberals** | 17.9 | 28 |
| Socialist Party | 6.3 | 9 |
| **List Pim Fortuyn** | 5.7 | 8 |
| Green Left | 5.1 | 8 |
| Democrats '66 | 4.1 | 6 |
| Christian Union | 2.1 | 3 |
| Political Reform Party | 1.6 | 2 |

*Source:* Statistics Netherlands, 2009, www.cbs.nl, accessed April 18, 2009.

*Note:* The parties in the governing caretaker coalition are boldface; the parties in coalition talks are boldface italic. Only those parties receiving seats in the parliament are included.

*Dutch Foreign Policy*

Christian Democrats had supported the United States in 2002 from the cabinet positions this party controlled (see table 4.7). As early as September of that year, one Dutch news source commented on the position of the Christian Democratic foreign minister: "In De Hoop Scheffer the Netherlands appears to have a clear-cut pro-US foreign affairs minister."[246] Prime Minister Balkenende went on record a number of times in the fall of 2002 to support Dutch military involvement in a U.S.-led intervention. The other parties in the outgoing coalition, the VVD and LPF, were generally right of the Christian Democrats on defense issues and supported Dutch participation in Iraq. Defense Minister Korthals of the Liberals (who served in that position until being replaced by Kamp in December 2002) also was on record as supporting the U.S. plans and Dutch participation in them. Although the Labour Party had become more pragmatic on foreign policy issues than was the case during the 1970s, it strongly opposed the Iraq War and Dutch participation in it.[247] In August 2002, the Labour opposition in parliament called for a parliamentary debate on the issue.[248]

TABLE 4.7. Members of the Balkenende II Cabinet of the Netherlands (2002–3)

| Ministry | Individual | Party |
|---|---|---|
| Prime minister | Balkenende | Christian Democrats |
| Deputy prime minister, Social Affairs and Employment, Health and Sport | de Gues | Christian Democrats |
| Deputy prime minister, Internal Affairs and Kingdom Relations | Remkes | Liberals |
| Deputy prime minister, Public Works | de Boer | List Pim Fortuyn |
| External Affairs | de Hoop Scheffer | Christian Democrats |
| Defense, Spatial Scheduling, Environment, Housing | Kamp | Liberals |
| Finance, Economic Affairs | Hoogervorst | Liberals |
| Justice | Donner | Christian Democrats |
| Education and Science | van der Hoeven | Christian Democrats |
| Agriculture, Fishing and Nature | Veerman | Christian Democrat |
| Foreigners Policy and Immigration | Nawijn | List Pim Fortuyn |

*Source:* Government of the Netherlands, Minister of General Affairs, "Cabinets Since 1945," http://minaz.nl/Onderwerpen/Ministerraad/Kabinetten_sinds_1945, accessed April 15, 2009.

*Note:* The individuals listed are those that occupied these ministerial positions at the time of the case.

*Disagreements and Decision Making*

After the January 2003 elections, and amid the growing popular opposition to the Iraq War, the outgoing caretaker government softened its stance, saying that the international community should give Iraq time to comply with UN resolutions.[249] In February 2003, however, a majority in parliament supported the government's decision to ship to Turkey antimissile batteries and approximately three hundred Dutch soldiers to man the batteries. Prime Minister Balkenende said the February 2003 deal to provide missile batteries and soldiers did not require parliamentary approval. However, "under Dutch law parliament members can demand a debate about a government decision after it has been taken and possibly put it to a vote."[250] The motions introduced by opposition parties to stop the deal, however, failed to gain a majority.[251]

At this time, the government also allowed the United States to move supplies to the Middle East via the Netherlands. The Labour Party disagreed and along with one other opposition party introduced two motions demanding a freeze on the shipment of weapons to Turkey and any other action that might assist the United States in its military preparations. The shipment of missiles and the use of the Netherlands as a supply route became an issue of contention in the coalition talks as Labour, along with the Greens and the Socialists, voted against the decision.[252]

Prime Minister Balkenende "said troop movements through the Netherlands should be seen as a way to keep the pressure on Saddam Hussein and not as a preparation for war."[253] Defense Minister Kamp of the Liberal Party agreed, saying, "The Americans are our friends. . . . It goes without saying that if they want to move whatever supplies and personnel they have in Europe, we will help them."[254] Indeed, the two main parties in the caretaker government, the Christian Democrats and the Liberals, consistently and strongly supported the war following the elections.[255]

On March 18, at the start of the war, the prime minister announced that the Netherlands would give political but not military support to the war.[256] This announcement was taken as the official government decision, coming after a three-hour cabinet meeting.[257] The Christian Democratic Party in parliament said it fully backed the cabinet decision.[258]

The decision, however, was criticized from the left and the right both inside and outside the cabinet. Liberal party leader Gerrit Zalm said the decision was "half-hearted and hypocritical."[259] The Liberals wanted outright military support and participation[260] but realized that this decision was the best the party could get.[261] Although considerably weakened by its electoral losses, the List Pim Fortuyn Party also backed military support.[262] According to LPF leader Mat Herben, by offering only political support, the Netherlands was isolating its important ally, the United States.[263] Outside the cabinet, in the opposition, the leader of the Socialist Party said of the policy, "'This is an implausible, unique position, which nobody else in the world has taken,' . . . adding that the stance was 'cowardly' and 'weak.'"[264] The Greens criticized the decision for contributing to violation of international law.[265]

Although the prime minister claimed that public opinion was constraining his government, the "political but not military support" policy was widely seen as a "classic Dutch compromise,"[266] a concession to the Labour Party, with whom the Christian Democrats were in coalition negotiations: "The government stance is clearly a compromise made to accommodate Labour's anti-war stance, as they pursue talks to form a coalition."[267] "The concession was necessary if Dutch policy on Iraq was to be consistent after a centre-left Cabinet assumed power."[268]

Yet "Labour has given little impression of being moved by the gesture and continues to firmly oppose the government position."[269] Indeed, at the time of the decision, Labour leader Bos argued "that there should be no Dutch political or military support for the war. 'No people, no equipment.' Meanwhile, Labour's parliamentary party said it had additional questions about the government's 'political support' of military action."[270] According to the Labour Party, the government decision went too far in supporting the United States, and the party stressed the need for a total rejection of support, making coalition formation less likely.[271]

Indeed, the coalition talks almost collapsed over the issue following intense parliamentary debate, with the Christian Democrats calling Labour's position "sad."[272] Iraq became the primary topic of negotiations between the Christian Democrats and Labour following the March 18 decision.[273] "Bos said the talks concerning Iraq were 'crucial' in the ongoing bid to form a government, and that Labour wanted guarantees that The Netherlands will not be dragged into the 'US doctrine of rogue states.'"[274] Bos repeatedly called the U.S. intervention "unjustified."[275] The CDA demanded that Bos rescind such statements.[276] Foreign Minster de Hoop Scheffer said of Labour, "They are completely the opposite of our position."[277]

Relations between the parties were further complicated when despite the compromise, a Dutch air force officer appeared with U.S. General Tommy Franks at a press conference, along with representatives of Britain, Denmark, and Australia, which more clearly supported the United States in the war. Balkenende admitted that he was unaware that the officer was meeting with the U.S. Central Command and Kamp apologized for the incident.[278] The government also deployed a submarine and frigate to the Middle East under U.S. military command. Labour balked, arguing that this action violated the agreement because it went beyond political support.[279]

Yet within a week, Labour seemed to soften its stance when Balkenende and Bos agreed that the Netherlands was part of the U.S.-led coalition and that the U.S. intervention was justified under UN Resolution 1441. Discussion on the formation of the new government thus continued. Labour clearly gave in to some extent with this declaration.[280] Bos had already given some inconsistent signals. Although he argued that the intervention was unjustified, he also stated that the Netherlands would support its allies if war occurred.[281] "And in a further sign of a shift in his position, Bos told the NRC Handelsblad newspaper, he had still not decided whether or not to attend Saturday's anti-war demonstration[, saying,] 'At the last demo it was a question of opposing the war in principle. The difference now is that in a choice between Saddam and Bush, we take the US's side.'"[282] Yet soon thereafter, Bos returned to being very critical of the decision and "despite moving towards the CDA in his support for the allies, Bos said it was essential that the Netherlands did not supply military help and was not included in the 'committee of the willing.'"[283]

Despite the Christian Democrats' concession to Labour on Iraq and Labour's change in position regarding the UN justification for the war, the coalition talks broke down in April 2003 over spending cuts.[284] The Christian Democrats and the Liberals convinced the D66 (a small center-left party with six seats in Parliament) to join the coalition, which had a slim majority.[285] D66 had strongly opposed the war but agreed to concede the issue in exchange for a role in the government.[286] Soon after the new coalition was formed, the United States claimed "victory" in dismantling the Iraqi regime and the Dutch sent eleven hundred troops to Iraq,[287] later extending the deployment for six months.[288] Not until the summer of 2004, when the UN Security Council approved the handover of sovereignty to the new Iraqi government, did the Dutch announce that they would withdraw from Iraq in early 2005.[289] The United States was shocked by the Dutch decision, thinking the handover of sovereignty to the Iraqi government would be an opportunity to deepen the Dutch presence in Iraq.[290]

*Role of Coalition Politics*

The decision to offer political but not military support to the U.S. intervention in Iraq was not a compromise between the parties in the existing (caretaker) government, as all three coalition partners backed full military support. It was nevertheless affected by coalition politics since the position was a compromise between two potential coalition partners. In other words, the particular decision directly resulted from the compromise that the Christian Democrats felt they had to make with Labour to keep alive the possibility of a grand coalition between the two parties.

In terms of images about coalition politics and foreign policy, the decision is moderate, not extreme. It can be seen as cooperative in that the Dutch government did not participate in a military invasion of another country, yet it is also conflictual in that it offered political support for the military use of power.[291] The decision meets the expectation that coalition governments are highly constrained and that shared power between parties can result in meaningless compromise and constraint. The junior partner (Labour in this case) was not, however, able to blackmail the senior party (the Christian Democrats) to adopt its outright antiwar position because the Christian Democrats had a fairly strong pro–United States position. The Christian Democrats may also have wanted to avoid angering their other partner (the Liberals, who were more supportive of military backing) too much. In addition, Labour may not have been able to hijack the process because it did not yet have any institutional support (such as the control of the foreign or defense ministry) to put behind its position. Some of the inconsistency in Labour's position (arguing that the Netherlands should support its allies but that the intervention was unjustified) may have also been present in the run-up to the war and may have undermined the party's ability to influence the policy.

This case also fits the expectation that coalition governments are poor decision-making bodies—the compromise resulted from a papering over of differences and was not the preference of any actor. The case did not, however, see paralysis and excessive delay in decision making. The Dutch government made this statement at the start of the war. In this way, the case challenges some of the expectations about the quality of decision making.

In addition, the case arguably demonstrates the benefits of multiple advocacy. The introduction of the Labour Party into the process prevented (or reversed) premature closure on the pro-Iraqi position that would have come from a single-party (Christian Democratic) cabinet or even the governing (caretaker) center-right coalition. Furthermore, the decision was made in a fairly timely fashion. Not only is this a higher-quality decision-making process, but it may have been the better decision-making outcome. When the coalition talks fell apart and Labour was removed from the picture, the Dutch government proceeded militarily to support a war that many now believed was unjustified and poor policy. Indeed, the Christian Democrats eventually changed their position on the war. In 2005, the foreign minister announced that in hindsight, the Iraq invasion was not "wise," although the next day he said the United States had a right to invade.[292] Even the Liberal defense minister, Kamp, changed his mind about the war and supported withdrawal of Dutch troops (although his party opposed withdrawal). Kamp believed that the Dutch military was overstretched and that something similar to the disaster of Srebenica might occur in Iraq.[293] In 2010, a Dutch independent inquiry into decision making on the Iraq war concluded that the invasion had no basis in international law and that cabinet ministers misled parliament. "The report was vehemently critical of the manner in which the government defended its position with regard to the invasion. The Dutch cabinet was 'so determined' to retain its positions on the matter that 'no substantial exchange of ideas between government and parliament with regard to the policy on Iraq' ever took place."[294]

## TROOP DEPLOYMENT TO URUZGAN, AFGHANISTAN

In January 2006, the Netherlands became the focus of considerable international attention. UN secretary-general Kofi Annan, NATO secretary-general Jaap de Hoop Scheffer (who previously served as Dutch foreign minister), NATO supreme allied commander James Jones, and half of the cabinet of the Afghan government met with Dutch leaders and appealed to public opinion in an attempt to influence Dutch foreign policy. The United States also sent numerous officials to persuade the government; Paul Bremer, former U.S. ambassador to the Netherlands and U.S. administrator in Iraq, unofficially warned the Netherlands that it was risking economic sanctions.[295]

World leaders were asking the Dutch government to agree to NATO's request to send troops to Uruzgan, a southern Afghanistan province considered a Taliban stronghold. The Dutch had previously pledged to make this troop contribution to the NATO effort but were now reconsidering. This mission was important to Afghanistan. The foreign and defense ministers stressed that the mission was critical to the stability of the post-Taliban government.[296] It was also important to the United Nations and the international community. According to Annan, "No one can afford to see a destabilized Afghanistan," and a Dutch refusal "would mean that the international efforts in Afghanistan, after all the investment we put in, may not be successful."[297] de Hoop Scheffer agreed: "This is an extremely important mission. We should not grant the terrorists, the Taliban, victory."[298] For NATO, the Dutch decision was also a matter of alliance solidarity, already in danger after divisions over Iraq. According to NATO officials, a no vote would also delay the operation.[299] Said one NATO diplomat, "No one should pretend that if the Dutch don't go, it will not be a big problem."[300] To the United States, the Dutch debate over deployment became "a test of the transatlantic alliance's efforts to find new missions and credibility in the post–Cold War era, and a referendum on President Bush's war against terrorism. U.S. officials consider[ed] the vote a crucial measure of allies' willingness to share the risks and costs of stabilizing troubled nations and combating terrorism."[301] More practically, the United States was counting on allied contributions to Afghanistan to allow it to shift its troops to a destabilizing Iraq.[302]

In the face of this international pressure, the Dutch government repeatedly delayed the decision, and the outcome was far from certain, even though "failure to contribute troops to NATO's expansion into southern Afghanistan could severely tarnish the Dutch standing in the alliance."[303] This delay occurred despite the support for deployment from the prime minister, the foreign minister, and the defense minister and the two governing parties that they represented, the Christian Democrats and the Liberals. The delay stemmed from the opposition to deployment from a junior party in the coalition, the D66. This party, which held six seats in parliament, was critical to the maintenance of the governing coalition's slim four-seat parliamentary majority (see table 4.8). The D66 threatened to withdraw from the cabinet over the Afghan troop decision; withdrawal would lead to new elections. The coalition partners finally agreed to defer the decision to parliament. Parliament supported the deployment after

Labour, the major opposition party, shifted away from its earlier resistance to the policy.

*Players and Positions*

While the parties and the Dutch people generally supported the effort in Afghanistan that began in 2001 (all but the Socialist Party supported the original troop commitment to Afghanistan in December 2001),[304] post-Srebrenica cautiousness was ever present, and by late 2005, the mission in Afghanistan had become the most accident-prone and expensive in Dutch history. In November 2005, a report issued by the Dutch military intelligence and security service declared that the Uruzgan province would be "too dangerous" for Dutch soldiers. "The Dutch intelligence report highlights the serious contradiction inherent in concentrating on nation-building in an area where Taliban and Al-Qaeda forces remain active."[305]

The public and opposition parties continued to oppose the Dutch mission in Iraq, which had seen the death of two Dutch soldiers, and public discontent over Iraq weighed "heavily on the parties as they head[ed] toward elections in 2007."[306] In 2006, the United States was sharply criticized in Europe (and elsewhere) for its policies in Iraq and its treatment of prisoners. The Netherlands was not immune to the growing anti–United States sentiment. In an early January 2006 interview, Labour leader Wouter Bos expressed the sentiment from the left:

**TABLE 4.8. Dutch National Election Results, 2003**

|  | Votes (%) | Seats |
|---|---|---|
| **Christian Democrats** | 28.6 | 44 |
| Labour | 27.3 | 42 |
| **Liberals** | 17.9 | 28 |
| Socialist Party | 6.3 | 9 |
| List Pim Fortuyn | 5.7 | 8 |
| Green Left | 5.1 | 8 |
| **Democrats '66** | 4.1 | 6 |
| Christian Union | 2.1 | 3 |
| Political Reform Party | 1.6 | 2 |

*Source:* Statistics Netherlands, 2009, www.cbs.nl, accessed April 18, 2009.

*Note:* The parties in the coalition are boldface; only those parties receiving seats in the parliament are included.

The United States would still be our friend and partner in NATO, but there would be a different balance here. I believe that the future of Dutch foreign policy is very much within European foreign policy and that's where we should go first to find our partners. We shouldn't, almost without any type of criticism, follow the Americans whenever they ask us something—which I am sad to say has been the pattern of the last few years in the Netherlands.[307]

This general distrust of the United States affected all of the political elite in the Netherlands, but the coalition that had come to power in the spring of 2003 included the most pro-Atlantic of the political parties, the Christian Democrats and the Liberals. The coalition, however, also included the D66, which had originally opposed Dutch participation in Iraq but agreed to concede the issue when it joined the coalition.[308] Foreign affairs generally was not a salient policy area for the D66.

The D66's two cabinet members held the positions of minister for economic affairs and minister for government reform (see table 4.9). The key foreign policy positions in the cabinet were controlled by the Christian Democrats (with Prime Minister Balkenende and Foreign Minister Bot) and the Liberals (with Defense Minister Kamp). Overall, the cabinet portfolios were divided among the coalition partners in a way that fairly reflected their relative parliamentary strength.

*Disagreements and Decision Making*

The release of the Dutch intelligence report in November 2005 came as NATO was pushing the Dutch government for a firm commitment on troop deployment to Uruzgan. The intelligence report was only one factor in the government's hesitation. Concerns were growing that the Dutch mission in Afghanistan was tainted by association with the United States and the rumors of secret rendition and detention centers and the use of torture on prisoners of war at Cuba's Guantánamo Bay and the Abu Ghraib prison in Iraq. At this time, concerns were shared across the political spectrum. Balkenende reportedly had serious doubts about the mission, and Bot said that a review of the Dutch position on troop deployment was triggered by concerns over treatment of Afghan prisoners by the United States.[309] Opposition parties in parliament and the coalition parties demanded an explanation and review before they would support a new mission.[310] In addition, members of the military and 71 percent of those polled in a survey expressed opposition to the deployment.[311] The opposition to the mission also stemmed from memories of the Srebrenica incident, as the Dutch wanted assurances that their troops would have sufficient support.[312] Wim van den Burg, head of a military union, expressed this concern in a radio interview: "In Srebrenica we had the wrong mandate, the wrong rules of engagement . . . the wrong weapons. I don't want us to get into the same situation in Afghanistan because we know what will happen."[313]

**TABLE 4.9. Members of the Balkenende III Cabinet of the Netherlands (2003–6)**

| Ministry | Individual | Party |
|---|---|---|
| Prime minister | Balkenende | Christian Democrats |
| Deputy prime minister, Finance | Zalm | Liberals |
| Deputy prime minister, Economic Affairs | Brinkhorst | D66 |
| External Affairs | Bot | Christian Democrats |
| Defense | Kamp | Liberals |
| Development Cooperation | van Ardenne/ van der Hoeven | Christian Democrats/ Christian Democrats |
| Internal Affairs and Kingdom Relations | Remkes | Liberals |
| Justice | Donner | Christian Democrats |
| Education, Culture and Science | van der Hoeven/ van Ardenne | Christian Democrats/ Christian Democrats |
| Housing, Spatial Planning and Environment | Dekker | Liberals |
| Public Works | Peijs | Christian Democrats |
| Government Reform and Relations with Monarchy | Pechtold | D66 |
| Food Quality, Nature and Environment | Veerman | Christian Democrats |
| Social Affairs and Employment | Jan de Geus | Christian Democrats |
| Public Health, Well-Being and Sport | Hoogervorst | Liberals |
| Immigration and Integration | Verdonk | Liberals |

*Source:* Government of the Netherlands, Minister of General Affairs, "Cabinets since 1945," http://minaz.nl/Onderwerpen/Ministerraad/Kabinetten_sinds_1945, accessed April 15, 2009.

*Note:* The individuals listed are those that occupied these ministerial positions at the time of the case.

NATO formally approved the expansion of its force into southern Afghanistan on December 8, and following a meeting between Dutch military officers and NATO, government leaders were more supportive and predicted that the cabinet would approve the deployment within a week.[314] Bot "said that the Netherlands had received guarantees that 1,100 of its troops likely to be working in the southern Oruzgan province would have the backing of [U.S.-led Operation Enduring Freedom] soldiers in any crisis. Any prisoners they hand over to Afghan police will also be treated humanely and not face the death penalty."[315] On December 9, however, the Dutch cabinet postponed the deployment decision and scheduled a special meeting on December 19 to decide the issue, but the cabinet was again unable to decide. On December 22, the cabinet declared its "intention" to deploy troops, but this was not its final decision. Instead, it announced that parliament would debate the issue in January and that the cabinet would make a final decision in early February.[316]

The cabinet was forced to delay a decision as a result of opposition from the D66 party and its two cabinet ministers.[317] Lousewies van der Laan, deputy D66 leader and a member of parliament, explained the party's position: "The NATO mission in Afghanistan is about peacekeeping and reconstruction. If we agree to send troops to southern Afghanistan, then we have to know under what conditions they would be sent."[318] Van der Laan later said, "The question here is: can a reconstruction mission be carried out successfully in a war zone? What we must avoid is fighting an American war under a NATO flag."[319] More bluntly, she asked, "If you are busy fighting the Taliban and al-Qa'ida, how do you have the space to win hearts and minds by building schools and hospitals?"[320] She also cited the U.S. suspected practice of renditions as a reason for her party's opposition.[321] Another spokesperson for the party claimed that "this mission is doomed to fail."[322] In addition, one party leader reportedly said that in opposing the deployment, the D66 party was standing against "the Bush, Blair and Balkenende axis."[323]

The D66 opposition threatened to bring down the government as the cabinet met again on January 13 to resolve the issue. "Bert Bakker, an MP with D66 . . . said his party would have no option but to quit the government if the troops were sent."[324] Bakker had led the commission that produced a critical report on the Dutch role in the Srebrenica crisis.[325] According to some observers, the D66's position was at least in part a strategy to increase its popularity with its constituency prior to the 2007 election.[326]

Dutch political scientist Rudy Andeweg's analysis was reported in the news: "It's a mixture of concern and party politics. The party needs to do something to attract attention."[327] Others also suggested that in addition to real concerns about the mission, the party's position was connected to internal leadership struggles and was consistent with isolationist, domestic-oriented, and anti-American trends among the Dutch public and political parties.[328]

The D66 was at odds with both of the Christian Democrats and the Liberals. Although the Christian Democrats were somewhat divided over the issue in December 2005 and January 2006, with some in parliament opposing the deployment, Prime Minister Balkenende came out firmly in support of the troop deployment by mid-January: "I want to make plain where I stand in the discussion. I want our Dutch troops to make a contribution to the reconstruction of Uruzgan."[329] In a letter to members of parliament, the prime minister wrote, "There have been some positive developments in the last few years. But this cannot continue without international aid, without international support. The United Nations called upon us not to forget Afghanistan, to be active in our support."[330] The Liberal Party expressed the most support for the deployment from the beginning.[331] Hans van Baalen, a party representative, explained the Liberals' position: "It's time for us to show some guts, let's do that. Fighting terrorism is in the Netherlands' interest and in the interest of Afghanistan."[332]

With the opposition to the deployment coming from within the cabinet and from the Dutch people, Balkenende decided to refer the decision to parliament, "an unusual step, since the Cabinet has the authority to deploy troops without a parliamentary vote."[333] Yet sending troops without support of the entire cabinet or a majority in parliament was risky for the prime minister. Such a move would likely further weaken the governing parties' popularity.[334] Furthermore, "while the formal approval of parliament is theoretically unnecessary, Dutch troop deployments abroad have in the recent past generally been on the basis of broad parliamentary support."[335]

Although the prime minister could get a positive decision from parliament without the D66 by relying on his own party, the Liberals, and small Christian parties, support from the largest opposition party, Labour, was required for a broad majority.[336] Indeed, the mission could not occur without the endorsement of either Labour or the D66.[337] Labour, however, was critical of troop deployment. Indeed, D66 calculated that moving the decision to parliament would kill the policy because of Labour's opposition.[338] From the beginning of the debate over the issue, Labour "expressed fears

Dutch Foreign Policy

that the NATO-led [International Stability Force] deployment could begin to be seen by Afghans as part of the U.S.-led Operation Enduring Freedom, which is seeking out Taliban remnants and al-Qaeda fighters."³³⁹ In December, the Labour Party signaled that it would likely vote against the troop deployment if the vote came to parliament.³⁴⁰ "Bert Koenders, a legislator with the . . . Labor Party and a member of Parliament's foreign and defense committee, said NATO's new mission in southern Afghanistan was 'foggy.' 'We don't want NATO to be mixed up with . . . Operation Enduring Freedom,' Koenders said. 'What would this do to NATO's ability to undertake any reconstruction, especially if the region is not even safe for carrying out any reconstruction? Our troops also need proper security. I am not sure Parliament will back the government in February.'"³⁴¹ In an early January 2006 interview, Bos fully explained the Labour Party's opposition to the deployment:

> We have got strong doubts about whether any proposal could meet our criteria. We are very concerned about having troops in one [of] the most difficult provinces of Afghanistan. . . . We would then have troops that are both peace-building and fighting and that is confusing. For the people living there it would not be clear when they deal with a Dutch soldier whether they are dealing with a peacemaker or a fighting soldier and that is a dangerous thing. Despite the guarantees we are getting from the Americans, we are also very worried about how the (NATO-led) international security force and (the U.S.-led) Enduring Freedom can remain separate exercises. The reason we in the Dutch Labor Party did not agree to send troops to participate in Enduring Freedom is that under no circumstances did we want to get involved in Guantanamo Bay type practices. If we cannot get a guarantee that by sending Dutch troops to Afghanistan they will not get mingled up in Enduring Freedom and Guantanamo Bay, then we shouldn't send them.³⁴²

Most of the other opposition parties—the Socialists, the Greens, and the LPF—opposed deployment.³⁴³ "The populist LPF said that The Netherlands shoulders too much of the burden for rebuilding Afghanistan, where 600 Dutch troops are already stationed. The GreenLeft party argued that the security conditions in Uruzgan would make it impossible for the ISAF mission to help reconstruction."³⁴⁴

Despite the cabinet's referral to parliament, the parties in the Tweede Kamer refused to vote on the issue without a firm decision from the cabinet.³⁴⁵ The Liberals specifically insisted on something beyond the "intention" issued at the end of December.³⁴⁶ On January 13, 2006, therefore, the cabinet met to endorse the decision so that parliament could vote on it. Prime Minister Balkenende announced that the cabinet now wholly supported troop deployment and said that "he hoped this announcement would end a long-running procedural controversy with parliament over the . . . deployment."³⁴⁷ The Liberals then agreed to debate the issue in parliament.³⁴⁸ Although the two ministers from the D66 agreed to the plan in the cabinet, their party continued to oppose it, with party leaders communicating that they would vote against it in parliament.³⁴⁹ The issue jeopardized the continuation of the government: "A vote against or a slim majority in favour would make it politically impossible for the centre-right coalition . . . to continue."³⁵⁰

Evidence of the significance of the vote was the eleven-hour closed briefing that members of parliament received from the NATO commander, the former commander of NATO troops in Afghanistan, and Afghanistan's foreign and defense ministers. Intense international pressure was also aimed directly at the parliament and the Dutch public.³⁵¹ Various leaders tried to appeal to the Dutch international commitment as well as reassure the country's leaders concerning the mission's risks. General Jones, the NATO commander, said, "I understand the particular signification of Srebrenica in the Netherlands [but] the comparison cannot be made. If the Dutch command in Afghanistan calls for reinforcements they will get them."³⁵² Bremer used a more coercive tactic when he said the Dutch might face economic sanctions if they refused to contribute to this mission.³⁵³ This tactic may have backfired, however: "Opponents of the Afghan mission have not taken kindly to what they view as diplomatic blackmail and bullying."³⁵⁴ Even supporters of troop deployment within the Dutch and U.S. governments regretted Bremer's threat and considered it counterproductive.³⁵⁵

The assurances from NATO and the United States and pleas from respected international leaders such as Annan did have some effect on public opinion and the political parties. By mid-January, only half of those polled in a public opinion survey expressed opposition to the deployment.³⁵⁶ By the end of January, 43 percent were in favor, compared to 26 percent in December.³⁵⁷ By the eve of the parliamentary vote in early February, the public was almost evenly divided on the matter.³⁵⁸

The Labour Party changed its position as well. By the end of January, analysts were predicting that Labour would support the deployment in the parliamentary vote. This change may have been made with an eye to the upcoming election. In early 2006, Labour enjoyed a strong lead in the polls and was predicted to come to power with the 2007 elections.[359] In the news, Dutch political scientist André Krouwel predicted that Labour "will want to show they are viable for government."[360] Bos indicated that his party was satisfied with the assurances he had received from NATO and the cabinet.[361] "According to Dutch television reports, Mr. Bos said the cabinet had moved in the right direction and that he was satisfied there was a distinction between counter-terror efforts and the reconstruction mission that would involve the Dutch troops."[362] At the end of the parliamentary debate, Bos argued that the Netherlands must live up to its rhetoric of international solidarity.[363]

As the parliamentary vote neared and Labour and the List Pim Fortuyn signaled their intention to approve the deployment, the D66 said it would not withdraw from the coalition if troops were sent to Afghanistan. "D66 spokesman Bert Bakker told the ANP news agency that a main argument for dropping the threat was 'that it would not help D66, the mission would continue regardless.'"[364] Yet previously unreleased reports by the Dutch military intelligence agency (MIVD) were seen by political leaders immediately before the vote. Defense Minister Kamp had refused to share the reports but gave in after Labour threatened to vote against the deployment if the reports were not made available to members of parliament. These reports reinforced the D66 opposition to deployment. After reading the reports, D66 leader Boris Dittrich said, "The [Afghan] population is wild, angry, and vengeful. The MIVD is very critical about the prospects of reconstruction."[365]

Despite the negative reports, the motion passed after a marathon debate, with 131 out of 150 members of parliament supporting deployment. All but one of Labour's 42 members of parliament voted for the decision, and the party said that it would agree only to a two-year mission.[366] Although the D66 did not leave the government over the decision, the party "reiterated its view that Uruzgan . . . is too unstable to allow reconstruction."[367] Following the vote, under heavy criticism, Dittrich resigned as the D66 parliamentary leader.[368] The coalition collapsed a few months later, in June 2006, when the D66 withdrew to protest the treatment of Ayan Hirsi Ali by the minister of immigration, a member of the Liberal Party. Ali, also from the Liberal Party, a member of parliament, and an outspoken critic of certain Islamic practices, admitted she had lied on her asylum application to flee an arranged marriage in Africa. The immigration minister, Verdonk, was campaigning for her party on the issue of tough immigration rules and moved to rescind Ali's citizenship and position in parliament. The D66's withdrawal forced early general elections and brought to power a new coalition, comprising Labour, the Christian Democrats, and the Christian Union.[369] This government collapsed in 2010 over the issue of Dutch troops in Afghanistan. The Labour Party withdrew from the government because it opposed a further extension of the Dutch troop commitment.[370]

*Role of Coalition Politics*

The case of Dutch troop deployment to Uruzgan, Afghanistan, can be characterized as extreme and conflictual as it committed troops to a military mission.[371] This case demonstrates the potential of constraint on military operations (the expectation of how coalition politics affects foreign policy that is consistent with democratic peace logic) and hijacking by a small coalition partner (the expectation consistent with other literatures, as discussed in chapter 2). In the end, however, the D66 was unable to constrain the Netherlands from sending troops and hijack this decision, even though the party threatened to withdraw from the coalition and was critical to sustaining its majority. There is no evidence that the D66 threat to leave the government was not perceived as credible, although the retraction of the threat in late January rendered any future use of this threat unlikely and ineffective.

The junior party's inability to influence the decision in this case can be explained by the willingness of the other coalition parties to go to parliament for support, by the D66's lack of institutional position to leverage its position (it held neither the defense or foreign ministries), and by the change of heart by the opposition Labour Party. This change was critical to the outcome and came about for reasons both substantive (Labour received assurances regarding some of the mission's risks) and political (changing public opinion combined with Labour's desire to look viable in the upcoming election). In addition, the international pressure tapped into Labour's identity and foreign policy orientation as a supporter of internationalist policies.[372]

This case met both positive and negative expectations about the effects of coalition politics on the quality of decision making. On the negative side, the delay in responding to NATO's request and international pleas was a direct result of the presence of a small junior party in the coalition. Although the government crisis was averted and the Netherlands ultimately made a meaningful foreign policy decision, the two-month deadlock, indecision, and uncertainty meant that, according to one NATO diplomat, "the Dutch have lost much credibility in NATO over this issue."[373] Moreover, the junior party's insistence on blocking this decision partly stemmed from the political necessity for small parties in a fragmented party system to appeal to their narrow constituency and look distinct. As D66 was not in good standing in the public opinion polls, it instrumentally used the controversial deployment to attract attention before the upcoming elections.[374]

Yet the party was also motivated by substantive concerns about the risky mission and played devil's advocate to prevent premature closure. Such actions arguably improved the decision making, forcing the discussion of contingencies and making clear some ambiguities in the form of assurances from NATO and the United States. As the D66's van der Laan said, "One lesson of Srebrenica is not to take decisions too quickly without studying the rules of engagement."[375] Another commentator noted, "In the Netherlands the issue could . . . bring down the government; in Britain it has hardly been discussed."[376] In this way, regardless of the D66's motivations, the party's position and presence in the coalition may have contributed to a more detailed debate on the issue, which is one hallmark of effective decision making.[377]

CONCLUSION

Overall, the Dutch cases support some key images of how coalition politics influence foreign policy but challenge others (see table 4.10). The cases were more moderate than extreme (according to WEIS coding classifications) but were both cooperative and conflictual in nature. Indeed, elements of conflict and cooperation could be seen in each case, since each decision involved cooperation in a multilateral framework in a hostile gesture toward a third party. In all cases, constraints on government action were attempted by actors in the coalition, and all attempted constraints were in the direction of peace, consistent with the logic of the democratic peace as it has been applied to coalitions. These attempts, however, did not always succeed. Compromise was the outcome in two of the four cases.

TABLE 4.10. Do the Dutch Cases Fit the Images of Coalition Politics and Foreign Policy?

| Questions | Cases | | | |
| --- | --- | --- | --- | --- |
| | South Africa | Cruise Missiles | Iraq | Afghanistan |
| Was the foreign policy cooperative or conflictual? | conflictual | cooperative | cooperative | conflictual |
| Was the foreign policy extreme or moderate? | moderate | moderate | moderate | extreme |
| Did coalition parties attempt to constrain the policy? | yes | yes | yes | yes |
| Were attempted constraints in the direction of peace? | yes | yes | yes | yes |
| Were the constraints successful? | yes | yes | somewhat | no |
| Was the decision a compromise? | yes | no | yes | no |
| Was there poor decision making? | yes (poor implementation) | yes (deadlock) | yes (paper over differences) | yes (delay) |
| Was there good decision making? | yes (divergent thinking) | somewhat (tensions contained) | yes (prevention of premature closure; timely) | yes (contingency planning) |
| What factors best explain the policy outcome and decision making quality? | locus of authority; sr. party disunity; divisibility of issue; political calculations | jr. party consistency and threat; sr. party disunity; coalition weakness | party unity; jr. party inconsistency; formation stage of coalition | political calculations; threats; locus of authority |

The Dutch cases exhibited some form of poor decision making that is often expected of coalition cabinets, including poor implementation (the South Africa case), deadlock (in the cruise missile case), papering over of differences (in the Iraq case), and delay (in the Afghanistan case). Yet each case showed some good decision-making practices as well, such as divergent thinking (in the South African case), prevention of premature closure (in the Iraq case), and contingency planning (in the Afghanistan case). Both the good decision making and the bad can be traced to the nature of coalition politics.

Several factors explain the outcome of the party conflicts. Although these factors vary across the cases, party unity, locus of authority, and distribution of ministries are important in more than one case. The Dutch cases certainly demonstrate the complexities of how coalition politics affects foreign policy and governance. In each case, however, the fact that the authority to make foreign policy was shared across political parties influenced the way the Dutch government reacted to internal and external pressures. In all four cases, the coalition's survival was threatened by the foreign policy issue. These cases also challenge some of the images of Dutch foreign policy: Although most of the cases exhibited deadlock, delay, or the viscosity often associated with Dutch foreign policy, not all of the cases ended in excessive compromise.

The cases also clearly show that even in a small state such as the Netherlands whose agency is constrained by the international environment (in both the Cold War and post–Cold War eras), domestic political actors can sharply disagree on the nature of that environment and how to respond to it. Furthermore, the cases illustrate that even in a democracy and with the public fairly united around a highly salient issue, governments do not respond to the will of the people in a deterministic fashion. In all four cases, the public's preference was not pursued. Public pressure was important in each case (as was international pressure) but was funneled through the coalition cabinets and their constituent political actors.

# 5
# *Japanese Foreign Policy: Paralyzed by Coalition Conflict?*

CHALLENGES AND FACTORS IN JAPANESE FOREIGN POLICY

Japanese foreign policy has provided international relations scholars with an interesting puzzle. Since the country's defeat in World War II, many observers have seen Japan as an enigma, since it did not translate its powerful capabilities—one of the largest economies and one of the highest absolute levels of defense spending—into political influence in global politics.[1] As Thomas Berger writes, "For more than thirty years the central puzzle in the study of Japanese foreign policy has been why Japan has chosen to play a relatively passive role in international affairs despite its impressive economic, political, and potentially military power. By almost any measure, Japan should be one of the world's leading powers."[2]

Japan's foreign policy choices in the Cold War were encapsulated in the Yoshida Doctrine, named for Shigeru Yoshida, the country's prime minister in the late 1940s and early 1950s. The Yoshida Doctrine was a strategic decision to focus on economic growth over self-security and to rely on the U.S. alliance. The policy was very successful in that Japan enjoyed decades of peace and prosperity, although internal and external critics charged that it was too dependent on the United States, labeling it "karaoke diplomacy."[3] Japan's Cold War foreign policy, based on the Yoshida doctrine, was challenged at times, with the United States pressuring Japan to open up its markets to foreign imports and to share more in the alliance's defense burden. Yet "these adjustments did not amount to a fundamental shift away from the country's neomercantilist foreign economic strategy and a pacific security policy. . . . Content with the prosperity and security that a recalibrated Yoshida doctrine brought, Japan refrained from vigorously seeking the international prestige and national security autonomy that would have been more commensurate with its economic capabilities."[4] Japan's most visible presence in the world came in the form of overseas development assistance; it became a world leader in this regard.[5]

The end of the Cold War called into question the bases of the Yoshida Doctrine. Without the Soviet threat, the purpose of the U.S.-Japanese alliance was less clear to either side. Economic interdependence and the rise of economic regionalism (with a more integrated EU and the development of NAFTA) challenged Japan's neomercantilist strategy for foreign economic policy and also brought it into "chronic friction with the United States over trade."[6] New regional threats and uncertainties also emerged: China's increased military spending, North Korean threats to acquire nuclear weapons and long-range missile capability, tensions between the United States and China over the Taiwan Straits, continued territorial disputes between Japan and South Korea and Japan and China, and Indian-Pakistani nuclear tensions.[7]

The post–Cold War international environment created conditions for Japan to reassess its foreign policy and its role in the world. The Gulf War of 1990–91 was a critical point in this regard. Mochizuki describes this event as "perhaps the most acute post–Cold War shock to Japanese foreign policy."[8] Despite pressure from the United States, Japan was unable to gain a majority of Diet members to support legislation that allowed for logistical assistance and traditional peacekeeping activities. Although Japan made a significant financial contribution to the war against Iraq, it was criticized for its "checkbook diplomacy." When Japanese diplomats were forced to wait in the hallways while the permanent members of the United Nations Security Council deliberated over the crisis and when Kuwait did not list Japan in its full-page *New York Times* thank you note, "a sense of impotence mixed with embarrassment and irritation led to a reconsideration of Japan's role in global security."[9]

The Gulf War spurred a debate on whether Japan should become a "normal power." Indeed,

> since the early 1990s, the idea of the "normal" state has been explicitly and implicitly appropriated by other sections of the policy-making community and is now the central reference point for the debate on the future of Japan's security policy. The different sections of policy opinion are united in that they take the developed states of the West as the (often ill-defined or

poorly understood) benchmark for "normalcy" in security policy to which Japan should aspire. Opinion is more strongly divided over how normalization should be achieved and the relative weight that should be ascribed in this process to greater independent Japanese defence efforts, the strengthening of US-Japan alliance cooperation and the development of multilateral security options.[10]

Japanese foreign policy did change in the 1990s. Japan broadened its military role, liberalized its foreign economic policy, and became somewhat more assertive of its interests regionally.[11] But the puzzle remained as to why Japan did not become even more "normal," why it remained a fairly passive player in global politics in the post–Cold War era.[12]

The primary explanations for Japan's foreign policy in the 1990s focus on its position in the international system, its political culture, and its domestic politics. Consistent with realist and neoliberal perspectives, Japan's passivity, even after the Cold War ended, has been attributed to the changing nature of the international environment and the challenges and opportunities it posed for Japan. According to Sato and Hirata, neorealist explanations emphasizing both realist security policy and neomercantilist economic policy were dominant in studies of Japanese Cold War foreign policy and continued for post–Cold War Japanese foreign policy.[13] Indeed,

> it is often taken for granted that the recent expansion of Japan's international contribution [in terms of both security and economic policies] has largely been a response to external pressures or *gaiatsu*, not based on Japan's own independent decision. This view is promoted most often by the "Iraqi shock" hypothesis . . . which suggests that a shocking external event, such as the Gulf War, was a necessary precondition for the public awareness to mature and the policy to change in Japan. But, more broadly, Japan is frequently seen as simply reacting to various strains imposed by the changes in the international environment, such as the ending of the Cold War and economic/technological globalization.[14]

In this way, Japan is portrayed as continuing as the "reactive state" it was during the Cold War but simply reacting to different international pressures.[15]

While much of the scholarship has focused on the role of *gaiatsu*, or pressure, and the constraints on Japan, one school of thought stresses the "rationality" of Japan's foreign policy choices. According to this perspective, Japan does not merely react; its "passivity" is a rational response to its international environment and is in its national interest.[16] In his argument against domestic-constructivist explanations and neorealist expectations of Japanese foreign policy, Kawasaki contends that postclassical realism, with its focus on security maximization, the probability of conflict, and sensitivity to economic costs, better accounts for Japan's foreign policy:

> The logic of post-classical realism still holds for post–Cold War Japan. The collapse of the Soviet Union has only reduced the intensity of the security dilemma that Japan used to face *vis-à-vis* the Soviet Union. . . . If Japan abandons its alliance with the United States and/or starts large-scale military build-up with clearly offensive weapons, such an action would ignite the serious intensification of the security dilemma in Northeast Asia . . . clearly undermining Japan's otherwise secure strategic position. In addition, the Japanese economy would face an enormous financial burden generated by such arms build-up programs. Thus, Japan as a security-seeker has no incentives to abandon its Cold War policy package.[17]

Offering a more neoliberal interpretation, Miyashita has argued that Japan's asymmetrical dependence on the United States for economic markets continued to constrain its foreign policy choices after the Cold War.[18]

Perhaps the dominant explanation of Japan's foreign policies in the 1990s focused on the role of political culture and domestic norms, consistent with constructivism. "In the past two decades or so, a growing number of scholars have focused on such intangible factors as norms and culture in explaining Japan's defense policy. . . . Constructivists hold that international position alone is insufficient to explain why Tokyo behaves the way it does and that collective identity as a peaceful trading nation and the norm of antimilitarism that emerged after its defeat in World War II have constrained Japan's postwar defense policy."[19] Peter Katzenstein and Thomas Berger are the most prominent scholars to argue that Japan's "passivity" stemmed from the antimilitarism and pacifism that developed in post–World War II Japan.[20] These earlier works focused on the enduring nature of these norms and ideas to explain continuity in Japanese foreign policy after the end of the Cold War. More recently, scholars have examined the changing nature of these norms and their effects. For example, Mochizuki discusses evolving internationalism in Japan, arguing that citizens have gradually switched from seeing Japan's international role as involving more environmental and economic issues to seeing that role as involving more security issues. At the same time, a new nationalism has emerged with the aim of asserting Japan's national identity and national interests and of making Japan into a "normal" power that does so.[21] Others have used the internalization of international norms, such as economic liberalism, to explain Japan's gradually changing foreign economic policies.[22]

The constructivist norm and culture arguments imply that public opinion is important and that leaders either represent or listen to the masses. Other explanations of Japanese foreign policy more explicitly point to the role of domestic politics and key domestic political actors. Indeed, Kent Calder's original *gaiatsu* thesis stressed a fragmented, factionalized, bureaucratized political system as the reason for Japan's reactive foreign policy during the Cold War.[23] According to Akihiko, "Why Japan tends to act only after international changes have occurred and seems hesitant to take the initiative cannot be understood without a proper examination of the domestic Japanese setting."[24]

In the 1990s, scholars stressed the changing domestic political conditions at both the elite and mass levels to account for Japan's foreign policy.[25] Kohno, for example, argues that there has been too much emphasis on international pressures to explain Japan's post–Cold War foreign policy: "A more sophisticated analysis of Japan's international behavior must take into account the political process in which these external forces affect the incentives of domestic actors, the power balance among them, and the foundations of existing political institutions."[26] Specifically, Kohno points to the electoral reforms that led to changes in who governed Japan and significant revisions in key party's foreign policy positions. He also notes that the bureaucracy and administrative institutions involved in Japanese foreign policy also underwent major reforms in the 1990s.[27]

Indeed, 1993 brought major changes to the Japanese political system. Most important, the thirty-eight-year single-party, majority rule by the Liberal Democratic Party (LDP) came to an end. A number of factors contributed to the end of the "1955 system," including economic decline, political corruption, the end of the Cold War, and internal LDP splits. The 1993 national parliamentary elections saw significant losses for both the LDP and the Socialist Party, the second-largest party under the 1955 system. Electoral reforms in 1994 contributed to greater volatility and political realignment.

Tsuchiyama contends that the identity crisis and internal debate over Japan's role in the world cannot be separated from this changing domestic political landscape. He points out that one of the factions that left the ruling Liberal Democratic Party was led by Ichiro Ozawa, a champion of reshaping Japan as a "normal" power. Ozawa helped engineer Japan's first coalition government in 1993.[28] With new parties in the government and changes in the old parties' positions, foreign policy was very much a contested issue in Japan during this time of domestic political upheaval.[29] Cortell and Davis also argue that domestic politics is key to understanding the internalization of international norms and external pressure. "The internalization of the GATT/WTO trade liberalization norm has followed a stop-and-go pattern in Japan. The halting nature of the process suggests that pre-existing norms are not easily pushed aside but continue to infuse the beliefs of domestic actors even after important elites have proclaimed their obsolescence."[30]

ACTORS IN JAPANESE FOREIGN POLICY

Domestic political actors play a prominent role in both domestic political and constructivist explanations of Japanese foreign policy. The constructivist-cultural perspective argues (or assumes) a strong, constraining role for public opinion. Accountable to and elected by the people, Japanese political elites are presumably sensitive to the views of the masses. Pacifist and economic nationalist sentiments have significant value in Japanese public opinion and have arguably prevented leaders and some political parties from endorsing and choosing more aggressive or "normal" security policies and more liberal economic policies.[31] Leader sensitivity to public opinion may have been particularly acute in the 1990s, during the period of volatile political realignment, as new parties and splinter parties competed to define their space on the ideological continuum. Furthermore, changes in electoral laws meant that "under the new system, the majority of parliamentarians have to win the plurality of the vote in their electoral district. ... As a result, for the first time candidates for office find themselves under pressure to craft a political message that goes beyond their core group of supporters."[32]

Yet even those who support the cultural explanation for Japanese foreign policy agree that "for decades, Japanese foreign policy by and large has been the preserve of the relatively small number of Japanese officials and politicians who make up the Japanese foreign policy establishment. Except in a very broad and general way, public opinion has traditionally had only limited impact on the making of different aspects of Japanese foreign policy."[33] While evidence shows that Japanese attitudes underwent change in the 1990s to embrace more nationalist or internationalist foreign policies and that the public became more engaged in foreign policy issues,[34] it is not clear that these changes were the primary drivers of Japanese foreign policy or were independent of other domestic political actors. Political parties and leaders, for example, may have played a role in shaping and changing public opinion. And without a consensus in the public on key foreign policy issues, leaders had room to maneuver and at times acted contrary to majority opinion.[35]

Other societal actors, in the form of organized interest groups, have long been considered important players in Japanese foreign policy. Organized peace movements were influential in the 1950s and 1960s and maintained strong relationships with trade unions and leftist opposition parties.[36] Business interests have also been particularly important in foreign economic policy. Federations of business groups, industry sectors, chambers of commerce, and employers' associations have articulated organized preferences on foreign and trade policies. Their influence in foreign policy has largely come through their close connections with political parties and leaders. Scholars of Japanese economic foreign policy have described "iron triangles" involving clientelistic relationships among domestic business groups, bureaucrats, and politicians.[37] Akihiko argues, however, that "with the end of the Cold War and the radically reduced ideological confrontation in domestic politics . . . the role of the *zaikai* [business groups] seems to be undergoing changes and has become more reluctant to side with political parties. Moreover, as globalization proceeds rapidly, it has become difficult to aggregate Japan's business interests."[38]

Changes in the post–Cold War era have opened up the policy-making process for input from other societal actors. According to Sato and Hirata, "Even though foreign policy has traditionally been an elite policymaking domain, calls to reform Japanese foreign policy since the 1980s have created openings for more participation by diverse societal groups. One of the most heralded recent examples of citizen participation in Japanese foreign policy is the role of nongovernmental organizations . . . in the making of

Japan's official development assistance . . . policy and implementation."[39] Domestic nongovernmental organizations have also become more important in foreign policy human rights advocacy and think tanks and media have actively advocated "normalization" of Japanese security policy.[40]

Interest and advocacy groups in Japan can have strong relationships with political parties represented in parliament. Parliament itself can be considered a foreign policy actor in Japan, although it is a relatively weak institution in this area. The Diet—consisting of the House of Representatives (lower house) and the House of Councillors (upper house) mattered little in foreign policy during the era of LDP dominance.[41] With the onset of coalition cabinets, the parliament, particularly the House of Representatives, became theoretically more important, and Diet members at key times used their positions in parliament to voice foreign policy opinions.[42] Parliament also had a formal role in the issues that dominated Japanese foreign policy in the 1990s, including constitutional revision and peacekeeping. Parliamentary approval is necessary to change Article 9, the constitution's "peace clause." Article 9 affirms that the Japanese people forever renounce war and the threat or use of force as sovereign rights and that military forces will never be maintained. With the passage of peacekeeping legislation in 1992, parliamentary approval was required for each dispatch, and parliament must reauthorize every two years.[43]

Parliament, however, serves less as an independent actor in Japanese foreign policy-making and more as a forum in which political parties and party factions interact.[44] Political parties are the primary locus for disagreements over foreign policy. Even during the strong consensus over foreign economic and security policy during the Cold War, the opposition parties in Japan consistently offered an alternative, leftist-pacifist vision. While they were unable to get around the Liberal Democratic's majority control, the Socialists, as the primary opposition party, often employed stalling techniques in parliamentary voting on LDP budgets as a way to criticize the government's foreign policies.[45] In this way, the Socialists "acquired a *de facto* veto power over any security measures: they could boycott Diet sessions or bring them to a halt with procedural delays if the LDP attempted to get an unpopular security measure passed."[46]

The LDP was far from united on foreign policy, although disagreements were more over tactics and were used instrumentally in factional rivalries.[47] Overall, "The LDP's strong factions arguably constrained prime ministers (who were usually faction leaders themselves) from taking decisive action in foreign affairs and weakened the party's ability to articulate a guiding foreign policy vision, beyond the flexible principles of the Yoshida Doctrine."[48] The LDP factions used the Diet's powerful caucuses (the *zoku*) to influence foreign policy even before issues reached the formal committee structure.[49]

With LDP dominance ending in the 1990s, factions became less coherent and important, but the greater number of parties represented in parliament and the changing electoral rules meant greater fragmentation on foreign policy issues.[50] While fragmented, partisan debate over foreign policy became less polarized than during the Cold War after the Socialists abandoned their strict interpretation of Article 9 (in exchange for partnership in a ruling coalition) and their long-held opposition to the military alliance with the United States and the maintenance of the Self-Defense Forces.[51]

Although opposition parties and party factions can play a role in Japanese foreign policy from their seats in parliament, real authority for political parties is found through representation in the cabinet, the chief policy-making body in Japan. As in other parliamentary systems, the cabinet is collectively responsible to the Diet and, according to the Japanese constitution, has the authority to "conduct affairs of state," "manage foreign affairs," and "conclude treaties."[52] At least half of the cabinet ministers, including the prime minister, must be representatives in the Diet, according to the constitution. Cabinet ministers are appointed and dismissed by the prime minister. The number of ministers in the cabinet is constitutionally limited, but this constraint is circumvented with the appointment of ministers without portfolio and the creation of agencies that are not formally ministries.

The Japanese prime minister heads the cabinet but in many ways is less powerful than prime ministers in other parliamentary systems.[53] According to Shinoda,

> The prime minister's direct authority over the executive is surprisingly limited. Although he often gives instructions to the ministries, theoretically he cannot directly control administrative operations. Executive power belongs to the cabinet, and administrative jurisdiction is divided among cabinet members who head administrative agencies. The prime minister controls administrative operations only through the cabinet, which operates under a rule of unanimity. Political reality further undermines his legal authority.

For example, although the Constitution gives the prime minister a free hand in appointing his cabinet members, intraparty politics generally do not allow him to exercise that freedom.[54]

In the 1990s, coalition politics arguably limited the prime minister's power even further.[55] According to Ahn, a prime minister cannot represent the collective will of the cabinet, as the constitution stipulates, when there is no interparty consensus within the cabinet.[56]

Yet the prime minister does have important formal powers as head of the cabinet, and coalitions may have enhanced informal powers by giving him a role in interparty bargaining.[57] Prime ministers' formal powers include presiding over cabinet meetings, dissolving the Diet, and serving as chief government spokesperson, chief diplomat, and commander in chief.[58] Informally, the prime minister can use his support as party leader and his popularity with the public and interest groups and can provide leadership to the bureaucracy to exercise influence.[59] Beginning in the mid-1980s, several Japanese prime ministers capitalized on these sources of power.

> As a result, the prime minister has over time become more active in parliamentary election campaigns and more extensively covered by the media, and his image now has a greater influence on elections. He has also become more active in chairing policymaking commissions, participating in overseas meetings, and hosting foreign guests, thus giving him more policy influence and media "photo ops." This has given him enhanced resources to exercise influence, especially in making foreign policy.[60]

The electoral reforms of the 1990s also considerably reduced the power of intraparty factions, thereby enhancing the power of prime ministers.[61] As in other parliamentary systems, the influence of Japanese prime ministers on foreign policy has varied among individuals with different leadership styles.[62] Overall, Akihiko argues that despite the constraints on leaders, "the prime minister is the single most important player in the game that is Japan's domestic politics, and particularly in the games of complex domestic/foreign policy interaction."[63]

Japanese prime ministers and other party leaders and the cabinet compete with a strong and independent-minded foreign policy bureaucracy. Indeed, bureaucratic actors have been extremely influential in Japanese foreign policy. Japanese bureaucrats tend to stay in their position much longer than politicians do, thereby acquiring expertise and control over implementation. Moreover, bureaucratic agencies' ties to business groups and to factions in political parties also enhance their powers. Yet "the bureaucracy in Japan does not act in chorus; because of the relative weakness of the central coordination of the prime minister, each ministry acts as if it were a sovereign state, especially where jurisdictional demarcation is clear."[64] The Ministry of Foreign Affairs (MOFA) and the Ministry of International Trade and Industry are particularly important. The Japanese Defense Agency is constitutionally an inferior institution; its director-general is a member of the cabinet but as a second-ranking secretary of state, not a full-fledged minister of defense.[65] With foreign policy issues that cut across jurisdictional boundaries, bureaucratic power, factionalism, and infighting are important constraints.

Bureaucratic dominance in Japanese foreign policy is, however, a contested issue. Some observers argue that bureaucratic control has been overstated and that politicians lead bureaucracies, rather than the other way around.[66] Part of this debate hinges on whether coalition government and other political and economic development in the 1990s decreased or enhanced bureaucratic influence. Berger, for example, argues that the poor economy and political corruption weakened the bureaucracy: "Even though the bureaucracy in Japan remains central to the policymaking process . . . , over the past decade its authority has been shaken and its ability to shape political decisionmaking sharply curtailed."[67] Dobson argues that coalition politics weakened bureaucratic control by making decision making more fractious and pluralist.[68] Drifte agrees: "The bureaucracy feels now more vulnerable than before because they are exposed to more rigorous scrutiny in the absence of political cover which they enjoyed before. Today politicians of changing coalition governments can score points against each other by attacking a ministry, particularly if it is headed by a politician from a rival party."[69]

Other scholars contend that coalition politics enhanced bureaucratic influence. Mochizuki, for example, argues that career bureaucrats had a distinct advantage over politicians during the time of fluid party realignment during the early 1990s.[70] Shinoda agrees that the inexperience of parties in the first coalitions yielded influence to the bureaucracy, although he concedes that major policy issues were decided by the political actors.[71] Ahn writes that coalition politics meant that the bureaucracy had to "lobby" political parties and developed two strategies to do so: "With its organizational strength in managing a concerted action, the bureaucracy plays one part against another to push its own agenda and policy. And, with its superior access to information and expertise, the bureaucracy helps political parties build intraparty consensus, thereby facilitating interparty policy coordination."[72] Overall, Berger believes that "the prolonged crisis and increased factionalism that has gripped Japanese politics since 1989 has further reinforced the system's tendency toward fragmented decision making. Each ministry continues to jealously guard its bureaucratic prerogatives, while lack of direction at the political center leads to a mode of policymaking in which new policies are made in ad hoc fashion."[73]

## COALITION POLITICS IN JAPANESE FOREIGN POLICY: GENERAL IMAGES AND FOUR CASES

Despite the other actors that influence Japanese foreign policy, the cabinet is the central authority for policy-making. As in other parliamentary systems, the influence of other players is typically funneled through the cabinet. With the changes in the party system and the political system in the 1990s, coalition cabinets governed Japan, and the central authority to make foreign policy was shared by multiple parties. Many analysts of Japanese foreign policy have consistently echoed the general images of the impact of coalition politics on foreign policy as presented in chapter 2. Most of these analyses emphasized negative effects. Japan was seen as too constrained by coalition politics to respond to demands from its international and regional environments. Its policy-making processes were characterized as paralyzed, as in "total confusion," and as "non-decision politics."[74] As Berger argues,

> Upheavals in the bureaucracy and the party political system initially paralyzed the Japanese political system. For more than a decade Japanese politicians and officials found themselves almost entirely focused on the task of trying to cope with these momentous changes in the political and economic environment. As a result, for much of the 1990s Japan arguably was even more of a reactive state than it had been at the time Kent Calder invented the phrase.[75]

According to Berger, "The prolonged crisis and increased factionalism that has gripped Japanese politics since 1989 has further reinforced the system's tendency toward fragmented decision making. Each ministry continues to jealously guard its bureaucratic prerogatives, while lack of direction at the political center leads to a mode of policymaking in which new policies are made in ad hoc fashion."[76] Mochizuki also argued that the fluid and weak governments generated ineffective policies.[77] Ahn wrote specifically that the factionalism and associated ineffective policy and policy-making were qualitatively different under coalitions than under the LDP's single-party rule. He points out that coalition parties were much more ideologically heterogeneous than LDP factions and that the LDP did have party leaders, particularly the prime minister, who could resolve differences among factions or overrule dissent. He cites foreign policy examples of this centralization and says that it was not possible in coalition cabinets.[78]

Green proposed that coalition politics in Japan created not only poor decision making but also opportunities for hijacked, extreme foreign policy:

> The limitations of coalition government and the pressing challenges of domestic economic restructuring have prevented sustained attention to international problems by senior political leaders. [These and other] trends have created a more pluralistic and less predictable foreign policy-making process, where contentious policies are more difficult to sustain and reactions to external shocks are often more assertive and even nationalistic.[79]

Similarly, Green argues that instead of creating constraints, weakened institutions made it more possible for a significant change in Japanese security policy.[80] Mochizuki agrees that more extreme foreign policy had more potential with coalition cabinets: "Fragmentation of the conservative forces could yield a stridently nationalistic force that would compete for support in the mainstream of electoral politics. . . . Voices for a more assertive and independent foreign policy backed by a stronger military could become more powerful."[81]

Conversely, Pekkanen and Krause contend that coalition politics decreased the polarization in debates over Japanese foreign policy, as the Socialist Party was forced to become more pragmatic as it moved out of opposition and into governance.[82] And Berger argues that despite the difficulties of coalition politics, the new political environment and players that were brought in to the foreign policy-making process allowed Japan finally to attend to matters (such as the issue of apologies for past actions and the revision of the constitution for peacekeeping participation) that were never addressed under single-party rule.[83]

In addition to these comments on the effects of coalition politics, a few studies have focused on coalition politics in particular cases,[84] while others have compared the decision-making processes of different coalitions.[85] No scholar, however, has conducted a systematic analysis of how coalition politics affected Japanese foreign policy according to the theoretical expectations outlined in chapter 2.

The Japanese cases for this project, listed in table 5.1, were chosen to investigate these expectations consistent with the case selection principles outlined in chapter 3. Each case is an instance of conflict among the political parties in the coalition over foreign policy. The cases come from three different coalition cabinets across the 1990s. They cover trade policy, Japan's role in the United Nations, and two aspects of peacekeeping policy—a decision on a particular peacekeeping mission and revision of the general guidelines that define the conditions under which Japan partici-

**TABLE 5.1. Japanese Cases**

| Case | Coalition Parties | (a) Prime Minister<br>(b) Foreign Minister<br>(c) Director, Defense Agency |
| --- | --- | --- |
| Liberalization of rice imports (1993) | Japan Socialist Party<br>Japan Renewal Party<br>Komeito<br>Democratic Socialist Party<br>Japan New Party<br>Sakigake<br>Shaminren | (a) Hosokawa (JNP)<br>(b) Hata (JRP)<br>(c) Nakanishi/Aichi (JRP) |
| Permanent UNSC membership (1993–94) | Liberal Democratic Party<br>Japan Socialist Party<br>Sakigake | (a) Murayama (JSP)<br>(b) Kono (LDP)<br>(c) Tamazawa (LDP) |
| Golan Heights peacekeeping (1995) | Liberal Democratic Party<br>Japan Socialist Party<br>Sakigake | (a) Murayama (JSP)<br>(b) Kono (LDP)<br>(c) Tamazawa (LDP) |
| Peacekeeping law (1998–99) | Liberal Democratic Party<br>Liberal Party<br>New Komeito | (a) Obuchi (LDP)<br>(b) Kono (LDP)<br>(c) Kawara (LDP) |

pates in international peacekeeping. All three cases involve the debates regarding Japan's identity and national role in the post–Cold War era. Even though three of the cases are similar in that they relate to peacekeeping and Japan's role in the United Nations, all four cases differ somewhat from each other in terms of the international and domestic contexts in which they occurred. Yet they all afford an opportunity to assess how coalition politics affects foreign policy and decision making in the Japan. There is no a priori reason to believe that the differences critically affect the relationships under investigation.

LIBERALIZATION OF RICE IMPORTS

In 1986, the United States issued a formal complaint against Japan's restrictions on its imports of various agricultural products, including rice. The U.S. government charged that these restrictions violated GATT rules. The ban on rice imports was put in place shortly after World War II and kept rice costs in Japan at more than eight times the international price.[86] Over the next seven years, Japan responded first by trying to prevent the issue of rice from reaching the bargaining table and then by seeking exceptions to rice in multilateral liberalization negotiations, including the Uruguay round of GATT talks.

Japan cited many reasons for its preference not to open up the rice market to foreign imports. These included historical and cultural significance of rice to Japan, Japanese laws identifying rice as a "basic food" and self-sufficiency in rice as a national security interest, and domestic opposition.[87] Indeed,

> for Japan, rice is a near-sacred product. Deeply embedded in Japanese history, culture, economics, politics, and symbolism. For the Japanese, rice is "our Christmas tree," and rice-producing land is reverently called "our holy land." In Japanese eyes, rice—far more than beef, citrus fruit, or textiles—represented the ultimate non-negotiable market-access topic. "Not a single grain of foreign rice shall ever enter Japan," was the solemn vow of Japanese politicians of all stripes, backed by public opinion, the press, the business community, academics, and the bureaucracy. Opposition to imported rice reflected a national consensus. Small wonder that American demands in

1986 for opening the Japanese rice market were seen as a frontal assault on Japanese culture itself.[88]

Japanese recalcitrance on the issue was strong and persistent. As "rice became a symbol of all that was wrong with U.S.-Japan trade relations, international attention increasingly focused on Japanese protectionism."[89] Under pressure, Japanese officials privately became resigned to some form of liberalization.[90] Nevertheless, the George H. W. Bush presidency "ended with a standoff with the Japanese side on the subject of rice imports, with Washington standing firmly behind its 'no exceptions' position and Tokyo doggedly continuing to seek preferential treatment on rice. The new Clinton administration trade team, working against the backdrop of the looming deadline for wrapping up the Uruguay Round multilateral negotiations, moved aggressively . . . to resolve the issue."[91] The United States, along with Canada and the European Community, proposed comprehensive negotiations to force Japan directly to confront the rice issue, which was becoming a key stumbling block in GATT negotiations.[92] A shortfall in domestic rice production in 1992 also forced the Japanese to import rice on an emergency basis, an event that perhaps chipped away at the taboo of foreign rice.[93] In addition, the United States offered a compromise (known as the O'Mara plan, after U.S. chief agricultural negotiator Charles O'Mara): Japan could delay implementing tariffs on rice for six years, during which time the United States would be granted minimum access to the Japanese rice market. Japan's Ministry of Agriculture responded positively to the offer, and additional talks, some of them secret, ensued between O'Mara and ministry officials to work out the details.

These developments occurred in the summer of 1993 at the same time as the domestic political upheaval in Japan in which the long-ruling Liberal Democrats went into opposition and Japan for the first time was ruled by a coalition government. The coalition was divided on the rice issue. Thus, although the O'Mara compromise led to a breakthrough in bilateral and multilateral negotiations, the domestic constraints remained operative and arguably became stronger. After all,

> of the many obstacles to rice liberalization that Japanese officials and politicians had listed repeatedly before and during negotiations . . . several were rooted in hard political reality. One was the Diet resolution on self-

sufficiency in rice, which remained in effect and which was taken seriously as a commitment. Another constraint stemmed from the long-term and unchanged public statements of many politicians and political parties opposing the importation of a single grain of rice, much less tariffication. The chief barrier to winning acceptance of the compromise draft, one which caused the premier to be "tied up in a rope" ... was disagreement within his governing coalition serious enough to threaten its continuation in power.[94]

*Players and Positions*

Following the July 1993 national elections to Japan's House of Representatives (see table 5.2), the Liberal Democrats, lacking majority for the first time, attempted to put together a coalition. The party failed and was forced into opposition. Although the Japan Socialist Party (JSP) was the second-largest party in the House of Representatives, it had suffered significant losses in the election and did not emerge as a coalition leader.[95] Instead, the Japan New Party, led by Hosokawa, was the key player: "The party's success made it inevitable that Hosokawa would play a pivotal role in the struggle over the composition of the new government."[96]

Hosokawa put together a seven-party coalition and became prime minister in August 1993. The other ministries were divided among the remaining parties, with the Socialists controlling six cabinet posts and the Japan

TABLE 5.2. Japanese National Election Results, 1993

|  | Votes (%) | Seats |
|---|---|---|
| Liberal Democratic Party | 36.6 | 223 |
| **Japan Socialist Party** | 15.4 | 70 |
| **Japan Renewal Party** | 10.1 | 55 |
| **Komeito** | 8.1 | 51 |
| **Japan New Party** | 8.0 | 35 |
| **Democratic Socialist Party** | 3.5 | 15 |
| Japan Communist Party | 7.7 | 15 |
| **Sakigake** | 2.6 | 13 |
| **Shaminren** | 0.7 | 4 |
| Others | 7.3 | 30 |

Source: J. A. Stockwin, *Governing Japan: Divided Politics in a Resurgent Economy*, 4th ed. (Oxford, UK: Blackwell, 2008).

Note: The parties in the governing coalition are boldface. An eighth party, Rengo, was also in the coalition but only had representation in the upper House of Councillors.

Renewal Party (JRP) five (see table 5.3). "The power of Ozawa's Japan Renewal Party in the coalition was reflected in its control over the most important cabinet posts, including ministers of finance, international trade and industry, foreign affairs, defense, and agriculture."[97] Ministries were also controlled by Komeito (Clean Government Party) and Shaminren (Social Democratic League). Takemura, head of Sakigake (New Party Harbinger) was also a key player in the new coalition. "With only thirteen members in the Diet, this party should have been too small to be a significant player in negotiations over the composition of a coalition government. But Sakigake was more important than its numbers indicated. For Hosokawa, alliance with the Sakigake increased his bargaining power because it gave

TABLE 5.3. Members of the Hosokawa Cabinet of Japan (1993)

| Ministry | Individual | Party |
|---|---|---|
| Prime minister | Hosokawa | Japan New |
| Foreign Affairs | T. Hata | Japan Renewal |
| Justice | Mikazuki | independent |
| Finance | Fujii | Japan Renewal |
| Education | Akamatsu | independent |
| Welfare | Ohuchi | Democratic Socialist |
| Agriculture, Forestry, and Fisheries | E. Hata | Japan Renewal |
| Trade and Industry | Kumagai | Japan Renewal |
| Transportation | Itoh | Japan Socialist |
| Posts and Telecommunication | Kanzaki | Komeito |
| Labor | Sakaguchi | Komeito |
| Construction | Igarashi | Japan Socialist |
| Home Affairs | Sato | Japan Socialist |
| Environmental Agency | Hironaka | Komeito |
| Hokkaido and Okinawa Development Agency | Uchara | Japan Socialist |
| Economic Planning Agency | Kubota | Japan Socialist |
| Science and Technology Agency | Eda | Shaminren |
| Minister (in charge of political reform) | Yamahana | Japan Socialist |
| Chief cabinet officer | Takemura | Sakigake |
| Director general of Defense Agency | Nakanishi/Aichi | Japan Renewal |
| Director general of Management and Coordination Agency | Ishida | Komeito |

Source: Rei Shiratori, "Japan," European Journal of Political Research 26 (1994): 355–60.
Note: Uchara (JSP) also served as director general of National Land Agency.

him a bloc of lower-house votes that was close in number to what the Japan Renewal Party and the Komeito each commanded."[98]

The parties represented in the cabinet held diverse policy positions. According to Christiansen, "The new coalition government spanned the ideological spectrum from former LDP members to the Socialist Party. The coalition had six major party members, three conservative/reformist parties, the Socialists (on the left wing), and the centrist Democratic Socialist and Clean Government Parties."[99] Prime Minister Hosokawa's Japan New Party was a conservative party, formed in 1992 from defectors of the Liberal Democratic Party and dedicated to political reform.[100] The party's platform "included decentralization to vent the collusive relationship between the central ministries and industries, deregulation to promote consumer interests, and opening Japanese markets to foreign enterprises. . . . Hosokawa was also explicitly neoconservative in foreign and defense policies."[101] The party was largely formed around and popular because of Hosakawa's charismatic personality.[102]

The JRP, led by Ozawa, was formed an 1993, also from a split within the Liberal Democratic Party. "The defection of this group was the most important factor leading to the ruling party's defeat in the July election. No doubt a principal motive for the formation of the JRP was Ozawa's desire to shake up the political system and form the nucleus of a credible alternative" to the Liberal Democrats.[103] Although he did not have a particular ministry, Ozawa's influence in the 1993 coalition was significant.[104] Sakigake, led by Takemura, was another party formed from defections from the Liberal Democratic Party in 1993.[105] "Its views were more 'progressive' than those of the JRP."[106] These three parties had differences over foreign policy. Ozawa and his party envisioned moving Japan toward a more assertive status of a "normal country," while Takemura preferred strengthening the United Nations and multilateralism. Hosokawa leaned toward Takemura on this issue.[107]

The Socialists were the ideological outlier in the coalition.[108] The JSP was always the largest party in opposition during the long era of Liberal Democratic rule. Consequently, "many of the JSP's policies were conceived in reaction against the conservative governments of the 1950s, particularly against the power of what the JSP chose to call 'monopoly capital.' It repeatedly inveighed against rearmament, which (in its view) defied the 'Peace Constitution,' Japanese membership in an anti-Communist alliance of nations led by the United States, erosion of the powers of the National

Diet, antilabor legislation . . . , exclusion of labor unions in general from central decision making . . . and so on."[109] Unlike many Western European socialist parties, the JSP retained strong elements of Marxism in its rhetoric and was seen as extremely left of center in the Japanese system, although the party contained leftist, centrist, and rightist factions.[110] Although the Socialist Party emerged as the largest party in parliament after the 1993 elections, it suffered an unambiguous defeat, losing almost half of its seats. The party "was bereft of attractive leadership, beholden to public-sector unions, torn internally by personal and ideological feuds, and unable to break away from policy positions that had been devised in the context of domestic and international conditions that no longer existed."[111]

Also new to governing was Komeito, the only religious party in modern Japanese politics. Komeito is a Buddhist-based party, with connections to the Buddhist organization Soka Gakkai. "At the core of this reconstructed religious movement, the Soka Gakkai's central objective is the improvement of Japanese society in particular and the world in general through the reformation of human character [and the Komeito Party] was formed to mold the environment toward acceptance of its religious objectives."[112] Soka Gakkai leaders argue that the Komeito resembles Western Europe's Christian Democratic parties.[113] Komeito's policy principles include "middle-of-the-road reformism," "humanitarian socialism," and "pacifism." At the national level, it usually adopts left-of-center positions, but observers and Komeito leaders have argued that the party is difficult to place on a left-right scale.[114] In the 1970s, Komeito officially shifted its stance on defense and security issues toward the center.[115]

The two other parties in the coalition, the Democratic Socialist Party and Shaminren, were fairly small. The Democratic Socialist Party was formed in 1960, drawing on support from some labor union federations, but was never a major party. It has been classified as just left of the Liberal Democratic Party. Expressing hawkish views on defense by the 1970s, it was in conflict with the Socialists.[116] The Shaminren was formed in 1977 to represent a less extreme form of democratic socialism.

With these parties in the cabinet,

> Hosokawa came to power as head of a motley coalition of reformers, political opportunists, socialists, pacifists, internationalists, and others. The potential for conflict within the coalition was obvious from the beginning. There were unresolved policy differences between the Socialists and former

LDP members who now were in the Japan Renewal Party. Many of the coalition's members were uneasy about alliance with the Soka Gakkai–supported Komeito. And there was a deep animosity between the two most important supporting players in the coalition that had put Hosokawa in power, Ozawa and Takemura, who represented two very different conceptions of political reform.[117]

In addition to policy differences, "personal antagonisms among the coalition's leaders made it difficult for them to agree on anything. Nor . . . were there institutionalized decision-making mechanisms that could restrain personal conflicts from dominating the policy process."[118] Indeed, there was little agreement on the process for making policy decisions. Although Hosokawa proposed a number of formal committees to manage party and legislative relations and to formulate policy, they never played a significant role. Instead, "Ozawa was able by the force of his personality, and because of his strategy of close alliance with the Komeito, to establish himself as the dominant figure in the coalition, exerting extraordinary power over its policies and its personnel decisions."[119] Hosokawa's preference for top-down decision making, particularly on controversial issues, and his "reliance on Ozawa's strong leadership, however, engendered a tenacious dissonance and distrust among the governing parties that ultimately led to the eight-party coalition's breakdown."[120]

Considerable disagreements also arose over the issue of rice imports. Both Hosokawa and Ozawa favored opening the rice market before they took office.[121] Hosokawa's Japan New Party platform included neoliberal commitments such as deregulation to serve consumer interests and opening Japan's markets to foreign imports. "Particularly significant was the fact that during the 1993 election campaign Hosokawa called for the opening of the Japanese rice market, hitherto regarded as a taboo by political parties."[122] This stance put the prime minister and his party in direct policy conflict with the Socialists, who relied on rural votes and had consistently opposed lifting the ban on rice imports.[123]

The Socialists were supported by the Liberal Democrats, now in opposition. "When the LDP raised the issue [of rice liberalization] in 1989, the shift of farmers' votes from the LDP to opposition parties led to the LDP's historic defeat in the Upper House election. After the 1989 election, the LDP shelved the issue."[124] After the 1993 elections, most LDP members of parliament remained opposed to tariffs, although some younger representatives supported liberalization.[125]

In the fall of 1993, the Japanese public was divided about

> whether to open their rice market to foreign countries, with 42 percent favoring and 44 percent opposing the idea [according to an] opinion survey. The poll, which was conducted on Nov. 7 and 8 by the Asahi Shimbun, a major Japanese daily, also revealed that 58 percent of respondents think Japan will have to accept tariffication of non-tariff barriers on rice imports in several years. Nonetheless, concerns about the safety of foreign rice is what comes to the minds of the highest percentage—30 percent—of respondents when they think about the market opening, according to the survey. . . . The percentage of people in favor of opening the rice market was the same as that revealed by a March survey, while that of those against it dropped slightly from 47 percent.[126]

Although rice farmers also believed that Japan would eventually have to open its market to foreign imports, they protested the lifting of the ban at key points in the fall of 1993.[127]

*Disagreements and Decision Making*

Taking office during the final round of the GATT negotiations, in which agricultural trade was the primary sticking point, Hosokawa's government faced significant international pressure to lift the ban on rice imports. But Hosakawa's public popularity and his apparent national mandate for political reform "did not translate into the political clout to force opponents in his multi-party government, especially on a subject as touchy as rice. The coalition was not unified on rice liberalization."[128] Hosokawa supported liberalization on rice. "Prime Minister Hosokawa personally placed the highest priority on the conclusion of the GATT Uruguay Round. To put it in his words: 'Japan is in the world system and I thought that we must show leadership by contributing to the successful conclusion of the Uruguay Round.'"[129]

Hosokawa could count on support from his own party, Komeito, and the Democratic Socialist Party.[130] To persuade Sakigake to join the coalition, Hosokawa had pledged to Takemura that he would oppose subjecting rice to tariffs (but did not rule out a compromise to delay that move).[131] Some hard-line opposition to tariffs arose in Ozawa's Renewal Party, "but Ozawa seemed able to contain his troops and kept them in the party and the coalition."[132] Ozawa also supported tariffs: "Ozawa said it would be 'undesirable' for Japan to comply with the proposal only after pressure from abroad"; instead, he argued, Japan should voluntarily impose tariffs and dismantle the ban on imported rice.[133] He warned that Japan would be isolated in the international arena if the United States and Europe reached an agreement on agricultural issues and argued that tariffs alone could protect Japanese rice farmers and ensure self-sufficiency while still maintaining the principle of free trade.[134] The Socialists were the main source of opposition to tariffs in the coalition and remained so until the decision was made in December.

Although Hosokawa favored liberalization, as prime minister he reiterated the official line of opposing the lifting of the ban.[135] In September 1993, while visiting New York, he repeated that Japan would respect parliament's resolution and not import rice.[136] Prime Minister Hosokawa, Foreign Minister Hata, and the chief cabinet secretary, Takemura, stressed that the fall 1993 emergency imports of rice did not portend permanent liberalization.[137]

When a report surfaced in October that Japan and the United States were negotiating a tariff deal, the Socialists warned "that Hosokawa risks undermining the governing coalition if he unilaterally endorses a lifting of the ban [and that] any move to lift the rice ban would run counter to an agreement among the coalition members to oppose liberalization."[138] Japanese officials denied the report, saying that Japan was merely communicating with GATT partners to seek an understanding of its position against lifting the ban.[139] The proposal, which leaked to the press in mid-October, included a six-year grace period during which Japan would accept imports equal to 3 to 5 percent of domestic consumption. The United States called the offer "a big step forward."[140]

After the GATT director-general visited Japan in October,

> Hosokawa felt compelled to reassure the press that "I told him . . . Japan would not accept tariffication." The prime minister's defensive and evasive public statements stemmed from the tightrope he was walking in domestic politics. Caught between his own preferences and stated commitments and his die-hard political opponents, Hosokawa was frustrated and cautious. He

also was pessimistic about the usefulness of continued Japanese stonewalling. He told one coalition party leader that Japan's merely saying "we oppose, we oppose" . . . will "not work." The hostile political and press backlash to reports of his remarks led Hosokawa to avoid comment on the subject.[141]

The opposition in Japan included rice farmers who protested in the streets of Tokyo in October, even though surveys showed that most farmers believed that opening the rice market was unavoidable at some point in the future.[142] The idea of lifting the rice ban also faced stiff opposition in the Diet: "A recent poll of Lower House politicians by the Asahi Shimbun daily found that, apart from Mr Hosokawa's own Japan New Party, as much as 80 per cent still oppose the liberalisation of Japanese rice imports. Many Socialist MPs . . . joined opposition LDP politicians in demanding, without success, that the government pass a parliamentary resolution to reaffirm its ban on rice imports."[143] In late November, LDP opposition members called on the cabinet to resign if it partially lifted Japan's ban on rice imports. This action followed Takemura's comments that Japan would have no choice but to liberalize its rice market.[144] Divisions existed among the Liberal Democrats, however, with some younger MPs favoring liberalization.[145]

Supporters of liberalization attempted to change domestic opposition. In late October, Hosokawa sent Agriculture Minister E. Hata on a surprise trip to Europe to again request for an exemption for Japanese rice. The prime minister reportedly had sent Hata on the trip "to show the domestic Japanese electorate that the coalition government had done its utmost to fight tariffication if Tokyo was forced to open its rice market."[146] In addition, the chief cabinet secretary, Takemura; Foreign Minister T. Hata; and the JRP's Ozawa hinted that Japan's acceptance of rice imports was inevitable.[147]

> The government is trying to convince those who oppose rice imports, by stressing the danger of Japan being blamed for the failure of the talks if it does not agree to a compromise deal on rice. Last weekend, Mr Takemura said Japan could not break up the Uruguay Round, and it would have to allow foreign access to the rice market. Mr Yuichi Ichikawa, secretary general of the Komeito, . . . also expressed support for a compromise deal. Mr Takemura said the partial lifting of the import ban would not contradict a parliamentary resolution and an agreement within the coalition opposing the replacement of the ban with tariffs.[148]

Throughout November, government leaders continued to deny they were in secret negotiations with the United States; during the middle of the month, Hosokawa again insisted that Japan would not replace the ban with tariffs and denied that a deal had been negotiated.[149] Not until late November did a senior government official reveal that Japan indeed was involved in negotiations with the United States regarding rice tariffs and was likely to accept a compromise deal that phased in tariffs over six years.[150] The compromise—known as "minimum access"—was officially presented in GATT talks in Geneva and in a cabinet meeting in Tokyo in early December 1993. Hosokawa argued that Japan had an obligation to uphold the world's free trade system.[151] The official announcement sparked protests in Japan, although industrialists reportedly responded favorably.[152]

The Socialists were decidedly opposed and threatened again to leave the coalition.

> Wataru Kubo, secretary general of the Social Democratic Party, the biggest partner in the seven-party coalition, reiterated his party's opposition to the compromise accepting minimum market access over a six-year grace period. "The minimum access idea constitutes part of the opening of the rice market," Kubo was quoted as saying by Kyodo News Service. "We cannot agree to the proposal in view of past Diet resolutions, which were designed to oppose allowing foreign rice growers access to the Japanese rice market, and the coalition government's policy agreement on the issue."[153]

Takemura countered that the coalition agreement to avoid liberalizing rice trade did not cover "minimum access." The Socialists were unconvinced: the minister of political reforms, Sadao Yamahana, disagreed with this interpretation of the compromise, arguing that it violated either the Diet resolution or the coalition agreement.[154] The Socialists reportedly warned Hosokawa that "there could be opinions emerging in our party to leave the coalition."[155] News agencies, however, reported that some Socialists were not ready to leave the coalition over the rice issue.[156]

Disagreement in the coalition and ambiguity about the compromise led Hosokawa to postpone a cabinet meeting to decide the issue:

> In a meeting at Prime Minister Morihiro Hosokawa's official residence, the leaders of the other coalition parties resisted a call from the premier and his supporters to reach a decision at Friday's regular cabinet meeting. . . . The

coalition leaders are reported to have criticized Hosokawa's failure to make clear that if Japan accepts the proposal it will have to make additional concessions to continue the exemption from tariffication after the seventh year. . . . Hosokawa apologized at the meeting for the government's failure to confirm that the clause was included in the proposal, saying Japan cannot destroy the Uruguay Round. . . . The premier also reportedly asked the coalition leaders to build a consensus among their respective parties on the partial opening of Japan's rice market.[157]

Amid the delay, GATT officials pressured Japan to reach a decision, and rice farmers were arrested for protesting on the grounds of the parliament building.[158] "Near the parliament building in Tokyo, some 5,000 farmers along with politicians from both the ruling and opposition parties, gathered at an outdoor amphitheater and accused the government of betrayal. There were cheers for SDP Chairman Tomiichi Murayama who said his party would do its 'utmost' to prevent Japan's rice market being opened. The move would lead to the 'destruction of Japanese agriculture,' he said."[159]

Although the Socialists at one point had hinted that they would not leave the coalition over the issue,[160]

> SDP secretary general Wataru Kubo has also pointed out that party members are now in a dilemma. The SDP had promised voters it would never give in to rice imports during past election campaigns. Most SDP members fear they will lose their supporters if they remain in the Hosokawa government. The SDP has noted a decline its popularity—down 30 percent in a recent poll—after it joined the coalition. Kubo says SDP legislators will have to make a major decision whether or not to stay with the Hosokawa administration. Upper House SDP member Masayoshi Ito has suggested the only way they can regain their reputation as "a party that stands up for the people" is to break away from the coalition and campaign as a powerful opposition.[161]

In early December, Hosokawa called for an emergency meeting with the Socialists on the issue. He also sent Foreign Minister Hata to Geneva to try to gain last-minute concessions on the proposal.[162] Hata returned with no alternatives, and the cabinet scheduled an extraordinary December 13 meeting to accept the proposal, even if the Socialists would not approve it.[163]

The Socialists remained divided and met in special session on the issue but were unable to reach an agreement and were split about whether to leave the coalition.[164] "Potential defectors were holding up the party's reluctant acceptance of the proposal. With Hosokawa only holding a slim parliamentary majority, political analysts said the departure of just a few SDP members would threaten the four-month-old government."[165] Finally, "the SDP's acceptance came during a meeting of the party executive in the early hours of Tuesday morning at the socialist party's headquarters in central Tokyo, where dozens of protesting farmers had set up an all-night vigil. A subsequent meeting of socialist members of parliament entrusted party chairman Tomiichi Murayama with the decision. In reluctantly accepting the view of Hosokawa and the other six parties in the coalition, the Socialists decided to remain in the government, news reports said."[166]

Shortly thereafter, the cabinet met at 3:16 A.M. on December 14 to approve the "minimal access" policy under which a quota equal to 4–8 percent of Japan's total rice consumption would be imported until 2000, at which time the policy would be renegotiated. "'We must do it for the sake of world trade,' Hosokawa said at a 4 A.M. news conference where he asked for the nation's understanding."[167]

*Role of Coalition Politics*

This case challenges many general images of coalition foreign policy as well as specific characterizations of Japanese coalition policy in the 1990s. The decision to concede on rice liberalization and grant minimal access as part of GATT negotiations can be classified as an extreme and cooperative foreign policy behavior, as it was a substantive agreement and quite a reversal from past Japanese foreign policy.[168] There is no evidence that this policy resulted from a diffusion of responsibility and accountability (although the seven-party coalition made it difficult for the wary public to hold one party accountable for this controversial policy), nor is there evidence that the extremity was a diversionary tactic or resulted from hijacking and minority influence by subsets of the coalition. The subset (primarily the Socialists) that attempted to constrain the coalition from making this decision failed despite the importance of those votes for the maintenance of the coalition. Moreover, the constraint was against the direction of cooperation, not for it, as is assumed by democratic peace research.

Two factors were particularly important in the outcome of this case.

First, Prime Minister Hosakawa's personal commitment to rice liberalization, his leadership style, and the decision-making processes he established in the coalition allowed him to prevail over the Socialists' objections.[169] Indeed, the rice case is a good example of the Hosakawa government's top-down policy-making processes and success in initiating change.[170] According to Shinoda, the "centralized nature of the coalition government helped in implementing Hosokawa's political decision to open the rice market."[171] The prime minister never met with officials from the agricultural ministry and for months denied that top-level negotiations were taking place.[172] This development is consistent with Shinoda's classification of Hosokawa as a "grandstander" who "goes directly to the public and the media in his search for support of his policy goals to supplement his lack of internal sources of power."[173] Yet in the rice case, he also tried to keep the issue out of public scrutiny.

> Hosokawa was certainly using his best spin-doctoring skills to obscure what had really been happening in the final stage of the negotiations on rice imports. Just a week before the Uruguay Round ended, Japanese government officials not only were denying reports of a compromise settlement but were asserting, in fact, that Tokyo was still engaged in final-hour attempts that somehow might improve rice-import-related terms in the document. As late as December 9 . . . Hosokawa himself publicly rejected reports of a final agreement. The Japanese leaders' claim strained credulity.[174]

In addition to Hosakawa's leadership style, characteristics of the Socialists' attempt to constrain this policy and the Socialists' political calculations were also important to the outcome of this case. The party adopted a fairly rigid negotiating style throughout the case: "The Socialists, known for nearly four decades as a party in perpetual opposition, were still playing that adversarial role—to the point of posing hostile queries about the state of the rice liberalization negotiations directly to the prime minister on the Diet floor. In the end, the negativistic politics of the Socialists left them out of the loop."[175] Although they threatened to leave the coalition over the rice issue, they calculated that doing so would be too costly. "In the end, the party decided that breaking with the popular prime minister and bearing the blame for the collapse of the world trade system would be much more dangerous politically than protecting rice farmers, giving Hosokawa his victory."[176] Younger members of the party apparently pushed to accept liberalization, calculating that "the party will not have much to gain by leaving the coalition government, and are calling for the party to accept liberalization."[177]

Public opinion and international pressure also played a role in this case, but they were filtered through the leadership and coalition politics. Hosokawa did not have to worry about general public opposition his position: "Every national poll taken in the months just prior to his announcement showed that most Japanese agreed that the time had come to import at least some rice."[178] At the same time, no politician seemed willing to stand up to the pressure of the international community and risk isolating Japan.[179] Yet the prime minister navigated both internal and external pressures. According to Nonaka, Hosokawa "neither obeyed the U.S. government, nor utilized *gaiatsu*, as external or U.S. government pressure for domestic reform."[180]

In this case, coalition politics was more important in terms of the quality of the decision-making process than in terms of the outcome. There are signs of good decision making for the reasons proposed in the literature. Because of the presence of the Socialists and other critics of rice liberalization in the coalition, multiple viewpoints certainly were considered (consistent with standard notions of rationality) and represented (consistent with normative democratic criteria). Furthermore, this decision is viewed as a major policy achievement and the Hosokawa government is characterized as "successfully" pursuing rice market liberalization, one of its chief goals.[181]

Yet the case also exhibited some of the characteristics of poor decision making that are often associated with coalitions. Largely as a consequence of opposition within the coalition, the government repeatedly delayed liberalization on rice. In addition to delay, considerable denial and even deception took place, with the prime minister keeping secret the ongoing negotiations—again, largely to keep his government together. This lack of transparency may have allowed Japan to sign such a substantive agreement conceding its earlier position, but it detracts from the legitimacy that an open process in coalition governments can have.

Despite the December 15 announcement of the agreement to allow minimal access, the issue of rice liberalization continued to cause problems for the coalition.

According to Hosokawa, two days before he announced his resignation, on April 6, 1994, JSP Chairman Murayama and two other Socialist Party leaders called on Hosokawa to ask him not to send Hata, who was then foreign minister, to the signing in Marrakesh, Morocco, of the Uruguay Round treaty that was scheduled to be held on April 10. They warned that if Hata went there and signed the treaty that the six JSP members of the cabinet would resign. Hosokawa reminded them that they had agreed the previous December 15, after Hosokawa had accepted a lot of their conditions . . . , to support the government on liberalizing the rice market. . . . Now, Hosokawa said, he told them to go ahead and resign if that is what they wanted to do. He said that he was proud of his decision to open the rice market and that it was all right with him if his government fell on this issue.[182]

In the end, the coalition fell because it was united only regarding the importance of reforming the electoral system. Hosokawa claimed that he resigned as prime minister to reduce the Socialist Party's ability to obstruct Japanese policy.[183] The rice liberalization issue weakened the Socialists' internal cohesion, and they were left out of the next coalition, which lasted only from April to June 1994.[184]

## PERMANENT UNSC MEMBERSHIP

The post–Cold War international environment, along with domestic political changes in Japan that opened the door for more voices, spurred an internal debate regarding Japan's role and identity in the world. This more philosophical debate was manifest in a number of specific policy questions, including whether and how Japan should pursue a permanent seat on the United Nations Security Council (UNSC). According to Drifte, "Japan's quest for permanent Security Council membership has undoubtedly been closely linked with the issue of prestige and status."[185] Green agrees: "The questions that emerged in pursuit of the UNSC seat are *the* fundamental questions about Japan's world role."[186] Yet this quest for membership was far from straightforward and embodied the many contradictions and frustrations of Japan's pursuit of multilateral diplomacy in the 1990s.[187]

International organizations had long been an important part of Japanese foreign policy after World War II and post–Cold War multilateralism heightened the UN role in international politics.[188] The prestige of gaining a seat in the elite group of Security Council members was particularly appealing to Japan, "which had been a member of the Council of the UN's predecessor organization, which has been eager to rehabilitate its reputation after the defeat in 1945 and which has been craving since the 1960s international recognition of its economic achievements and international contributions."[189] Many in Japan also felt that a permanent seat would reflect Japan's high levels of financial contributions to the United Nations. By the 1990s, Japan was one of the larger contributors to the UN budget.[190] Inside Japan, this argument became the chief rationale for a bid for UNSC membership.[191]

Some Japanese officials had argued for permanent membership even before the end of the Cold War. The Ministry of Foreign Affairs was particularly supportive of membership, without qualifications, and had paved the way for a bid for a seat during the 1980s by promoting Japanese nationals into UN positions and winning nonpermanent positions on the UNSC.[192] Under Liberal Democratic single-party rule, the Ministry of Foreign Affairs had submitted a position paper to the UN Secretariat that included an unqualified bid, hoping to secure a seat by the organization's fiftieth anniversary.[193] In the early 1990s, the ministry continued to work toward garnering international support and launched a campaign to "educate" Diet members on the importance of international organizations and on Japan's UN financial contributions.[194]

Yet the question of permanent membership was complicated by Japan's past, its views of the other members of the Security Council, its constitutional framework, and the different opinions in its fragmented party system. Indeed, internal debates on the issue became quite heated in the 1990s.[195] Opponents argued that it was not clear what a seat would allow Japan to do that it could not already do. They also suggested that pointing to Japan's contribution made it look like Japan was trying to buy a seat or that Japan was too eager.[196] "Other politicians, supported by many opinion leaders in the media and in academia, opposed the bid or at least urged restraint because they were receptive to the idea that the country was not yet ready, that there was no coherent concept for multilateral diplomacy, that the Ministry of Foreign Affairs was pursuing the campaign for prestige and to increase its own status, and that not enough discussion had taken place. Many thought, therefore, that Japan should wait, or that Japan should be invited to permanent Security Council membership rather than campaigning for it."[197] Article 9 of the Japanese constitution was also an issue, since many observers linked permanent Security Council membership with fully-fledged PKO [peacekeeping operations] involvement, which was seen as either in contradiction to the Japanese Constitution or at least threatening to lead to a further erosion of the Constitution. This link was made by many Japanese as a result of the chronological concurrence of the re-emergence of the government's intention to pursue the candidature for a permanent Security Council seat and, in the context of the allied action against Iraq in 1990–91, the need to respond positively to foreign pressure on Japan to do more international burden sharing. [Other political leaders] were opposed to UN-sanctioned actions involving the use of force and critical of a UN which seemed to become increasingly tilted towards more peace enforcement. As a result they pressed for the weakest wording possible in any expression of interest in permanent Security Council membership.[198]

Like their leaders, members of the Japanese public were divided over the issue of a permanent seat, although most polls showed that a majority supported membership by 1994.[199] According to Hiroshi, "The Japanese people are generally receptive to the idea of a permanent seat for Japan on the Security Council [but] they feel permanent membership should not push Japan beyond the limits imposed by the Constitution. . . . [W]ith almost one third . . . uncommitted, a sweeping consensus on the issue remains far off."[200]

The debates over a seat on the UN Security Council played out during the early years of coalition politics in Japan. During the tenure of the seven-party coalition led by Hosokawa, there was considerable disagreement over whether and how Japan should pursue a permanent seat. "Despite Prime Minister Hosokawa's own lukewarm interest in the bid and the reluctance if not opposition to it within his coalition, he decided to address the General Assembly in September 1993, his first visit abroad as prime minister."[201] Yet Hosokawa's speech included UN reform as a precondition as a consequence of an active intervention by Shusei Tanaka of the small Sakigake Party, who held a key position as chief cabinet secretary.[202] Tanaka, representing the position of many on the left, argued that permanent membership involved risks and would reignite militarism in Japan.[203]

The brief Hata-led government in April–June 1994 pursued a more aggressive policy of seeking a permanent seat. With the absence of the more pacifist-leaning Socialists and Tanaka's Sakigake, the Ministry of Foreign Affairs joined the prime minister and the foreign minister in backing permanent UNSC membership.[204] Indeed, this government "took a very positive attitude towards proclaiming Japan's candidature in an unconditional way. Both Prime Minister Hata and his foreign minister, Kakizawa Koji, left no opportunity unused to state publicly the candidature and to garner international support. [In the previous government], Hata had declared that it was only normal for Japan to become a permanent Security Council member. On his first visit to Europe as prime minister, he declared that Japan would do all it could to fulfill its responsibility if it were to become a permanent member of the Security Council."[205]

This unconditional bid for UNSC membership came to an end when the Hata cabinet fell and a coalition of the Liberal Democrats, the Socialists, and Sakigake came to power.[206] The three new coalition partners had no consensus on the issue internally or with each other.[207] Yet in a September 1994 speech at the United Nations, the Liberal Democratic foreign minister, Kono, formally announced Japan's bid for UNSC membership without reform as a condition.

*Players and Positions*

The coalition that came to power in 1994 was based on the same 1993 election results as the previous two cabinets. This time, the largest party in parliament, the Liberal Democrats, returned to power with the Socialists, the second-largest party, and Sakigake, a small party, as partners. The coalition controlled more than 59 percent of the seats in the Diet (see table 5.4). Hrebenar notes that this was an incredible surprise, as no one predicted a grand coalition between the former rivals.[208] Although the Liberal Democrats were the strongest party and controlled more ministries than their coalition partners, the Socialists' Tomiichi Murayama took the prime minister portfolio (see table 5.5). The foreign ministry was led by Kono, the LDP leader. The three-party coalition was not expected to last a year, given the policy differences among its members.[209]

The small Sakigake Party was a "progressive" party that had splintered off from the Liberal Democrats in 1993.[210] Shusei Tanaka, who served as Hosokawa's aide in the earlier government, had a record of opposing permanent UNSC membership without conditions for reform. In that cabinet's discussion of Hosokawa's speech on the subject, "Tanaka raised objections on the grounds that the extant structure and mission of the U.N. were obsolete in light of new problems in the post–Cold War world, and that Japan should formulate and promote the policy of 'a great UN reform aimed at serving mankind' rather than seek permanent membership to enhance its national status and prestige within the international community."[211] Tanaka also argued that if Japan made an aggressive bid for membership, the country would then be indebted to those countries that supported its pursuit.[212] In addition, "Tanaka argued that Japan will be forced to face the controversy over Article 9 of the Japanese Constitution once it becomes a permanent member whenever issues surrounding the settlement of international disputes arise."[213] Others in the party argued that UN reform was needed because the Security Council had allowed "superpower egoism to control it."[214] The Sakigake Party, however, was not united on the issue. Even though the leadership insisted on UN reform as a precondition for permanent membership, the party "could not find unanimity on the issue among its 16 Diet members."[215]

As early as 1993, the Socialists also had opposed an unconditional bid for permanent membership.

> The JSP's opposition at the time was based on grounds that the U.N. was being operated on the "principle of big-powerism." When the party set forth its "five conditions" for Japan's entry into the UNSC a year later, after the JSP had done an about-face in its previous stance on the Self-Defence Forces and the U.S.-Japan security treaty, the strongest opposition came from those who wanted to include Japan's right to claim the "illegality of the posses-

**TABLE 5.4. Japanese National Election Results, 1993**

|  | Votes (%) | Seats |
|---|---|---|
| **Liberal Democratic Party** | 36.6 | 223 |
| **Japan Socialist Party** | 15.4 | 70 |
| Japan Renewal Party | 10.1 | 55 |
| Komeito | 8.1 | 51 |
| Japan New Party | 8.0 | 35 |
| Democratic Socialist Party | 3.5 | 15 |
| Japan Communist Party | 7.7 | 15 |
| **Sakigake** | 2.6 | 13 |
| Shaminren | 0.7 | 4 |
| Others | 7.3 | 30 |

*Source:* J. A. Stockwin, *Governing Japan: Divided Politics in a Resurgent Economy*, 4th ed. (Oxford, UK: Blackwell, 2008).
*Note:* The parties in the governing coalition are boldface.

sion of nuclear arms" as one of the conditions. The JSP's overall stance on UNSC entry remained more rigid, its conditions tougher, and its opposition force larger than the LDP's, but the JSP was no better at reaching an intraparty consensus on the issue than the LDP, according to party polls.[216]

Indeed, there is no evidence that the Liberal Democrats, led by Foreign Minister Kono Yohei, had a consensus on the issue. The LDP's history was characterized by strong factional politics, and despite the defection of many factions in 1993 (which cast the LDP into opposition), the internal splits continued.[217] Many of LDP's factions were based on individuals, not

TABLE 5.5. Members of the Murayama Cabinet of Japan (1994–95)

| Ministry | Individual | Party |
| --- | --- | --- |
| Prime minister | Murayama | Japan Socialist |
| Foreign Affairs | Kono | Liberal Democrat |
| Justice | Maeda/Tazawa | Liberal Democrat |
| Finance | Takemura | Sakigake |
| Education | Yasano/Shimamura | Liberal Democrat |
| Welfare | Ide/Sakigake/Morii | Japan Socialist |
| Agriculture | Ohkawara/Norota | Liberal Democrat |
| Trade and Industry | Hashimoto | Liberal Democrat |
| Transportation | Kamei/Hiranuma | Liberal Democrat |
| Posts and Telecommunication | Ohide/Inoue | Japan Socialist |
| Labor | Hamamoto/Aoiki | Japan Socialist |
| Construction | Nosaka/ Mori | Japan Socialist/ Liberal Democrat |
| Home Affairs | Nonaka/Fukaya | Liberal Democrat |
| Chief cabinet officer | Igarashi/Nosaka | Japan Socialist |
| Defense Management and Coordination Agency | Tamazawa Yamaguchi/Eto | Liberal Democrat/ Japan Socialist/ Liberal Democrat |
| Hokkaido and Okinawa Development Agency | Ozato/Takagi | Liberal Democrat |
| Economic Planning Agency | Komura/ Miyazaki | Liberal Democrat/ Independent |
| Science and Technology Agency | Tanaka/Urano | Liberal Democrat |
| Environmental Agency | Sakurai/Miyashita | Liberal Democrat |
| National Land Agency | Ozawa/ Ikehata | Liberal Democrat/ Japan Socialist |

*Source:* Rei Shiratori, "Japan," *European Journal of Political Research* 30 (1996): 399–404.
*Note:* The cabinet was significantly reshuffled on August 8, 1995; this change in personnel only affects the final days of the Golan Heights case.

ideological differences, but there is evidence that the 1990s produced more ideological schisms, some along foreign policy lines, within the LDP.[218] On the issue of permanent membership,

> Kono represented the opinion of LDP "doves," who are not necessarily opposed to Japan's gaining permanent membership in the UNSC provided it does not entail an obligation to participate in U.N.-approved use of force, which they believe violates Japan's "peace" Constitution. LDP "hawks," on the other hand, seem to support Japan's entry to the UNSC even if it involves a reinterpretation or a revision of Article 9 to enable Japan to fulfill all of its UNSC obligations. A small group of LDP members—such as Koizumi Junichiro and others . . . —opposed Japan's entry to the Security Council without first "reforming" the U.N. The remainder of LDP members—perhaps a majority—seemed to be noncommittal on the issue, largely because they could not determine how their stance would affect their political survival in the next general election to be held under the new and hitherto untried single-member district system.[219]

*Disagreements and Decision Making*

The coalition agreement on the issue of a permanent seat reflected the cautious approach favored by the Socialists, Sakigake, and some in the LDP: "The new government, in accordance with the spirit of the Japanese constitution, strives for reform of the United Nations and aims at constructing a peaceful order of the world centered upon the United Nations. As for Japan's entry to the UNSC as a permanent member, we will not stretch ourselves, but will take a prudent approach by taking into consideration the progress of UN reform, the recommendation of neighboring Asian countries, and the consensus of the people."[220] This cautious approach was represented in Prime Minister Murayama's statements at the outset of the coalition, making it clear that this policy was in contrast to that of the preceding government.[221] The prime minister

> vowed in his inaugural speech Monday to pursue a dovish foreign policy, calling for a "minimum" self-defense force and pledging non-military global contributions. "We should strive not to be a powerful country but to be a caring country," he told the Japanese parliament. Murayama said that under him, Japan would "persistently maintain an exclusively defense-ori-

ented policy, study our defense posture for the future considering changes in the international situation, and work to build the necessary minimum defense capability." His speech marked a retreat from the previous government's position of pushing to take a permanent seat on the United Nations Security Council. "Japan needs to tackle this issue (the make up of the security council) on the basis of the support of its Asian neighbors and other members of the international community," he said.[222]

To carry out this prudent approach, Sakigake's leader, Tanaka, proposed the establishment of an advisory committee on the issue. The committee would be housed in the prime minister's office. "A storm of protest from MOFA and intervention by LDP politicians sympathetic to the Ministry's concern forced him to drop the proposal, but a month later he organized an LDP-JSP-Sakigake 'Study Group for the Deliberation of Japan's Entry to the UNSC,' designating LDP Diet member Junichiro Koizumi as its chairman and assuming the deputy chairmanship himself."[223] The study group consisted of sixteen LDP and SDP Diet members and called on Japan to make clear in the foreign minister's September UN speech that Japan was not willing to participate in UN military force. They also recommended that an advisory board should be established to further study the issue.[224]

At a meeting in late August, ministers agreed to "coordinate cabinet opinion" before Kono's September address to the United Nations. The finance minister, Takemura, and transport minister, Kamei, reportedly expressed support for a cautious stance at the meeting.[225] Also in August, Foreign Minister Kono predicted it would take a long time for Japan to secure permanent membership and said the government should be "more careful and exact than before."[226] He later denied that he opposed a permanent seat and said that there was little opposition inside Japan to permanent membership, although coalition partners differed about "how ardently" Japan should approach the issue.[227]

These differences were seen in statements coming from the foreign ministry. In late August, "A top Foreign Ministry official denied . . . that Japan has become cautious in its bid for a permanent seat on the U.N. Security Council after a remark by Prime Minister Tomiichi Murayama expressing concern about Japan's obligations. Vice Foreign Minister Kunihiko Saito told a press conference that Murayama's remark does not indicate a change in Japan's stance on its efforts to obtain permanent membership. He also said it is wrong to assume that Japan has backpedaled on its bid prior to the

U.N. General Assembly session opening next month."[228] Although the prime minister expressed agreement with the study group's recommendations in early September 1994, he also supported Japan's bid, mentioning the need for UN reform and the need to consider permanent membership within the framework of Japan's war-renouncing constitution. His words were interpreted as a shift from his earlier cautious approach.[229]

These statements, the Study Group's recommendations, and the upcoming General Assembly meeting led the prime minister's party, the Socialists, to meet on September 7, 1994, to clarify the party's conditions for supporting a bid for a permanent seat. "The main points were that Japan should be recognized for its right to declare the illegality of nuclear weapons, that it should be allowed to fulfill only non-military obligations, and that it should obtain support for its entry to the UNSC as a permanent member from its neighbors, including China and South Korea, as well as from the Japanese people."[230] In a September 9 meeting of all the coalition partners, the parties "agreed on an active stance in seeking permanent Council membership, provided the scope of Japan's contribution was kept within the scope of Article 9 of the Constitution," despite the varying opinions expressed by cabinet members.[231] Specifically, news reports indicated that the agreement said that

> Japan will take the initiative of proceeding with drastic reform of the United Nations so that the world organization can better cope with global challenges . . . and the post–cold war international situation. To these ends, Japan will strive to revise the U.N. Charter. . . . As the sole country in the world to be struck by an atomic bomb, Japan will make efforts to promote the reduction and control of nuclear and conventional weapons. . . . In honor of the principles of its pacifist constitution, Tokyo will clarify its determination to refuse to participate in military actions involving the use of force. . . . Based on these principles, Japan is prepared to fulfill its responsibilities on the Security Council positively on condition that the country's bid for permanent membership has consensus support from its people and the backing of many other countries.[232]

Sakigake leader Tanaka, however, believed that the parties agreed that UN reform was a precondition for Japan's entry into the Security Council. This basic disagreement of interpretation would become a problem for the coalition.[233]

In the interim, Murayama and Kono agreed that Japan would officially put forward an application for a UNSC seat at the UN General Assembly meeting, although Kono reportedly agreed only on the condition that Japan would not engage in military action.[234] Since the cabinet agreement expressed the need for international support, Japanese leaders began seeking backers. More than forty states, including the United States, publicly supported a seat for Japan.[235] According to the *Economist*, external support also allowed the policy's advocates to "finesse" the objections of some in the cabinet, in the parties, and in the public: UN Secretary-General Boutros-Ghali "helpfully emphasised that permanent membership of the Security Council does not necessarily entail sending troops abroad.... This offered Mr Murayama a way to marry national ambition with pacifist principle. One of the cabinet colleagues, Ryutaro Hashimoto, argues that Japan should use a permanent seat as a platform to argue for world disarmament."[236] While key international players expressed support, a September public opinion poll showed that only 37 percent of the Japanese public backed the policy, and nongovernmental organizations protested outside the foreign ministry.[237] Another September public opinion survey, however, indicated 70 percent support for a bid.[238]

Aware of the various opinions within the coalition, Foreign Minister Kono announced that he was bound by the tripartite agreement and would present a draft of his General Assembly speech to the cabinet. He stressed that the speech would clarify that Japan would not participate in the use of force since doing so was constitutionally prohibited.[239] Tanaka, however, claimed that Kono never allowed cabinet members to comment on a draft.[240] The Ministry of Foreign Affairs claimed that Kono altered the draft of the speech. "According to MOFA's side of the story, the original draft prepared by the Ministry was not acceptable to Kono, who subsequently altered it considerably. Kono, known as a pacifist representing the 'dovish' wing of the LDP and opposing any change in Japan's 'peace' Constitution, may be wary of entry to the UNSC lest it entail revisions of the Constitution to fulfill UNSC obligations. But Kono has not publicly declared any allegiance to the idea that U.N. reform should be a precondition for Japan's entry to the UNSC."[241] Kono did not publicly respond to these charges and "was apparently under cross-pressure from Tanaka and MOFA officials."[242]

Kono's September 27 speech to the General Assembly created considerable friction in the coalition.[243] Unlike Hosokawa's 1993 speech, Kono's address did not contain UN reform as a precondition.[244] "Tanaka complained about the omission, saying that U.N. reform was a crucial requisite. He argued that what Kono had said was comparable to 'a non-smoker avowing his intention to remain a non-smoker, whereas what the coalition parties had agreed upon constituted a challenge to the heavy smoker, the UNSC, to quit smoking.' The Sakigake Party itself published a 'position paper' charging that Kono's failure to clarify Japan's intention to reform the U.N. had created a misleading perception of Japan's eagerness to join the UNSC without reforming it."[245] The status of Japan's candidacy implied in the speech also "gave rise to conflicting interpretations in Japan. While Chief Cabinet Secretary Igarashi Kozo (JSP) and Prime Minister Murayama interpreted it as only indicating Japan's readiness to become a permanent Security Council member but not as a candidature, Kono himself was quoted as having wanted to express his intention that Japan be accepted as a new Council member. The Sakigake Party criticized the speech as emphasizing the candidature too much."[246]

*Role of Coalition Politics*

This case is consistent with some images of coalition politics but challenges the characterization of Japanese foreign policy in the 1990s as paralyzed by multiple viewpoints. The policy announced in the foreign minister's speech is difficult to categorize in terms of extremity and degree of cooperation. Objectively, it can be characterized as very moderate and neutral.[247] Yet in the context of Japanese foreign policy, it was "aggressive" and more extreme in that it signaled a significant change in Japan's international orientation and was in line with those advocating a more nationalistic foreign policy and a "normal power" role for Japan. Compared to alternatives, it was more moderate than proposals that did not stress Japan's inability to participate in the use of force but more extreme than proposals that predicated permanent membership on UN reform. The Socialists and leaders of the Sakigake Party attempted to constrain Japan's foreign policy from seeking a permanent seat without reform. These attempts were not in the direction of peace (objectively defined) and were unsuccessful.

The nature of the foreign policy in this case—the announcement that Japan sought a permanent seat, stressing the inability of Japan to participate in the use of force, but without UN reform as a condition—can best be explained as the successful hijacking by a subset of the coalition. According to Ahn, "Kono's actions, as shown by his 1994 U.N. speech, indicated that decisions made by the coalition parties had no binding effect on a cabinet minister who chose to stand apart. It also suggests that decisions made by any of the coalition's liaison councils could not be enforced against a dissenting party within the coalition."[248] Kono, representing the dovish wing of the LDP, seemed to steer this policy away from what the cabinet agreed and from what the foreign ministry advocated. He was able to do so because of the nature of the coalition and its parties.

The decision-making mechanisms established to coordinate policy in the Murayama cabinet were quite elaborate, but they failed in this case.[249] Ahn argues that "Japanese policy on UNSC permanent membership has suffered from a failure in policy coordination that . . . manifested itself not only among cabinet members but also in the triangular grid linking the cabinet, the chief cabinet secretary, and the bureaucracy."[250] Not only did Kono deviate from the collective cabinet stance, he also did not coordinate with his own ministry. His actions may have resulted from Japan's lack of history of coalitions. Indeed, MOFA was inexperienced at confronting political parties after years of single-party rule. It is generally disadvantaged because it has no specific interest group constituency, and in this case it could not rely on foreign pressure. There were also suspicions within Japan that the ministry would use a permanent UN seat to increase its role in the Japanese bureaucracy.[251]

Kono's ability to hijack policy also stemmed from the lack of consensus between and within parties. "This dissent between the coalition parties and within them gave extraordinary leeway to LDP Foreign Minister Kono Yohei in instructing the Ministry of Foreign Affairs . . . on how to proceed with the bid. . . . Since Prime Minister Murayama was not able to muster consensus among his coalition parties on the bid, Foreign Minister Kono was left free to shape the Ministry's policy."[252] The lack of party consensus within the LDP also facilitated Kono's influence.[253] In the end, "the only way Murayama could have prevented Kono from acting on his own would have been to dismiss him—which the Constitution allows the prime minister to do—but at the risk of bringing down the coalition."[254] But Murayama did not have a consensus in his own party to force the issue.

> That neither the LDP nor the JSP had a strong intraparty consensus on the UNSC issue probably protected the Murayama coalition from unraveling after Foreign Minister Kono delivered his 1994 U.N. speech. If the coalition's two major partners had had strong but mutually opposing intraparty con-

sensuses for and against Japan's entry . . . the failure of policy coordination in the liaison councils and Kono's subsequent action at the U.N. would not have been tolerated by the JSP or even by the LDP.[255]

In terms of the quality and effectiveness of decision making in this case, there is no evidence of incomplete information search or a lack of consideration of alternatives. Yet the implementation of the cabinet's agreement was circumvented by Kono's speech. Although all viewpoints were considered in the process (which therefore met standards of democratic representation and legitimacy), the output did not reflect these viewpoints. The government generally appeared ineffective, with confusing statements coming out of cabinet and coalition party Diet members regarding whether Kono's speech was declaring a bid for membership or just launching discussion of the issue.[256] Even if Kono had respected the cabinet's wishes, this compromise approach resulted from the contending positions that arose partly because of Japan's "confused domestic situation."[257] Overall, these actions "simply reinforced the impression that Japan was not yet ready for a permanent Security Council seat."[258] In this way, the foreign policy can be judged as poor quality, since it did not effectively address the issue and produced unwanted consequences for Japan.

Japan was not able to more successfully pursue permanent membership during the remainder of the LDP-JSP-Sakigake coalition. At the beginning of 1995, the parties again agreed to take a cautious and passive approach on this issue.[259] Moreover, the parties continued to disagree on the subject. When Kono next addressed the General Assembly on September 26, 1995, "the coalition's failure to reach any sort of consensus on the UNSC issue was still apparent. Kono repeated his previous year's statement almost verbatim. . . . Kono did mention U.N. reform again in his speech but not the same measure of reform Tanaka claimed to have been agreed upon among the three coalition parties."[260] The Sakigake leader even declared that "Japan should give up the idea of winning permanent membership."[261]

## GOLAN HEIGHTS PEACEKEEPING

The three-party coalition that came to power in 1994 also faced the issue of directly participating in United Nations peacekeeping. As with permanent membership in the Security Council, Japan confronted this issue in the context of the post–Cold War international environment, the debates over Japan's role in the world, and the changing domestic political landscape.[262] "For most countries, committing forces to U.N. peacekeeping operations entails a policy decision with fairly confined defense and budgetary implications. For Japan the ripples from any expansion in peacekeeping activity ... extend well beyond practical considerations relating to peacekeeping itself. The Japanese debate is primarily a political one touching on some of the most sensitive issues in domestic and defense politics and potentially generating fundamental divisions in Japanese society."[263] Indeed, participation in peacekeeping has been a contentious issue in Japan. The debate revolves around those who believe Article 9 of the constitution (rightly) restricts peacekeeping, those who want to revise the constitution, and those who believe that the constitution already allows for an expansion of Japan's peacekeeping roles.[264]

This debate has been ongoing in Japan since the establishment of the Self-Defense Forces (SDF) in 1954. Although conservative groups argued that Japan had a responsibility to cooperate within the framework of the United Nations to promote global security, Japanese PKO participation was effectively barred throughout the Cold War by progressive forces advocating the restraint of military force.[265] Japan did send civilians to Namibia in 1989 and to Nicaragua in 1990, but "the dispatch of Japanese military personnel was at that time unthinkable, mainly because of constitutional constraints."[266] The 1990–91 Gulf War crisis was a turning point in the PKO debate in Japan. When Japan was severely criticized for its inability to respond to requests for peacekeeping assistance, a sense of humiliation prompted calls for a reconsideration of Japan's global role.[267]

As a result, the Japanese government passed the Peacekeeping Operations Cooperation Law in 1992. This legislation was the result of many compromises and put numerous restrictions on the role that Japanese troops could play in peacekeeping. Nevertheless, it allowed Japan to dispatch six hundred SDF personnel to Cambodia in 1992. More PKO participation followed: in El Salvador (1993), in Mozambique (1994), and in Zaire (1994) for the Rwandan relief effort.[268]

Japan's contributions to PKO in the 1990s occurred in the context of cross-cutting international and domestic pressures. Some Asian states were mildly supportive, while others (including China and South Korea) were skeptical or critical. Outside of Asia, there was more support for Japan to share the PKO burden. Britain and France were particularly critical of Japanese reluctance to share the risks of peacekeeping. The United States was an important source of support for an expanded role for Japan in the post–Cold War era. This support included but was not limited to Japanese peacekeeping contributions.[269]

Inside Japan, there were considerable reservations about PKO. According to Mulgan, "The most important limiting factor is the national defense consensus, particularly public attitudes to the overseas dispatch of Japanese military forces and associated constitutional questions."[270] The collective memories of World War II and related suspicions of military actions are one source of the public's resistance to contributing troops to PKO.[271] As a result, "although opinion polls show high rates of support for the U.N. among the Japanese public, the level of popular reservation about the SDF engaging in international military action is still too high to permit rapid movement toward more ambitious peacekeeping engagements for the SDF. In a 1994 public opinion survey, 65% of the respondents were in favor of PKO, but according to the Foreign Ministry, there is a general understanding among the public that SDF personnel will not be dispatched to a war zone."[272] At this same time, the public was almost evenly divided between those who believed PKO were constitutionally problematic and those who believed that the constitution allowed for them.[273] Although public divisions remained prominent, support for PKO had gradually risen through the early 1990s.[274]

The Japanese bureaucracy has been another important source of opinion on the PKO issue.[275] The Ministry of Foreign Affairs was a strong advocate of Japanese PKO participation and played an important role in all PKO decisions.[276] The Japanese Defense Agency is a less important actor generally (without representation in the cabinet), but it became more assertive of the military perspective in the PKO debates.[277] The Japanese military "wants to become a normal military establishment and have its role and status eventually secured as it feels the long-standing constraints on its activities very keenly. As a respectable and honorable activity, U.N. peacekeeping offers an unparalleled opportunity for rehabilitating the SDF in the eyes of the regional and global communities as well as the Japanese public."[278]

The PKO issue was difficult enough under single-party rule. With the changing domestic political landscape, decision making become more complicated with multiparty rule. According to Mulgan, "The post-1991 crisis of political leadership in Japan, compounded by the advent of a coalition government in 1993, makes resolution of issues associated with peacekeeping options extremely difficult."²⁷⁹ The first coalition (under Prime Minister Hosokawa) generally supported Japanese PKO participation and considered but ultimately rejected sending personnel to the UN mission in the former Yugoslavia. Prime Minister Murayama's Liberal Democrat–Socialist–Sakigake coalition agreed to send SDF personnel to Zaire to aid Rwandan refugees, "but some coalition members later claimed that they had not known of the risks that former Rwandan government soldiers posed to SDF personnel, and accused MOFA of withholding information. The subsequent tension between the politicians and bureaucrats complicated the decision on the Golan Heights" peacekeeping mission.²⁸⁰

In early 1994, the United Nations requested that Japan send troops to the UN peacekeeping force in the Golan Heights (the UN Disengagement Force, UNDOF). The mission was established in 1974 to monitor the cease-fire and disengagement agreements between Israel and Syria. The troops would replace a Canadian logistics battalion.

> Japanese domestic politics once again proved to be a major obstacle to sending the SDF abroad. [A] decision on participating in the Golan Heights operation was delayed for over a year before the government was finally able to reach agreement. In August 1995 the coalition parties finally negotiated a compromise. In order to ensure that SDF personnel did not become entangled in conflict, they would not be allowed to transport ammunition or foreign combat troops, nor would they be permitted to join UN training exercises in which live ammunition was used. On the basis of this agreement, a 45-person SDF contingent arrived in the Golan Heights in February 1996 on a two-year mission.²⁸¹

*Players and Positions*

The parties in power and the distribution of ministries were basically the same for the Golan Heights PKO case as they were for the previous case (see tables 5.4 and 5.5). As with the issue of permanent UNSC membership, the three coalition parties disagreed about peacekeeping generally and on the specific question of participation in the Golan Heights mission. According to Berger, despite the Socialist Party's major concessions and reversals that it made to join with the LDP in coalition, "beneath the surface, tensions remained and the two partners clearly held very different views on security issues."²⁸²

The Liberal Democrats, the largest party in the coalition, were generally more supportive of full peacekeeping participation and quickly agreed that Japan should dispatch troops to the Golan Heights.[283] Others in the coalition disagreed: "Significant opposition existed within the Cabinet citing public attitude and also criticizing the manner in which MOFA was behaving without reference to the government stressing that only one PKO would be contemplated at a time and SDF troops would have to return from Mozambique beforehand."[284] This opposition came primarily from Prime Minister Murayama's Socialist Party. Historically, the Socialists were the primary advocates of antimilitarism in post–World War II Japan and opponents of the Self-Defense Forces and the alliance with the United States. The post–Cold War environment and particularly a role in government led the party to renounce many of its long-held philosophies and policy preferences soon after the Murayama government was formed. These changes to the Socialists'

> credo of anti-militarism had their origins in the report entitled *Choices for the 21st Century* submitted to the Temporary Party Congress in September 1994, which recognised participation in operations like Cambodia and promised a review of the idea of creating a separate organization for peacekeeping duties. This position was adopted officially at a party conference in the same month. Pledges were made to maintain the security relationship with the US and to recognise the SDF with over 60 per cent of the party agreeing to these changes.[285]

However, the Socialist Party retained a residual element of antimilitarism and of opposition to peacekeeping operations.[286] Indeed, the party kept

> much of its traditional reluctance to consider any expansion of the international role of the SDF and is still playing the role of pacifist watchdog on the LDP, even though this is being done from within the governing coalition. While the SDP has been forced to adopt the long-standing planks in the defense and security policies of the LDP—namely constitutionality of the SDF and the reliance on the security treaty with the United States—the broader significance of the Murayama government is that it has enabled the SDP's more pacifist ideology to exert more influence over government policy.[287]

For the SDP, "a modest and restricted role in international peacekeeping is a means whereby Japan can demonstrate its peaceful international intentions, offer reassurance of its adherence to the limits of its 'peace' Constitution, reassert the restraints on Japan as a military power, and keep a brake on the designs of the Japanese nationalists."[288]

In the case of the Golan Heights, the JSP's central executive committee directly expressed its opposition to Japanese participation.[289] "Socialist members [of the coalition] raised objections over the potential dangers of having SDF personnel handle transport duties. In a crisis, they pointed out, SDF drivers might be asked to carry ammunition or armed soldiers, which under Japanese law could be considered tantamount to using force and therefore prohibited by the constitution. An additional concern was that the head of UNDOF wanted Japan to commit to a two-year stint, which some felt could undermine the government's right to withdraw the SDF if trouble arose."[290]

The third coalition partner, the Sakigake Party, remained skeptical of peacekeeping operations. "The ideal of Japan as a global civilian power is strongly supported by the Shinto Sakigake (New Harbinger Party), which drafted a platform of policies in February 1995 supporting the current constitution and stressing the importance of Japan's non-military international contribution."[291] This document advocated participation in "green PKO," with Japan helping out internationally by cleaning up the environment. The views in this document were similar to those expressed in 1994 by the Sakigake leader, Takemura, who envisioned Japan as a "small but shining country" that would contribute to international social development and environmental protection.[292] With this orientation, Sakigake expressed opposition to participation in the Golan Heights mission.[293]

*Disagreements and Decision Making*

For more than a year, the coalition remained divided on the Golan Heights issue. In November 1994, the coalition passed "an amendment to the SDF legislation to enable the overseas dispatch of SDF transport planes for the purpose of airlifting Japanese nationals when their lives are threatened in a local conflict. These ground-breaking steps were taken partly in an effort to sustain the peculiar coalition between the prime adversaries of the cold war days, the Socialists and the Liberal Democrats."[294] But the question of participation in UNDOF remained unresolved. In early 1995, a fact-finding team traveled to the PKO site to make a recommendation to the cabinet. Most teams are composed of bureaucratic officials, but "some politicians felt that they were not receiving adequate information. As a result, a fact-finding team composed of politicians went to the Golan Heights in April 1995 in order to provide an alternative source of information."[295] As late as May 1995, Japan informed the United Nations that it would not take part in the UNDOF mission.[296]

The impasse was finally broken in August 1995, when the Social Democrats changed their position:

> The Japanese Cabinet approved the mission after the Social Democratic Party dropped its opposition to the deployment, ending months of agonizing over the decision. . . . Only Friday, the Socialists approved the dispatch of Japanese peacekeepers to the Golan Heights, abandoning their previous opposition. "There is still opposition within the party but we will honor the decision by the party's central committee," said SDP Secretary General Wataru Kubo announcing the decision. The change by the SDP leadership marked a major policy shift by the staunchly pacifist party previously opposed to the dispatch of Self-Defense Forces to the Syria-based UNDOF. Murayama's SDP, a minor player in the coalition, only last year recognized the constitutionality of Japan's Self-Defense Forces, but many lawmakers are opposed to peacekeeping missions. The Socialists agreed to the deployment on three conditions: Japanese forces will use their own judgment on use of weapons and on the withdrawal of personnel; they will not participate in joint practices that involve the use of weapons; they will not be required to transport weapons, ammunition and armed peacekeepers of other nations.[297]

The conditions on the mission and the other coalition partners' acceptance of these compromises were critical to the SDP's decision.[298] According to Mulgan, "Clearly, the LDP has been forced to compromise its policy objective of a more active role for the SDF by accommodating the cautious positions and reservations of the SDP and Sakigake that share some common ground with more dovish elements within the LDP itself."[299] In February 1996, forty-five SDF personnel were dispatched to the Golan Heights for a two-year mission (later extended).

*Role of Coalition Politics*

The decision to send Japanese SDF personnel to the Golan Heights peacekeeping mission was consistent with many of the images of coalition politics and foreign policy. Objectively, it can be characterized as an extremely cooperative decision,[300] although in the Japanese historical and political context, more nationalist groups supported this policy.[301] The dispatch of Japanese troops was not as extreme, however, as most in the senior party (the Liberal Democrats) desired, and the conditions on which the Socialists insisted resulted in a compromise among the coalition partners. It is not clear that this extreme policy resulted from a diffusion of responsibility and accountability, from diversion as a result of weakness, or from uncertainty. Support for the policy came from a subset of the coalition, but this backing was from the senior party. Consistent with the democratic peace, the multiple voices in the coalition did act as a constraint in the form of conditions for participation. According to Mulgan,

> The political effects of these internal divisions [in the coalition] have been a moderation of the more expansionist plans for the SDF. . . . Furthermore, the exigencies of gaining and retaining power on both sides mean that concessions have to be made to political grouping favoring the constitutional status quo and a more modest role for the SDF. In other words, . . . the more dovish factions are in the minority but actually hold the balance of power.[302]

But the coalition partners were unable to prevent peacekeeping participation. Instead, the Socialists dropped their opposition (although with conditions) for political reasons: "In the case of dispatching troops to the UNDOF operation, the [JSP] demonstrated how it was now unable to maintain the norm of anti-militarism and preferred to protect its presence in the government by eventually compromising with its coalition government partners over allowing SDF personnel to carry arms, and thereby acquiescing in the coalition's drawing-up of plans for the SDF's dispatch."[303]

Yet the Socialists' opposition did draw out the decision and contributed to deadlock on the issue for more than a year. This delay may have added to the legitimacy of the decision-making process, as it represented the views of many Japanese, but it did make for a slow response. In effect, "coalition politics to a degree brought about immobilism in Japan's UN [PKO] policy for a period with bureaucrats forced into a position where they must 'do the rounds' and visit each party with the aim of describing the ministry's objectives and inquiring as to the particular party's agenda. The ascendancy of the LDP after the 1997 election partly served to surmount this problem."[304] Mulgan agrees: "As the record shows, the political leverage that the LDP's coalition partners have been able to extract from its lack of a governing majority is having a visible impact on the pace of development in Japan's international peacekeeping policy. There was a delay of more than a year in sending the SDF to the Golan Heights."[305] In this way, the decision-making process in this case was of low quality as a consequence of coalition politics.

## REVISION OF THE PEACEKEEPING LAW

In addition to decisions over Japan's contributions to specific peacekeeping operations, debate continued throughout the 1990s on the general questions of the constitutionality of peacekeeping and the scope of Japan's involvement. The 1992 peacekeeping law (the PKO Law) established five principles for participation: (1) cease-fire agreement among the parties in conflict; (2) consent by all conflict parties to peacekeeping forces and to Japan's involvement; (3) strict neutrality by the peacekeeping force; (4) Japan's right to withdraw if the principles are violated; and (5) the use of weapons permitted only at a minimal level for the protection of personnel lives. These principles were taken seriously and affected policy decisions. Japan "turned down two informal requests from the UN Secretariat, both strongly supported by MOFA, to consider sending troops to the United Nations Preventative Deployment Force (UNPREDEP) mission in Macedonia and the United Nations Operation in Somalia II (UNOSOM II) mission. In each case, political leaders decided that one or more of the five principles of the PKO Law could be perceived to be violated if the troops were sent."[306] The law also stipulated the role of the prime minister and the Diet in the dispatch of peacekeepers. The PKO Law included a "freeze," stating specifically that any other PKO activities going beyond logistical support were prohibited until new legislation was passed.[307]

This freeze was the subject of much debate inside Japan.

> Although the passage of the [PKO Law] was the first success for those who supported a greater Japanese role in multilateral security affairs, it did not solve the legal ambiguity concerning Japan's participation in collective security, nor end political sensitivity about collective security. Rather, the law reflected a political compromise among the parties which, far from thinking clearly about collective security and Japan's role therein, decided to avoid critical issues such as Japan's participation in mainbody peacekeeping.[308]

In 1998, the PKO Law was amended to allow participation in election-monitoring missions organized by regional organizations, to allow provision of material assistance in situations where no cease-fire agreement exists, and to allow SDF personnel to follow orders from the force commander rather than acting individually. These changes allowed Japan to participate in election monitoring in Bosnia and East Timor, to take part in civilian police tasks in East Timor, and to contribute air transport in East Timor and Pakistan. These amendments, however, did not "unfreeze" the PKO legislation to allow regular contributions to UN missions.[309]

Little movement on new PKO legislation occurred until Prime Minister Keizo Obuchi's conservative coalition government between the Liberal Democratic Party and the new Liberal Party was formed in 1998.[310] The Liberal Party, led by Ichiro Ozawa, made revision of the PKO law a condition for joining the coalition. This agreement was complicated when a third party, New Komeito, entered the coalition in October 1999. The differences between the parties led the government to announce the following month that it would postpone any legislative action on PKO.

*Players and Positions*

The three-party coalition between the LDP, the Liberals, and New Komeito was based on the results of the 1996 national election (see table 5.6). The LDP remained the largest party in the Diet, and the New Frontier Party was the second-largest party. New Frontier, however, split into several smaller parties, including the Liberal Party, in 1998. New Komeito was also formed from New Frontier factions as well as other Diet members who had previously been part of the earlier Komeito.[311] New Komeito was an addition to the two-party minority coalition between the LDP and the Liberals that had formed in early 1999. The LDP-Liberal coalition already controlled a majority in the lower house of the Diet, but New Komeito was needed for a majority in the House of Councillors.[312] The LDP dominated the cabinet, with only one ministry controlled by the Liberals and one by New Komeito (see table 5.7).

The parties in the coalition had some disagreements over the scope of peacekeeping operations and revision of the PKO Law.[313] By 1999, the Liberal Democratic party was on record favoring constitutional revision to expand Japanese peacekeeping participation.[314] And in a compromise to lure the Liberal Party into the government, the LDP agreed to support expansion of peacekeeping operations.[315] Yet

> coalition talks had been stalled for weeks over the Liberal Party's demand to expand Japan's international military role, which the Liberal Democratic Party insisted was unconstitutional. The two parties reached a compromise that would allow Japan to participate in U.N. peacekeeping operations. . . . The two sides agreed . . . to allow Japan's Self Defense Forces to "actively participate and cooperate" in United Nations peacekeeping missions if asked to do so by the United Nations. The Liberal Party had wanted to allow Japan's Self Defense Forces to be able to provide medical aid to combat areas during multinational military missions. But the Liberal Party backed down from the demand. The ruling party had feared the Liberal Party's proposal would contravene Japan's constitution, which prohibits the country from participating in missions that use force to settle international disputes.[316]

**TABLE 5.6. Japanese National Election Results, 1996, and Seats After Realignment**

| 1996 Election Results | Votes (%) | Seats |
|---|---|---|
| **Liberal Democrats** | 32.8 | 239 |
| New Frontier Party | 28.0 | 156 |
| Democratic Party of Japan | 16.1 | 52 |
| Japan Communist Party | 13.1 | 26 |
| Social Democratic Party | 6.4 | 15 |
| Seats of New Parties after Realignment | | |
| **New Komeito** | | 52 |
| **Liberal Party** | | 39 |

*Source:* J. A. Stockwin, *Governing Japan: Divided Politics in a Resurgent Economy*, 4th ed. (Oxford, UK: Blackwell, 2008); Junko Kato, "Japan," *European Journal of Political Research* 38, no. 3–4 (2000): 443–52.

*Note:* The parties in the governing coalition are boldface. Two coalition parties, New Komeito and the Liberal Party, were formed after the 1996 elections from splits and mergers of other parties; the numbers of seats they controlled by the time the cabinet was formed in 1999 are shown here.

Throughout the LDP-Liberal coalition, the LDP continued to disagree with Ozawa's interpretation of the constitution.[317]

Ozawa was well known for advocating for "normal country" status for Japan.[318]

> The 1998 Liberal Party Basic Policy document pushes for an assertive foreign and security policy. The striking difference from other parties is the Liberals' call for active and expanded participation in UN peacekeeping, including the use of force under UN collective security. Most members also harbor a preference for constitutional revision. On their activist view of security policy, the Liberal Party members overlap with many of their former colleagues on the right of the LDP, and this is both the party's great strength and its great weakness. In certain circumstances, the Liberal Party might attract ideologically motivated conservatives to defect from the LDP, but the LDP might just as easily lure power-hungry Liberals back into the government party.[319]

TABLE 5.7. Members of the Obuchi Cabinet of Japan (October 1999)

| Ministry | Individual | Party |
|---|---|---|
| Prime minister | Obuchi | Liberal Democrat |
| Foreign Affairs | Kono | Liberal Democrat |
| Justice | Usui | Liberal Democrat |
| Finance | Miyazawa | Liberal Democrat |
| Education | Naksone | Liberal Democrat |
| Welfare | Niwa | Liberal Democrat |
| Agriculture | Tamazawa | Liberal Democrat |
| Trade and Industry | Fukaya | Liberal Democrat |
| Transportation | Nikai | Liberal |
| Posts and Telecommunication | Yashiro | Liberal Democrat |
| Labor | Makino | Liberal Democrat |
| Construction | Nakayama | Liberal Democrat |
| Home Affairs | Hori | Liberal Democrat |
| Financial Reconstruction | Ochi | Liberal Democrat |
| Chief cabinet officer | Aoki | Liberal Democrat |
| Defense Agency | Kawara | Liberal Democrat |
| Management and Coordination Agency | Tsuzuki | New Komeito |
| Environmental Agency | Shimizu | Liberal Democrat |

Source: Junko Kato, "Japan," European Journal of Political Research 38, no. 3–4 (2000): 443–52.
Note: Nakosone (LDP) also served as director general of Science and Technology Agency; Nikai (LP) also served as director general of Hokkaido Development Agency; Aoki (LDP) also served as director general of Okinawa Development Agency.

Indeed, when Ozawa left the coalition in April 2000, half of his party stayed with LDP. Ozawa's "support for the coalition was widely believed to be premised upon the government's willingness to submit legislation that would allow greater participation of Japanese forces in peacekeeping and widen the area of responsibility within peacekeeping operations."[320]

The third coalition partner, New Komeito, was much more centrist on the issue of PKO revision. New Komeito's 1998 "Basic Policy Outline stresses the theme of 'humanism,' which for foreign policy means an emphasis on 'soft power.' The [party] platform emphasizes nuclear disarmament and multilateralism in Asia . . . and the establishment of 'independent foreign policy from the United States' but based on 'partnership with the United States.' . . . On the other hand, [New Komeito] also emphasizes PKO and collective security under the United Nations, including full membership in the UN Security Council."[321]

*Disagreements and Decision Making*

In August 1999, before New Komeito entered the LDP-Liberal coalition, the LDP and New Komeito agreed "to work for the lifting of a restriction on the full participation of Self-Defence Forces (SDF) in UN peacekeeping forces. The agreement was reached by officials in charge of policy from the two parties during talks to prepare for the New Komeito's participation in the coalition government between the LDP and the Liberal Party (LP), officials of the LDP and New Komeito said."[322] Following this agreement, several prominent LDP politicians, in the context of the party's internal election, recommended revising the five principles in the PKO legislation.[323] Prime Minister Obuchi also indicated that he would support lifting the ban on full Japanese PKO participation.[324] He stated that the three parties had already agreed to this revision.[325]

Komura, who served as foreign minister before New Komeito entered the coalition, however, disagreed and stated that although he believed the time was ripe for lifting the freeze, a revision of the five principles was out of the question. He also ruled out dispatching personnel to East Timor because there was no cease-fire, in violation of the principles.[326] The foreign minister's remarks sparked public debate among Liberal Party and LDP politicians about whether and how the principles should be revised.[327]

In early October 1999, the three parties announced they had agreed on a new coalition. The agreement included a pledge to introduce legislation on PKO participation.[328] Yet soon after the coalition formed, "Chief Cabinet Secretary Mikio Aoki [LDP] rejected a call for revision of the government's five-point principles on Japanese roles in U.N. peacekeeping operations. The principles are a key part of the country's international peacekeeping law ensuring that Japan will not resort to the use of force as banned by its constitution, Aoki said in a press interview."[329] Aoki acknowledged that submission of a new bill to the next extraordinary session of the Diet depended on more negotiations among the three coalition partners.[330]

Efforts to proceed with legislation deadlocked over the Liberal Party's insistence on abandoning the principles underlying the 1992 PKO law and New Komeito's position that these principles should remain law.[331] "The rift apparently forced the ruling camp to give up efforts to submit legislation during the ongoing extraordinary Diet session" and to respond to requests to send troops to join the multinational force in East Timor.[332] Although the government said it would submit legislation in early 2000, not until 2001 did Japan "unfreeze" the PKO Law's provisions concerning regular peacekeeping activities.[333]

*Role of Coalition Politics*

This case is consistent with many of the general images of coalition politics and foreign policy and with images of paralyzed Japanese foreign policy in the 1990s. The result in this case, to postpone any revision of the PKO legislation, can be classified as neutral and moderate.[334] The attempt to constrain the government from revising the PKO Law to be less restrictive came from a junior partner, New Komeito, as well as from factions inside the senior party, the LDP. This attempted constraint succeeded in that it blocked further discussion. Its direction is more difficult to assess. Although fewer restrictions on peacekeeping participation can be classified objectively as more peaceful (by allowing more military assistance to the United Nations), in the context of Japanese foreign policy debates at the time, fewer restrictions were seen as more nationalistic. The decision was not a compromise but instead a result of irreconcilable viewpoints within the coalition.

Indeed, the best explanation for the outcome of this case highlights the distribution of viewpoints across the three parties and the divided senior party. With New Komeito on one side of the LDP and skeptical of PKO revisions that would alter the peacekeeping principles, the Liberals on the other side pushing for revisions, and the LDP itself divided over the issue, no meaningful decision could be made. This was true even though the junior partners did not control key ministries and New Komeito was not technically needed to maintain a majority in the Diet. Political calculations may have been important in this case, as the next general election was scheduled for October 2000, although "each of the coalition members will be calculating whether to try to force an earlier election."[335]

For these same reasons, the quality of decision making in this case also conforms to the expectations that coalitions are poor policy-making units. Because of the multiple viewpoints on peacekeeping principles, Japan did not effectively address legislation that most parties agreed was in need of revision. The government deadlocked on this important issue. On other criteria of quality decision making, however, the case fares better. Multiple viewpoints were represented and considered, and a decision was not made without consensus. Furthermore, there is no evidence that standard notions of rationality, such as information search, were not met.

CONCLUSIONS

The Japanese cases in this project support some images of how coalition politics influence foreign policy but challenge other images (see table 5.8). Half of the cases were extreme, while half were moderate (by WEIS coding rules). The most extreme behavior was sending troops to the Golan Heights to participate in limited peacekeeping activities.

Most of the foreign policies were cooperative, not conflictual, and two cases really involved no significant commitment of resources in either a peaceful or aggressive direction. The cooperative and neutral behaviors in these cases did not result from successful constraints in the direction of peace. Constraints were attempted by junior parties in most cases (i.e., the Socialists against rice liberalization and Sakigake against a bid for a permanent UNSC seat without reform as a precondition). But contrary to the logic of the democratic peace as it has been applied to coalitions, these actors were not attempting to constrain the country in the direction of peace—the main party was more peaceful (offering economic cooperation or participation and assistance with multilateral organizations), and the attempted constraint was for a more conflictual policy. And just as important, the constraint from the coalition was not necessarily successful—it failed in all instances except the revision of the peacekeeping legislation case.

TABLE 5.8. Do the Japanese Cases Fit the Images of Coalition Politics and Foreign Policy?

| Questions | Cases | | | |
|---|---|---|---|---|
| | Rice | UNSC | Golan Heights | PKO Bill |
| *Was the foreign policy cooperative or conflictual?* | cooperative | neutral | cooperative | neutral |
| *Was the foreign policy extreme or moderate?* | extreme | moderate | extreme | moderate |
| *Did coalition parties attempt to constrain the policy?* | yes | yes | yes | yes |
| *Were attempted constraints in the direction of peace?* | no | no | no | no |
| *Were the constraints successful?* | no | no | no | yes |
| *Was the decision a compromise?* | no | no | yes | no |
| *Was there poor decision making?* | yes (delay; secrecy) | yes (implementation) | yes (delay) | yes (deadlock) |
| *Was there good decision making?* | yes (multiple views) | yes (multiple views) | yes (representative) | yes (multiple views) |
| *What factors best explain the policy outcome and decision making quality?* | leader style; rigidity; political calculations | locus of authority; hijacking; coordination; party disunity | inconsistency; political calculations | distribution of viewpoints; party disunity political calculations |

The Japanese cases all showed signs of the poor decision making often expected of coalitions. In both the rice liberalization case and the Golan Heights case, decision making involved considerable delay as a consequence of differences in the coalition. In the case of the PKO Law, differences resulted in deadlock. The case of the bid for a permanent seat in the UNSC differs because the primary problem in decision-making quality was in terms of implementation; the compromise agreed upon was circumvented by the foreign minister. In all cases, however, multiple viewpoints were considered, in accordance with democratic notions of representation.

The factors that explain the outcome of the party conflicts varied across the cases. In the rice liberalization case, the leadership style, the rigidity in the Socialists' negotiating styles, and political calculations were important. Political calculations also played a key role in the Golan Heights and peacekeeping legislation cases. Divisions within the parties were important in both the UNSC case and the peacekeeping legislation case. Hijacking and coordination failure played a part in the Security Council case, as did inconsistency in the Golan Heights case and the particular distribution of viewpoints in the peacekeeping legislation case.

As in the Dutch cases, the Japanese cases demonstrate the complexities of coalition politics and foreign policy, clearly show that coalition politics matters, and challenge the simplistic notions of how multiparty governance plays out in the decision-making processes and the foreign policy outcomes of parliamentary democracies. The Japanese cases also challenge some of the images of Japanese foreign policy in the 1990s: Not all foreign policy decision making was paralyzed, but much of it involved deadlock, delay, and ineffective decision making. These cases also speak to the general theoretical perspectives that are often used to explain Japanese foreign policy. Specifically, they demonstrate that cultural identity and other ideational factors as well as realist and liberal international systemic factors are not automatic determinants. Rather, their impact on Japanese foreign policy can be traced through the central decision-making authority, the cabinet. When that cabinet is a coalition of multiple political parties and those parties disagree on foreign policy, the process by which those disagreements are negotiated (or not) is critical to a complete account of why Japan acts as it does in international politics.

# 6

# *Turkish Foreign Policy: Hijacked by Ideological Extremes?*

CHALLENGES AND FACTORS IN CONTEMPORARY
TURKISH FOREIGN POLICY

At the geographical junction of Europe and Asia, Turkey has long been an important state in international politics. Turkey's significance in the world was certainly evident after the end of the Cold War, particularly with the first Gulf War in the early 1990s and the Iraq War beginning in 2003.[1] Partly as a consequence of its geographical position, Larrabee and Lesser argue, Turkey is a "pivot" state in world politics, with the capacity to significantly affect international and regional stability.[2] After the Cold War, Turkey has experienced a rise in status, particularly in the eyes of the United States, but this change has come with many new challenges for Turkish foreign policy. Turkey now has more opportunities for assertive leadership in the region as well as a greater range of foreign policy concerns.[3] In the 1990s, Turkey coped with the expansion of the European Union without Turkish membership, an uncertain future for NATO, ethnic conflict in the region (in Eastern Europe, the former Soviet Union, and southeastern Turkey and Iraqi Kurdistan), opportunities for energy cooperation with the Caucasian region, the rise of political Islam both externally and internally, continuing conflict with Greece regarding Cyprus, and the strengthening international norm of human rights.[4] "For a state of its size and strength, Turkey had to deal with an extraordinarily wide range of international questions, mainly due to its geographical position."[5]

What explains Turkey's responses to these challenges? In addition to conventional explanations based on material interests and international structural imperatives, scholars of Turkish foreign policy have focused on the importance of history, ideology, and national identity and more recently on the role of domestic political actors.[6] As a long-standing state, Turkey's history undoubtedly affects its contemporary foreign policy and may account for great continuities in Turkish foreign policy.[7] Turkey's poor past relations with the Arab world and with Western Europe, for example, continue to affect Turkey today.[8] History is important in Turkish foreign policy not only because it provides a backdrop for current relations but because it affects perceptions of events and others.[9] Turkish mistrust of Western Europe, for example, has roots in the days of the Ottoman Empire and in particular the ill-fated Treaty of Sèvres (1920), which would have partitioned Anatolia, given the Greeks rights in western Anatolia, put the Bosporus and the Dardanelles Straits under the administration of the League of Nations, and put Armenia and Kurdistan under Great Power mandates.[10] "Though the treaty was never implemented, Turks have continued to live with the phobia that it never quite died and could be revived at any moment."[11] The "Sèvres syndrome" has served as a lens for understanding more recent history:

> The brooding suspicion of the Western Europeans has been periodically reinforced by Turkish experience since, again often interpreted as fleeting glimpses of the real European agenda for Turkey. The decision of Western European governments to give political asylum to a range of Turkish émigré political activists in the 1980s and 1990s, especially those of Kurdish ethnicity linked to the PKK and its front organizations, is perceived as showing a fundamental sympathy for those groups who would impose the Sèvres blueprint by stealth and from within.[12]

Turkey's history of mistrust of the European Union, however, has not prevented the country from seeking EU membership. Scholars of Turkish foreign policy recognize that Turkey's historical experiences have not determined its orientation toward Europe and have pointed to the significance of ideational factors that in many ways have overcome poor historical relations and are arguably more important drivers of Turkish foreign policy than are economic interests.[13] Hale, for example, argues that "although Turkey's relationship with the EU is one of its most tangled and conflicted, as well as crucial, it is generally accepted that neither Turkey's links with the EU nor its hope to attain full membership are primarily the result of economic interests. The main motivation [at least for elites] is likely the 'Kemalist imperative'—the aim of making Turkey a respected member of the Western community of democratic nations—rather than a desire for Western levels of prosperity or access to financial assistance."[14]

Kemalism was the set of beliefs of Mustafa Kemal Atatürk, who founded the Republic of Turkey in 1923 and ruled until his death in 1938. During Atatürk's leadership and throughout the Cold War, his ideas on Turkish foreign policy served as the dominant ideology, providing a consensus on most issues for the Turkish elite and public and a main driver of Turkey's external relations.[15] Kemalist principles include nationalism, republicanism, populism, secularism, statism, and revolutionism and translated into foreign policies that would use the world power balance to maintain independence and territorial integrity, realistic goals denouncing both pan-Islamism and pan-Turkism, and the goal of "modernizing" Turkey, which could be accomplished in part via strong ties to the West.[16] The nationalism of Kemalism "is perhaps most evident in the case of Cyprus, where Ankara, apparently supported by the bulk of the population, defiantly maintains its right and duty to protect the Turkish population of the island. Other illustrations of this proud nationalism would range from the haughty dismissal of the criticisms of Turkey's human-rights record . . . to Turkey's almost routine military incursions across the border into northern Iraq in search of PKK commandos."[17]

Kemalism remains a strong ideological orientation in Turkey today, particularly in the Turkish military, broadly among the elites, and especially in the Republican People's Party (originally founded by Atatürk). Kemalism, however, is no longer the sole lens through which the world is seen. By the end of the 1980s, foreign policy became a contested domain in Turkey as a consequence of the rise of political Islam within Turkey and of the end of the Cold War.[18] "The profound changes in domestic and international politics meant that the old consensus on foreign policy was breaking down just at a time when an ideological competition over the strategic direction the country should take was both emerging and becoming more intense."[19] Democratization of Turkey's internal politics in the late 1980s and 1990s facilitated the articulation of more viewpoints on Turkish foreign policy along with competing conceptions of national identity, including internationalism and Islamism.[20] According to Robins, "Foreign affairs have been an important and potent symbol of the growing divergence in outlook and values between the Kemalist establishment and the emerging Islamist movement in Turkey."[21]

## ACTORS IN TURKISH FOREIGN POLICY

Changing external and internal politics, new political actors, and the breakdown of the Kemalist foreign policy consensus brings to the forefront the domestic political sources of Turkish foreign policy. Only recently, however, have scholars included internal factors in explanations of Turkish external affairs.[22] International relations generalists and foreign policy analysts have largely ignored Turkish foreign policy, and Turkish specialists have favored systemic explanations.[23] But according to Robins, "systemic factors have clearly not been the only ones of significance in shaping Turkish foreign policy during this time. Indeed, at a time of systemic uncertainty and change there have arguably been added opportunities for other factors to make their mark. Key among these have been domestic factors."[24] Robins argues that in addition to the ideational conflict occurring within Turkey, domestic political actors, in the form of individuals and institutions, have significantly influenced contemporary Turkish foreign policy. Çalış agrees:

> When one looks at the map and the location of Turkey and studies Turkish history, one would naturally expect the country's foreign policy to be shaped by these visible factors. Geography and history have perhaps had considerable impact, but these factors have been filtered by the founding mentality of the Turkish Republic, through institutions defending a Kemalist world outlook and rules defining the identity of the state. Likewise, the impact of personalities and leadership on the shaping of foreign policy cannot be ignored.[25]

Although scholars of Turkish foreign policy have recently recognized the importance of domestic actors, very little research has examined the process of foreign policy decision making, particularly from a theoretical perspective. Instead, "these studies have concentrated either on descriptive or historical analyses. Hardly any work has been done on the decision and policy-making mechanisms and process of Turkish foreign policy."[26] Hale agrees: "The process of foreign policy-making is one of the least well-studied aspects of Turkish foreign policy."[27] Studies have, however, identified the principal actors that shape Turkey's foreign relations. These actors include the military, the president, the prime minister and the cabinet, the foreign minister and the foreign ministry, and the political parties and the

Parliament. Outside government, some have described the role of public opinion, the media, and interest groups in foreign policy.

Turkish foreign policy-making has been dominated historically by a tripod of actors—the military, the prime minister, and the foreign ministry.[28] Robins classifies these actors as "primary" and Parliament, public opinion, media, and interest groups as "secondary."[29] Among parliamentary democracies, Turkey is unique in terms of the role that the military plays in domestic politics and in foreign policy. Since the founding of the modern Turkish Republic, the military has held special place and influence as the custodian of Atatürk's secular vision and of an independent Turkey. Since the 1960 coup, the military has directly participated in governance and has again intervened either directly (in 1980) or indirectly (in 1971 and 1997) to bring about a change in government. With its history of interventions, the military enjoys an ability to intimidate in military and security areas, including domestic security issues broadly defined.[30] Elites often defer to or hide behind the military.[31] According to Makovsky, "A policy strongly advocated by the military will almost certainly be implemented; a policy strongly opposed by the military almost certainly will not."[32]

The military's role in Turkish foreign policy is institutionalized in the National Security Council (NSC), in which half of the members were military leaders before the constitutional changes in 2001.[33] NSC members also include the president, the prime minister, and the ministers of foreign affairs, defense, and internal affairs. The NSC is arguably "the most important institution in the policy-making process."[34] The NSC "exists as a conduit through which the military can give their views on a range of policy matters. . . . It may dispense 'advice,' but in practice it is virtually unheard of for cabinets and parliaments publicly to question its views, and it is a proud claim made by the NSC secretariat that there are no examples of recommendations in the realm of foreign policy that have remained unimplemented."[35] The military has been especially influential in policy in northern Iraq, in policy with Syria and Israel, and in security-related issues with the United States and Greece and PKK-related issues in Turkey's relations with the European Union.[36] "One consequence of the military's extraordinary role has been a marked asymmetry in Turkey's dialogue with allies on regional and defense matters. Whereas Western governments generally view their high civilian officials as the key interlocutors on foreign and security policy, the corresponding civilian officials in the Turkish Ministry of Defense are, in practical terms, subordinate to the leadership of the Turkish General Staff.... This is almost certainly one of the factors responsible for the continued predominance of security issues in Turkish-American relations."[37]

The military is certainly a powerful actor on issues that it deems important. According to Robins, however, the military tends to be less interested and less influential in foreign policy that is not directly linked with external or domestic security issues.[38] "On the whole..., both the ministry and the generals regard it as being the responsibility of government to make and preside over foreign policy."[39] There is also considerable disagreement within the military on strategic issues, and "the role of the military in Turkish society and politics is changing and is likely to change further under the pressures of modernization and with the emergence of competing policy elites."[40] Even in the past, the military shared the political stage with other actors. On rare occasions, this sharing has resulted in a loss of military influence. In 1990, President Özal, who supported the U.S. action against Iraq and the anti-Iraq coalition's use of Turkish bases and Turkish troops, "defied the military and forced the resignation of its commander-in-chief, as well as the foreign minister, in gaining acceptance for his policy."[41]

The foreign ministry is generally responsible for the daily execution of Turkey's foreign policy and has been regarded as source of elite and highly professionalized expertise. "The Foreign Ministry is razor sharp in its handling of certain portfolios and its performance in certain capitals and at certain forums. On issues relating to the EU, NATO, Cyprus, ... and the UN, and relations with the main European powers, the US and Russia, the ministry attains a level of activity well in excess of the often quite modest size of the genuinely diplomatic staff in its relevant missions would suggest."[42] While other ministries may also have a role in policy-making and implementation, depending on the specific foreign policy issue area, the foreign ministry and the foreign minister are key players at the cabinet level.[43]

The prime minister, as the third leg of the classically defined tripod in Turkish foreign policy-making, heads the cabinet and can be quite influential.[44] "Both the Prime Minister and the Council of Ministers are empowered to determine and then implement foreign policy goals and principles."[45] As in other parliamentary democracies, the prime minister's power derives from control of the largest political party, political patronage, the role of spokesperson for the government, and the ability to set the cabinet agenda. Yet like prime ministers in other parliamentary systems, the "influence of Turkish prime ministers in shaping their country's relations with the world have varied significantly according to the intensity of their interest in foreign affairs."[46] Prime Minister Ecevit, for example, was much more interested in foreign affairs than was Prime Minister Demirel.[47]

Scholars of Turkish foreign policy have recently included the Turkish president as a fourth major player in foreign policy.[48] The powers of the president, who is elected by Parliament, were increased in the 1982 constitution, and the powers of the NSC, which the president chairs, were enhanced in a 1983 law.[49] According to the constitution, the president, together with Parliament, has the authority to endorse international agreements and to call a meeting of the Council of Ministers. However, the constitution does not give the president any further explicit exclusive authority in foreign policy.[50] Yet "the possibilities for the president to play an activist role in foreign-policy-making became clear during the presidencies of Turgut Özal (1989 to 1993) and [Süleyman] Demirel (1993 to 2000). As politicians who vaulted from the prime ministry to the presidency, thanks to their parties' parliamentary voting strength, Özal and Demirel publicly broke the mold of the 'above-parties' presidency that took hold after the 1961 constitution, when the office was largely ceremonial and invariably held by retired military men."[51] As with prime ministers, presidential influence in foreign policy has varied according to the individual interest of the president.[52] "Bülent Ecevit and Turgut Özal showed great interest in the making of foreign policy, while Süleyman Demirel always left foreign affairs to his foreign ministers."[53] Özal was particularly interested in international affairs and was quite influential during the Gulf War, supporting the United States despite concerns from the Turkish military.[54]

Beyond the military, the prime minister and the cabinet, and the president, few other actors have consistent influence on Turkish foreign policy.[55] Parliament (the Turkish Grand National Assembly [TGNA]) generally does not play a major role, serving more as a forum for debate.[56] It does have the constitutional authority to approve declarations of war, commitment of troops, and foreign troops on Turkish soil, but the parties in Parliament tend to take the lead from their leaders, from the government, and from the military.[57] According to Çalış, "In practice, the TGNA looks very much like a talking chamber. Its members speak a lot, but in the end they endorse what the cabinet or the chief executive proposes."[58] The most notable exception to this was Parliament's 2003 refusal to ratify the government's decision to permit the United States to use Turkey as a base for its northern front as part of the U.S. intervention in Iraq.[59]

Historically, public opinion has not been very influential in Turkish foreign policy. The public's "views rarely appear to have an impact on either policymakers or the policymaking process. It is as if the elite does not expect to take such views into account, while the mass of the population does not expect its views to be taken on board."[60] Although the public is not very interested in foreign policy issues generally, "national pride" can draw the public's attention to policies on Greece and Cyprus and to a lesser extent in Turkish foreign policy toward the Muslim populations in Bosnia, Kosovo, and Chechnya.[61] Indeed, these identity-based issues, "spurred by the expansion of the private media and its growing role as a shaper of opinion,"[62] may have increased the role that public opinion is playing in Turkish foreign policy. According to Larrabee and Lesser, Turk sympathy for Muslims in Bosnia, Chechnya, and Kosovo "galvanized Turkish opinion and encouraged a more active, albeit multilateral, stance from Ankara."[63] Throughout the 1990s, public opinion was vocal on key issues, and in 2003, 83 percent of the public opposed the U.S. use of Turkish air bases for the Iraqi intervention. Winrow argues that this opposition influenced the Parliament's March 1 vote to not allow American use of Turkish soil.[64] How much the public can force a government to do what it otherwise would not do, however, remains an open question. Most scholars generally agree that "the ability of Turkish foreign policy elites to manage public opinion is mostly intact."[65] According to Robins, "In the 1990s, there was a growing debate about whether such factors as public opinion, the media, and organized lobby groups were becoming more influential in foreign policymaking than before. It may be the case that this was true, but incrementally so and starting from a very low base."[66]

Political parties lie at the center of all of the foreign policy players in Turkey except the military. Parties are represented in Parliament, and because they are elected democratically, they are representative of and accountable to the public. Although the president of Turkey is expected to operate separate from partisan politics, most recent presidents have come to the post through leadership positions in one of the political parties.[67] Most important, political parties are represented in the position of prime minister and in the cabinet, controlling the foreign ministry, the defense ministry, and other cabinet portfolios and bureaucratic agencies that can influence foreign policy decision making. According to Özkeçeci-Taner, political parties in Turkey are "*highly* interested in foreign policy issues and want to shape policy. In fact, one of the most important issues during coalition formation stages concerned negotiations about the distribution of the ministries of Foreign Affairs, Defense, and Finance, which [are] directly involved [in] Turkish foreign policy making vis-à-vis international entities. Coalition partners usually agreed to a distribution where each party was able to hold at least one of these ministries."[68] Although the cabinet is not the sole actor in Turkish foreign policy, it does include some of the most significant players, and as a collective, it has considerable power, and its deliberations and decisions are critical. According to Özcan, "As in all parliamentary democracies, Turkey's foreign and security decisions are made by the prime minister and cabinet members, who are responsible to the national legislature."[69] At times, the Turkish cabinet is controlled by a single party—most notably, during the late 1960s and the late 1970s, from the end of military rule in 1983 until 1992, and from 2002 until today. At other times, however, democratic elections have resulted in a fragmented Parliament with no single party controlling the majority. From 1961 to 1963, from 1974 to 1978, and from 1991 to 2002, the Turkish cabinet and all of its ministries were shared by two or more parties.[70]

## COALITION POLITICS IN TURKISH FOREIGN POLICY: GENERAL IMAGES AND FOUR CASES

There is little research on how multiparty cabinets make foreign policy in Turkey. According to Çuhadar-Gürkaynak and Özkeçeci-Taner, "For a country frequently ruled by coalition governments since the 1970s, there are hardly any significant studies on the influence of coalition decisionmaking structures in Turkish foreign policymaking."[71] Yet scholars of Turkish foreign policy have made claims regarding the effects of coalition politics on foreign policy and these claims are consistent with the expectations, detailed in chapter 2, that coalition cabinets are ineffective at policy-making. There has also been concern that the ideological fragmentation in Turkey in the 1990s and the rise of coalition government created the conditions for hijacking by ideologically extreme political parties, particularly those with political Islamist orientations.

Aydın, for example, states that "due to the major ideological differences between Turkey's various political parties, the long periods of coalition rule created an atmosphere within which a general consensus on policy, either foreign or domestic, was rarely reached. This, of course, created ineffectiveness and inactivity in Turkish foreign policy during the 1970s."[72] Bahceli extends this sentiment to the next period of coalition rule in Turkey: "During the 1990s, weak coalition governments shuffled in and out of office at the average rate of one per year. Eleven governments, including nine coalitions, and eleven different foreign ministers held office in Ankara during the decade. This made any major policy changes toward Greece most unlikely, since only a strong government could undertake bold policy departure."[73] Similarly, Atila Eralp blames coalition politics, along with EU's "ambivalent attitude," for Turkey's inability to secure EU membership.[74] Hale states that Turkey's democratic nature and the divided opinion among the Turkish public "turned out to be the Achilles heel of Turkish foreign policy, since external problems were seriously exacerbated by internal weaknesses and conflicts. In the search for effective democratic government, the record of the 1990s was a generally dismal one. No single party won an overall majority in Parliament in any of the three general elections, held in 1991, 1995, and 1999, and Turkey slipped back into the position of chronic governmental instability which it had experienced during the 1970s."[75]

The fragmented party system, the turnover in foreign ministers, and the weak coalition governments made it "difficult to establish effective or sustained initiatives abroad."[76] Indeed, according to Robins, "it has become a cliché of political commentary to say that in Turkey the state is strong and government is weak. . . . [G]overnments are indeed often weak, especially when they exist within a fragmented political-party system. For long periods of Turkey's recent history . . . multiparty coalitions of divergent ideological components have uneasily presided over the executive branch."[77] Only Dodd has noted some of the trade-offs regarding coalition governance in Turkey:

> Whether the coalition period is successful depends on the criteria by which it is judged. A single-party government might have governed more positively and have got more done, but would it have provided sufficient opportunity to represent, and meet, the many political demands that were made during this period of re-settlement after the revolution? The coalition system did not in fact break down, which meant that there was no successful challenge to the democratic political system itself. Looked at in the broad, the period 1961–1965 was one of marked political success.[78]

Özkeçeci-Taner is the only scholar who has seriously examined decision making by coalition cabinets in Turkey. She has argued that coalitions in Turkish foreign policy are an excellent "laboratory" in which to study the ideational conflict that came to the fore in Turkey by the 1990s as a consequence of changes in the internal and external environments.[79] She has detailed the different worldviews on Turkish foreign policy as they are institutionalized in political parties, demonstrating that "ideas matter" in Turkish coalitions when the issue is of high salience to the political parties and when they show consistency in their position. Like Özkeçeci-Taner's research, this book examines foreign policy-making by Turkish coalitions and includes some of the same cases.[80] While her research focuses on the factors that explain when ideas matter in coalitions, the Turkish case studies in this chapter explore the specific expectations regarding conflict and cooperation and regarding the quality of decision making set out in chapter 2.

The Turkish cases for this project, listed in table 6.1, were chosen according to the principles discussed in chapter 3. Each case is an instance of

**TABLE 6.1. Turkish Cases**

| Case | Coalition Parties | (a) Prime Minister (b) Foreign Minister (c) Defense Minister |
|---|---|---|
| Customs Union agreement (1995) | True Path (DYP) + Republican People's Party (CHP) | (a) Çiller (DYP) (b) Karayalçın/ İnönü (CHP) (c) Gölhan (DYP) |
| Islamic opening (1996–97) | Welfare Party (RP) + True Path (DYP) | (a) Erbakan (RP) (b) Çiller (DYP) (c) Tayan (DYP) |
| Helsinki Summit offer of EU Candidacy (1999) | Democratic Left (DSP) + Nationalist Action Party (MHP) + Motherland Party (ANAP) | (a) Ecevit (DSP) (b) Cem (DSP) (c) Çakmakoğlu (MHP) |
| Death penalty abolition (1999–2002) | Democratic Left (DSP) + Nationalist Action Party (MHP) + Motherland Party (ANAP) | (a) Ecevit (DSP) (b) Cem (DSP) (c) Çakmakoglu (MHP) |

*Turkish Foreign Policy* 191

conflict among the political parties in the cabinet over a foreign policy decision. The cases come from three different coalition cabinets across the 1990s and cover economic, identity, and Cyprus issues related to relations with the European Union, Turkey's general orientation toward the West versus the Islamic world, and the human rights issue of the death penalty, particularly as it was related to the death sentence of PKK leader Öcalan. The cases differ somewhat from each other in other ways. The Islamic Opening case, for example, is composed of several independent foreign policy actions (such as the prime minister's trip to Libya, a broad initiative to create an Islamic Union, and reassurances to the West of Turkey's continued commitment to the EU and NATO), while the Helsinki case is a specific decision to accept an EU agreement while issuing a separate statement on Cyprus. The death penalty case could easily be treated as a domestic issue, as criminal justice and legal policies generally are. Yet this case clearly shows the intermestic nature of many contemporary foreign policies. While Turkey's death penalty certainly affects people and politics within Turkey's borders, the death penalty also became a foreign policy issue for Turkey, since the EU viewed it as abusive of human rights and demanded its abolition as a condition for membership. Despite these differences, all of the cases afford an opportunity to assess how coalition politics affects foreign policy and foreign policy decision making. There is no a priori reason to believe that the differences critically affect the relationships under investigation.

*The Customs Union Agreement*

As early as 1959, Turkey applied for membership in the European Economic Community. In 1963, the Ankara Association Agreement granted Turkey associate membership and provided the legal basis for eventual full membership, with the establishment of a customs union as an important step toward that objective.[81] However, numerous political and economic obstacles delayed the start of a customs union for thirty-three years.[82] In 1987, Turkey again applied for full membership, only to be rejected by the European Community (EC). "Turkey's 1987 membership application, although dismissed by the EC, at least succeeded in goading the EC (and then the EU) to work with Turkey in completing customs union arrangements. Efforts began in earnest after 1992, and by early 1995 Turkey and the EU had reached agreement on the terms."[83] These efforts included internal reforms by Turkey, international negotiations between Turkey and the EC, and internal EU bargaining regarding the Cyprus issue.[84] The customs union agreement went into effect on January 1, 1996.

Turkey's interest in participating in post–World War II European integration efforts was part of the Kemalist Western orientation toward "modernizing" Turkey, and the goal of Westernization has been a dominant factor in the way the Turkish elite perceives its relations with Europe.[85] In this view, "closer association with Europe is above all a 'civilizing mission' that brings an increasingly larger section of the population into contact with Western lifestyles, behavior, and methods. But this goal was [also] shaped by political and economic considerations. Efforts toward Westernization would bring economic development and greater political stability, Turkish leaders believed."[86]

As EU-Turkish relations soured in the 1970s, however, and membership talks were further delayed, voices inside Turkey began to question the Kemalist consensus supporting union with Europe.[87] What was left of this "broad consensus that existed among political and economic elites during the 1987 membership application effort came apart during the customs union negotiations."[88] Indeed, the customs union negotiations became controversial and politicized.[89] "Many Turks derided the value of a customs union that did not foresee eventual full membership and that thus forced Turkey to obey economic rules it would never be able to influence. Turks increasingly viewed the customs union merely as an EU effort to compensate Turkey for nonparticipation in the membership process."[90] The customs union agreement also touched a nerve in Turkey when the matter became linked to the future of Cyprus. Greece continued to veto the customs union agreement between Turkey and the EU until Greece convinced the EU to remove the condition that there should be a political settlement on Cyprus before Cypriot accession.[91] On the same day the EU issued its resolution on the customs union with Turkey, it declared that membership negotiations with the Greek Cypriot government would begin.[92]

According to Öniş, "The interplay between domestic politics and foreign policy is crucial to an understanding of Turkey-EU relations."[93] In the case of the customs union agreement, the coalition government between the True Path Party (DYP) and the Republican People's Party (CHP or SHP)[94] was divided over whether to accept the agreement, given that it was linked to the start of Cyprus membership negotiations.[95] One coalition partner favored the agreement, but the other had deep reservations. Thus, the "government was faced with a difficult decision to make. They were to decide whether they would *accept* or *reject* the Customs Union Agreement with the *preconditions attached to it*. It was a critical decision for the ... coalition government to make because their determination to make Turkey a full member of the EU and their sensitivities regarding Cyprus [were] in conflict."[96] According to Kramer, the internal debate in Turkey over the customs union was much more shaped by these political issues than by economic considerations.[97] Uslu argues that because of the domestic opposition to the agreement, "it was rather surprising that Turkey gave the green light to the continuation of the membership negotiations of the Greek Cypriots in return for signing the Customs Union agreement with the EU in March 1995."[98]

*Players and Positions*

First elected in 1991, the coalition between True Path and the Republican People's Party ruled until March 1996.[99] Table 6.2 provides the 1991 election results. The portfolios were divided to reflect True Path's senior status in the coalition (see table 6.3). The prime ministership and ten other ministries, including those of defense and finance, were controlled by True Path, while eight ministries, including foreign affairs and trade, were controlled by the Republican People's Party. "Both parties seemed to be satisfied with the ministerial positions they possessed although it was obvious that [the] DYP wing of the coalition was very reluctant to let the SHP control the Ministry of Foreign Affairs."[100]

The coalition agreement forged between the parties was fairly ambigu-

**TABLE 6.2. Turkish National Election Results, 1991**

|  | Votes (%) | Seats |
|---|---|---|
| **True Path Party** | 27.0 | 178 |
| Motherland Party | 24.0 | 115 |
| **Social Democratic Populist/** | | |
| **Republican People's Party** | 20.8 | 88 |
| Welfare Party | 16.9 | 62 |
| Democratic Left Party | 10.8 | 7 |
| Independents | 0.1 | 0 |

*Source:* Turkish Statistical Institute, http://www.turkstat.gov.tr, accessed November 24, 2008.
*Note:* The parties in the governing coalition are boldface.

ous on foreign policy issues. Instead, the first prime minister in the coalition "plainly stated that the government partners would be in *constant dialogue* with each other regarding Turkish foreign policy matters."[101] The agreement referred to Turkey's special relationship with the United States (which was more in line with the True Path's positions) and to the importance of maintaining the status quo in Turkish foreign policy (which was more in line with the orientation of the Republican People's Party).[102] It also gave prominence to improving relations with the EU, stating, "Turkey's further integration with Europe . . . is one of the primary targets of our government."[103] The coalition partners, however, differed in how they perceived Turkey's relationship with Europe and the importance of

TABLE 6.3. Members of the 50th Cabinet of the Republic of Turkey (1993–95)

| Ministry | Individual | Party |
| --- | --- | --- |
| Prime minister | Çiller | True Path |
| Deputy prime minister | Karayalçın/Çetin | Republican People's |
| Foreign Affairs | Karayalçın/İnönü | Republican People's |
| National Defense | Gölhan | True Path |
| Justice | Moğultay | Republican People's |
| Interior | Menteşe | True Path |
| Finance | Attila | True Path |
| National Education | Ayaz | True Path |
| Public Works and Housing | Sahin/Çulhaoğlu | Republican People's |
| Health | Dinç/Baran | True Path |
| Transportation | Köstepen/Erek | True Path |
| Agriculture and Rural Affairs | Şahin | True Path |
| Labor and Social Security | Gürkan/Halis | Republican People's |
| Industry and Trade | Dönen/Akyol | Republican People's |
| Culture | Karakaş/Cem | Republican People's |
| Tourism | Ulusoy/Gürpinar | Republican People's |
| Forestry | Ekinci | True Path |
| Environment | Akçalı | True Path |
| Energy and Natural Resources | Atasoy | True Path |

*Source:* Turkish Grand National Assembly website, http:www.tbmm.gov.tr/hukumetler/HB50.htm, accessed January 15, 2009.

*Note:* There were several changes in personnel throughout this cabinet's tenure. The individual(s) during the later part of the coalition, when the negotiations were most intense, are presented here. For example, Süleyman Demirel was the first prime minister in this coalition but was replaced by Çiller in July 1993. There was no change in the distribution of ministries across parties. In addition to the cabinet positions listed, the 50th cabinet included 16 state minister portfolios. These were divided between the coalition partners as follows: 10 for True Path and 6 for the Republican People's Party.

the Cyprus issue.[104] The Republican People's Party viewed "the EC question in political rather than economic terms. It supported EC views on democracy and human rights but equivocated regarding the economic consequences of membership. As heir to Atatürk's Kemalism [the party] stressed the need for a largely indigenous industrialization capacity and fretted that integration with the EC would undermine Turkish industries, which were comparatively weaker than their European counterparts."[105] Yet the party also saw the customs union as a key step for Turkey's membership in the "civilized" world, an objective rooted in Kemalism.[106] Overall, the Republican People's Party did not advocate aggressive policies and by no means wanted a confrontation with the EU. Instead, the party generally supported a cautious handling of relations with the EU.[107] As for Cyprus, the Republican People's Party's position was "uncompromising," arguing the legal position that as a unified state composed of two separate entities, Cyprus could not become part of any international organization without Turkey.[108]

The True Path Party's foreign policy orientation, conversely, was "more open to outside influence and less skeptical about the threats to Turkey's political independence."[109] Özkeçeci-Taner classifies the True Path Party as the most Western-oriented party in Turkey and characterizes its interest in completing the customs union agreement as "obsession-like."[110] Indeed, Turkey's integration into the EU was the top issue on the party's agenda, and the customs union was the critical step.[111] Party leaders argued that the agreement "was one of the most important documents that the Turkish Republic would sign in its history."[112] Regarding the Cyprus issue, although some party members felt that the island's future should be treated as a "national cause" on which Turkey should not compromise, the majority in the party believed that the future of Cyprus could best be resolved within the framework of the EU. Indeed, "according to some DYP members, a united Cyprus joining the EU was an asset rather than a liability to Turkey."[113] Overall, the True Path Party focused on the economic and political benefits of the customs union agreement and suggested that Cyprus should not be an obstacle to its conclusion.[114]

*Disagreements and Decision Making*

Consistent with the coalition partners' different foreign policy orientations, the parties had divergent assessments of the customs union agreement during Turkey's negotiations with the EU in 1995. The Republican

People's Party expressed skepticism, most critically on the issue of Cyprus. Here, the party's behavior was inconsistent both over time and internally. In March 1995, the Turkish foreign ministry, controlled by the Republican People's Party, issued a statement objecting to any further moves toward Cypriot membership in the EU and warned that "if the Greek Cypriot application is processed further despite the objections of Turkey, Turkey will be left with no option but to take steps towards achieving a similar integration with the Turkish Republic of Northern Cyprus."[115] At another point, however, the deputy prime minister and foreign minister, Karayalçın, of the Republican People's Party, stated that he would not consider the EU's designation of Cyprus as a candidate for membership the same as actual membership. Many of the party's members in the Turkish Parliament criticized their leaders for making this "concession" and called on them to resign.[116] The Republican People's Party also did not like the EU's decision to send the agreement to the EU Parliament for ratification and objected to the idea that the ratification of the agreement would be based on the Parliament's assessment of Turkey's progress in meeting several criteria established for entry into the customs union. The party considered such assessment as an overt intervention in Turkey's domestic affairs and argued that there was no need for ratification because the Ankara agreement, which provided for a customs union, had already been accepted by all sides.[117]

For its part, the True Path Party emphasized Turkey's economic and political gains rather than focusing on problematic issues. "The DYP leadership . . . argued that the Turkish leadership should approach any decision that gives Turkey a chance to get closer to the EU positively."[118] Yet both coalition partners felt the pressure of criticisms from opposition parties and from the media that they had had sold out on the Cyprus issue. As a result, according to Özkeçeci-Taner, "to regain domestic legitimacy," the coalition "was compelled to take some actions" against Greece.[119] In the summer of 1995, for example, the coalition said that it viewed the extension of Greek territorial waters to twelve miles (consistent with the Greek ratification of the Law of the Sea Treaty) as a casus belli. "However, even these diversions did not help [the Republican People's Party] to successfully face the criticisms it received from its party members and the constituents. As a result, [the party] decided to break up" the coalition.[120]

Although the charges of selling out were speculation throughout most of 1995, it was clear that the coalition government had indeed accepted the customs union agreement with conditions in March 1995. Specifically, the coalition had agreed to work toward a political solution of the Kurdish issue, improve human rights and democratic standards, and solve the Cyprus issue within the EU framework. When these conditions were finally published in late 1995, following the ratification of the agreement by the European Parliament, Turkish media and opposition parties were highly critical.[121] According to Özkeçeci-Taner, the Republican People's Party was "uncomfortable" with these conditions and Turkey's signing of the agreement, which was against the junior partner's wishes, and this discomfort "led to the dissolution of the . . . coalition government in September 1995."[122]

*Role of Coalition Politics*

Although the customs union agreement can be characterized as somewhat extreme state behavior in that it is extremely cooperative for one state to merge its trade policies with a regionally integrated entity,[123] it does not fit most expectations for how coalition politics influences foreign policy and decision making. The extremity in this case did not result from hijacking or blackmail by the junior party—indeed, the junior party opposed this foreign policy. Moreover, diffused accountability or uncertainty and weakness did not play into the decision. True Path was ready to accept responsibility for this policy, which was a stated goal of their party. The coalition was in fairly good shape politically, having survived two elections, and economic reasons existed for joining the customs union, the agreement was not used as a diversion away from particular economic or other problems that the government was facing. Nor is this extremely cooperative behavior a product of institutional constraint, as the logic of some democratic peace research would suggest. Although the junior party opposed this decision, it opposed it in the direction of less cooperation, and its opposition did not constrain the final decision.

Negative rhetoric against Greece in the summer of 1995 was related to this decision and arguably stemmed from the government's need to divert attention from the domestic criticism of the customs union agreement. It is not clear, however, that coalition politics lay at the root of the decision. In other words, a single-party government consisting solely of the True Path Party might have also engaged in this diversionary, extremely conflictual behavior. In any event, this foreign policy was only a spinoff of the customs union agreement and not the direct subject of the case under investigation here.

The evidence available for this case does not explain exactly why the Republican People's Party failed to constrain, either through deadlock or compromise, the government from making concessions that the party opposed. Two explanations are plausible, however. The first concerns the consistency of the junior partner's position. The Republican People's Party was both internally and temporally inconsistent in its opposition. Without a unified party, and especially with a wavering party leadership, the Republican People's Party would have difficulty making a credible threat in this case. Despite the party's eventual departure from the coalition, influence arose not from this strategy but instead from internal opposition to the decision that had already been made. Consistency is a key condition of minority influence in social psychological research, and previous research on junior parties confirms the importance of consistency in influence in foreign policy.[124] A second explanation concerns the leadership style of Prime Minister Çiller. Çiller is generally characterized as authoritarian and power-oriented.[125] "During her tenure as Prime Minister, Tansu Çiller continuously tried to bypass the Ministry of Foreign Affairs," which was controlled by the Republican People's Party.[126] In the case of the customs union agreement, Çiller appointed one of her advisers, Ali Tigrel, to oversee Turkish-EU relations in early 1994 as a means of overcoming the foreign ministry's possible resistance to relations with EU.[127] These manipulations of the decision-making process may have hindered the ability of the Republican People's Party to influence this case.

This change in the locus of decision-making authority out of the hands of the Republican People's Party–controlled Ministry of Foreign Affairs, may have prevented the ineffective policy-making that is expected of coalition cabinets. The decision was not a meaningless compromise or fragmented action. There was no significant delay or deadlock in the process. The cabinet seemed to agree to the conditions without delay, in March 1995. The delay that occurred after this (from March to January) resulted from negotiations between the EU and Turkey and within the EU and from the steps that Turkey had to take to meet the criteria for membership (which it did fairly quickly and easily). The decision making in this case cannot, however, be characterized as especially high in quality. Although the junior party did offer an alternative position (opposing the agreement), it did not act as a devil's advocate in the sense that it avoided premature closure on an option or stimulated creative and divergent thinking. By being a member of the coalition, the junior party arguably made the policy more legitimate, as the government at least included representation for Turkey's anti-EU sentiment. The manipulations of the decision-making process, however, to some extent excluded this representation.

Coalition politics in Turkey may have also been important to the EU's decision making on the customs union agreement. After the breakup of the coalition in September 1995, the European Parliament voted on the union before new national elections in Turkey. In this way, the European Parliament's decision was closely tied to Turkish domestic politics, as Prime Minister Çiller and many leaders argued that a no vote from the Parliament would strengthen Islamic and anti-European groups within Turkey.[128] Indeed, the December 1995 national elections would significantly change Turkey's domestic political landscape and set the stage for an Islamist-oriented party to participate in a coalition cabinet.

ISLAMIC OPENING

One of the most significant challenges to traditional Turkish foreign policy came in the mid-1990s with the coming to power of the Welfare Party (RP), in coalition with the True Path Party (DYP). The dimensions of the post–Cold War world were still unfolding, relations with the European Union were mixed, and Turkey remained at the crossroads between Western global actors and the Islamic and Middle Eastern worlds. Inside Turkey, the domestic political situation did not provide a stable ground from which policy-makers could face these challenges. In particular, "the entry of the Welfare Party into government and the role of Erbakan as Turkey's prime minister clearly brought a new dimension to Turkish foreign policy decision-making."[129]

During the 1996–97 coalition, called "one of the oddest couples in Turkey,"[130] the Welfare Party attempted to reorient Turkish foreign policy away from the West and toward the Middle East and the broader Islamic world. This policy, known as the Islamic Opening, intended increased cooperation between Turkey and Islamic states such as Iraq, Iran, Nigeria, and Libya. The True Path Party resisted this reorientation and attempted to reassure the West that Turkey remained its ally. Indeed, this coalition "highlighted the division between pro-Western forces that tried to preserve the

Western identity of the Turkish State and Islamists who wanted to change it. While the Western-oriented Deputy Prime Minister [and foreign minister], Tansu Çiller, was visiting European leaders to confirm Turkey's Europeanness, [Prime Minister] Necmettin Erbakan was receiving the leader of the Muslim Brotherhood as his first foreign visitor. When Çiller was visiting Western capitals and institutions, Erbakan was heading to Islamic countries such as Iran and Libya, implying that Turkey is essentially a Muslim country."[131] Unlike the other cases in this book, this case does not rest on a single decision. Instead, it covers a general policy that was pursued by one coalition partner and countered by another throughout the cabinet's tenure.

*Players and Positions*

The coalition between Welfare and True Path that came to power in June 1996 resulted from significant changes in the Turkish political landscape. According to Yavuz, "This coalition government between the pro-Islamic Necmettin Erbakan and the Europhile Tansu Çiller indicates the duality of Turkish identity and marks a turning point in the history of the Turkish Republic. On June 28, 1996, for the first time, the Turkish republic had a prime minister whose political philosophy was based on Islam. This even marked a psychological break in Turkish history that was the outcome of a search for new relations between state and society."[132]

The rise of the Welfare Party stemmed from a number of factors, including changing views in the military regarding the need for democracy and tolerance for Islam and the ineffectiveness of other political parties.[133] It also stemmed from the more general rising importance of Islam in Turkey.[134]

> The main goals of the [Welfare Party] have been the externalization of Islamic identity in the public domain and the construction of a moral and virtuous community. . . . It acts as a conveyor of the voices of Islamist groups to the public sector; it represents Islamist interests in the Turkish parliament; and it has become a vehicle for Islamists to move into the administration of local municipalities and the larger national bureaucracy. However, paradoxically, the process of externalization has helped promote the inner secularization of Islam. Necmettin Erbakan and his associates

reimagined Islamic tradition as a modernist discourse to solve Turkey's temporal problems of identity and justice.[135]

In contrast, True Path, was a much more traditional Turkish political party, with connections to Islam but committed to secular government. True Path is categorized as a center-right party, typically defending conservative traditional and religious values.[136] This division meant that "the nature of the polarization [in the 1990s] was quite different from that which prevailed two decades earlier when Turkish politics was immersed in ideological battles between the left and the right. Polarization in party politics during the 1990s was based largely on the growing conflict between the secularists and the Islamists."[137] The Erbakan-Çiller coalition was the most visible manifestation of this division and held implications for domestic and foreign policy. "While one component of society is staunchly secular and believes that the future of Turkey lies in the West, another part believes that religion should play a greater role in Turkish society and that Turkey should enhance its relations with Islamic countries."[138]

Although the Welfare Party had emerged as the largest party in the 1995 national elections (see table 6.4), it did not immediately come to power in the cabinet. "Despite finishing first . . . , the Islamist RP/FP displayed—in Sartorian terms—limited 'coalition potential,' for the pro-secular parties appeared reluctant to enter into partnerships with the Islamists."[139] Negotiations between Erbakan and other party leaders proved fruitless.[140] In-

TABLE 6.4. Turkish National Election Results, 1995

|  | Votes (%) | Seats |
|---|---|---|
| **Welfare Party** | 21.4 | 158 |
| Motherland Party | 19.6 | 132 |
| **True Path Party** | 19.2 | 135 |
| Democratic Left Party | 14.6 | 76 |
| Republican People's Party | 10.7 | 49 |
| Nationalist Action Party | 8.2 | 0 |
| People's Democracy Party | 4.2 | 0 |
| Others | 1.6 | 0 |
| Independents | 0.5 | 0 |

*Source:* Turkish Statistical Institute, http://www.turkstat.gov.tr, accessed November 24, 2008.
*Note:* The parties in the governing coalition are boldface.

stead, the outgoing prime minister, True Path's Tansu Çiller, remained in power by forming a minority coalition with the Motherland Party. But the True Path–Motherland Party coalition was plagued by personal rivalries and financial scandals. After only a few months, the coalition collapsed, and True Path was forced to negotiate with the largest party in the Turkish Parliament, the Welfare Party.[141]

Despite their differences, Welfare and True Path formed a coalition, thus sharing the cabinet's authority to make policy. Ministries were distributed fairly evenly between the coalition partners (see table 6.5). Party leaders divided up the top posts with, Erbakan becoming prime minister and Çiller serving as deputy prime minister and minister of foreign affairs. Although the Welfare Party was the senior partner in the coalition, with twenty-three more seats in Parliament, Erbakan agreed to switch positions with Çiller after two years. However, the coalition collapsed before any change in the prime ministership could take place.

Necmettin Erbakan was not new to Turkish politics. "Erbakan started

TABLE 6.5. Members of the 54th Cabinet of the Republic of Turkey (1996–97)

| Ministry | Individual | Party |
|---|---|---|
| Prime minister | Erbakan | Welfare |
| Deputy prime minister, foreign affairs minister | Çiller | True Path |
| National Defence | Tayan | True Path |
| Justice | Kazan | Welfare |
| Interior | Ağar/Akşener | True Path |
| Finance | Şener | Welfare |
| National Education | Sağlam | True Path |
| Public Works and Housing | Ayhan | Welfare |
| Health | Aktuna/Karakuyu | True Path |
| Transportation | Barutçu | True Path |
| Agriculture and Rural Affairs | Demirci | Welfare |
| Labor and Social Security | Çelik | Welfare |
| Industry and Trade | Erez/Gönül | True Path |
| Culture | Kahraman | Welfare |
| Tourism | Yücel | True Path |
| Forestry | Dağlı | True Path |
| Environment | Tokar | Welfare |
| Energy and Natural Resources | Kutan | Welfare |

*Source:* Turkish Grand National Assembly website, http:www.tbmm.gov.tr/hukumetler/HB50.htm, accessed January 15, 2009.

out at the end of the 1960s as the leader of the National Order Party . . . , continued his struggle during the 1970s as leader of the National Salvation Party . . . , and gathered his supporters around the Welfare Party . . . during the 1980s and 1990s."[142] As leader of the National Salvation Party, Erbakan had participated in a coalition with the Republican People's Party. Throughout his political career, Erbakan has been described, somewhat contradictorily, as both pragmatic (willing to make ideological sacrifices for the sake of power) and as risk-taking (willing to sponsor bold, eye-catching, and controversial policies).[143] According to Robins, Erbakan's rhetoric on foreign policy has been "repetitive and largely consistent" throughout his political career and thus "gives us real insight into Erbakan's attitudes and feelings" as "a mixture of pious Islamism, 1950s style Third World Struggle and truculent, xenophobic Turkish nationalism."[144]

Erbakan's personal beliefs became the policies and orientations of his Welfare Party—pro-Islamic and nationalist. Erbakan was especially vocal on foreign policy, "apparently perceived by . . . Erbakan and his supporters as an area where they could speak more freely,"[145] and Turkey's relations with the West.

> He argued that "Turkey should cooperate with Muslim countries through which she can realize the goal of being a leader, instead of being a servant in the EU." He also accused other political parties of imitating Western mentality and advocating full membership in the EU. "To become a member in the EU by leaving the Community of Muslim countries," he continued, means to lose the very essence of our identity and to accept a "Second Sevres." He promised to turn Turkey into a leader in the Muslim world through the establishment of an Islamic Union that would include an Islamic United Nations, an Islamic defense organization, a common Islamic currency, and an Islamic common market.[146]

Erbakan had a number of complaints against the European Union, including the treatment of Muslims by EU member states, the effects the customs union might have on Turkey's small- and medium-sized businesses (which were electorally important for his party), and the closed nature of the EU's decision-making processes (in which Turkey would not be able to participate even as part of the customs union).[147] More basically, however, Erbakan opposed association with Europe for cultural, religious, and ideological reasons.[148] "In the December 1995 election campaign, Erbakan's

Welfare Party had strongly opposed the project to gain full membership of the EU, which it characterized as a 'Christian Union,' and called instead for a 'Union of Muslim Countries,' though it did accept the need to remove barriers to trade with Europe. Erbakan had also suggested that Turkey might leave the customs union, or at least revise it (quite how was unclear)."[149] Erbakan's views on Europe were shared by others in his party and in the cabinet. State Minister Abdullah Gül, viewed as a party moderate who confronted Erbakan on other foreign policy issues, had agreed with him that "our opposition to the European Union is based on the idea that we are from a different culture, we have a different identity and a different economic structure than European countries."[150]

Çiller was quite different in political background and beliefs. "Tansu Çiller gained prominence in Turkish politics by becoming the country's first female prime minister and the first woman to head a major political party. Her rapid rise to the chairmanship of the center-right True Path Party . . . and the prime minister's office surprised many since she had no prior experience in politics."[151] Before becoming party leader and prime minister, Çiller was a party technocrat and a state minister in charge of economic policies. Her election in the party resulted in part from the lack of any other strong candidates and in part from a move by the party to capture more of the urban sector of the Turkish electorate. Çiller had received her doctoral degree in economics in the United States and expressed favorable views of American society and economy.[152] Most observers of Çiller during her time as prime minister and foreign minister describe her personality in largely negative terms—authoritarian, deceitful, and self-interested. She often promoted her "decisiveness," "toughness," and "self-determination."[153] After becoming True Path's leader, Çiller led the party in line with some of her personal beliefs. Unlike her predecessor, Süleyman Demirel, "Çiller's political discourse emphasized conservative-populism, commitment to economic liberalism and close cooperation with the armed forces to win a military victory in the Kurdish conflict."[154] She was also strongly committed to moving Turkey toward a closer connection with the European Union.

*Disagreements and Decision Making*

Generally, the coalition between Welfare and True Path was "wracked by dissent between the two constituents" from the start.[155] Once in office, Erbakan made no moves to revise Turkey's customs unions agreement with the EU but also did not advance negotiations on accession. "Welfare Party spokesmen made it clear that they were opposed to the idea in principle on 'cultural' grounds."[156] Instead of Europe, Erbakan looked to make his mark on foreign policy in the Islamic world. One of his goals was to establish the Developing Eight (D8), which would include Turkey, Bangladesh, Egypt, Indonesia, Iran, Malaysia, Nigeria, and Pakistan and would "ensure cooperation among member states on a wide range of issues including banking, equity markets, and privatization through trade promotion, tourism and energy."[157] Indeed, the prime minister "promised to turn Turkey into a leader in the Muslim world through the establishment of an Islamic Union that would include an Islamic United Nations, an Islamic defense organization, a common Islamic currency, and an Islamic common market."[158] Such rhetoric alarmed the West, particularly the United States. Morton Abramowitz, former ambassador to Turkey, summarized much of the concern: "How do you deal with a NATO ally led by a man who is fundamentally anti-NATO, fundamentally anti-Semitic and fundamentally pro-Islamist, even when he's largely behaving himself?"[159]

While the prime minister indeed "behaved himself" by not pursuing or implementing many of the most extreme positions he had articulated during the election, Erbakan did pursue policies distancing Turkey from Israel (by, for example, supporting Palestinians opposing the peace process) and reached out to the Islamic states seen as radical by the West.[160] Erbakan's first official foreign visit, in August 1996, was to Iran, part of a tour of Muslim countries that also included Pakistan, Malaysia, and Indonesia. Although this trip was generally well received at home, from abroad, "this visit was particularly alarming because it led to the signing of a $20 billion agreement for Turkey to buy natural gas from Iran. Coming less than a week after the passing of a law by the U.S. Congress . . . intended to isolate sponsors of international terrorism (mainly Iran and Libya) by barring other countries from trading with them, Erbakan's deal with Iran openly flouted the wishes of the United States."[161] Later that year, Erbakan again angered the West when he instructed Turkey's delegation at the United Nations to vote against a resolution condemning Iran, North Korea, China, Cuba, and Libya for their human rights record.[162]

Erbakan's second foreign trip, to Libya, Egypt and Nigeria in October 1996, proved even more controversial both at home and abroad. In Libya, "Erbakan became one of the few world leaders to extend a friendly hand to Colonel Muammar al-Qaddafi, and referring to the American bombing of

Tripoli in 1986, he declared that Libya, instead of being a terrorist state, was in fact a victim of terrorism."[163] Qaddafi, however, publicly criticized Turkey for its traditional pro-Western stance and its treatment of Kurds. Political opponents at home condemned Erbakan for humiliating Turkey and called for his resignation.[164] Even before his trip to Africa, Erbakan faced resistance from within the coalition and from within his own party. Both Çiller and Gül opposed the visit to Libya: "Gül considered such a visit 'misguided' coming, as it did, against a backdrop of Colonel Qadhafi's encouragement of Kurdish separatism."[165] Although Erbakan ignored this advice, Gül and "senior members of the foreign ministry" convinced the prime minister not to visit Sudan.[166]

The prime minister also challenged U.S. policy in Iraq. Erbakan advocated lifting the UN embargo against Iraq and began negotiations to open the oil pipeline that had been closed by UN resolutions.[167] Erbakan also wanted to discontinue Turkey's support for Operation Provide Comfort to protect Kurds in northern Iraq. Before coming to power, Erbakan had condemned the operation as a "sinister Western plot to divide the Muslim countries."[168] Once in office, however, he reluctantly agreed to renew support for the U.S. policy, bowing to pressure and persuasion from the military and the foreign ministry, "although the government managed to extract some cosmetic changes, and the name of the operation was changed to 'Northern Watch' as from the beginning of 1997."[169]

While the prime minister was distancing himself from Europe and pursuing his Islamic Opening, Çiller maintained close relations with the West.[170] The foreign minister, for example, attended the reopening of talks with the International Monetary Fund in Washington, D.C., in September 1996 and the EU Dublin summit dinner in December 1996.[171] In general, Çiller represented the "secularist opinion, particularly in the military and the foreign ministry, [which] strongly opposed Erbakan's policies, mainly because they alienated Turkey from the West."[172]

*Role of Coalition Politics*

Welfare's Islamic Opening and True Path's attempts to counter it are consistent with many of the images of coalition foreign policy. Most of the foreign policy outputs in this case took the form of statements and visits—only a few high-commitment behaviors (such as the $20 billion natural gas agreement with Iran) materialized.[173] Although the tone was often extreme, the tangible outputs were not. The direction of conflict and cooperation depends on the target. Visits and agreements with the Islamic world, for example, would be seen as cooperative gestures (and would be coded as such in event data sets) but were certainly viewed as hostile by the West.[174] Foreign Minister Çiller's reassurances toward Europe and the United States, however, were highly cooperative, but her threats with regard to Cyprus were extremely negative. Thus, coalition politics did not lead Turkey to engage in either excessively peaceful policies or excessively aggressive policies; rather, both coalition partners were pursuing both positive and negative foreign policies that were mostly moderate or minimal in commitment.

Some of the factors that account for Turkish foreign policy during the Erbakan-led coalition are consistent with the theoretical literature. There is no evidence of hijacking by the junior party. In fact, the senior party, Welfare, was more important in generating the more extreme and conflictual foreign policy—hostile to the West and cooperative to Islamic countries. Nor is there direct evidence that the extremity stemmed from a feeling of unaccountability. Indeed, Erbakan may have felt accountable to the military that was critical of his foreign policies and represented a standing threat to intervene in the civilian government, as it had done before.[175] Although it is not clear that the coalition's general political weakness played a role in foreign policy, uneasiness within the Welfare Party at Erbakan's failure to follow through on some of his campaign rhetoric may have pushed him to some of his high-profile foreign adventures. According to Robins, "Mindful of Welfare's looming fifth party conference, and the almost unprecedented challenges emerging from below to the party machine, Erbakan became increasingly keen to achieve some success. Given the nature of the audience, that success had to be ideological in content. The result was the two major foreign tours of Erbakan's premiership" (to Asia and to Africa).[176]

Most important, the constraints that are assumed to be operating in coalitions were apparent in this case. Compared to his previous statements, Erbakan pursued a fairly mild path in his foreign policy choices as prime minister. "Once in power, Erbakan, a pragmatic politician with decades of experience, immediately backpedaled on his more extreme positions."[177] He did not revise the customs union agreement, pull Turkey out of NATO, establish an anti-Western Islamic Union, or end military cooperation and trade agreements with Israel, as he had indicated he would do when he was on the campaign trail.[178] Mufti argues that Erbakan's prime ministership represented more rhetorical challenge than substantive change.[179] Other observers suggest that Erbakan restrained himself once in office. Robins, for example, argues that the prime minister favored longevity in government over his Islamist principles and was thus willing to compromise on many policies in the interest of personal political gain.[180]

Yet Robins and others also interpret any constraint on Erbakan in terms of the power of the military.[181] "What Erbakan ignored while making promises and attempting to establish close ties with other Muslim countries was the power of the military, the guardian of Atatürk's secular vision, which defends the Kemalist ideology and the national interest prescribed by it by every means available, including the use of force."[182] The military was particularly resistant to any change in relations with Israel and in Turkey's support for Operation Provide Comfort.[183] "In essentials of security policy, Erbakan completely bowed to the demands of the military, be it with regard to the continuation of the fight against the PKK and the allied supervision of the Kurdish safe haven in northern Iraq or strengthening ties to Israel."[184] Hale argues that the military's opposition to Erbakan's Islamist overtures to the Middle East was an important part of his downfall.[185] Indeed, "the military used every economic, legal, constitutional, and political means in their campaign against Islamic fundamentalism and the WP [Welfare Party]. The top military officers, for example, sued their enemies in Turkish courts and boycotted firms that were believed to support the Islamic cause and the WP. Through the NSC, the military pressured the government to curb Islamic radicalism and purged some military officers from the army for activities that violated secular principles. As a result, Erbakan resigned in June 1997."[186]

Yet the military's pressure on Erbakan (often referred to as a silent coup) stemmed as much or more from its concern about the Welfare Party's challenge to domestic politics. Hale argues that "the alignment of Erbakan's party with Iran and the militant Palestinians played a part (though probably not a decisive one) in Erbakan's fall from power."[187] According to Robins, "the government eventually fell more as a result of conflict in the realm of education than foreign policy."[188] And while the military certainly criticized Erbakan's foreign policy positions, he was not so constrained by the threat of military intervention that he refrained from pursing some of those goals.

In addition to self-restraint and military opposition, the difference between Erbakan the candidate and Erbakan the prime minister may be attributed to coalition politics. In particular, Erbakan needed his partner to maintain a majority coalition. Moreover, the junior partner's leader, Çiller, held the post of foreign minister and had prior experience in government. In this position, Çiller "worked to balance Erbakan's Islamist tendencies"[189] and "sought to act as a check on" the prime minister so that Erbakan "did not violate Turkey's secular tradition."[190] "The DYP's moderating influence on its larger coalition partner—strengthened by the strong state's looming presence—was nowhere more dramatic than at the news conference at which the coalition protocol was published. Time and again Erbakan mouthed the platitudes of Kemalism in committing his government to 'Atatürk's principles,' while reaffirming the coalition's commitment to all existing agreements and binding treaties."[191] Thus, the presence of the Turkish military and its history of ending civilian rule, somewhat unique in the family of contemporary parliamentary democracies, cannot be underestimated as a source of constraint outside of coalition politics. Yet it was not the only source, as the junior partner voiced its own opposition and as Erbakan constrained himself to maintain the coalition and the Welfare Party's participation in it.

Another underlying factor for the coalition's pattern of conflictual and cooperative foreign policy behavior was the division of labor between the two parties. Indeed, the "political actors involved in foreign policy making took initiatives, mostly not even in consultation with each other. On many occasions, the RP wing of the coalition government did not even inform" Çiller.[192] With both coalition partners pursuing fairly independent foreign policy courses, they worked in different directions. Overall, "in foreign policy Çiller and Erbakan developed a kind of division of labor, with the deputy prime minister taking care of relations with Europe and the Western allies, while the prime minister tried to establish the first elements of what could be termed a more Islamic foreign policy."[193]

The division of labor in the coalition not only helps explain the content of the foreign policy but also was a source of poor decision making. The Erbakan-Çiller cabinet did not really suffer from the excessive compromises and entrapment that are often associated with coalition politics, but it did suffer from inconsistent and fragmented action.[194] The coalition guided the country's foreign policy in opposite directions because both party leaders were quite active and influential in foreign policy. There is no evidence that the cabinet was plagued by conflict in an attempt to reconcile the differences. Instead, the parties apparently operated quite independently.

In Turkey's foreign policy toward the European Union, for example, "Çiller, as the foreign minister and the main architect of the customs union on the Turkish side, seemed to be caught between two fires, as Erbakan attempted to launch a pan-Islamist project which was clearly at variance with her ideas, rendering her previous claim that the customs union would stem the tide of Islamism quite hollow. In effect, the Turkish government looked like a car with two drivers, each trying to steer it in opposite directions."[195] Indeed, the Erbakan-Çiller coalition was notable for its "wavering or inconsistent policies."[196] Thus, coalition politics in this case conformed to the image of fragmented action and poor decision making. This negative judgment on coalition politics in Turkey in the 1990s, particularly with regard to the coalition between the Welfare Party and True Path, is dominant. Yet Yavuz argues that the Welfare Party's rise to power preserved Turkish democracy by integrating Islam into the political system.[197] In this way, the cabinet represented the multiple voices that many see as an advantage to coalition governments.

This division of labor, important for both inconsistency and extremity, does not occur in all coalition cabinets but can be explained by a couple of factors operating in this case. First, while it is not unusual for the junior party to control the foreign ministry, the foreign minister in this case was relatively experienced in government affairs. Having previously served as prime minister and foreign minister, Çiller may have felt more comfortable operating independently from Erbakan and the cabinet as a whole, and Erbakan may have had difficulty challenging this independence. Second, the division of labor may also reflect the very different orientations of the two coalition partners. While most political parties disagree with one another on some aspects of politics and policies, the differences between the Welfare Party and the True Path Party were so fundamental that any attempt to reconcile them or compromise on them in cabinet might appear futile. Indeed, the parties represented Turkey's "identity crisis," with disagreements over Turkey's role in the world and on the role of Islam in the domestic political system. This fundamental difference may have contributed to the coalition's division of labor, with Erbakan talking to the Islamic world and Çiller to the West. It may also explain the way in which the coalition seemed extreme in rhetoric (with each party emphasizing and advertising its competing Turkish identity) yet constrained in behavior (with little room for compromise on any meaningful policy initiative).

RESPONSE TO THE HELSINKI SUMMIT OFFER OF EU CANDIDACY

Turkey's relations with the European Union hit a low point in 1997, when, at the Luxembourg Summit, the EU did not include Turkey in its list of candidate countries for enlargement but instead declared a separate "European Strategy for Turkey" that stressed the need for Turkey to resolve its regional problems and commit to further democratization. Cyprus, however, received candidacy status. "The Turkish government regarded the Luxembourg decision as discriminatory and politicized, and made under the influence of Greece. . . . The Turkish government also thought that the Copenhagen criteria, which were said to be objective bases of the Luxembourg Summit, were implemented rather subjectively. . . . [T]he inclusion of Cyprus created a deep feeling of resentment. Cyprus was not merely a candidate, but was among the first rank of candidates."[198]

Turkey rejected the decision, froze political contact with the EU, and even considered revisiting the customs union agreement. Relations between Turkey and the EU were poor and the future of Turkey's status in the EU unclear.[199]

> Following the Luxembourg summit, there were two possible options for EU-Turkish relations. The first was Turkey's exclusion from the emerging European project. Increasing marginalization of Turkey in post–Cold War Europe and growing anti-European feeling among Turks pointed to this as a possibility. The second option was to establish a working arrangement that goes beyond customs union, incorporating political and security dimensions and keeping open the prospect of Turkish membership. With the December 1999 Helsinki summit which acknowledged Turkey, at last, as a "candidate State destined to join the Union on the basis of the same criteria as applied to the other candidate States"—the EU and Turkey seem definitively to have chosen the second option.[200]

This choice for Turkey was not easy, however. Although Turkey welcomed the offer of official candidacy, the conditions attached to the offer—including referral of Aegean disputes with Greece to the International Court of Justice (ICJ) and the accession of Cyprus to the EU—were seen as problematic by the Turkish government.[201] Prior to the Helsinki Summit, Turkish officials had made it clear that they would not accept EU candidacy if it were based on discriminatory criteria or if it included preconditions connected to Cyprus or Kurdish issues.[202] The conditions attached to the offer were deliberately ambiguous in the original declaration sent to Turkey from the Helsinki Summit. Turkey wondered whether it was obliged to go to the ICJ by 2004, whether the resolution of the Aegean issue had to precede negotiations for full EU membership, and whether Cyprus could become an EU member before any political resolution.[203] A response was required from Turkey before the end of the Helsinki Summit. The decision to accept with conditions or reject the Helsinki Declaration was critical "because of Turkey's determination to become a full member of the EU and her sensitivities on the Aegean and Cyprus" issues.[204] Turkey's acceptance was also important to the EU.[205] When the EU released its declaration from Helsinki, the EU high representative for foreign affairs and security, Javier Solana, flew to Ankara to address Turkey's potential concerns about the membership offer.[206]

Solana was greeted by a ruling coalition that was divided along party lines over the interpretation of the conditions and how to respond to the offer. Since national elections in early 1999, a three-party coalition between the Democratic Left Party (DSP), the Nationalist Action Party (MHP), and the Motherland Party (ANAP) controlled the cabinet. Within a few days, the parties resolved their disagreement and responded to the EU offer. The coalition compromised and accepted the Helsinki Summit Declaration but issued a separate statement renouncing Cyprus's EU membership.

*Players and Positions*

Each of the three parties in the ruling coalition was critical to maintaining the cabinet's parliamentary majority of 64 percent (see table 6.6). The Democratic Left was the largest party in the coalition and controlled the prime ministership (Bülent Ecevit) and the foreign ministry (İsmail Cem). The Nationalist Action Party held the key post of minister of national defense, and its leader (Devlet Bahçeli) was a deputy prime minister (see table 6.7). Other key ministers in the Helsinki case included Minister Gürel (DSP), responsible for Cyprus affairs, and Minister İrtemçelik (ANAP), responsible for EU affairs.[207]

The cabinet made the final decision in Turkey's response to the Helsinki

Declaration. In addition to the cabinet members, the leader of the Motherland Party, Mesut Yılmaz, who was not an official member of the cabinet, was present.[208] The military had no direct involvement in this issue, and cabinet discussions remained largely out of the public's eye.[209] Furthermore, there is no evidence that the party leaders consulted their parties outside of the cabinet: Time pressures prevented such consultations.[210] Turkey's president, Süleyman Demirel, was involved in the discussion. According to Çuhadar-Gürkaynak and Özkeçeci-Taner, "Demirel's position was independent of the political parties and most of the people in the group saw him as neutral, above bureaucratic interests and political parties. Demirel also perceived himself as the representative of the 'State.'"[211]

The issues involved in the Helsinki Summit case were highly salient for all three coalition partners. The parties were, however, divided along a hawk versus dove distinction that was connected to more general ideological differences.[212] The coalition included two parties—Democratic Left and Nationalist Action—that were quite nationalist in their foreign policy orientations.[213] "One can argue that the 1999 election took place at a time when the increasingly *nationalistic* tendency in Turkey was growing" and that this growth, at least in part, stemmed from the EU's 1997 decision to reject Turkey's bid for candidacy status."[214] The coalition agreement between the parties made it clear that the "national interest" would be a guiding principle in Turkish foreign policy, much more than in previous governments and coalition agreements, despite the presence of the Motherland Party and its decidedly more internationalist foreign policy

TABLE 6.6. Turkish National Election Results, 1999

|  | Votes (%) | Seats |
|---|---|---|
| **Democratic Left Party** | 22.2 | 136 |
| **Nationalist Action Party** | 18.0 | 129 |
| Virtue Party | 15.4 | 111 |
| **Motherland Party** | 13.2 | 86 |
| True Path Party | 12.0 | 85 |
| Republican People's Party | 8.7 | 0 |
| Democratic People's Party | 4.7 | 0 |
| Others | 4.8 | 0 |
| Independents | 0.9 | 3 |

*Source:* Turkish Statistical Institute, http://www.turkstat.gov.tr, accessed November 24, 2008.

*Note:* The parties in the governing coalition are boldface.

orientation.[215] At the time the coalition was formed, the parties agreed on issues related to Cyprus and the EU. "All three leaders agreed that the 57th government would be more assertive in their relations with Greece, especially Cyprus."[216] "The DSP-MHP-ANAP coalition also made it clear that full membership in the EU was not an *obsession*.... MHP had always been suspicious of the intentions of the EU vis-à-vis Turkey, and DSP also had mixed feelings toward the Union. ANAP's position, on the other hand, was more pro-EU. However, ANAP's leadership had to compromise its position on Turkish-EU relations in this coalition," at least at the outset.[217]

Özkeçeci-Taner classifies the Democratic Left Party as nationalist in its foreign policy orientation, largely because of its position on the Kurdish question, attitudes toward human rights, and suspicions of the EU and the EU's treatment of Turkey's candidacy. Indeed, the "DSP has been suspicious of EU intentions toward Turkey and believes that Turkey becoming a re-

TABLE 6.7. Members of the 57th Cabinet of the Republic of Turkey (1999–2002)

| Ministry | Individual | Party |
|---|---|---|
| Prime minister | Ecevit | Democratic Left |
| Deputy prime minister | Özkan/Gürel | Democratic Left |
| Deputy prime minister | Bahçeli | Nationalist Action |
| Deputy prime minister | Ersumer/Yılmaz | Motherland |
| Foreign Affairs | Cem/Gürel | Democratic Left |
| National Defense | Çakmakoğlu | Nationalist Action |
| Justice | Türk | Democratic Left |
| Interior | Tantan/Yücelen | Motherland |
| Finance | Oral | Motherland |
| National Education | Bostancıoğlu | Democratic Left |
| Public Works and Housing | Aydın/Akcan | Motherland |
| Health | Durmuş | Nationalist Action |
| Transportation | Öksüz | Nationalist Action |
| Agriculture and Rural Affairs | Gokalp | Nationalist Action |
| Labor and Social Security | Okuyan/Arseven | Motherland |
| Industry and Trade | Tanrıkulu | Nationalist Action |
| Culture | Talay/Çağlayan | Democratic Left |
| Tourism | Mumcu/Taşar | Motherland |
| Forestry | Çağan | Democratic Left |
| Environment | Aytekin | Democratic Left |
| Energy and Natural Resources | Ersümer | Motherland |

*Source:* Turkish Grand National Assembly website, http://www.tbmm.gov.tr/hukumetler/HB57.htm, accessed January 15, 2009.

gional leader and having relations with many regional institutions better serves Turkey's interests. According to DSP, however, membership in the EU is a natural right of Turkey given to her by the 1963 Ankara Agreement."[218] Some in the party even criticized the existing customs union agreement and suggested, at the time of coalition formation, a review of that arrangement.[219] "It is also important to point out that DSP has always considered the EU, and especially Greece, to be *unreliable*. To say that the Party is *anti-Greek* and *anti-European* would not be an exaggeration."[220] Dunér and Deverell also categorize the "left-wing nationalists" in the Democratic Left party as "Euroskeptics," and Tachau discusses nationalism as a central part of Prime Minister Ecevit's ideological outlook.[221]

The Nationalist Action Party was also nationalist in orientation, influencing the party's position toward the EU.[222] The "MHP was eminently suspicious of the European powers and believed that Turkey's full membership in the European Union would result in Turkey's loss of *independence* and *national integrity.*"[223] The party's leader, Bahçeli, had made clear before the Helsinki Summit that his party would regard concessions on Cyprus as unacceptable.[224] "For [the] MHP, Cyprus is a 'national cause,' meaning that MHP strongly supports the independence of the Turkish Republic of Northern Cyprus and is against any kind of compromise with the EU or Greece. The party's position on the island is so strict that those who support compromise are considered to be traitors."[225]

Özkeçeci-Taner classifies the Motherland Party as internationalist and pro-EU.

> Contrary to MHP and DSP, ANAP believes that Turkey's integration with the EU would increase Turkey's prestige and standing in the international arena. Many ANAP members, including those having positions in the coalition government, stated many times that keeping Turkey outside of the Union will not help to resolve bilateral problems with any of the EU members, particularly Greece. . . . ANAP also thinks that Turkey's national security syndrome is an obstacle rather than an advantage in making Turkey a full member of the Union. . . . ANAP's position was that the resolution of the Aegean and the Cyprus problems had a better chance if worked out in an institutional setting like the EU. For ANAP, there is no pure national *independence* in the world anymore because countries are *interdependent*. . . . However the party also believes that the EU is guilty of ethnocentrism and using double standards against Turkey.[226]

The Motherland Party argued that the EU's decision in and Turkey's response to the Helsinki Summit would be critical, "suggesting that the party would do everything it could to influence the coalition's position vis-à-vis the EU."[227]

*Disagreements and Decision Making*

After the offer of membership in the EU's Helsinki Declaration, the Turkish government held an emergency cabinet meeting to discuss the conditions attached to the candidacy, and members' first impressions were decidedly negative.[228] Given the different general ideological orientations of the coalition parties, it is not surprising that the cabinet was divided about how to respond. The parties also disagreed regarding the interpretation of the conditions, such as whether the Helsinki Declaration required resolution of the Aegean issue as a precondition for membership.[229] "There was still a major debate between *nationalist/Kemalists* and *internationalist* factions in the government as to the most appropriate Turkish response to the draft declaration. Since the coalition had to respond to the EU Council before the Helsinki Summit ended, no one knew whether the Cabinet would reach a decision amenable to all the coalition members or even if the DSP-MHP-ANAP coalition government stayed intact."[230]

The Nationalist Action Party maintained, as it had throughout the EU negotiations, that membership requiring concessions on Cyprus was unacceptable. The party also rejected the apparent fact that Cyprus could become an EU member without a political settlement. For the MHP, "the existence of the Turkish State is the primary goal, with the emphasis on *independence, national unity,* and *non-interference* in Turkish domestic politics. MHP was particularly disturbed by the EU Council's 'suggestion' of taking the Greek-Turkish dispute in the Aegean Sea to the ICJ. In addition, for MHP, Cyprus is a 'national cause,' meaning that MHP strongly supports the independence of the Turkish Republic of Northern Cyprus and is against any kind of compromise with the EU or Greece."[231]

In the Motherland Party, the minister responsible for EU Affairs, İrtemçelik, was more favorable toward the decision, urging a positive response from Turkey. Yılmaz, the leader of the Motherland Party and a participant at the cabinet meeting, agreed.[232]

The position of the principal players in the Democratic Left Party changed over time. Prime Minister "Ecevit was initially skeptical and suspicious of the Helsinki deal. Even Cem, who as foreign minister might have been regarded as having a bureaucratic vested interest in Helsinki, was also reluctant."[233] According to Cem, the conditions on Cyprus in the Helsinki Declaration were unacceptable and indicated the EU's continued discriminatory treatment of Turkey.[234] The position of the prime minister and the foreign minister was shared by the other members of the Democratic Left Party. "The DSP wing of the coalition, led mainly by Şükrü Sina Gürel, the state minister responsible for Turkey-Cyprus relations, maintained that Turkey should reject the offer . . . immediately because of the Cyprus and the Aegean articles attached to it."[235]

The positions of the foreign minister and the prime minister, however, were not strongly argued throughout the deliberations. "Although FM Cem expressed his concerns in the beginning . . . he resisted complete rejection of the EU offer. PM Ecevit was initially closer to the pessimists, but his position shifted during the course of the decisionmaking process."[236] Robins credits Solana's trip to Ankara as key to helping persuade Ecevit to come to Helsinki and accept the offer.[237] Gürel, however, maintained his opposition to the declaration, and "there is no question that Gürel's views were taken seriously especially on the issues regarding Cyprus, but he played more of an advisory role based on his expertise on the issue."[238]

President Demirel also participated in the discussions regarding the Helsinki Declaration. Demirel supported the declaration's acceptance, in line with the Motherland Party's position: "President Demirel's instant reaction was that the offer was decisively in Turkey's interest, and he set about giving a positive lead."[239] Demirel argued that the declaration fulfilled the primary expectations for Turkey and that "accepting the document would not alter the *de facto* situation in Cyprus anyway. Demirel also drew . . . attention to the likely domestic consequences of rejection: such as the public rage against the EU and the West, and the slowing down of the economic and democratic reforms."[240]

Demirel also supported a compromise that was first introduced by the minister of state, the Motherland Party's İrtemçelik, and "wholeheartedly supported" by his party. The idea was to accept the Helsinki Declaration but to issue a separate memorandum denouncing the preconditions concerning Cyprus.[241] This became the final decision of the cabinet. "The DSP-MHP-ANAP coalition government decided to welcome the EU's decision to accept Turkish candidacy for full membership, but negotiated with the EU officials on issuance of a declaration perpetuating the Turkish position on

Cyprus. With the concurrence of the EU Council, the issue was separated from EU membership. The . . . coalition also made it clear to EU officials that Turkey. . . . repudiated *parts* of the agreement related to the transfer of the disputes to the ICJ, and did not fully support the full text of the Helsinki Summit Declaration. Thus the final outcome. . . . was a *mutual compromise* representing the range of foreign policy objectives guided by the *ideational orientations* of the three parties that made up the governing coalition."[242] Prime Minister Ecevit, Foreign Minister Cem, and other members of the cabinet insisted that the government had not accepted any concessions in exchange for the EU's offer of candidate membership.[243]

The two most vocal and steadfast opponents to the decision, Gürel (Democratic Left) and Bahçeli (Nationalist Action) did not oppose the decision but did monitor the implementation phase to "further push their preferences."[244] "Despite their furiousness about the EU's 1999 Helsinki Conclusions with regard to Turkey's membership, both [the Democratic Left Party and the Nationalist Action Party] listened to [the Motherland Party's] position and agreed to integrate it in their response to the EU Council. Although their earlier announcements suggested that they would reject any offer that put preconditions in front of Turkey's full membership to the Union, their commitment to the [coalition] government was one of the factors why they agreed to accept the offer with a memorandum on Cyprus."[245]

*Role of Coalition Politics*

The final response to the Helsinki Summit and the offer of EU candidacy can be classified as moderate foreign policy behavior, in both a cooperative direction (acceptance candidacy) and a conflictual direction (denouncing the position on Cyprus).[246] This response was certainly affected by coalition politics. Both junior parties, Motherland and Nationalist Action, influenced the decision and attempted to constrain the response. ANAP was "influential in pointing out the importance of the Helsinki decisions and the responsibility of the Turkish government to accept the EU Council's declaration."[247] "Without the presence of ANAP, there may have been more retaliatory response to the EU's Helsinki Declaration, with possible damaging effects for the future of Turkey-EU relations."[248] And the position of the Nationalist Action Party also made unlikely any response that completely ignored the issue of Cyprus. Indeed, "a declaration unacceptable to any coalition party leader . . . would have jeopardized not only the legitimacy of the decision, but also the survival of the coalition government."[249]

It is not the case, however that either the Motherland Party or the Nationalist Action Party hijacked the cabinet to the extremes of either outright acceptance or rejection. Rather, this case fits the expectation that coalitions often compromise. In this case, though, the compromise was not a meaningless papering over of differences. In some respects, such a compromise was not expected. "The fact that the major parties of the coalition, the far-right MHP and the center-left DSP, cooperate is surprising. The parties share a history as hardened enemies during the political violence that threw the country into turmoil in the 1970s."[250] The compromise can be explained by the parties' commitment to the coalition. "The party leaders were as much loyal to the coalition as to their own parties. . . . Devlet Bahçeli was quick to note that even though he had the power to block the decision, MHP's commitment to the coalition was an important factor in his taking into consideration the views supported by his coalition partners. Same thing can also be said about the rather extreme position taken by some of the DSP members like Sina Gurel."[251] The compromise was also possible because the senior party, Democratic Left, was somewhat divided and because its most important leaders, Prime Minister Ecevit and Foreign Minister Cem, gravitated toward the Motherland Party's position during the decision-making period.

The solution of accepting the declaration but issuing a separate memo on Cyprus also allowed both sides to get something out of the decision. This solution conforms to the expectation that a creative solution can emerge from dissent. Divergent thinking may have occurred so that the original, dichotomous choice of accept or reject was replaced by a third alternative of accept and reject. Again, the commitment to the coalition was probably the factor behind this process. In addition, all three parties seemed to want the EU candidacy that was being offered, though they disagreed about whether this offer was worth the preconditions. The divisible nature of the offer—the ability to separate candidacy from the preconditions—allowed the parties to find this acceptable hybrid outcome. The coalition did not succumb to the expectations of negative decision making; it responded without much delay and without a meaningless compromise or fragmented, inconsistent action. Furthermore, the presence of the Motherland Party as a junior partner in the coalition may have prevented the cabinet from outright rejection, which some observers would have seen as an overreaction to the conditions and which would have caused severe damage to Turkey's relations with the EU.[252] In this way, the presence of dissenting position, possible only because of the nature of the coalition, may have prevented premature closure on an option and produced higher-quality decision making.

## DEATH PENALTY

The acceptance of the Helsinki Declaration paved the way for negotiations to begin on Turkey's EU candidacy. In March 2001, the EU agreed on the Accession Partnership for Turkey. This framework established the necessary economic, legal, and political reforms, consistent with the EU's Copenhagen criteria, that Turkey had to complete for membership. Although all of Turkey's political parties generally supported EU membership, some reforms were contentious, particularly in the area of human rights policy.[253] Throughout 2001 and 2002, the measures to bring Turkey's constitution in line with EU expectations "were dramatic compared with previous efforts and they were engineered by a relatively weak coalition government of three different political orientations. . . . While dramatic in Turkish terms, critical areas were still left contested between the EU and Turkey, such as the abolishment of the death penalty."[254]

The EU, in its Accession Partnership document, required absolute abolition of the death penalty. "The problem thus became a black-and-white issue without any of the areas of doubt left in other parts of the EU's list of requirements: either Turkey abolished the death penalty . . . or it did not."[255] The 1997–99 coalition had already attempted and failed to deal with this issue. That government had prepared a draft bill to lift the death penalty, but the effort could not get enough support even from within the cabinet.[256] President Demirel said at the time, "Turkey is not ready for the lifting of the death penalty."[257] Indeed, Turkish public opinion was not very supportive of a complete lifting of the death penalty.[258] According to Mehmet Güner, director of an organization for families of soldiers and police killed in the line of duty, "We do not accept any good will for those who want to divide this country and pull down our flag. . . . Ending capital punishment should not be a precondition to enter the European Union. If they like us, they better accept us, the way we are."[259]

The issue of the death penalty became connected to Turkey's right to deal with convicted terrorists and the Kurdish nationalist problem. Members of the Kurdistan Worker's Party (PKK), the political and terrorist organization in Turkey seeking Kurdish independence, were found guilty of terrorist acts against the state and had been sentenced to death. Most important, the PKK's leader, Abdullah Öcalan, was captured in Kenya in February 1999 and brought to Turkey. Öcalan was sentenced to death and was awaiting this punishment when the EU issued its demands to Turkey regarding the death penalty. According to Dunér and Deverell, "Carrying out the death sentence against Öcalan is one of the most sensitive political issues in Turkey."[260]

Although the death penalty is certainly domestic policy, as it is part of the legal justice system, it also became a foreign policy issue. The EU's requirement that the law be abolished became one of the focal points in European-Turkish relations. At the 1999 Helsinki Summit, Solana, then serving as the EU's president, stated the position of all member states: "It would be very difficult to have a member in the European family who does not have the same respect for life."[261] The death penalty also became a foreign policy issue in Turkey's bilateral relations. When Öcalan was arrested in Rome in 1998, for example, Turkey requested extradition. Italy refused because Italian law forbids extradition of anyone who might face capital punishment. Turkey then threatened a trade war against Italy, its third-largest trading partner, and Prime Minister Yılmaz called on Turks across Europe to protest Italy.[262] Turkish-Belgian relations were also strained in 2000, when Belgium rejected Turkey's demand to extradite Fehriye Erdal, another wanted criminal, because of Turkey's death penalty. More generally, Turkey found itself out of step with the liberal international norms of human rights and the growing norm that domestic political conditions should be a topic in foreign relations. According to Robins, "Turkey just did not connect with the spirit of these normative changes."[263] And Rumford argues "the lack of consistency in Turkey's approach to aligning domestic demojcratic norms with those of the EU is the result of divisions within the political elites."[264]

The cabinet that came to power in 1999—the coalition between the Democratic Left Party, the Nationalist Action Party, and the Motherland Party—attempted to commute existing death sentences to life in jail but failed because of disagreements among coalition members. Once the Helsinki Summit Declaration was accepted in late 1999 and the EU agreed on the specific criteria for reforms in 2000 and 2001, the cabinet faced pressure to act from the EU. In October 2001, Parliament passed thirty-four amendments to the constitution to conform to EU requirements, and the death penalty was restricted to crimes committed in cases of war or the imminent threat of war and terror crimes. The caveat of terrorist crimes reflected the Nationalist Action Party's position to follow through on Öcalan's execution.[265] The EU was not satisfied. "At a meeting of the Turkish-EU Association Council in April 2002, the EU side emphasized that Turkey still had to allow Kurdish broadcasting and other cultural rights, to abolish the death penalty in law, and withdraw the emergency regime in the south-eastern provinces. . . . If Turkey wanted to be set for the start of the accession process, then it had to achieve these reforms first—preferably by September 2002, by which time the Commission would be preparing its next annual report on Turkey."[266]

The conflict between the coalition partners over the death penalty, however, remained unresolved.[267]

> In the midsummer of 2002 . . . the cabinet was gravely weakened and divided . . . by disagreements over the completion of political reforms which were required by the European Union (EU) as a prerequisite for the start of accession negotiations. Two of the ruling parties [Democratic Left and Motherland] claimed they were fully prepared to enact the required human rights improvements. Nonetheless, the way was effectively blocked by the third coalition partner [the Nationalist Action Party]. Since Ecevit refused to dismantle his government by excluding the MHP, the process of preparing Turkey for eventual accession seemed to have reached an impasse. The widening of human rights thus became Turkey's most pressing political question alongside the survival of the government.[268]

This impasse was broken in August 2002, when terror crimes as an exception to the death penalty was removed from the law and conformity with the Sixth Protocol of the European Convention of Human Rights was attained. Atila Eralp calls Parliament's decision "historic."[269]

> The period from the beginning of 2000 onwards could be described as a period of profound and momentous change in Turkish history, a process that was ironically engineered by a relatively weak coalition government. . . . During the summer of 2002, the process of change appeared to gather further momentum with the controversial harmonization laws having been

approved by the parliament over an unexpectedly short period of time considering the depth of resistance involved. Particularly striking in this context was the August 2002 removal of the death penalty, including for those convicted of terrorist activity. This particular element of reform encountered major opposition from the military and nationalist parties, notably the ultra-nationalist Nationalist Action Party. . . . Indeed, the MHP has been playing a major role as a key member of the coalition government in terms of explicitly blocking some of the major political reforms needed to meet the EU's democratic norms in the post-1999 era.[270]

*Players and Positions*

Although the final approval of the change to the death penalty law lay with the Parliament,[271] the cabinet was critical to the decision. From the time it came to power until July 2002, the coalition held a majority in the Turkish Grand National Assembly (see tables 6.6 and 6.7). After July 2002, the cabinet lost its majority when a group of deputies from the Democratic Left Party bolted and established the New Turkey Party.[272] Both before and after this development, the support of the Nationalist Action Party was not necessary for the legislation to succeed in Parliament, as the opposition parties generally backed the measure.[273] "Ecevit, and his deputy premier Mesut Yılmaz, who favoured reform on most of the points demanded by the EU, had either to persuade Bahçeli and his colleagues to change their minds, by citing the need to meet the Copenhagen criteria if Turkey were serious in its aim of gaining accession to the EU, or to appeal to support from the opposition parties, at the risk of provoking serious splits in the government."[274] Prime Minister Ecevit, however, did not want to risk the dissolution of the government by excluding and essentially overruling this junior party; coalition politics thus were critical to the policy-making process.[275]

There is no evidence of direct presidential or military pressure or involvement in this case. "In issues like the death penalty (especially the Öcalan issue) and legalizing the use of Kurdish, the military has been particularly hesitant" to adopt policies demanded by the EU.[276] A spokesperson for the military, the secretary-general of the National Security Council, voiced his opinion about Turkish-EU relations in March 2002, sparking controversy and a range of reactions from the coalition parties. The general stated that Turkey has never been assisted by the EU, that the EU was a neocolonial force that wanted to divide Turkey, and that Turkey should search for new allies, such as Iran and Russia.²⁷⁷ Although the general claimed that he was speaking personally, not for the military, "his words shocked the Turkish establishment. First, because they differ[ed] sharply from the army's usual claims to be pro-European. Second, because it is common knowledge in Turkey that the army speaks with one voice."²⁷⁸ Ecevit responded that there were no alternatives to the pro-EU path. The Motherland Party's Yılmaz reacted that an alliance with Iran and Russia would be "a nightmare scenario," and the Nationalist Action Party's Bahçeli "remained silent."²⁷⁹

> The parties in the coalition disagreed on the issue of the death penalty. While all the major political parties in Turkey displayed a vague commitment on the issue of EU membership, when it came to the sensitive issues [such as the death penalty], there was a lack of consensus. The coalition was clearly fragmented on these issues. The MHP opposed the abolition of the death penalty. . . . The DSP was more favorable regarding the death penalty. . . . Only ANAP had a clear pro-EU attitude. Within this climate, it became increasingly difficult for the government to move forward in the reform process on these key political issues.²⁸⁰

The parties' positions on the death penalty stemmed from their more general ideological differences, as discussed in the Helsinki Summit case. The Democratic Left Party and the Nationalist Action Party were more nationalistic, with the former holding deep suspicions of the EU and the latter concerned that EU membership would mean a loss of Turkish independence and national integrity. The Democratic Left Party, however, saw the death penalty as a problem for Turkish foreign relations and for Turkey's internal security. When he was in the previous government, Democratic Left leader Ecevit argued that it was necessary to abolish the death penalty so that Turkey could easily press Italy, which then held Öcalan, to extradite the PKK leader.²⁸¹

According to Hale, "Opposition to reform of the human rights regime came almost exclusively from the MHP, which regarded any constitutional liberalization—especially on the Kurdish issue—as an insult to those who had died during the long struggle" against the PKK.²⁸² The Nationalist Action Party's position on the death penalty directly stemmed from the party's anti-Kurd orientation. The party wanted to retain the death penalty and the right to execute Öcalan.²⁸³ "Bahçeli stated Turkey wants to unite with Europe in an honorable, fair and full membership. However, there would be 'no bargaining concerning Öcalan.'"[284] During the campaign for the 1999 elections, the Nationalist Action Party had campaigned on a "hang Öcalan" ticket.[285] "Officially, the MHP supported Turkey's application for eventual accession, but party spokesman maintained that, since the EU was unlikely to admit Turkey anyway, there was no point in making these 'concessions.'"[286] More generally, the Nationalist Action Party believed that the death penalty should not be abolished, especially for crimes against the state, a category that embraces a wide spectrum of political activity. The Motherland Party, the other junior coalition partner, was more internationalist in orientation and supported Turkey's alignment with international human rights norms.[287]

*Disagreements and Decision Making*

These basic differences between the coalition partners persisted throughout the cabinet's attempts to deal with the issue of the death penalty. In 1999, during the coalition's first year in office, the Democratic Left Party wanted to pass special legislation to commute death sentences to life in jail before Parliament went on summer recess. According to Prime Minister Ecevit, "It is out of the question to withdraw or delay" the law.[288] For the Nationalist Action Party, however, this bill would only frustrate the public, since a death sentence had already been imposed on Öcalan. Thus, this party believed that the bill should be postponed to avoid adverse public reaction.

Following the Helsinki Summit, the parties again expressed their positions. Ecevit stated that "it is clear that the capital punishment cannot go with EU membership" and called the two a "contradiction." He continued, "God willing, we will overcome this contradiction soon."[289] The minister of justice, also a member of the Democratic Left Party, agreed: 'Turkey, as being a member of both the Council of Europe and a candidate country to the EU, has to review the death penalty in its legal system."[290] For Ecevit and his party, the outcome of the summit was "a landmark event," and he promised that he would do his best to repeal capital punishment. He also stressed that such a move would depend on support from the other members of his coalition government.[291] The Motherland Party could be counted on to provided that support. According to Öniş, no party "actively promoted EU-related reforms as vocally as ANAP" during this period.[292]

The Nationalist Action Party signaled that it would be willing to consider the abolition of the death penalty but not the commutation of Öcalan's sentence.[293] A Nationalist Action deputy who served as the chair of a joint EU-Turkey commission stated, "First execution. Then we can abolish the death penalty."[294] Bahçeli too stood firm on Öcalan, stressing that "the sentence which the murderer deserved cannot be changed with pretexts" and that "efforts by some EU circles to present this (sparing Öcalan) as a basic condition for Turkey's EU membership are the indication of double standards which contradict Europe's own human rights and democracy values."[295]

Over the next two and a half years, the Democratic Left Party continued to make the case for the death penalty's abolition. In the summer of 2000, for example, Prime Minister Ecevit argued that "one of the difficulties in our path towards (membership of) the EU would disappear."[296] Justice Minister Turk, referring primarily to the disagreement between Belgium and Turkey over the extradition of Fehriye Erdal, also argued that the abolition of the death penalty would open the way for improved Turkish relations with the EU countries.[297] As opposition from the Nationalist Action Party became more vocal, Ecevit expressed hope that the penalty could be lifted by reaching a consensus in Parliament for the sake of EU membership.

The Nationalist Action Party, however, did not compromise its position, and when the Turkish Parliament passed a package of EU-compliant constitutional amendments in October 2001, terrorist crimes were added to the conditions under which the death penalty could be imposed. In 2002, the party signaled that it was considering withdrawing from the coalition if the prime minister submitted a constitutional amendment to outlaw capital punishment.[298] According to İsmail Köse, deputy chair of the Nationalist Action Party, "Yes to EU, but you can't accept demands which overlap with those of the PKK. We will certainly continue to oppose lifting the death penalty in crimes committed against the state."[299] In the summer of 2002, Bahçeli argued that there was no need to rush ahead with EU-demanded reforms like the death penalty since Turkey would not be able to enter the EU for another decade anyway: "This murderer has become a condition for Turkey even to be given a date to start membership talks. If that is not injustice and disrespect to our country, then what is it?" He continued, "The nationalists will under no circumstances be part of such a move."[300]

According to Avcı, the Nationalist Action Party "did suggest at some point that it would not oppose abolishing the death penalty if the DSP and

ANAP legislated it through Parliament with the support of the opposition, but it has changed its position during the course of the discussion."[301] Bahçeli's threat to break up the coalition over the abolition of the death penalty contrasted starkly with the efforts of his coalition partners: "Bahçeli's coalition partners both favor swift moves to meet the EU's criteria, in an effort to secure a date for opening membership negotiations."[302]

Over the objections of the Nationalist Action Party, the Motherland Party introduced an August 2002 package of reforms in Parliament that included the complete abolition of the death penalty. With support from the Democratic Left Party, Motherland, and the opposition parties, the legislation passed. The Nationalist Action Party voted as a bloc against the reforms, and "Bahçeli said that the MHP would appeal to the Constitutional Court in a bid to force parliament to reverse its decision regarding the death penalty and minority rights."[303] "Addressing a crowd of supporters in the central Anatolian province of Kayseri the following day [Bahçeli] described the reforms as harmful to Turkey's 'national unity and existence' and blasted those who had opposed Öcalan's execution for 'doing evil to the country.'"[304] The coalition fell shortly after this case as a result of partisan differences regarding EU-related reforms.[305]

*Role of Coalition Politics*

In the end, Turkey made a decision on abolition of the death penalty that was cooperative but not extreme despite the change's profound effects on the domestic justice system.[306] One junior party attempted to constrain the government but in the direction of conflict. Despite vocal opposition from a junior party critical to the maintenance of the coalition and threats to leave that coalition, the issue was not hijacked in an extreme, conflictual direction. Nor is there any evidence that the coalition felt that accountability could be diffused by making this decision. The coalition's weakened nature by 2002 may have played a role in the eventual decision, as general elections were approaching and the government was still dealing with the economic consequences of the 2001 financial crisis. In other words, the parties supporting the death penalty may have felt it was time to risk the coalition and pass reforms that were necessary for membership. Although abolition of the death penalty itself was not particularly popular in Turkey, the Democratic Left Party and the Motherland Party may have calculated that their constituency would see the pro-EU policy favorably. Also, as the election neared, the Nationalist Action Party's threat to withdraw from the coalition became less meaningful—the coalition was not likely to survive anyway.

The coalition might have survived its disagreements on this issue for so long because of a commitment to the coalition and norms of trust. One Nationalist Action Party member remarked, "We trust Ecevit. He too trusts us. This government helped us develop a culture of coalition."[307] According to Başkan, "Ecevit and Bahçeli acted like a state elite in emphasizing that the country's interests were more important than each party's interests."[308] Prime Minister Ecevit refused to dismantle the coalition to move forward on the reforms, and his "strong words to the PKK appear to be an attempt to placate MHP and its grassroots supporters."[309] Early on, Bahçeli apparently overruled the rest of his party by agreeing to postpone a final decision on Öcalan.[310] The Nationalist Action Party did, however, become more vocal and insistent in its opposition in 2002. With elections approaching and the party facing grassroots pressure, it may have felt the need to distinguish itself from its coalition partners.[311] The nature of this issue may have also played a role in this case. Although a compromise was attempted, with the 2000 legislation abolishing the death penalty except for terror crimes, the EU rejected the deal. The black-and-white choice facing Turkey prevented compromise between the parties. Finally, the fact that Parliament would be the final locus of authority for this decision and that the opposition parties supported the abolition of the death penalty allowed the coalition to escape a decision that would have risked the survival of the government.

The decision making in this case conforms with two somewhat contradictory images of coalition policy-making. On the one hand, considerable deadlock and delay occurred. After the Helsinki Summit in December 1999, Turkey knew it would have to abolish the death penalty so that membership negotiations could begin. But it did not act decisively for more than a year and a half. This delay stemmed directly from the opposition of the Nationalist Action Party as a junior coalition partner. On the other hand, the decision that was made was "historic," and the time it took to pass the entire set of reforms was shorter than expected, given the significant opposition.[312] That such a weak coalition was able to make this reform runs contrary to the image that divided coalitions are likely to deadlock or pursue only fragmented action.

## CONCLUSIONS

In general, the Turkish cases in this project support some images of how coalition politics influence foreign policy but challenge other images (see table 6.8). Most of the foreign policies in these cases were not extreme (by WEIS coding rules). The most extreme behavior was the customs union agreement with the EU. The Islamic Opening case includes some more extreme behaviors (such as the $20 billion natural gas agreement with Iran), but most of this coalition's foreign policy outputs took the form of rhetoric or visits. Most of the foreign policies across the cases were cooperative, not conflictual, although some cases included both (such as the Islamic Opening and the response to the Helsinki offer).

Yet the cooperation in these cases did not result from successful constraints in the direction of peace. Constraints were attempted by junior parties in most cases (i.e., the Republican People's Party against the customs union agreement, the True Path Party against the Islamic Opening, and the Nationalist Action Party against the Helsinki offer and the death penalty). But contrary to the logic of the democratic peace as it has been applied to coalitions, these actors were not attempting to constrain the country in the direction of peace. Instead, the main party was more peaceful and the attempted constraint was for a more conflictual policy. (The Islamic Opening case is the exception here, as True Path attempted to constrain against hostility toward the West.) And just as important, the constraint from within the coalition was not necessarily successful—it failed in the customs union and death penalty cases, it was somewhat successful in the Helsinki case, and it worked at times in the Islamic Opening case.

The Turkish cases are mixed in terms of whether they exhibited poor decision making. Decision making was fragmented and inconsistent during the Islamic Opening case, and considerable delay occurred in the death penalty case. In the other cases, the government was able to make a fairly meaningful decision without much delay, despite the differences between the parties. And some signs of good decision making were evident. In the Helsinki case, the Motherland Party arguably prevented premature closure on outright rejection, and the separate memo on Cyprus can be seen as a creative solution that came about only because of coalition differences.

The factors that explain the outcome of the party conflict varied across the cases. In the customs union case, the inconsistency in the junior party's

TABLE 6.8. Do the Turkish Cases Fit the Images of Coalition Politics and Foreign Policy?

| Questions | Cases | | | |
|---|---|---|---|---|
| | Customs Union | Islamic Opening | Helsinki Offer | Death Penalty |
| *Was the foreign policy cooperative or conflictual?* | cooperative | conflictual and cooperative | conflictual and cooperative | cooperative |
| *Was the foreign policy extreme or moderate?* | extreme | moderate | moderate | moderate |
| *Did coalition parties attempt to constrain the policy?* | yes | yes | yes | yes |
| *Were attempted constraints in the direction of peace?* | no | yes | no | no |
| *Were the constraints successful?* | no | somewhat | no | no |
| *Was the decision a compromise?* | no | no | yes | no |
| *Was there poor decision making?* | yes (process manipulation) | yes (fragmented) | no | yes (deadlock; delay) |
| *Was there good decision making?* | no | no | yes (prevention of premature closure; creative; timely) | somewhat (substantive reform) |
| *What factors best explain the policy outcome and decision making quality?* | inconsistency; leadership style; locus of authority | division of labor; extreme differences between parties | disunity; commitment to coalition; divisibility of issue | commitment to coalition; indivisibility of issue |

position and the prime minister's leadership style were important. In the Islamic Opening case, the extreme differences in the parties' positions and the related division of labor in the coalition were critical. In the Helsinki case, the division in the senior party at the beginning of decision making on the issue, the divisibility of the issue, and the commitment to maintaining the coalition were important. Commitment to the coalition was also important in the death penalty case, as was the black-and-white nature of the issue (which meant that no compromise was possible).

Like the Dutch and Japanese cases, the Turkish cases demonstrate the complexities of coalition politics and foreign policy. They certainly challenge the simplistic notions of how multiparty governance plays out in the decision-making processes and the foreign policy outcomes in parliamentary democracies. But they also clearly show that coalition politics matter. Even when the attempted constraints by junior parties are unsuccessful, the policy conflict can affect the timing of the decision and the stability of governance. In the death penalty case, for example, even though the Nationalist Action Party ultimately failed to prevent the EU-mandated reform, the party's position delayed the decision for many months and led to the collapse of the government. These cases also challenge some of the images of Turkish foreign policy in the 1990s: Not all foreign policy decision making was hijacked by ideologically nationalist or Islamist parties.

According to Robins, "With the exception of Germany, surely no other Western state has been as much affected by the recent changes in the international system as Turkey."[313] These systemic changes, however, were filtered through Turkey's domestic political institutions and actors. Ruled by coalition governments throughout the 1990s and into the new century, Turkey's reaction to its international environment was a product of partisan conflicts over Turkey's identity, role, and priorities in its foreign affairs.

# 7

# Challenging and Unpacking Images of Coalition Foreign Policy: Implications for International Relations and Governance

When the authority to make a country's foreign policy is divided among political parties, there are implications for decision making and for foreign policy behavior. The existing images of the effects of coalition politics on foreign policy offer alternative expectations of these implications. These expectations include the simplistic image that foreign policy by coalition is characterized by moderate, cooperative policy as a consequence of inherent constraints and the equally naive notion that coalitions are hijacked by ideologically extremist small parties that blackmail the cabinet into adopting aggressive foreign policy. There are also strong negative images of decision making by coalitions: They are expected to be poor policy-making bodies, with endemic deadlock and delay that can contribute to ineffective governance and even government instability. These expectations are widespread—in scholarship and in journalistic accounts—and are linked to various theoretical traditions and research programs in the study of politics and international relations. They are, however, rarely examined, despite the important decisions made by coalition cabinets that govern influential countries in world politics.

The central argument of this book has been that these images are incorrect and incomplete. The research presented in earlier chapters challenges these expectations of the effects of coalition politics on foreign policy and begins to unpack the patterns of policy and policy-making by multiparty cabinets as well as the underlying causal mechanisms that translate divided cabinet authority and policy disagreements into foreign policy decisions. In this conclusion, I assimilate the results from the chapters on Dutch, Japanese, and Turkish foreign policy and identify themes

# Challenging and Unpacking Images of Coalition Foreign Policy 233

and key factors in the presence of which different images of coalition politics are likely to prevail. I also return to the results from the quantitative studies (presented in chapter 3) and put them in the context of the theoretical perspectives. This chapter concludes with implications for the study and practice of international relations and with insights on broad issues of governance and institutional design.

## CHALLENGING IMAGES OF COALITION POLITICS AND FOREIGN POLICY

This book adopted a multimethodological approach to examine the existing images of foreign policy by coalitions. The quantitative, cross-national studies were important to establish the general differences in foreign policy behavior between multiparty and single-party cabinets. Past quantitative studies that investigated the democratic peace expectation of peaceful foreign policy by coalitions yielded mixed results. For this project, a quantitative study was designed to overcome limitations in previous research. Specifically, the assumption that the built-in constraints on coalitions operate only in the direction of peace was discarded, so that whether coalitions were more moderate or more extreme—in either the direction of peace or the direction of conflict—became the question. This study also investigated the effect of coalition politics on foreign policy broadly, using the WEIS events data set, which captures a full range of foreign policy behaviors, not just behaviors in conflict situations.

The findings from the first quantitative study challenge the democratic peace expectation and other images of coalition foreign policy. In the many events the study examined, coalition cabinets did behave significantly differently from single-party governments, although they were neither more conflictual (as was expected by some theoretical perspectives) nor more cooperative (as was expected by the logic of the democratic peace theory). Coalitions were nonetheless more extreme. This result also challenges the expectation that coalitions are so riddled by conflict that they can take only moderate, if any, action.

The second quantitative study was designed to assess the causes of extremity by comparing different types of coalition cabinets. The three characteristics of coalitions examined (cabinet strength, the number of parties in the coalition, and the ideological location of the junior partner) correspond to the three dominant explanations (diversion, diffusion, and hijacking) that have theoretical bases in both political science and social psychology. The findings were consistent with some of these explanations but challenged others. Consistent with the idea that coalitions diffuse authority and responsibility more easily, higher numbers of parties in coalitions were more likely to engage in extreme behavior generally and conflictual foreign policy more specifically in the events analyzed in this study. This finding suggests that fragmentation and diffusion of responsibility and accountability lead coalitions to riskier, aggressive behaviors. This study also found that coalitions with higher levels of parliamentary support were associated with foreign policy behaviors involving high levels of commitment, contrary to the diversionary theory. Finally, coalitions with rightist junior parties pursued more cooperative foreign policy. Although this result suggests a challenge to the expectation that ideologically right parties can hijack foreign policy in the direction of aggression, chapter 3 presented several operational and theoretical caveats to this finding.

Taken together, the quantitative analyses show that coalitions behave differently than single-party cabinets and that characteristics of these coalitions help to unpack what underlies these differences. While this information takes us much further down the road to an understanding of how coalition politics affects foreign policy, the results do not provide definitive answers and do not address the operating causal mechanisms and microfoundations assumed by existing images of coalitions. At the heart of these mechanisms lies the decision-making process. The comparative case studies in this book traced the process to specifically examine how disagreements between coalition parties affect foreign policy-making and choice. For each case study, I examined existing theoretical expectations and assumptions and discovered the most important factors that affected the outcome and process. The answers to the questions derived from these theories are summarized across the cases in table 7.1.

In general, the case studies demonstrate that coalition politics affected the process, outcome, or both in these disagreements between coalition partners. By tracing the process, a plausible case was made that events would have unfolded differently if foreign policy authority were not shared across political parties.

These cases also challenge the simple versions of images of coalition foreign policy. While half of the cases were cooperative, the others were conflictual or neutral or included both cooperative and conflictual behav-

## Challenging and Unpacking Images of Coalition Foreign Policy 235

iors. And while most outcomes were moderate, several were extreme. The expectation, based on the logic of the democratic peace, that multiple voices in the cabinet constrain governments from pursuing noncooperative and extreme foreign policies clearly is not supported by these cases. This result reinforces the finding in the first quantitative study.

Perhaps more important, while coalition parties attempted to constrain their partners from taking action in all twelve cases, in most of those cases, these constraints were not in the direction of peace. In many cases, junior

TABLE 7.1. Do the Cases Fit the Images of Coalition Politics and Foreign Policy?

| Questions | Categories and Number of Cases | | |
|---|---|---|---|
| Was the foreign policy cooperative or conflictual?[a] | Cooperative: 6 | Conflictual: 2 | Neutral/Both: 4 |
| Was the foreign policy extreme or moderate? | Moderate: 8 | Extreme: 4 | |
| Did coalition parties attempt to constrain the policy? | Yes: 12 | No: 0 | |
| Were attempted constraints in the direction of peace? | Yes: 5 | No: 7 | |
| Were the constraints successful? | Yes:[b] 5 | No: 7 | |
| Was the decision a compromise? | Yes: 4 | No: 8 | |
| Was there poor decision making? | Yes: 11 | No: 1 | |
| Was there good decision making? | Yes:[c] 10 | No: 2 | |

[a]The classification of cases as cooperative or conflictual is based on WEIS codings, as they are presented in the tables at the end of each country chapter. Some of the case studies discuss alternative interpretations of the foreign policy behavior, according to the historical or situational context of the case. In two cases, the WEIS coding was neutral; in two other cases, more than one foreign policy action resulted from the decision; at least one action was cooperative and one was conflictual in these cases.

[b]In order to simplify the presentation of the results, two cases (the Dutch Iraq case and the Turkish Islamic opening case) that were categorized as having "somewhat" successful constraint are classified as "successful" here. Some constraint was evident in both of these cases, even though the coalition partners were not able to completely constrain the other parties from taking foreign policy behaviors consistent with their policy positions.

[c]In order to simplify the presentation of the results, two cases (the Dutch cruise missile case and the Turkish death penalty case) that were categorized as having "somewhat" good decision making are classified as having good decision making here.

parties attempted to constrain their partners from making cooperative policy. This finding also challenges the assumption that constraints result in peaceful foreign policy. Instead, we see attempts to hijack foreign policy in the conflictual direction. Yet these attempted constraints did not always succeed. In fact, they failed in a majority of the cases. This result is inconsistent with both the democratic peace-constraint image and with the hijacking image of coalition politics.

The case studies also challenge the expectation that shared authority leads to excessive compromise. Compromise was the outcome in some of the cases, but not in the majority. The cases generally confirm the negative image of coalition decision making. Almost all of the cases featured examples of poor decision making that could be traced to coalition politics, with deadlock, delay, and general viscosity appearing most frequently. Yet all of the cases also showed signs of good decision making. Beyond meeting democratic standards of good governance by representing multiple viewpoints, the presence of additional positions prevented premature closure in some cases and led to divergent, creative policymaking in a few instances. And despite the differences among parties, some of the coalitions made historic, substantively meaningful decisions, and some did so in a timely fashion.

## KEY FACTORS IN COALITION FOREIGN POLICY DECISION MAKING

The case studies probed the reasons behind the process and outcomes for these decision-making episodes. This exercise was necessarily exploratory, given the level of theoretical development and understanding of coalition decision making, but it was guided by extant expectations, and it revealed some patterns across the cases. Table 7.2 summarizes the factors that emerged as important for explaining the outcomes in all twelve case studies. Although some explanations were limited to only one or two cases, other factors operated in several cases. These factors are distributed across the countries, indicating general patterns of the effects of coalition politics on foreign policy.

The explanations that occurred most frequently across the cases are party disunity, issue divisibility, locus of authority, political calculations, and consistency of the junior party's position. Parties that were divided internally were less able to advocate for or force their position or block advocacy by coalition partners. In some instances, such as the Helsinki Declaration, the embargo on South Africa, and the peacekeeping operations case, division in the senior party was important. In the Iraq case and the UN Security Council case, critical divisions occurred in the junior party.

The nature of the issue and the party disagreement over the issue were also important in a number of cases. When positions were irreconcilable, as in the Islamic Opening and peacekeeping operations cases, fragmented action resulted. When the issue was indivisible, as in the death penalty case, one side prevailed. Divisible issues, as in the embargo on South Africa and Helsinki Declaration cases, allowed the parties to make meaningful compromises. The locus of authority was also important. Where the decision took place (for example, if it was taken away from the foreign ministry, as in the customs union case; shifted to Parliament, as in the Afghanistan deployment and South African embargo cases; or moved outside of clear lines of coordination, as in the UN Security Council case) was critical for the results of the party disagreements.

Political calculations played a role in several cases. In the South African embargo and Golan Heights peacekeeping cases, for example, key players sacrificed policy positions to maintain power in the government. In the Afghanistan deployment case, political calculations arguably propelled the junior party to push the position to the point of coalition crisis. Political calculations are not the same as the "commitment to coalition" factor, which occurred in only two of the cases and refers to parties' loyalty to the

**TABLE 7.2. What Factors Explained the Case Study Outcomes?**

| Explanatory Factors | Distribution of Cases | | | |
| --- | --- | --- | --- | --- |
| | Netherlands | Japan | Turkey | Total |
| Party disunity | 2 | 2 | 1 | 5 |
| Issue divisibility | 1 | 1 | 3 | 5 |
| Locus of authority | 2 | 1 | 2 | 5 |
| Political calculations | | 2 | 3 | 5 |
| Consistency of jr. party | 2 | 1 | 1 | 4 |
| Jr. party threat | 2 | | | 2 |
| Commitment to coalition | | | 2 | 2 |
| Leadership style | | 1 | 1 | 2 |
| Coalition weakness | | 1 | | 1 |
| Formation stage of coalition | | 1 | | 1 |
| Rigidity | | | 1 | 1 |

coalition and its culture of consensus. Finally, when junior parties inconsistently argued their position, as in the customs union, Iraq, and Golan Heights cases, they failed completely to constrain their coalition partners. Consistent advocacy, as in the cruise missile case, helped junior parties influence foreign policy.

These dominant explanatory factors reflect institutional, ideational, psychological, and political aspects of decision making, suggesting that all of these aspects are key in our understanding of coalition politics and foreign policy. Moreover, three of these factors—party unity, locus of authority, and junior party consistency—also emerged as important explanations in my previous research on junior party influence in German and Israeli foreign policy. Özkeçeci-Taner's research also found that consistency, locus of authority (in terms of control over key ministries), and the ideological distance between political parties (which may relate to issue divisibility) were important for understanding when ideas are influential in Turkish foreign policy.[1] This finding provides further confidence that the results from this research are not unique to the cases and countries covered in this book.

Some of the factors are noteworthy because they appear in only one or two cases despite existing theoretical expectations. Threats to leave the coalition, for example, were important in only two cases, even though it is often assumed that junior parties (especially those in minimum winning coalitions) frequently use this threat—and use it successfully—to blackmail senior partners for policy outcomes. The weakness of the coalition played an important role in only one case, which is inconsistent with the diversionary theory as it has been applied to coalition politics and foreign policy.

Few clear patterns emerge if we examine these explanatory factors across the different outcomes of the cases. In other words, it is not clear that certain factors are associated with conflict, for example, and others are associated with cooperation. Most of the variables appear uniformly across cases of different outcomes and policy-making processes. The clearest distinction is between moderate and extreme cases: in six of the eight moderate cases, one or more of the coalition parties was internally divided; there was no party division in any of the four extreme cases. This finding reinforces the importance of party unity in coalition foreign policy and suggests that only unified parties are able to hijack the coalition, resist constraint, or logroll for extreme policies. The nature of the issue was also important in five of the eight moderate cases, and it was not important in all four of the extreme cases, although the issue was divisible in just some of the moderate cases. This finding suggests that moderate foreign policies can come from irreconcilable differences so that no meaningful decision can be made or compromises made between two compatible positions.

Interesting patterns appear when the cases are compared in terms of the three cabinet characteristics used in the second quantitative study. For example, the coalitions in cases of extreme foreign policy behavior involved more parties.[2] This finding is consistent with the quantitative study. However, the case studies that featured cooperative foreign policy also featured more parties, whereas higher numbers of parties were associated with conflictual foreign policy in the quantitative study.[3] Higher numbers of parties also occurred in cases with no constraints in the direction of peace, with unsuccessful constraints, and with no compromises.[4] The case studies do not offer clear clues as to why the number of parties in the coalition correlates with these different outcomes and processes, and the Japanese case of rice liberalization may be driving this distinction, with seven parties in the coalition.

Patterns are evident with regard to the strength of the coalition as measured by the percentage of parliamentary seats that all parties control. In the case studies, higher levels of support were associated with cooperative behaviors and with more moderate behaviors.[5] This finding is consistent with the diversionary expectation—that weak coalitions will be more extreme generally and more conflictual specifically. In contrast, in the quantitative study, higher parliamentary support was associated with foreign policy behaviors involving high levels of commitment, with no clear relationship to extremity and conflict.

The third cabinet characteristic examined in the quantitative study was ideological placement of the junior party. As with the quantitative data, junior parties to the right of senior parties were present in more cases of cooperation than of conflict.[6] Furthermore, rightist junior parties in the cases were associated with more extreme foreign policy, constraints not in the direction of peace, unsuccessful constraints, and no compromises.[7]

The case studies allow exploration of the reasons behind the unexpected finding on rightist junior parties and cooperative behavior. In chapter 3, I speculate that rightist junior parties may in fact not be more hawkish on foreign policy. The case studies demonstrate the complexities: the conservative junior parties in the Turkish case studies did advocate more hawkish foreign policies (such as the Welfare Party in the Islamic Opening case and the National Action party in the death penalty case), and their attempted constraints were not in the direction of peace. In Japan, however, the conservative junior party in the coalition in the rice liberalization case was advocating more cooperation in the form of liberalization and acquiescence to GATT. And in the peacekeeping cases, the conservative, rightist parties were also advocating cooperation (contribution to multilateral missions), but in the context of the political debate, this was a very conservative-nationalist position. The Netherlands adds another wrinkle to the relationship between ideological placement and specific policy positions. The "centrist" Liberals, who were junior parties in many coalitions, can be regarded as left of the senior party when in coalition with the Christian Democrats and often advocate the most hawkish positions in foreign policy, as seen in the case studies on South Africa, the cruise missile crisis, and Afghanistan. Thus, some junior parties in the quantitative study may have also been technically left of the senior party but still right of center on foreign policy issues.

Another explanation for the presence of rightist junior parties in cooperative cases is that they advocate more conflictual policies yet fail to have influence (as discussed in chapter 3). The Turkish cases are consistent with this explanation. In the customs union and the death penalty cases (the two cooperative cases with rightist junior parties), the conservative junior parties failed to influence their senior partners.[8] And one general finding is that more of the attempted constraints were unsuccessful than were successful. Something about rightist junior parties may create a backlash or boomerang effect, since their presence in the cases was associated with extreme foreign policies and no compromises.[9]

These results from the cases studies are not, of course, statistically significant given the small number of instances examined, but they do suggest patterns that might be generalizable. While each case has idiosyncratic elements, there is nothing to suggest that as a set, these cases are unique instances of coalition foreign policy-making. And all of the cabinet characteristics were meaningful in both the case studies and the quantitative studies, and some were in the same direction across these multiple methods. The findings from this research are not tidy; no single factor distinguishes one type of coalition foreign policy-making from another. Yet this research provides a much more detailed picture of the effects of coalition politics on foreign policy and begins to trace the causal mechanisms of how a divided cabinet negotiates its differences.

Future research should focus on the factors that were important in the empirical record of the cases and the quantitative analyses presented in this book. Party disunity, the nature of the issue and partisan positions, how the locus for decision-making authority is used and manipulated by political actors, political calculations for staying and leaving the coalition, and the consistency in the junior party's position should be the focus of subsequent studies. The number of coalition partners, the strength of the coalition, and the ideological placement and position of the players are also candidates for future research. Taken together, this list of factors suggests that institutional, political, psychological, and ideational aspects all play a part in coalition decision making. They are dynamic; how they play out in the decision-making process is key to the production of foreign policy by multiparty cabinets.

## THEORETICAL AND POLICY IMPLICATIONS (BRITAIN IS NOT IN "CRYOGENIC SUSPENDED ANIMATION")

Each of the case studies and each of the events in the quantitative analyses in this book has an alternative explanation. External pressures and relationships, public opinion, and leader beliefs, for example, no doubt affect Dutch, Japanese, Turkish, and other countries' foreign policies. Yet these other factors are funneled through the decision-making unit. The cases presented here clearly show that the actors who have the power to make foreign policy do not always agree. Their disagreement itself is evidence that factors exogenous to decision makers are not deterministic.

Recognition that foreign policy is contested and that it plays out in cultural, historical, and institutional contexts is not enough. After all, the images of how coalition politics affects foreign policy based on the democratic peace and diversionary theory acknowledge the importance of domestic political divisions. Yet they assume much about the nature and operation of those divisions, and as this book has demonstrated, these assumptions are often incorrect. Built-in institutional constraints are not always successful, attempted constraints are not necessarily in the direction of peace, ideologically extreme parties do not always hijack foreign policy, and divided coalitions can make meaningful and creative policies. Yet these assumptions undergird much research and expectations about coalition decision making.

To gain a full understanding of coalition foreign policy, attention to decision-making processes is necessary. In these processes, institutional, ideational, psychological, and political factors shape contestation, choice, and behavior. The broadest theoretical implication from this book is that decision-making processes are foundational to international relations. They are not a separate area of inquiry but are the ground for all else.[10] In the research presented here, important world issues of trade, peacekeeping, shaming and sanctions, military buildup, war, governance, regional and political integration, ideological alliances, and diffusion of norms hinged on foreign policy choices, which in turn hinged on how coalition partners negotiated their differences. More specifically, this book reinforces arguments for the importance of partisanship, ideas, domestic structures, and group-level dynamics.

Although this book has focused on foreign policy and on states, its insights can be applied to other policy domains and to other types of actors. Although cabinets might be more insulated from domestic pressures on foreign policy issues, there is no reason to believe that the consequences of coalition disagreement are not similar in domestic policy disputes. Indeed, some of the cases in this book could be classified as domestic policy (e.g., the Turkey death penalty case and Japan's liberalization of its rice imports). As discussed in chapter 2, research on cabinets in comparative politics has paid little attention to decision-making dynamics and the consequences of a divided cabinet for either foreign or domestic policies, although correlational, quantitative studies have found that coalitions are associated with more extreme spending policies.

More broadly, similar effects of disagreements in a policy-making group may occur in single-party cabinets and other types of decision units. Coalition cabinets are distinct from single-party cabinets (as demonstrated in Study 1 in chapter 3), but this standard dichotomous categorization may mask what is more of a dimension of "coalitionness." According to Nousiainen and Blondel, "There are many types of coalitions and what appears in the first instance to be a dichotomy is in reality a continuous dimension. Governments are not only of the single-party or the coalition type: they have, in a sense, more or less of a coalition character, as coalitions can be more or less extreme, more or less ideologically diverse, and composed of partners who are more or less equal."[11] Single-party cabinets divided by factions with policy disagreements, for example, may behave similarly to the coalitions in this study. Small advisory groups, town councils, committees of bureaucratic agencies, and international organizations with national or organizational veto players may also exhibit similar policy-making processes and outcomes. Extensions of this book's approach to these other decision-making forums have the potential to reshape the way students of politics think about policy disagreements.

From the standpoint of policymakers, this book offers several takeaways. First, this research provides policymakers who deal with coalition governments a more nuanced understanding of what is going on when coalition partners disagree. My research questions the stereotypical images of coalitions that policymakers may hold. Moreover, it gives leaders and policy analysts a framework within which to focus on key factors so that they can better track the other in any two-level game. When Paul Bremer, former U.S. ambassador to the Netherlands, threatened the Dutch government if it did not commit troops to Afghanistan, some in the U.S. government understood that his remarks might only complicate the interparty negotiations on the policy; others, apparently including Bremer, did not understand this point. When other actors deal with Israel in the Middle East peace process, try to build multinational alliances for intervention and peacekeeping missions, or pressure Ireland to deal with its economic crisis, knowing the nature of the decision-making conditions important in the cases and events in this book will help them understand and predict foreign policies of concern to other policymakers.

This research suggests that policymakers who are part of coalitions consider these factors when making bids for or blocking influence. Small junior parties can affect policy, but their influence is not automatic, even with threats to leave the coalition. Party unity is important for influence, as is party consistency. The case studies demonstrate that fighting over procedures—where the decision will take place—can be an effective strategy in coalitions, since procedures can matter to the outcome of the policy. Other research suggests that procedural manipulation is an especially attractive and effective tool for junior parties because it takes less status and authority to initiate these changes than substantive changes and because indirect changes provoke less opposition from the senior party than would direct policy attacks.[12]

Finally, this book provides some lessons for general issues of governance and institutional design. Coalition cabinets provide an excellent laboratory for investigations of the promises and pitfalls of dissent. How many players should be at the table? What are the trade-offs between diversity and dissent? These enduring questions apply to many levels of governance—local, national, and international—that have authority over a variety of political issues and are critical to questions of effective governance and institutional design.

Electoral systems are often created amid debate over the trade-offs between the enhanced legitimacy that comes with proportional representation and multiple voices in the government, on the one hand, and the coherence of vision and purpose and stability associated with majority rule, on the other hand. Arguments citing the drawbacks of coalition cabinets stemming from policy conflict and weak rule frequently invoke foreign policy scenarios—coalitions are seen as too ineffective to deal with severe economic development challenges or security threats. Weimar Germany and Fourth Republic France are the negative anecdotes used to warn against the dangers of a coalition government in, for example, Iraq or Afghanistan. They may become threats to others or threats to themselves. Or they may be unable to deal with pressing international issues and pursue national interests. After the 2010 British election, when a coalition governed the country for the first time in seventy years, the *New York Times* predicted, "The government is . . . likely to be less influential on the international stage than its predecessors. As a Tory-Liberal alliance could be broken by arguments over the European Union, Britain's relationship with Brussels will be placed in cryogenic suspended animation with the label, 'Do Not Waken Before 2015.'"[13]

The research here suggests that coalitions are not as bad as they are often portrayed in these debates. There is certainly some truth to the image that coalitions can be ineffective—they are prone to deadlock and delay. But they also show signs of good decision making that might have not occurred without the multiple viewpoints inherent to their design. In short, Britain will not be in "cryogenic suspended animation." Something will "wake" it before 2015, and it is not doomed to deadlock or even compromise. How the British coalition will play its role on the international stage and pursue the national interest will turn on key factors presented in the research in this book.

In the study of foreign policy, scholars continue to stress the dangers of a lack of multiple advocacy. Schafer and Crichlow's study of groupthink in recent U.S. foreign policy clearly shows the risks of groups that lack or discourage dissent; these groups tend to make poor policies.[14] Although coalition partners do not always disagree on foreign policy, and disagreement can certainly occur in all types of governments, coalitions have built-in conditions that foster disagreement. By design, they allow for the representation of multiple and sometimes minority views. Clashing views can now be seen in coalitions governing states around the globe, and coalitions may govern many more countries in the future. How disagreements are negotiated provides the foundations for state choices and for international relations.

# Appendix: Goldstein Conflict-Cooperation Scale for WEIS Event Data

| Event Type | Weight |
|---|---|
| Military attack; clash; assault | −10.0 |
| Seize position or possessions | −9.2 |
| Nonmilitary destruction/injury | −8.7 |
| Noninjury destruction action | −8.3 |
| Armed force mobilization, exercise, display; military buildup | −7.6 |
| Break diplomatic relations | −7.0 |
| Threat with force specified | −7.0 |
| Ultimatum; threat with negative sanction and time limit | −6.9 |
| Threat with specific negative nonmilitary sanction | −5.8 |
| Reduce or cut off aid or assistance; act to punish/deprive | −5.6 |
| Nonmilitary demonstration, walk out on | −5.2 |
| Order person or personnel out of country | −5.0 |
| Expel organization or group | −4.9 |
| Issue order or command, insist, demand compliance | −4.9 |
| Threat without specific negative sanction stated | −4.4 |
| Detain or arrest person(s) | −4.4 |
| Reduce routine international activity; recall officials | −4.1 |
| Refuse; oppose; refuse to allow | −4.0 |
| Turn down proposal; reject protest, demand, threat | −4.0 |
| Halt negotiation | −3.8 |
| Denounce; denigrate; abuse | −3.4 |
| Give warning | −3.0 |
| Issue formal complaint or protest | −2.4 |
| Charge; criticize; blame; disapprove | −2.2 |
| Cancel or postpone planned event | −2.2 |
| Make complaint (not formal) | −1.9 |
| Grant asylum | −1.1 |
| Deny an attribute policy, action, role, or position | −1.1 |
| Deny an accusation | −0.9 |
| Comment on situation | −0.2 |

| Event Type | Weight |
|---|---|
| Urge or suggest action or policy | −0.1 |
| Explicit decline to policy | −0.1 |
| Request action; call for | −0.1 |
| Explain or state policy; state future position | 0.0 |
| Ask for information | 0.1 |
| Surrender, yield to order, submit to arrest | 0.6 |
| Yield position; retreat; evacuate | 0.6 |
| Meet with; send note | 1.0 |
| Entreat; plead; appeal to; beg | 1.2 |
| Offer proposal | 1.5 |
| Express regret; apologize | 1.8 |
| Visit; go to | 1.9 |
| Release and/or return persons or property | 1.9 |
| Admit wrongdoing; apologize, react statement | 2.0 |
| Give state invitation | 2.5 |
| Assure; reassure | 2.8 |
| Receive visit; host | 2.8 |
| Suspend sanctions; end punishment; call truce | 2.9 |
| Agree to future action or procedure, to meet or to negotiate | 3.0 |
| Ask for policy assistance | 3.4 |
| Ask for material assistance | 3.4 |
| Praise, hail, applaud, extend condolences | 3.4 |
| Endorse other's policy or position; give verbal support | 3.6 |
| Promise other future support | 4.5 |
| Promise own policy support | 4.5 |
| Promise material support | 5.2 |
| Grant privilege; diplomatic recognition; de facto relations | 5.4 |
| Give other assistance | 6.5 |
| Make substantive agreement | 6.5 |
| Extend economic aid; give, buy, sell, own, borrow | 7.4 |
| Extend military assistance | 8.3 |

*Source:* Modified from Joshua S. Goldstein, "A Conflict-Cooperation Scale for WEIS Events Data," *Journal of Conflict Resolution* 36 (1992): 369–85.

# Notes

## Preface

1. Stieg Larsson, *The Girl Who Kicked the Hornet's Nest* (New York: Knopf, 2010), 282.

## Chapter 1

1. "Pressure Mounts"; Harding, "Analysis."
2. "Pressure Mounts."
3. "Pressure Mounts."
4. "Netherlands to Send More Troops."
5. Molly Moore, "Dutch Debate."
6. Molly Moore, "After Long Debate"; interview, U.S. embassy personnel, the Hague, March 2006.
7. Kulish, "Dutch Pull-Out."
8. Nousiainen and Blondel, "Conclusion," 307.
9. Blondel and Müller-Rommel, "Introduction," 1.
10. Müller, Bergman, and Strøm, "Coalition Theory."
11. A single-party minority government is another possible outcome when no single party controls a parliamentary majority. For the factors that promote minority government, see Strøm, *Minority Government*. In addition, the largest party in the parliament does not necessarily form a coalition. On the significance and distinctiveness of small parties in coalitions, see Bolleyer, "Small Parties."
12. Lanny W. Martin and Vanberg, "Coalition Policymaking," 94.
13. Hagan, "Does Decision Making Matter?"; Ripsman, *Peacemaking;* Elman, "Unpacking Democracy"; Susan Peterson, "How Democracies Differ"; Perkovich, *India's Nuclear Bomb*.
14. Müller, Bergman, and Strøm, "Coalition Theory," 8.
15. Putnam, "Diplomacy."
16. For other recent arguments consistent with this approach, see Hagan, "Does Decision Making Matter?"; Margaret G. Hermann, "How Decision

Units"; Hudson, "Foreign Policy Analysis"; Margaret G. Hermann and Kegley, "Rethinking Democracy"; Schafer and Crichlow, *Groupthink.*

17. Rathbun, *Partisan Interventions,* 2.
18. Rathbun, *Partisan Interventions,* 6. Rathbun argues that although international norms are undoubtedly important in his case studies of humanitarian interventions, "equally important, however, is cross-national and cross-temporal variation in its embrace. Who takes up these principles and puts them into practice?"
19. Schuster and Maier, "Rift"; see also Therien and Noel, "Political Parties."
20. Rathbun, *Partisan Interventions,* 8.
21. Kaarbo, "Power and Influence."
22. See, for example, Adler, *Power of Ideology;* Finnemore, *National Interests;* Wendt, *Social Theory;* Haas, *When Knowledge Is Power;* Judith Goldstein and Keohane, *Ideas and Foreign Policy;* Katzenstein, *Culture of National Security.*
23. Rathbun, *Partisan Interventions,* 7.
24. Özkeçeci-Taner, *Role of Ideas;* Özkeçeci-Taner, "Impact."
25. Özkeçeci-Taner, "Impact," 250; see also Özkeçeci-Taner, "Role."
26. Strøm, *Minority Government,* 116–20; see also Damgaard, "Cabinet Termination," 308.
27. Exceptions include Hagan et al., "Foreign Policy by Coalition"; Margaret G. Hermann, "How Decision Units"; Özkeçeci-Taner, "Impact"; Kaarbo, "Power and Influence"; Kaarbo, "Influencing Peace"; Özkeçeci-Taner, "Role."
28. Chapter 2 provides details and full references for the images of coalition politics discussed in this section.
29. Maoz and Russett, "Normative and Structural Causes."
30. Chapter 2 provides details and full references on this point.
31. The quantitative studies in this project were conducted jointly with Ryan Beasley.

## Chapter 2

1. Müller, Bergman, and Strøm, "Coalition Theory."
2. Blondel and Müller-Rommel, "Introduction," 4.
3. Frognier, "Single Party/Coalition Distinction," 43.
4. For reviews, see Müller and Strøm, "Coalition Governance"; Timmermans, *High Politics.*
5. Gallagher, Laver, and Mair, *Representative Government,* 4th ed.
6. For overviews, see Laver and Budge, *Party Policy;* Laver and Schofield, *Multiparty Government;* Lanny W. Martin and Stevenson, "Government Formation"; Müller, Bergman, and Strøm, "Coalition Theory."
7. There are too many studies in this area to cite here. Some of the seminal and/or recent works include de Swann, *Coalition Theories;* Gamson, "Theory"; Riker, *Theory;* Axelrod, *Conflict of Interest;* Strøm, Budge, and Laver, "Constraints"; Strøm and Swindle, "Strategic Parliamentary Dissolution"; Tavits,

"Role"; Laver and Schofield, *Multiparty Government;* Mitchell and Nyblade, "Government Formation." According to Laver and Schofield, *Multiparty Government*, research on coalitions has typically fallen into two categories: the "European politics" tradition of cross-national empirical research and the "game-theoretic tradition." Good examples of the "European politics" tradition are the country-by-country volumes edited by Laver and Budge, *Party Policy*, and Müller and Strøm, *Coalition Governments*. A good example of the game-theoretic tradition is Laver and Shepsle, *Making and Breaking Governments*.

8. Research on the distribution of ministries has revolved around how proportional the distribution is to each parties' electoral and parliamentary strength and the salience and value of particular ministries. See, for example, Warwick, "Coalition Policy"; Warwick and Druckman, "Portfolio Salience"; Druckman and Warwick, "Missing Piece"; see also Laver and Schofield, *Multiparty Government;* Verzichelli, "Portfolio Allocation." For work on coalition agreements, see Strøm and Müller, "Keys"; Müller and Strøm, "Coalition Agreements."

9. Gallagher, Laver and Mair, *Representative Government*, 4th ed., 410. See also Saafeld, "Institutions."

10. Warwick, *Government Survival*.

11. Lupia and Strøm, "Coalition Termination"; Laver and Shepsle, *Making and Breaking Governments;* Tavits, "Role"; Damgaard, "Cabinet Termination."

12. Many comparativists have made this observation. See, for example, Lanny W. Martin, "Government Agenda"; 445–46; Strøm and Müller, "Keys"; Müller and Strøm, "Coalition Governance"; and most recently Müller, Bergman, and Strøm, "Coalition Theory."

13. Baylis, *Governing by Committee*, 62.

14. Andeweg, "Centrifugal Forces," 125.

15. Warwick, "Coalition Policy," 1214.

16. Timmermans, *High Politics*.

17. Hofferbert and Klingemann, "Policy Impact"; Strøm, "Behavioral Theory."

18. Müller and Strøm, *Coalition Governments*.

19. Müller, Bergman, and Strøm, "Coalition Theory."

20. Blondel and Müller-Rommel, "Introduction."

21. Frognier, "Single Party/Coalition Distinction," 64.

22. Lanny W. Martin, "Government Agenda," 457. The "ministerial government" argument is often attributed to Laver and Shepsle, *Making and Breaking Governments*.

23. Lanny W. Martin, "Government Agenda," 457.

24. Gallagher, Laver, and Mair, *Representative Government*, 4th ed, 388.

25. Bawn and Rosenbluth, "Short versus Long Coalitions," 262.

26. Bawn and Rosenbluth, "Short versus Long Coalitions."

27. Iversen and Soskice, "Electoral Institutions."

28. Hofferbert and Klingemann, "Policy Impact."

29. See Russett, *Controlling the Sword*, 89; Maoz and Russett, "Normative and Structural Causes"; Owen, *Liberal Peace;* Bueno de Mesquita et al., "Institutional Explanation"; Rosato, "Flawed Logic."
30. Maoz and Russett, "Normative and Structural Causes," 626.
31. Ripsman, *Peacemaking*, 46.
32. Auerswald, "Inward Bound"; Elman, "Unpacking Democracy"; Ireland and Gartner, "Time to Fight"; Reiter and Tillman, "Public, Legislative, and Executive Constraints"; Leblang and Chan, "Explaining Wars"; Glenn Palmer, London, and Regan, "What's Stopping You?"
33. Auerswald, "Inward Bound," 477–78.
34. Auerswald, "Inward Bound," 488.
35. Auerswald, "Inward Bound," 489.
36. Elman, "Unpacking Democracy," 101.
37. Elman, "Unpacking Democracy," 121.
38. Elman, "Unpacking Democracy," 122–23.
39. Prins and Sprecher, "Institutional Constraints," 275.
40. Hagan, *Political Opposition*, 27.
41. Stinnett, "International Uncertainty."
42. Levy, "Diversionary Theory."
43. Hagan, *Political Opposition*, 30–31.
44. Hanreider and Auton, *Foreign Policies*.
45. Prins and Sprecher, "Institutional Constraints," 275.
46. Susan Peterson, "How Democracies Differ," 17–18.
47. Elman, "Unpacking Democracy," 97.
48. Kaarbo, "Power and Influence"; Kaarbo, "Influencing Peace"; Kaarbo and Lantis, "'Greening.'"
49. Browne, "Considerations"; Hofferbert and Klingemann, "Policy Impact."
50. For a discussion of this strategy in the context of international negotiations, see Lindell and Persson, "Paradox."
51. Wallfish and Segal, "Cabinet Approves Treaty."
52. Maoz, "Framing," 77; see also Hoyt, "Political Manipulation"; Garrison, *Games Advisors Play*.
53. Asmus, *Politics;* Saafeld, "West German Bundestag."
54. Maoz, "Framing."
55. This idea is consistent with research on minority influence in small groups; see Wood et al., "Processes"; Kaarbo and Beasley, "Political Perspective."
56. Prins and Sprecher, "Institutional Constraints"; Glenn Palmer, London, and Regan, "What's Stopping You?"
57. Ireland and Gartner, "Time to Fight"; Reiter and Tillman, "Public, Legislative, and Executive Constraints"; Glenn Palmer, London, and Regan, "What's Stopping You?"; Clare, "Ideological Fractionalization."
58. Leblang and Chan, "Explaining Wars."
59. Charles F. Hermann, "International Crisis"; Vertzberger, *World;* Verbeek, *Decision-Making*.

60. Kaarbo and Lantis, "'Greening.'"
61. Elman, "Unpacking Democracy," 125.
62. Clare, "Ideological Fractionalization."
63. This chapter's comparison of psychological and political perspectives on coalition politics has also been published in Kaarbo, "Coalition Cabinet Decision Making."
64. Blondel and Müller-Rommel, "Introduction," 1.
65. 't Hart, Stern, and Sundelius, "Foreign Policymaking," 5.
66. Brown, *Group Processes*.
67. Myers and Lamm, "Group Polarization Phenomenon," 603.
68. Myers and Lamm, "Group Polarization Phenomenon"; Brauer and Judd, "Group Polarization."
69. Vertzberger, "Collective Risk Taking," 281–82. Vertzberger notes that "it is not the actual probability of adversarial consequences of the decision (policy risk) that is reduced, but the anticipated adversarial personal consequences to the decision maker (political risk)."
70. Vertzberger, "Collective Risk Taking," 282.
71. Janis, *Victims*.
72. Metselaar and Verbeek, "Beyond Decision Making," 109.
73. Brown, *Group Processes*, 219.
74. Brown, *Group Processes*. Other explanations of group polarization include group decision rules, interpersonal comparison, familiarization, and intergroup differentiation. For reviews, see Myers and Lamm, "Group Polarization Phenomenon"; Vertzberger, "Collective Risk Taking"; Brown, *Group Processes*.
75. Myers and Lamm, "Group Polarization Phenomenon," 611.
76. Vertzberger, "Collective Risk Taking," 284. For an example of the persuasive ability of a committed minority in Israeli cabinet deliberations during the Israeli-Egyptian war of attrition, see Maoz, "Framing."
77. Maass and Clark, "Hidden Impact"; Crano, "Social Influence."
78. Milgram, "Behavioral Study"; Milgram, "Some Conditions."
79. Asch, "Opinions"; Asch, "Studies."
80. Moscovici, *Social Influence;* see also Moskowitz and Chaiken, "Mediators." Moskowitz and Chaiken suggest that Moscovici's ideas provided a "European perspective" to correct the North American bias on power, pressure, and conformity ("Mediators," 60).
81. Moscovici, *Social Influence*, 45.
82. Brown, *Group Processes*, 145.
83. De Dreu and De Vries, *Group Consensus*, 3. For a recent review on Moscovici-inspired research and dual-process models of social influence, see Wood, "Attitude Change"; Crano and Seyranian, "Majority and Minority Influence"; Crano and Prislin, "Attitudes and Persuasion."
84. Levine and Kaarbo, "Minority Influence."
85. Kerr, "Is It What One Says?," 207.
86. Kerr, "Is It What One Says?," 207.

87. Tindale, Sheffey, and Scott, "Framing." More evidence of this idea comes from research on jury decision making; see Tindale et al., "Shared Representations"; Kerr and MacCoun, "Effects"; Christine M. Smith, Tindale, and Anderson, "Impact," 189.

88. De Dreu and Beersma, "Minority Influence."

89. Clark and Maass, "Social Categorization"; Clark, "Few Parallels."

90. This research in social psychology is consistent with recent work in foreign policy decision making on problem representations. Studies of political decision making suggest that the ways in which individuals and groups represent a problem is key to understanding the policy choices that are considered and eventually chosen. Scholars who have examined the role of problem representation in the group setting (for example, Burnstein and Berbaum, "Stages"; Sylvan and Thorson, "Ontologies"; Beasley, "Collective Interpretations") have noted that much of the group process revolves around negotiation among competing problem representations rather than among competing policy choices.

91. For a review of research on personality factors in negotiation, see Spector, "Negotiation."

92. Morton Deutsch and Shichman, "Conflict"; Fisher, *Social Psychology;* Bazerman et al., "Negotiation."

93. Spector, "Negotiation"; Jervis, "Deterrence and Perception"; Morton Deutsch and Shichman, "Conflict"; Bazerman et al., "Negotiation."

94. For a review, see Bazerman et al., "Negotiation."

95. Bazerman et al., "Negotiation," 301.

96. 't Hart, "From Analysis to Reform."

97. 't Hart, "From Analysis to Reform"; Randall Peterson, "Directive Leadership Style"; Verbeek, *Decision-Making;* Schafer and Crichlow, *Groupthink.*

98. Janis, *Victims.*

99. See, for example, Gaenslen, "Democracy vs. Efficiency."

100. Schafer and Crichlow, *Groupthink;* see also Randall Peterson, "Directive Leadership Style."

101. The link between the quality of the decision and its outcome is often questioned. Nevertheless, those who have directly investigated the link between the quality of the decision-making process and the quality of the outcome have found support for Janis's original proposition. See Herek, Janis, and Huth, "Decisionmaking"; Randall Peterson, "Directive Leadership Style"; Schafer and Crichlow, "Process-Outcome Connection"; Schafer and Crichlow, *Groupthink.*

102. Perhaps as a result of these negative judgments, coalition formation often creates a great deal of uncertainty among economic actors in parliamentary democracies, which can, in turn, affect economic outcomes such as exchange rate volatility. See Hallerberg and Von Hagen, "Electoral Institutions"; Will H. Moore and Mukherjee, "Coalition Government Formation"; Laver and Shepsle, *Making and Breaking Governments.*

103. Andeweg, "Centrifugal Forces"; Gallagher, Laver, and Mair, *Representative Government*, 3rd ed.
104. Charles F. Hermann, "Avoiding Pathologies," 189.
105. Destler, "Comment," 789.
106. Gaenslen, "Democracy vs. Efficiency."
107. Hagan, *Political Opposition;* Elman, "Unpacking Democracy"; Hagan et al.,"Foreign Policy by Coalition"; Ripsman, *Peacemaking.*
108. Prins and Sprecher, "Institutional Constraints," 274.
109. Elman, "Unpacking Democracy," 103.
110. Hagan, *Political Opposition.*
111. Hagan, *Political Opposition,* 26.
112. Ripsman, *Peacemaking,* 219.
113. Elman, "Unpacking Democracy," 102.
114. See Hagan, *Political Opposition,* 26–27; Ahn, "Government-Party Coordination"; Berger, "Alliance Politics"; Green, *Japan's Reluctant Realism.*
115. Gallhofer, Sairs, and Voogt, "From Individual Preference," 168.
116. Sathe, "For a Directly Elected President."
117. Lardeyret, "Problem," 88.
118. See, for example, Lardeyret, "Problem"; Quade, "PR and Democratic Statecraft"; for a summary of this argument, see Powell, *Elections.*
119. Linz, "Virtues"; Blondel and Müller-Rommel, "Introduction"; for a summary of this argument, see Powell, *Elections.*
120. Blondel and Müller-Rommel, "Introduction," 4.
121. Blondel, "Introduction," 3.
122. Dodd, *Politics,* 103.
123. Andeweg, "Centrifugal Forces."
124. Kameda and Sugimori, "Psychological Entrapment," 284, quoting Janis, *Victims,* 215. For a summary of the benefits of advocacy in small groups, see Gaenslen, "Democracy vs. Efficiency," 25.
125. Nemeth and Kwan, "Minority Influence."
126. Butera and Mugny, "Conflicts," 164–65.
127. Robin Martin and Hewstone, "Afterthoughts," 30.
128. Nemeth and Chiles, "Modeling Courage"; De Dreu and Beersma, "Minority Influence."
129. Gruenfeld, "Status"; Gruenfeld, Thomas-Hunt, and Kim, "Cognitive Flexibility."
130. Pérez and Mugny, "Paradoxical Effects"; De Dreu and De Vries, "Numerical Support"; Crano and Chen, "Leniency Contract."
131. De Dreu et al., "Convergent and Divergent Processing," 329.
132. Schweiger, Sandberg, and Ragan, "Group Approaches"; Schwenk, "Effects"; Williams and O'Reilly, "Demography and Diversity"; Dooley and Fryxell, "Attaining Decision Quality"; Randall Peterson et al., "Group Dynamics."
133. De Dreu and Beersma, "Minority Influence," 274.

134. Billings and Hermann, "Problem Identification"; Beasley et al., "People and Processes."
135. Kameda and Sugimori, "Psychological Entrapment," 284.
136. Alvaro and Crano, "Indirect Minority Influence."
137. Brockner and Rubin, *Entrapment*.
138. Kameda and Sugimori, "Psychological Entrapment."

## Chapter 3

1. For a history of mixed-method approaches, see Tashakkori and Teddlie, *Mixed Methodology;* Tashakkori and Teddlie, *Handbook*.
2. Levy, "Qualitative Methods," 447.
3. Tarrow, "Bridging"; Levy, "Qualitative Methods," 447; see also Tashakkori and Teddlie, *Mixed Methodology*.
4. Lieberman, "Nested Analysis," 436. Comparativists have recently suggested that "coalition studies are well suited for 'nested analysis'—which implies moving back and forth between statistical analyses and case study research."
5. Prins and Sprecher, "Institutional Constraints"; Glenn Palmer, London, and Regan, "What's Stopping You?"; Ireland and Gartner, "Time to Fight"; Reiter and Tillman, "Public, Legislative, and Executive Constraints"; Leblang and Chan, "Explaining Wars."
6. One exception is Clare, "Ideological Fractionalization."
7. Prins and Sprecher, "Institutional Constraints"; Ireland and Gartner, "Time to Fight"; Reiter and Tillman, "Public, Legislative, and Executive Constraints"; Glenn Palmer, London, and Regan, "What's Stopping You?"
8. Leblang and Chan, "Explaining Wars."
9. Charles A. McClelland, *Theory and the International System* (New York: Macmillan, 1966); Charles A. McClelland, *The Anticipation of International Crises: Prospects for Theory and Research* (Fort Belvoir, Va.: Defense Technical Information Center, 1976); Rodney G. Tomlinson, "World Event/Interaction Survey (WEIS) Coding Manual" (Manuscript, Department of Political Science, U.S. Naval Academy, Annapolis, 1993).
10. This study was previously published in Kaarbo and Beasley, "Taking It to the Extreme."
11. Because of extensive missing data for 1990 and 1991, this analysis does not include these years.
12. The sources used were Ahmad, *Turkish Experiment;* Close, *Greece;* Derbyshire and Derbyshire, *Encyclopedia;* Dodd, *Politics;* Dodd, *Crisis;* Hale, *Turkish Foreign Policy;* Hideo, *Power Shuffles;* Mershon, *Costs;* Moon and Sharmon, *Australian Politics;* Müller and Strøm, *Coalition Governments;* Roozendaal, *Cabinets;* Strøm, *Minority Government*.
13. Joshua S. Goldstein, "Conflict-Cooperation Scale." See appendix for complete scale.

14. Absolute values of the cooperation-conflict scales were used so that both the highest levels of conflict and the highest levels of cooperation received the same score (+10).

15. Schrodt and Gerner, "Event Data Analysis."

16. East, "Size."

17. The following action categories were coded as low commitment: comment, consult, approve, promise, agree, request, propose, reject, accuse, protest, deny, demand, warn, threaten. The action categories coded as high commitment were: yield, grant, reward, demonstrate, reduce relations, expel, seize, force.

18. The variables Commitment and Extremity of Behavior are correlated (Pearson correlation .694) but are not identical.

19. J. David Singer, Stuart Bremer, and John Stuckey, "Capability Distribution, Uncertainty, and Major Power War, 1820–1965," in *Peace, War, and Numbers*, ed. Bruce Russett (Beverly Hills, Calif.: Sage, 1972), 19–48; J. David Singer, "Reconstructing the Correlates of War Data Set on Material Capabilities of States, 1816–1985," *International Interactions* 14 (1987): 556–76.

20. East, "Size."

21. Monty G. Marshall and Keith Jaggers, *Polity IV Project* (College Park, Md.: Center for International Development and Conflict Management, 2002). Not all of the targets of the actions were states. All nonstate actors were therefore not coded for this control variable, and these events were not included in the analysis of cooperative behavior.

22. A separate analysis with all the events treated equally was also performed. In this analysis, coalition cabinets were significantly related to conflictual behavior, extremity in terms of conflict-cooperation, and high commitment behaviors. These results are presented in full in Kaarbo and Beasley, "Taking It to the Extreme," but are omitted here because of the disproportionate influence of Israel, Great Britain, and West Germany. In an additional set of analyses, all events, unweighted and unaggregated, except those in which the actor was Germany, Israel, and the United Kingdom were examined. Leblang and Chan, "Explaining Wars" likewise omit Israel from their analyses of war involvement for similar reasons. This analysis revealed the same pattern as the weighted analyses. With the three most dominant actors omitted, across 7,691 events, the relationship between cabinet type and level of conflict-cooperation is no longer significant ($p = .5$). The relationships between cabinet type and extremity of behavior, however, remain significant. As before, coalitions are more likely to engage in more extreme conflict-cooperation behaviors ($n = 10,106$; $p = .003$) and more extreme commitment behavior ($n = 10,454$; $p = .03$).

23. The CINC data are annual. In those instances when a government was in power through two or more calendar years, the average CINC value was used.

24. The mean number of events for the 217 cabinets was 123.

25. Kaarbo, Beasley, and Cantir, "Explaining."

26. See Kaarbo, "Influencing Peace"; Kaarbo, "Power and Influence."

27. Hofferbert and Klingemann, "Policy Impact."
28. Zaller, "Information."
29. Glenn Palmer, London, and Regan, "What's Stopping You?," 5, citing Eichenberg, *Public Opinion;* Klingemann, Hofferbert, and Budge, *Parties;* Bjereld and Ekengren, "Foreign Policy Dimensions"; Schultz, *Democracy.*
30. Glenn Palmer, London, and Regan, "What's Stopping You?," found that the political orientation of the cabinet was a significant predictor of state behavior in militarized disputes. As they hypothesized, right governments were more likely to be involved in militarized disputes than were left governments, but left governments were more likely to escalate disputes than were right governments. See also Rathbun, *Partisan Interventions,* 21–25.
31. Glenn Palmer, London, and Regan, "What's Stopping You?," 11.
32. Glenn Palmer, London, and Regan, "What's Stopping You?," n. 22.
33. Clare, "Ideological Fractionalization."
34. Sources used to code for critical party and ideological position are *Keesing's Record of World Events* (Cambridge, UK: Kessing's Worldwide, various years); Gould and Ganguly, *India Votes;* Mershon, *Costs;* Moon and Sharmon, *Australian Politics;* Müller and Strøm, *Coalition Governments;* Strøm, *Minority Government;* Dodd, *Politics;* Dodd, *Crisis;* Ahmad, *Turkish Experiment;* Close, *Greece;* Adam Carr, *The Australian Election Archive* (2004; www.elections.uwa.edu.au); W. Nordsieck, *Parties and Elections in Europe* (2004; www.parties-and-elections.de); Huber and Inglehart, "Expert Interpretations"; Kalaycioglu, "Elections"; Woldendorp, Keman, and Budge, *Party Government;* Rahat, "Determinants." For the majority of the countries, this study used tables from Müller and Strøm, *Coalition Governments,* which relies on Laver and Hunt, *Policy and Party Competition,* and the contributors to Laver and Hunt's volume to classify parties' ideological orientation. Placement was based on the parties' positions on "pro public ownership vs. anti public ownership" or "increase services vs. cut taxes" policy scales. I thank Binnur Özkeçeci-Taner for her help with Turkey.
35. Sources used to code the percentage of seats and the number of parties are Woldendorp, Keman, and Budge, *Party Government; Keesing's Record of World Events;* Gould and Ganguly, *India Votes;* Mershon, *Costs;* Moon and Sharmon, *Australian Politics;* Müller and Strøm, *Coalition Governments;* Strøm, *Minority Government;* Dodd, *Crisis;* Dodd, *Politics;* Ahmad, *Turkish Experiment;* Close, *Greece;* Carr, *Australian Election Archive;* Nordsieck, *Parties and Elections;* Huber and Inglehart, "Expert Interpretations"; Kalaycioglu, "Elections." I thank Binnur Özkeçeci-Taner for her help with Turkey.
36. East, "Size."
37. An unweighted analysis was also performed with similar control variables. In this analysis, the presence of a critical junior party ideologically to the right of the senior party is significantly related to more cooperative foreign policy. The strength of the coalition is statistically significant for cooperation, extremity, and commitment; weaker coalitions are more cooperative, stronger coalitions are more extreme and committed. The number of parties is also im-

portant; more parties is associated with extreme behavior, but in the direction of cooperation. This analysis is reported in full, in Kaarbo, Beasley, and Cantir, "Explaining."

38. Analyses of this relationship without the other two independent variables in the regression model were also conducted. Support for this relationship was confirmed in both unweighted and weighted analyses in these tests.

39. Stinnett, "International Uncertainty."

40. Glenn Palmer, London and Regan, "What's Stopping You?"

41. Snyder, *Myths*.

42. Support for this relationship was also confirmed in weighted and aggregated-by-coalition analyses in these tests without the other two independent variables in the regression model.

43. Kaarbo, "Influencing Peace"; Kaarbo, "Power and Influence."

44. George and McKeown, "Case Studies"; George and Bennett, *Case Studies*; Levy, "Qualitative Methods"; Tarrow, "Bridging."

45. Levy, "Qualitative Methods," 436.

46. Shively "Case Selection," 346.

47. Achen and Snidal, "Rational Deterrence Theory," 169.

48. George and Bennett, *Case Studies*.

49. Levy, "Qualitative Methods," 443.

50. Bennett and Elman, "Complex Causal Relations"; see also Bäck and Dumont, "Combining." Of course, case studies, like all other methods, have their limitations. For a summary of the most commonly cited limits, see Bennett and Elman, "Complex Causal Relations."

51. Levy, "Qualitative Methods."

52. See Przeworski and Teune, *Logic*.

53. Levy, "Qualitative Methods," 439.

54. Ragin, *Comparative Method*.

55. The attempted revision of the Japanese peacekeeping law (chapter 5) is the sole exception.

56. An important practical criterion in choosing cases in comparative research is the availability of sources. These three countries and the decisions in the cases are sufficiently important for information to be available on the positions of the parties and at least parts of the decision-making process. The availability of English-language sources for these cases is a function of both their significance and the academic culture in these countries that promotes English-language publication. In this way, the case selection may be biased, and we should have less confidence in generalizing findings to cases of trivial or mundane conflicts between coalition parties and to "less important" countries that are generally not covered by English-language academic or journalistic sources.

57. See Andeweg and Irwin, *Governance and Politics*, 2nd ed.; Gladdish, *Governing*; Anderson and Kaeding, "Belgium"; Rochon, *Netherlands*.

58. Ahn, "Government-Party Coordination."

59. Adamson, "Democratization"; Charlton, *Comparing Asian Politics*.

60. George, "Causal Nexus"; George and Bennett, *Case Studies.*

61. For the Dutch cases, government and party officials and Dutch political scientists were interviewed for additional information on the cases. For the Turkish cases, Turkish political scientists were consulted for additional information. Every case selected had sufficient published information on it to complete the case study; interviews and consultations served as an additional check on the insights gained from the other forms of evidence.

62. George, "Causal Nexus"; Levy, "Qualitative Methods."

63. For a discussion of concept validity as a strength of case studies, see George and Bennett, *Case Studies,* 19–20.

## Chapter 4

1. Voorhoeve, *Peace.*
2. Andeweg and Irwin, *Governance and Politics,* 2nd ed., 205. For a discussion of traditions and continuity in Dutch foreign policy, see Hellema, *Dutch Foreign Policy.*
3. Tonra, *Europeanisation,* 58.
4. Rochon, *Netherlands,* 234.
5. Baehr, "Foreign Policy," 3–4; see also Andeweg and Irwin, *Governance and Politics,* 2nd ed., 215; Deboutte and Van Staden, "High Politics," 56.
6. Van Staden, "Changing Role," 99; see also Tonra, *Europeanisation,* 170; Siccama, "Netherlands Depillarized."
7. Andeweg and Irwin, *Governance and Politics,* 2nd ed., 205; see also Everts, *Public Opinion;* Pijpers, "Netherlands"; Rochon, *Netherlands.*
8. For a detailed analysis of Dutch European policy through the late 1970s, see Jonas, "Denial."
9. Pijpers, "Netherlands," 249; see also Rochon, *Netherlands;* Jonas, "Denial"; Tonra, *Europeanisation;* Everts, *Public Opinion.*
10. Everts, *Public Opinion,* 28; see also Baehr, "Foreign Policy."
11. Pijpers, "Netherlands," 250; Andeweg and Irwin, *Governance and Politics,* 2nd ed.; Van Staden, "Changing Role," 100; see also Siccama, "Netherlands Depillarized."
12. Pijpers, "Netherlands"; Andeweg and Irwin, *Governance and Politics,* 2nd ed.
13. Van Staden, "Changing Role," 100.
14. Andeweg and Irwin, *Governance and Politics,* 2nd ed., 208; See also Hellema, *Dutch Foreign Policy.* For a criticism of Laqueur's thesis, see Van Staden, "Changing Role," 102–3.
15. Everts, *Public Opinion,* 27–38; Tonra, *Europeanisation,* 69; Siccama, "Netherlands Depillarized," 139.
16. Pijpers, "Netherlands," 251–52; see also Andeweg and Irwin, *Governance and Politics,* 2nd ed.; Verbeek and van der Vleuten, "Domesticization"; Van Staden, "Changing Role," 108.
17. Pijpers, "Netherlands," 247; see also Rees, "Netherlands."

18. See Andeweg and Irwin, *Governance and Politics*, 2nd ed.; Verbeek and van der Vleuten, "Domesticization."
19. Andeweg and Irwin, *Governance and Politics*, 2nd ed., 215.
20. Pijpers, "Netherlands," 257; see also Rochon, *Netherlands*, 253–55.
21. Verbeek and van der Vleuten, "Domesticization," 363.
22. "Srebrenica—A 'Safe' Area: Reconstruction, Background, Consequences, and Analyses of the Fall of a Safe Area," Netherlands Institute for War Documentation (NIOD), http://srebrenica.brightside.nl/srebrenica/.
23. Andeweg and Irwin, *Governance and Politics*, 2nd ed., 217; see also Verbeek and van der Vleuten, "Domesticization," 366.
24. Andeweg and Irwin, *Governance and Politics*, 2nd ed., 218.
25. Rochon, *Netherlands*, 255.
26. Tonra, *Europeanisation*, 66.
27. Van Staden, "Changing Role," 101. See also Hellema, *Dutch Foreign Policy*.
28. Jonas, "Denial," 246; see also Baehr, "Foreign Policy"; Siccama, "Netherlands Depillarized."
29. Pijpers, "Netherlands," 248–51.
30. Pijpers, "Netherlands," 262; see also Rochon, *Netherlands*.
31. For general criticisms of the focus on history and traditions as explanations of Dutch foreign policy, see Van Staden, "Changing Role." For a critique of the idea of a lingering great power, colonial nostalgia, see Tonra, *Europeanisation*, 69.
32. Jonas, "Denial," 246–47; see also Baehr, "Foreign Policy."
33. Jonas, "Denial," 247–54; Rochon, *Netherlands*.
34. Rochon, *Netherlands*, 231.
35. Verbeek and van der Vleuten, "Domesticization."
36. Rochon, *Netherlands*, 232; see also Van Staden, "Changing Role," 99, 103.
37. Rochon, *Netherlands*, 232; see also Jonas, "Denial," 258.
38. Andeweg and Irwin, *Governance and Politics*, 2nd ed., 206.
39. Baehr, "Foreign Policy," 7.
40. Van Staden, "Changing Role," 100.
41. Andeweg and Irwin, *Governance and Politics*, 2nd ed., 218; see also Rochon, *Netherlands*, 247. For an analysis of foreign aid rhetoric in the Netherlands, see Breuning, "Words and Deeds."
42. Andeweg and Irwin, *Governance and Politics*, 2nd ed., 216; see also Verbeek and van der Vleuten, "Domesticization." The Dutch may have also felt obligated to provide troops since they had supported the idea of safe areas. I thank Bertjan Verbeek for pointing out this idea.
43. Jonas, "Denial," 259; see also Rochon, *Netherlands*.
44. Van Staden, "Changing Role," 109; for a critique of the size factoring Dutch foreign policy, see also Deboutte and Van Staden, "High Politics."
45. Dutch foreign policy prior to the 1970s was not immune to the effects of domestic politics and partisan divisions, which were important, for example, in policy toward Indonesia.
46. Verbeek and van der Vleuten, "Domesticization," 361; see also Andeweg

and Irwin, *Governance and Politics*, 2nd ed., 209; Tonra, *Europeanisation*, 67; Van Staden, "Changing Role," 104; Deboutte and Van Staden, "High Politics," 74–75; Siccama, "Netherlands Depillarized," 135; Voorhoeve, *Peace*, 59–63. The classic work on the pillar system is Lijphart, *Politics*.

47. Van Staden, "Changing Role," 104; see also Siccama, "Netherlands Depillarized."
48. Van Staden, "Changing Role," 105.
49. Voorhoeve, *Peace*, 63.
50. Baehr, "Foreign Policy," 4.
51. Andeweg, "Centrifugal Forces," 135.
52. Baehr, "Foreign Policy," 4.
53. Everts, *Public Opinion*, 27; see also Everts, *Controversies*.
54. Verbeek and van der Vleuten, "Domesticization," 375; see also Rochon, *Netherlands*.
55. Verbeek and van der Vleuten, "Domesticization."
56. As reported in Voorhoeve, *Peace*, 87; see also Soetendorp and Hanf, "Netherlands," 40–41.
57. Deboutte and Van Staden, "High Politics"; Everts, *Public Opinion*; Van Staden, "Changing Role"; Hellema, *Dutch Foreign Policy*; for an argument and evidence that a consensus on many issues remained, see Cohen, *Democracies*.
58. Everts, *Public Opinion*, 40.
59. Cohen, *Democracies*; see also Voorhoeve, *Peace*.
60. Everts, *Public Opinion*, 40; see also Voorhoeve, *Peace*, 89–91; Van Staden, "Changing Role," 104; Cohen, *Democracies*, 137.
61. Baehr, "Foreign Policy"; Voorhoeve, *Peace*; Cohen, *Democracies*.
62. Voorhoeve, *Peace*, 88.
63. Voorhoeve, *Peace*, 88. Furthermore, Verbeek and van Ufford argue that Dutch development aid is somewhat corporatized, including in a policy system that includes state and nonstate actors; see Verbeek and van Ufford, "Non-State Actors."
64. Cohen, *Democracies*, 70.
65. Cohen, *Democracies*, 152.
66. Cohen, *Democracies*, 143.
67. Andeweg and Irwin, *Governance and Politics*, 2nd ed., 132.
68. Rochon, *Netherlands*; Everts, *Public Opinion*; Tonra, *Europeanisation*, 68; Van Staden, "Changing Role," 104, 107; Deboutte and Van Staden, "High Politics," 75; Hellema, *Dutch Foreign Policy*.
69. Rochon, *Netherlands*, 262–63.
70. Voorhoeve, *Peace*, 58.
71. Jonas, "Denial," 263.
72. Voorhoeve, *Peace*, 82.
73. Voorhoeve, *Peace*, 82; Cohen, *Democracies*, 87; Tonra, *Europeanisation*, 68.
74. See Kesgin and Kaarbo, "When and How."
75. Rochon, *Netherlands*, 261.

76. Andeweg and Irwin, *Governance and Politics*, 2nd ed.; see also Jonas, "Denial," 263.
77. Cohen, *Democracies*, 88.
78. Jonas, "Denial," 263.
79. Andeweg and Irwin, *Governance and Politics*, 2nd ed., 141.
80. Cohen, *Democracies*, 74–86.
81. Rochon, *Netherlands*, 261–63; see also Everts, *Controversies*; Tonra, *Europeanisation*, 69.
82. Verbeek and van der Vleuten, "Domesticization," 362.
83. Andeweg and Irwin, *Governance and Politics*, 2nd ed., 123–24; Soetendorp and Hanf, "Netherlands," 40–41; Jonas, "Denial," 263; Andeweg, "Centrifugal Forces," 137.
84. Andeweg and Irwin, *Governance and Politics*, 2nd ed., 125.
85. Baehr, "Foreign Policy," 8. For an analysis of the importance of foreign affairs to the Dutch cabinet, see Voorhoeve, *Peace*, 63–65. European Union issues are treated differently, as most EU policies are composed in interdepartmental committees; the full cabinet considers only the most sensitive topics.
86. Tonra, *Europeanisation*, 71; Andeweg, "Centrifugal Forces," 139.
87. Andeweg and Irwin, *Governance and Politics*, 2nd ed., 122. See also Everts, *Controversies*, 91.
88. Andeweg and Irwin, *Governance and Politics*, 2nd ed., 122–23. See also Voorhoeve, *Peace*, 76; Gallhofer, Saris, and Voogt, "From Individual Preference," 156.
89. Rochon, *Netherlands*, 122.
90. Baehr, "Foreign Policy," 9; see also Rochon, *Netherlands*, 261; Tonra, *Europeanisation*, 71–73.
91. Baehr, "Foreign Policy," 11.
92. Jonas, "Denial," 263.
93. Cohen, *Democracies*, 34; for a detailed description of the organization of the Dutch foreign ministry, see Deboutte and Van Staden, "High Politics."
94. Rochon, *Netherlands*, 262.
95. Rochon, *Netherlands*, 262; Voorhoeve, *Peace*, 75.
96. Rochon, *Netherlands*, 262.
97. Cohen, *Democracies*, 35.
98. Cohen, *Democracies*, 41.
99. Pijpers, "Netherlands," 264; see also Deboutte and Van Staden, "High Politics," 66–68.
100. Verbeek and van der Vleuten, "Domesticization," 362.
101. Voorhoeve, *Peace*, 75.
102. Gallhofer, Saris, and Voogt, "From Individual Preference," 156.
103. Rochon, *Netherlands*, 120; see also Andeweg, "Centrifugal Forces"; Gallhofer, Saris, and Voogt, "From Individual Preference."
104. Voorhoeve, *Peace*, 75.

105. Andeweg, "Centrifugal Forces," 143–46; Gallhofer, Saris, and Voogt, "From Individual Preference," 167.
106. Andeweg and Irwin, *Governance and Politics*, 2nd ed., 110.
107. Andeweg, "Centrifugal Forces," 134.
108. Gallhofer, Saris and Voogt, "From Individual Preference."
109. Gladdish, *Governing*, 177.
110. Timmermans, *High Politics*; Andeweg and Irwin, *Governance and Politics*, 2nd ed.
111. Andeweg, "Centrifugal Forces," 142.
112. Cohen, *Democracies*, 35.
113. Timmermans, *High Politics*; Andeweg and Irwin, *Governance and Politics*, 2nd ed.; Blondel and Müller-Rommel, "Introduction."
114. Rochon, *Netherlands*, 123.
115. Andeweg, "Centrifugal Forces," 135–36.
116. Rochon, *Netherlands*, 120. Rochon cites the Dutch-language study by Timmermans and Bakema, "Conflicten."
117. Van Staden, "Changing Role," 107.
118. Verbeek and van der Vleuten, "Domesticization," 363; for further examples, see Metselaar and Verbeek, "Beyond Decision Making"; Everts and Walraven, *Politics*; Voorhoeve, *Peace*; Deboutte and Van Staden, "High Politics"; Everts, *Controversies*; Hellema, Duco, and Witte, *Netherlands and the Oil Crisis*; Gladdish, *Governing*; Hoekema, "Srebrenica."
119. Kulish, "Dutch Pull-Out."
120. Rochon, *Netherlands*, 278; Putnam, "Diplomacy."
121. Schie, interview.
122. Interview, U.S. embassy personnel, the Hague, March 2006.
123. Andeweg and Irwin, *Governance and Politics*, 2nd ed., 149; Gladdish, *Governing*, 144.
124. Anderson and Kaeding, "Belgium," 117.
125. Rochon, *Netherlands*, 120; Gladdish, *Governing*, 178.
126. Andeweg and Irwin, *Governance and Politics*, 2nd ed., 224 (although Dutch *stroop* is much thicker than U.S. syrup).
127. Rochon, *Netherlands*, 278–79.
128. Everts, *Controversies*, 91.
129. Andeweg and Irwin, *Governance and Politics*, 2nd ed., 128.
130. Andeweg and Irwin, *Governance and Politics*, 2nd ed., 222.
131. Tonra, *Europeanisation*, 201.
132. Tonra, *Europeanisation*, 218; see also Everts, *Controversies*, 215.
133. Tonra, *Europeanisation*, 219.
134. Voorhoeve, *Peace*, 225; for a good summary of the history of Dutch relations with South Africa, see 225–31.
135. Tonra, *Europeanisation*, 201.
136. Everts, *Controversies*, 215.

137. Tonra, *Europeanisation,* 205; Voorhoeve, *Peace,* 230; Kremer and Pijpers, "South Africa."
138. Kremer and Pijpers, "South Africa," 310.
139. Everts, *Controversies,* 217.
140. Hellema, *Dutch Foreign Policy.*
141. In the 1977 elections, three parties ran a common list of candidates. In 1980, they officially merged into one, the Christian Democratic Appeal. For a history of the Christian Democratic Appeal, see ten Napel, "Development."
142. The dynamic and open-ended process of coalition formation in the Netherlands frequently produces a government with the largest party in opposition. See Andeweg and Irwin, *Governance and Politics,* 2nd ed., 111.
143. Laver and Mair, "Party Policy"; Daalder and Koole, "Liberal Parties," 168.
144. Wolinetz. "Netherlands," 150.
145. Daalder and Koole, "Liberal Parties," 171.
146. Van Staden, "Changing Role," 106.
147. Kremer and Pijpers, "South Africa," 310–11.
148. Kremer and Pijpers, "South Africa," 311.
149. Tonra, *Europeanisation,* 207.
150. Everts, *Controversies,* 225.
151. Everts, *Controversies,* 223–24.
152. Everts, *Controversies,* 229.
153. Everts, *Controversies,* 229.
154. Kremer and Pijpers, "South Africa," 311.
155. Everts, *Controversies,* 220.
156. Everts, *Controversies,* 216.
157. Kremer and Pijpers, "South Africa," 311.
158. Everts, *Controversies,* 224.
159. Tonra, *Europeanisation,* 205.
160. Tonra, *Europeanisation,* 207.
161. Kremer and Pijpers, "South Africa," 311.
162. Everts, *Controversies,* 61; see also Van Staden, "Changing Role," 106.
163. Everts, *Controversies,* 220.
164. Everts, *Public Opinion,* 307.
165. Everts, *Public Opinion,* 307.
166. Everts, *Controversies,* 218.
167. Kremer and Pijpers, "South Africa," 310.
168. Everts, *Controversies,* 218.
169. Everts, *Controversies,* 218.
170. Kremer and Pijpers, "South Africa," 311.
171. Everts, *Controversies,* 218.
172. Kremer and Pijpers, "South Africa," 311.
173. Everts, *Controversies,* 218–19.
174. Everts, *Controversies,* 218.

175. Everts, *Controversies*, 220; Kremer and Pijpers, "South Africa," 311.
176. Kremer and Pijpers, "South Africa"; Everts, *Controversies*.
177. Tonra, *Europeanisation*, 205.
178. In terms of the Goldstein-WEIS scale, the decision is consistent with "urge or suggest action or policy" (−0.1).
179. The *Economist* called this position "eccentric" ("Holland: Island Mentality," 49).
180. Everts, *Controversies*, 135.
181. Everts, *Controversies*, 133.
182. Andeweg and Irwin, *Governance and Politics*, 2nd ed., 208.
183. Soetendorp, "NATO 'Double Track' Decision," 152–53; Everts, *Controversies*, 151; Hellema, *Dutch Foreign Policy*.
184. Everts, *Controversies*, 140–41.
185. "Holland: Dutch Dilemma," 40.
186. Soetendorp, "NATO 'Double Track' Decision," 155.
187. Everts, *Controversies*, 136.
188. Everts, *Public Opinion*, 341.
189. Gladdish, *Governing*, 171; see also Van Staden, "Changing Role," 101.
190. Andeweg and Irwin, *Governance and Politics*, 2nd ed.
191. Van Staden, "Changing Role," 106; for a review of the evolution of the PvdA, see Van Praag, "Conflict"; for a discussion of the rise of the "New Left" within Labour, see Siccama, "Netherlands Depillarized."
192. Van Staden, "Changing Role," 100.
193. Andeweg and Irwin, *Governance and Politics*, 2nd ed.; see also Daalder and Koole, "Liberal Parties."
194. Daalder and Koole, "Liberal Parties," 170.
195. Everts, *Controversies*, 136.
196. Everts, *Public Opinion*, 310–11.
197. Timmermans, *High Politics*, 79; see also Everts, *Controversies*, 136.
198. Everts, *Public Opinion*, 309; see also Hillebrand and Irwin, "Changing Strategies," 117; John Palmer, "Holland."
199. Everts, *Controversies*, 136.
200. Soetendorp, "NATO 'Double Track' Decision," 154.
201. Everts, *Controversies*, 139–40.
202. Rochon, *Netherlands*, 264.
203. Everts, *Public Opinion*, 309.
204. Everts, *Public Opinion*, 309–10; see also Timmermans, *High Politics*, 79.
205. Everts, *Public Opinion*, 309; see also Timmermans, *High Politics*, 79.
206. Everts, *Public Opinion*, 310–11.
207. Everts, *Controversies*, 142; see also Andeweg and Irwin, *Governance and Politics*, 2nd ed.
208. Everts, *Controversies*, 142–43; see also Van Staden, "Changing Role," 105.
209. Everts, *Controversies*, 145–46, 151–52; Andeweg and Irwin, *Governance and Politics*, 2nd ed.; Barton, "Nuclear Message."'
210. Everts, *Controversies*, 146.

211. Everts, *Controversies,* 154–55.
212. Everts, *Controversies,* 139–42; Rochon, *Netherlands,* 266.
213. Timmermans, *High Politics,* 79; see also "Holland: Queen's Men Try Again," 42.
214. Quoted in Everts, *Public Opinion,* 329.
215. Everts, *Public Opinion,* 329.
216. Siccama, "Netherlands Depillarized," 143.
217. Timmermans, *High Politics,* 79; see also James F. Smith, "Three Parties."
218. Daalder and Koole, "Liberal Parties," 170.
219. James F. Smith, "Dutch."
220. Hagan et al., "Foreign Policy by Coalition," 186.
221. Everts, *Controversies,* 137.
222. Everts, *Controversies,* 137.
223. Timmermans, *High Politics,* 98–99.
224. In terms of the Goldstein-WEIS scale, this behavior can be classified as "postpone planned event" (−2.2).
225. Of course, the effect was also constraint on a cooperative policy—that is, cooperation with NATO allies.
226. Andeweg and Irwin, *Governance and Politics,* 2nd ed., 208.
227. Apple, "U.S. Missiles."
228. Hagan et al., "Foreign Policy by Coalition," 187.
229. Andeweg and Irwin, *Governance and Politics,* 2nd ed.
230. Hagan et al., "Foreign Policy by Coalition," 188.
231. Hagan et al., "Foreign Policy by Coalition," 188.
232. Andeweg and Irwin, *Governance and Politics,* 2nd ed., 211.
233. Van Holsteyn and Irwin, "Never a Dull Moment."
234. Andeweg and Irwin, *Governance and Politics,* 2nd ed.
235. "Eighty Percent."
236. Rochon, *Netherlands,* 255.
237. "Dutch Opposition MPs."
238. Hellema, *Dutch Foreign Policy,* 375.
239. Schlaghecke, "Dutch Join."
240. "Dutch Would Back War."
241. Van Holsteyn and Irwin, "Dutch Parliamentary Elections"; "Return to the Centre."
242. Van Holsteyn and Irwin, "Dutch Parliamentary Elections"; "Rapport Commissie-Davids (Rapport Commissie Van Onderzoek Besluitvorming Irak)," http://www.rijksoverheid.nl/onderwerpen/irak/commissie-davids.
243. Hennink, "Dutch Cabinet."
244. "Dutch Parliament Will Not Block Patriot Missile Shipment."
245. "Eighty Percent."
246. Schlaghecke, "Dutch Join."
247. Van Staden, "Changing Role," 109; see also van Praag, "Conflict"; Hillebrand and Irwin, "Changing Strategies."
248. "Dutch Opposition MPs."

249. Hennink, "Dutch Cabinet."
250. "Dutch Parliament Will Not Block Patriot Missile Shipment."
251. "Dutch Parliament Will Not Block Patriot Missile Shipment."
252. "Dutch Parliament Will Not Block Patriot Missile Shipment"; Hennink, "Dutch Cabinet"; Couch, "Dutch Help."
253. Quoted in Couch, "Dutch Help."
254. Quoted in Couch, "Dutch Help."
255. Van den Berg, "Talks"; Schie, interview.
256. "Netherlands Prime Minister."
257. "Dutch Government."
258. Cooper, "Iraq War Threat."
259. Cooper, "Iraq War Threat."
260. Cooper, "Iraq War Threat."
261. Schie, interview.
262. Cooper, "Iraq War Threat."
263. Beunderman, "Crisis."
264. Quoted in Cooper, "Iraq War Threat."
265. Beunderman, "Crisis."
266. Hoekema, interview.
267. Van Den Berg, "Iraq War"; see also Beunderman, "Crisis"; Van den Berg, "Talks." This view was also supported by Bolkestein (interview). See also "Rapport Commissie-Davids."
268. Beunderman, "Crisis."
269. Van den Berg, "Iraq War."
270. Cooper, "Iraq War Threat."
271. Beunderman, "Crisis"; "Dutch Cabinet Formation under Pressure."
272. Beunderman, "Crisis."
273. "Dutch Cabinet Formation under Pressure."
274. Van den Berg, "Iraq War."
275. Van den Berg, "Talks."
276. Van den Berg, "Iraq War."
277. Van den Berg, "Iraq War."
278. Van den Berg, "Iraq War."
279. Piggot, "Dutch Navy Submarine."
280. Van den Berg, "New Dutch Government"; see also "Dutch Cabinet Formation Goes Ahead"; Piggot, "Dutch Navy Submarine."
281. Cooper, "Iraq War Threat"; Pascoe, "Dutch Back War."
282. Pascoe, "Dutch Back War."
283. Pascoe, "Dutch Back War."
284. Van den Berg, "Talks."
285. "Netherlands Christian Democrats." By 2003, the Democrats '66 party was referred to simply as D66.
286. Hoekema, interview.
287. "Netherlands to Send 1,100 Troops."
288. "Deployment of Dutch Troops."

289. "Dutch Troops to Leave."
290. Interview, U.S. embassy personnel, the Hague, March 2006.
291. In terms of the Goldstein-WEIS scale, this decision is consistent with "endorse other's policy or position; give verbal support" (+3.6), if the United States is the target. If Iraq is the target, it might be considered a "nonmilitary demonstration" (−5.2).
292. "Dutch FM"; "In About-Face."
293. Hoekema, interview; interview, U.S. embassy personnel, the Hague, March 2006.
294. "New Invasion Report: Dutch Government Misrepresented Case for Iraq War," NRC Handelsblad, January 13, 2010. The Davids report can be found (in Dutch) at http://www.nrc.nl/multimedia/archive/00267/ rapport_commissie_i_ 267285a.pdf.
295. "Pressure Mounts"; Harding, "Analysis."
296. "Pressure Mounts."
297. Quoted in "Pressure Mounts."
298. Quoted in Ames, "NATO Chief."
299. "Netherlands to Send More Troops."
300. Quoted in Dempsey, "Dutch Future."
301. Molly Moore, "Dutch Debate."
302. Molly Moore, "After Long Debate"; interview, U.S. embassy personnel, the Hague, March 2006.
303. Anthony Deutsch, "Dutch Premier."
304. "Parliament Agrees." In December 2001, 61 percent of the Dutch public supported sending troops to Afghanistan, as reported by Global News Wire's abstract from De Telegraaf in Dutch, "Dutch Population."
305. Michael Smith, "Afghan Posting."
306. "Afghanistan Is Netherlands' Most Disastrous Overseas Mission"; Max, "Military Ambition"; Anthony Deutsch, "Dutch Premier."
307. Harding, "Interview."
308. Hoekema, interview.
309. "Netherlands Hesitant"; Beeston, "Dutch Think Again"; "Dutch Prime Minister Cautious."
310. "Netherlands Hesitant."
311. "Netherlands Expected to Decide"; "Netherlands Again Puts Off Decision."
312. Watt, "'Shades of Srebrenica.'"
313. "Dutch Discord Fuels Doubts."
314. "NATO Approves Plan"; "Netherlands Expected to Decide."
315. "NATO Approves Plan."
316. "Netherlands Postpones Decision"; "Netherlands Again Puts Off Decision"; Bickerton, "Dutch Delay"; Anthony Deutsch, "Dutch Premier."
317. "Netherlands Postpones Decision"; "Netherlands Again Puts Off Decision"; Bickerton, "Dutch Delay."
318. Quoted by Dempsey, "Dutch Future."
319. Castle, "Dutch Government."

320. Castle, "Why."
321. Dempsey, "Dutch Down."
322. Andor Adiraal, quoted in Harding, "Analysis."
323. Smyth, "1,400 Dutch Troops."
324. Bickerton and Dombey, "Afghan Mission Doubts."
325. "Dutch Discord Fuels Doubts."
326. "Dutch Discord Fuels Doubts"; Bolkestein, interview; Hoekema, interview; interview, U.S. embassy personnel, the Hague, March 2006.
327. Quoted in Molly Moore, "Dutch Debate."
328. Edwin Baker of the Clingendael Institute, quoted in "Dutch Discord Fuels Doubts"; Schie, interview; Hoekema, interview; interview, U.S. embassy personnel, the Hague, March 2006; interview, member of the Democrats '66, the Hague, March 2006.
329. "Netherlands Again Puts Off Decision"; "Dutch Cabinet for Sending Troops"; "Dutch PM Firmly Backs Controversial Military Mission."
330. Harding, "Analysis."
331. Bickerton, "Dutch Delay." According to one source, Kamp, the leader of the Liberals, also had some early reservations about the mission, but after he received assurances about some of the specifics, he came to support the policy, and the rest of his party followed his lead (Schie, interview).
332. Quoted in Smyth, "Dutch Poised."
333. Anthony Deutsch, "Dutch Premier."
334. Bickerton, "Dutch Delay."
335. "Dutch Cabinet for Sending Troops." According to Hoekema (interview), the issue of who has the authority to commit Dutch troops was a contested one in this case and at the time of the decision; see also Hoekema, "Srebrenica."
336. Bickerton, "Dutch Delay."
337. "Dutch Discord Fuels Doubts."
338. "Dutch Parliament Approves Afghanistan Mission." One source, however, argued that the D66 continued to try to convince the cabinet to oppose deployment (interview, member of the Democrats '66, the Hague, March 2006).
339. "Dutch Cabinet for Sending Troops."
340. "Netherlands Again Puts Off Decision."
341. Quoted in Dempsey, "Dutch Future."
342. Harding, "Interview."
343. "Dutch Cabinet for Sending Troops"; "Netherlands Again Puts Off Decision."
344. "Dutch Parliament Appears Set."
345. "Dutch PM Firmly Backs Controversial Military Mission."
346. Bickerton and Dombey, "Afghan Mission Doubts."
347. "Dutch Premier Says."
348. "Dutch Troops Planned."
349. Castle, "Dutch Government."
350. Castle, "Dutch Government."

351. "Pressure Mounts."
352. Quoted in "Pressure Mounts."
353. Harding, "Analysis."
354. Harding, "Analysis."
355. Interview, U.S. embassy personnel, the Hague, March 2006.
356. "Dutch Premier Says."
357. Poll by Maurice de Hond, reported in "Dutch Discord Fuels Doubts."
358. Poll by Maurice de Hond, reported in "Dutch Parliament Appears Set."
359. Harding, "Interview."
360. "Dutch Discord Fuels Doubts."
361. Harding, "Analysis."
362. Bickerton and Dombey, "Dutch Edge Closer."
363. Quoted in Molly Moore, "After Long Debate."
364. Quoted in "Dutch Parliament Appears Set"; "Netherlands to Send More Troops."
365. Quoted in Traynor, "Netherlands Votes."
366. Bickerton, Dombey, and Morarjee, "Dutch MPs"; "Netherlands to Send More Troops." The U.S. government viewed Labour's limit of two years as a compromise (interview, U.S. embassy personnel, the Hague, March 2006).
367. Bickerton, Dombey, and Morarjee, "Dutch MPs."
368. Bickerton, Dombey, and Morarjee, "Dutch Decision."
369. Van Holsteyn, "Dutch Parliamentary Elections."
370. Kulish, "Dutch Pull-Out."
371. In terms of the Goldstein-WEIS scale, this decision can be categorized as "armed force mobilization, exercise" (−7.6).
372. Hoekema, interview, March 2006; interview, member of the Democrats '66, the Hague, March 2006; interview, U.S. embassy personnel, the Hague, March 2006.
373. Quoted in Dempsey, "Dutch Future."
374. Rudy Andeweg, quoted in Molly Moore, "Dutch Debate"; Schie, interview; Bolkestein, interview; Hoekema, interview; interview, U.S. embassy personnel, the Hague, March 2006.
375. Castle, "Dutch Government."
376. Castle, "Why."
377. This party, however, cannot claim sole responsibility for the assumptions that were questioned, since other political parties also demanded assurances (Hoekema, interview).

## Chapter 5

1. Miyashita, "Japanese Foreign Policy"; Berger, *Cultures*.
2. Berger, "Pragmatic Liberalism," 262.
3. Mochizuki, "Japan's Changing International Role," 12; Inoguchi and Jain, "Introduction."

4. Mochizuki, "Japan's Changing International Role," 2.

5. See, for example, Akiko Fukushima, "Official Development Assistance (ODA) as a Japanese Foreign Policy Tool," in *Japanese Foreign Policy Today*, ed. Inoguchi and Jain.

6. Miyashita, "Japanese Foreign Policy," 153; see also Mochizuki, "Japan's Changing International Role," 4; Lind, "Pacificism."

7. Miyashita, "Japanese Foreign Policy," 151; see also Mochizuki, "Japan's Changing International Role."

8. Mochizuki, "Japan's Changing International Role," 4.

9. Heinrich, Shibata, and Soeya, *United Nations Peace-Keeping Operations*, 19; see also Mochizuki, "Japan's Changing International Role"; Akihiko, "UN Peace Operations."

10. Hughes, *Japan's Re-Emergence*, 50.

11. Lind, "Pacifism," 114; see also Hughes, *Japan's Re-Emergence*; Hughes, *Japan's Remilitarization*.

12. See, for example, Katzenstein, *Cultural Norms*; Berger, *Cultures*; Green, *Japan's Reluctant Realism*; Miyashita, "Japanese Foreign Policy"; Lind, "Pacifism."

13. Sato and Hirata, "Introduction"; see also Midford, "Logic"; Twomey, "Japan"; Heginbotham and Samuels, "Mercantile Realism."

14. Kohno, "Domestic Foundations," 27.

15. Miyashita, "Where Do Norms Come From?," 29.

16. For a review of this "strategic" and "realist" perspective, see Berger, "Japan's International Relations."

17. Kawasaki, "Postclassical Realism," 231.

18. See Miyashita, "Gaiatsu"; Miyashita, "Japanese Foreign Policy."

19. Miyashita, "Where Do Norms Come From?," 22. For a useful summary of constructivist explanations of Japanese foreign policy, see Lind, "Pacifism." On the importance of Japan's conception of its role in the world, see Green, *Japan's Reluctant Realism*, 11.

20. Katzenstein, *Cultural Norms*; Berger, *Cultures*; Berger, "Japan's International Relations."

21. Mochizuki, "Japan's Changing International Role," 9.

22. Cortell and Davis, "When Norms Clash," 21. For an examination of the role of international and domestic norms across several issue areas in Japanese foreign policy, see Sato and Hirata, "Introduction."

23. Calder, "Review."

24. Akihiko, "Domestic Politics," 3.

25. Miyashita, "Where Do Norms Come From?," 36–39; Berger, *Cultures*, 178–81.

26. Kohno, "Domestic Foundations," 27.

27. Kohno, "Domestic Foundations," 37–40.

28. Tsuchiyama, "War Renunciation," 61; see also Hughes, *Japan's Re-Emergence*.

29. See, for example, Mochizuki, *Japan.*
30. Cortell and Davis, "When Norms Clash," 21.
31. See, for example, Risse-Kappen, "Public Opinion."
32. Berger, "Japan's International Relations," 272.
33. Berger, "Japan's International Relations," 274.
34. See, for example, Mochizuki, *Japan,* especially chapter 4; Hughes, *Japan's Re-Emergence;* Berger, "Japan's International Relations," 272.
35. Pekkanen and Krauss, "Japan's 'Coalition,'" 430.
36. Risse-Kappen, "Public Opinion."
37. Calder, "Review," 530; Green, *Japan's Reluctant Realism.*
38. Akihiko, "Domestic Politics," 14; see also Green, *Japan's Reluctant Realism.*
39. Sato and Hirata, "Introduction," 10; see also Jain, "Emerging Foreign Policy Actors."
40. Dalpino, "Role"; Hughes, *Japan's Re-Emergence,* 57–58.
41. Akihiko, "Domestic Politics," 11.
42. Akihiko, "Domestic Politics," 11; see also Ahn, "Government-Party Coordination," 381.
43. Hayes, *Introduction,* 266.
44. Hayes, *Introduction.*
45. Green, *Japan's Reluctant Realism,* 38; Berger, "Japan's International Relations," 271.
46. Pekkanen and Krauss, "Japan's 'Coalition,'" 42–43.
47. Stockwin, *Governing Japan,* 4th ed., 139.
48. Green, *Japan's Reluctant Realism,* 37.
49. Green, *Japan's Reluctant Realism,* 48.
50. Stockwin, *Governing Japan,* 4th ed., 139; Green, *Japan's Reluctant Realism,* 49.
51. Berger, "Japan's International Relations," 271.
52. Akihiko, "Domestics Politics," 4.
53. Hayes, *Introduction,* 56; Stockwin, *Governing Japan,* 4th ed., 139; Akihiko, "Domestic Politics," 4–5.
54. Shinoda, *Leading Japan,* 47. See also Green, *Japan's Reluctant Realism;* Akihiko, "Domestic Politics"; Pekkanen and Krauss, "Japan's 'Coalition.'"
55. Akihiko, "Domestic Politics," 4.
56. Ahn, "Government-Party Coordination," 380.
57. Pekkanen and Krause, "Japan's 'Coalition,'" 439.
58. Shinoda, *Leading Japan;* Green, *Japan's Reluctant Realism.*
59. Shinoda, *Leading Japan.*
60. Pekkanen and Krause, "Japan's 'Coalition,'" 438; see also Mochizuki, "Japan's Changing International Role," 6.
61. Pekkanen and Krause, "Japan's 'Coalition,'" 439.
62. Shinoda, "Japan's Decision Making"; Shinoda, *Leading Japan;* Mochizuki, "Japan's Changing International Role."
63. Akihiko, "Domestic Politics," 7.

64. Akihiko, "Domestic Politics," 7.
65. Calder, "Institutions," 5; for a discussion of the changing status of the JDA, see Green, *Japan's Reluctant Realism*, 62–64; Hughes, *Japan's Re-Emergence*, 60–62.
66. For a review of this debate, see Maswood, "Japanese Foreign Policy," 21–23.
67. Berger, "Japan's International Relations," 271; see also Green, *Japan's Reluctant Realism*, 43.
68. Dobson, *Japan*, 137.
69. Drifte, *Japan's Foreign Policy*, 17.
70. Mochizuki, *Japan*, 19.
71. Shinoda, "Japan's Decision Making," 705.
72. Ahn, "Government-Party Coordination," 378.
73. Berger, "Alliance Politics," 201.
74. Tadokoro, "End," 1002.
75. Berger, "Japan's International Relations," 272.
76. Berger, "Alliance Politics," 201; see also Ahn, "Government-Party Coordination."
77. Mochizuki, *Japan*, 23. See also Green, *Japan's Reluctant Realism*; Charlton, *Comparing Asian Politics*.
78. Ahn, "Government-Party Coordination," 379.
79. Green, *Japan's Reluctant Realism*, 8.
80. Green, *Japan's Reluctant Realism*, 75.
81. Mochizuki, *Japan*, 4.
82. Pekkanen and Krauss, "Japan's 'Coalition,'" 444.
83. Berger, "Japan's International Relations," 272.
84. Ahn, "Government-Party Coordination"; Ahn, "Interministry Coordination."
85. Shinoda, "Japan's Decision Making"; Naoto, "Characteristics."
86. Keohane and Milner, *Internationalization*.
87. Blaker, "Negotiating," 216.
88. Blaker, "Negotiating," 215. For more on the sacrosanct nature of rice in Japanese politics, see Schwartz, *Advice*, especially chapter 6. For a review of the rice issue and Japan's evolving orientation toward GATT/WTO liberalization norms, see Cortell and Davis, "When Norms Clash." For more history of Japan's positions in the Uruguay round and the domestic groups for and against liberalization, up until 1992, see Rapkin and George, "Rice Liberalization."
89. Schwartz, *Advice*, 260.
90. Schwartz, *Advice*, 260; see also Blaker, "Negotiating."
91. Blaker, "Negotiating," 223; for more details on the positions and bargaining styles in the rice negotiations between 1986 and 1994, see Blaker "Negotiating."
92. Blaker "Negotiating"; "Hosokawa Rules Out."
93. Blaker, "Negotiating," 231; see also Schwartz, *Advice*, 260.

94. Blaker, "Negotiating," 226.
95. Curtis, *Logic*, 108; Christensen, *Ending*, 14. The Socialist Party renamed itself the Social Democratic Party of Japan in 1991, but many analysts still referred to it as the Socialist Party. For simplicity, I will refer to it as the Japan Socialist Party (JSP).
96. Curtis, *Logic*, 104.
97. Curtis, *Logic*, 114.
98. Curtis, *Logic*, 107.
99. Christensen, *Ending*, 14–15.
100. Hrebenar, *Japan's New Party System*, 150; Stockwin, *Governing Japan*, 4th ed., 200.
101. Hideo, "Political Realignment," 142.
102. Curtis, *Logic*, 106.
103. Stockwin, *Governing Japan*, 4th ed., 200; see also Hideo, "Political Realignment," 138–39.
104. Stockwin, *Governing Japan*, 4th ed., 200.
105. Hrebenar, *Japan's New Party System*, 150.
106. Stockwin, *Governing Japan*, 4th ed., 200.
107. Mochizuki, *Japan*, 9–10, 50; Berger, *Cultures*, 184; Hughes, *Japan's Re-Emergence*.
108. See Tadokoro, "End."
109. Hrebrear, *Japan's New Party System*, 212; see also Miyashita, "Where Do Norms Come From?," 36–39.
110. Hrebenar, *Japan's New Party System*, 212–41.
111. Curtis, *Logic*, 101.
112. Hrebenar, *Japan's New Party System*, 168–69; see also Curtis, *Logic*, 102–4.
113. Hrebenar, *Japan's New Party System*, 169.
114. Hrebenar, *Japan's New Party System*, 190–202.
115. Hrebenar, *Japan's New Party System*, 195–96; see also Miyashita, "Where Do Norms Come From?," 36–39.
116. Stockwin, *Governing Japan*, 4th ed., 199; Hideo, "Political Realignment," 127.
117. Curtis, *Logic*, 114.
118. Curtis, *Logic*, 125.
119. Curtis, *Logic*, 121; see also Naoto, "Characteristics"; Shinoda, "Japan's Decision Making."
120. Naoto, "Characteristics," 109, 115; Shinoda, "Japan's Decision Making."
121. "Battle over Rice Imports."
122. Hideo, "Political Realignment," 142.
123. "Battle over Rice Imports"; Naoto, "Characteristics," 107.
124. Naoto, "Characteristics," 107.
125. "Battle over Rice Imports."
126. "Japan Split"; see also Cortell and Davis, "When Norms Clash."
127. "Battle over Rice Imports"; "Japan Delays."

128. Blaker, "Negotiating," 226.
129. Shinoda, "Japan's Decision Making," 705; see also Stockwin, *Governing Japan* [1999 ed.], 84; "Battle over Rice Imports"; Blaker, "Negotiating," 226; "Japan Adopting."
130. Shinoda, "Japan's Decision Making," 706.
131. Blaker, "Negotiating," 227.
132. Blaker, "Negotiating," 227.
133. *Japan Economic Newswire,* October 9, 1993.
134. *Japan Economic Newswire,* October 9, 1993.
135. "Japan Adopting."
136. "Hosokawa Says."
137. "Japan Says"; "Hosokawa Rules Out."
138. "Hosokawa Rules Out."
139. "Japan Renews Opposition."
140. "Battle over Rice Imports."
141. Blaker, "Negotiating," 228.
142. "Battle over Rice Imports."
143. "Japan Adopting."
144. "Japan Opposition."
145. "Battle over Rice Imports."
146. "Japan Adopting."
147. "Japan Adopting."
148. "Japan May Partially Lift."
149. "Japan Adopting"; "No Change."
150. Emiko "Japan to Offer"; Landers, "Japan Moves."
151. "Japan Bound."
152. "Opening of Rice Market."
153. "Japan's Socialists."
154. "Japan to Make Final Decision."
155. "Japan's Socialists."
156. Landers, "Japan Moves."
157. "Japan's Decision"; see also "Japan Delays"; "Prime Minister Delays."
158. "GATT Chief Urges Japan to Reach Early Decision on Rice," *Japan Economic Newswire,* December 13, 1993; "Japan Delays."
159. "Japan Delays."
160. "Japan Delays"; "Prime Minister Delays."
161. Kakuchi, "Trade."
162. "Japan Has Already Agreed"; Talmadge, "In Major Concession."
163. "Opening Rice Market"; "Japan to Decide."
164. Kin, "Japan's Socialists"; Blaker, "Negotiating," 227.
165. "Opening Rice Market."
166. "Japan's Fragile Coalition"; see also Naoto, "Characteristics," 107–8.
167. Talmadge, "In Major Concession."

168. In terms of the Goldstein-WEIS classification, the acceptance could be coded as +6.5 (make substantive agreement).
169. On his personal commitment, see Shinoda, "Japan's Decision Making," 705.
170. Naoto, "Characteristics," 109.
171. Shinoda, "Japan's Decision Making," 706-7.
172. Blaker, "Negotiating," 229.
173. Shinoda, "Japan's Decision Making," 722.
174. Blaker, "Negotiating," 230.
175. Blaker, "Negotiating," 89.
176. Shinoda, "Japan's Decision Making," 706-7.
177. "Battle over Rice Imports."
178. Shinoda, "Japan's Decision Making," 706-7.
179. Blaker, "Negotiating," 230.
180. Nonaka, "Negotiating," 108.
181. Curtis, *Logic*, 134; Naoto, "Characteristics," 109; for an analysis of the longer-term effects in Japanese rice trade, see Bullock, "Market Opening," 47-49; Schwartz, *Advice*, 260.
182. Hosokawa, interview, as reported by Curtis, *Logic*, 264.
183. Curtis, *Logic*.
184. Mochizuki, *Japan*, 10.
185. Drifte, *Japan's Quest*, 95.
186. Green, *Japan's Reluctant Realism*, 200.
187. Green, *Japan's Reluctant Realism*, 200.
188. See Newman, "Japan and International Organizations"; Ogata, "Japan's Policy."
189. Drifte, *Japan's Quest*, 95.
190. Kawashima, *Japanese Foreign Policy*, 139.
191. Drifte, *Japan's Quest*, 102.
192. Green, *Japan's Reluctant Realism*, 202; Drifte, *Japan's Quest*, 125-30.
193. Masahiko Ishizuka, "Security Council Issue."
194. Drifte, *Japan's Quest*, 128-29.
195. Akiko Fukushima, *Japanese Foreign Policy*, 98.
196. Drifte, *Japan's Quest*, 103-23.
197. Drifte, *Japan's Quest*, 122-23.
198. Drifte, *Japan's Quest*, 122.
199. Green, *Japan's Reluctant Realism*, 205; Drifte, *Japan's Quest*; Akiko Fukushima, *Japanese Foreign Policy*, 102; "53% Support Permanent Seat."
200. Hiroshi, "UN Reform," 438.
201. Drifte, *Japan's Quest*, 126.
202. Ahn, "Government-Party Coordination," 369-70; Akiko Fukushima, *Japanese Foreign Policy*, 99.
203. Green, *Japan's Reluctant Realism*, 204.

204. Ahn, "Government-Party Coordination," 371; see also "Hata Pushes."
205. Drifte, *Japan's Quest*, 129.
206. Ahn, "Government-Party Coordination," 371; for more on decision making regarding this issue in the Hosokawa and Hata coalitions, see Ahn, "Government-Party Coordination"; Mochizuki, *Japan*; Drifte, *Japan's Quest*.
207. Drifte, *Japan's Quest*, 130.
208. Hrebenar, *Japan's New Party System*, 91.
209. Di Cicco, "Japan's PM."
210. Hrebenar, *Japan's New Party System*, 150; Stockwin, *Governing Japan*, [1999 ed.], 200.
211. Ahn, "Government-Party Coordination," 369–70.
212. Akiko Fukushima, *Japanese Foreign Policy*, 99.
213. Akiko Fukushima, *Japanese Foreign Policy*, 99; see also Drifte, *Japan's Quest*, 125.
214. Drifte, *Japan's Quest*, 127.
215. Ahn, "Government-Party Coordination," 377.
216. Ahn, "Government-Party Coordination," 377; see also Drifte, *Japan's Quest*, 131; Dawkins, "Japan Scales Down."
217. Hrebenar, *Japan's New Party System*; Stockwin, *Governing Japan* [1999 ed.].
218. Green, *Japan's Reluctant Realism*, 55; Ikuo, "Ideological Survey."
219. Ahn, "Government-Party Coordination," 376–77; see also Drifte, *Japan's Quest*, 131.
220. Quoted in Ahn, "Government-Party Coordination," 371 n. 5; see also Drifte, *Japan's Quest*, 131.
221. Masahiko Ishizuka, "Security Council Issue"; "Japan's Stance on UNSC Membership."
222. Tazaki, "Japan's Socialist Premier."
223. Ahn, "Government-Party Coordination," 371.
224. Ahn, "Government-Party Coordination," 371; "Japan UNSC Membership Studied"; Drifte, *Japan's Quest*, 131.
225. Quoted in "Kono Sees Some Time."
226. Quoted in "Kono Sees Some Time."
227. "Kono Not Opposed."
228. "Japan's Stance on UNSC Seat."
229. Ahn, "Government-Party Coordination," 371; "Japan UNSC Membership Studied"; Drifte, *Japan's Quest*, 131; "Murayama Turns Positive"; "Murayama Sounds Strong Support."
230. Ahn, "Government-Party Coordination," 372; Drifte, *Japan's Quest*, 131.
231. Drifte, *Japan's Quest*, 131 "Kono to Voice Japan's Wish."
232. "Coalition Agrees."
233. Drifte, *Japan's Quest*, 131; see also Ahn, "Government-Party Coordination," 372.
234. Donnet, "Japan."
235. "Japan and the UN."
236. "Japan and the UN."

237. Donnet, "Japan."
238. "Kono to Voice Japan's Wish."
239. "Kono to Voice Japan's Wish"; "Kono to State Japan Cannot Play Combat Role."
240. Drifte, *Japan's Quest,* 132–33; Ahn, "Government-Party Coordination," 373.
241. Ahn, "Government-Party Coordination," 373.
242. Ahn, "Government-Party Coordination," 373.
243. Ahn, "Government-Party Coordination."
244. Ahn, "Government-Party Coordination."
245. Ahn, "Government-Party Coordination," 373; see also Dobson, *Japan,* 137
246. Drifte, *Japan's Quest,* 132–33.
247. In terms of the Goldstein-WEIS classification, the behavior would be coded as 0.0 (state policy).
248. Ahn, "Government-Party Coordination," 376.
249. Ahn, "Government-Party Coordination," 375–76.
250. Ahn, "Government-Party Coordination," 375.
251. Ahn, "Government-Party Coordination," 370.
252. Drifte, *Japan's Quest,* 132–33.
253. Ahn, "Government-Party Coordination," 376.
254. Ahn, "Government-Party Coordination," 381.
255. Ahn, "Government-Party Coordination," 377.
256. Ahn, "Government-Party Coordination," 374.
257. Drifte, *Japan's Quest,* 124.
258. Drifte, *Japan's Quest,* 124.
259. Drifte, *Japan's Quest,* 133; Mulgan, "International Peacekeeping," 1108.
260. Ahn, "Government-Party Coordination," 374.
261. Ahn, "Government-Party Coordination," 375.
262. Dobson, *Japan;* Mulgan, "International Peacekeeping"; Takahara, "Japan"; Inoguchi, "Japan's United Nations Peacekeeping and Other Operations"; Ogata, "Japan's Policy."
263. Mulgan, "International Peacekeeping," 1104.
264. Newman, "Japan's Multilateral Politics," 228; Newman, "Japan and International Organizations," 55–56.
265. Heinrich, Shibata, and Soeya, *United Nations Peace-Keeping Operations,* 1–2; see also Takahara, "Japan"; Leitenberg, "Participation"; Song, "Japanese Peacekeeping Operations"; Katzenstein and Okawara, "Japanese Security Issues."
266. Takahara, "Japan," 52.
267. Heinrich, Shibata and Soeya, *United Nations Peace-Keeping Operations,* 19; see also Akihiko, "UN Peace Operations"; Mochizuki, "Japan's Changing International Role"; Katsumi Ishizuka, "Japan's Policy."
268. Newman, "Japan and International Organizations," 56.
269. Mulgan, "International Peacekeeping," 1112–14.

270. Mulgan, "International Peacekeeping," 1117.
271. Zisk, "Japan's United Nations Peacekeeping Dilemma," 23–24.
272. Mulgan, "International Peacekeeping," 1112.
273. Takahara, "Japan," 65.
274. Dobson, *Japan*, 134; Song, "Japanese Peacekeeping Operations," 64.
275. Zisk, "Japan's United Nations Peacekeeping Dilemma," 23–24.
276. Song, "Japanese Peacekeeping Operations," 63; Heinrich, Shibata, and Soeya, *United Nations Peace-Keeping Operations*, 35.
277. Mulgan, "International Peacekeeping," 1110.
278. Mulgan, "International Peacekeeping," 1110.
279. Mulgan, "International Peacekeeping," 1105.
280. Heinrich, Shibata, and Soeya, *United Nations Peace-Keeping Operations*, 39.
281. Heinrich, Shibata, and Soeya, *United Nations Peace-Keeping Operations*, 28–29.
282. Berger, *Cultures*, 184.
283. Dobson, *Japan*, 138.
284. Dobson, *Japan*, 150.
285. Dobson, *Japan*, 132–33; see also Song, "Japanese Peacekeeping Operations," 62; Akihiko, "Domestic Politics," 4–5; Hideo, "Political Realignment," 112.
286. Dobson, *Japan*, 131–32.
287. Mulgan, "International Peacekeeping," 1106.
288. Mulgan, "International Peacekeeping," 1105.
289. Dobson, *Japan*, 132.
290. Heinrich, Shibata, and Soeya, *United Nations Peace-Keeping Operations*, 28–29.
291. Mulgan, "International Peacekeeping," 1106; see also Song, "Japanese Peacekeeping Operations," 62.
292. Mulgan, "International Peacekeeping," 1106.
293. Dobson, *Japan*, 138.
294. Takahara, "Japan," 62–63.
295. Heinrich, Shibata, and Soeya, *United Nations Peace-Keeping Operations*, 34.
296. "Japan Unlikely to Send Troops."
297. "Japan Peacekeepers Get OK"; see also Heinrich, Shibata, and Soeya, *United Nations Peace-Keeping Operations*, 28–29.
298. Kin, "Japan Set."
299. Mulgan, "International Peacekeeping," 1107.
300. In terms of the Goldstein-WEIS classification, sending of troops to UNDOF would be coded as +8.3 (extend military assistance).
301. Leitenberg, "Participation," 30.
302. Mulgan, "International Peacekeeping," 1108.
303. Dobson, *Japan*, 131.
304. Dobson, *Japan*, 138.

305. Mulgan, "International Peacekeeping," 1106.
306. Zisk, "Japan's United Nations Peacekeeping Dilemma," 30.
307. See Tanaka, "UN Peace"; Cooney, *Japan's Foreign Policy Maturation*; Inoguchi, "Japan's United Nations Peacekeeping and Other Operations"; Song, "Japanese Peacekeeping Operations."
308. Aoi, "Asserting Civilian Power," 117.
309. Aoi, "Asserting Civilian Power," 117.
310. Grimes, "Institutionalized Inertia."
311. Curtis, *Logic*; Stockwin, *Governing Japan* [1999 ed.].
312. "Japan: Parties to End Restrictions."
313. Dobson, *Japan*.
314. Grimes, "Institutionalized Inertia," 373.
315. "Japan: Government May Consider Lifting Ban"; "Japan Backs Its Wider Role."
316. Sakurai, "Japan Governing Party"; see also Barr, "Japan Plots," 1.
317. "Japan Should Fully Join."
318. Newman, "Japan and International Organizations," 46; Stockwin, *Governing Japan* [1999 ed.], 201; Hughes, *Japan's Re-Emergence*, 49–50.
319. Green, *Japan's Reluctant Realism*, 53.
320. Newman, "Japan and International Organizations," 46, 56; Newman, "Japan's Multilateral Politics," 229.
321. Green, *Japan's Reluctant Realism*, 54.
322. "Japan: Parties to End Restrictions"; see also "LDP, New Komeito to Work."
323. "Yamasaki Eyes Removal"; "Japan: Ruling Party Official Calls for Review."
324. Aoki, "Obuchi Willing to Remove Ban."
325. "Japan to Revise Law."
326. "Japan: Foreign Minister Views."
327. Iitake, "Japan."
328. "Japan LDP Confirms Agreement."
329. "Chief Cabinet Secretary Vows."
330. Aoki, "Aoki Favors Lifting Limit"; Aoi, "Asserting Civilian Power," 117–18.
331. "Japan: Ruling Coalition Delays Plan."
332. "Japan Gives Up."
333. Hughes, *Japan's Re-Emergence*, 125; Katsumi Ishizuka, "Japan's Policy."
334. In terms of the Goldstein-WEIS classification, this result would be coded as 0.0 ("explain or state policy") and involved no commitment of resources.
335. Struck, "Japan Forms a New Government," A30.

## Chapter 6

1. See, for example, Robins, "Confusion at Home"; Robins, "Foreign Policy"; Lenore G. Martin, "Turkey's Middle East Foreign Policy"; Hale, *Turkey*.

2. Larrabee and Lesser, *Turkish Foreign Policy*, 2; see also Gözen, "Turkish Foreign Policy"; for an analysis of Turkey's geographical exceptionalism, see Yanık, "Metamorphosis."

3. Lesser, "Beyond 'Bridge or Barrier,'" 219; see also Makovsky and Sayarı, "Introduction," 2; Kut, "Contours." Çelik, *Contemporary Turkish Foreign Policy*, xv, argues that Turkey became more secure than ever at the end of the Cold War.

4. See Lesser, "Beyond 'Bridge or Barrier'"; Hale, *Turkish Foreign Policy*.

5. Hale, *Turkish Foreign Policy*, 327. For more on the significance of geography and a criticism of its often exaggerated importance, see Soysal, "Future."

6. For fairly descriptive discussions of the role of economic and military capabilities and constraints in Turkish foreign policy, see Çelik, *Contemporary Turkish Foreign Policy*, chapter 1; Hale, *Turkish Foreign Policy*, chapter 6. A more focused discussion of international and regional system constraints on Turkish foreign policy across time can be found in Robins, "Foreign Policy," 312–17.

7. Hale, *Turkish Foreign Policy*; see also Lenore G. Martin, "Turkey's Middle East Foreign Policy"; Özcan, *Harmonizing*. For an overview of the history of Turkish foreign policy, see Ahmad, "Historical Background."

8. Soysal, "Future."

9. Robins, *Suits*, 94.

10. For a discussion of the "Sèvres syndrome" among the Turkish public and elite, see Soysal, "Future."

11. Ahmad, "Historical Background," 9.

12. Robins, *Suits*, 105; see also Rumford, "Failing."

13. For a general discussion of the importance of ideational factors in Turkish foreign policy, see Hale, *Turkish Foreign Policy*, 331; Bozdağlıoğlu, *Turkish Foreign Policy*; Özkeçeci-Taner, *Role*; Robins, *Suits*. According to Robins, "Ideology is at least as important as geopolitics in the formulation and pursuit of Turkish foreign policy" (159).

14. Hale, "Economic Issues," 29.

15. Robins, *Suits*, 138; see also Özcan, *Harmonizing*; Çalış, "Turkish State's Identity."

16. Özkeçeci-Taner, *Role*; Bozdağlıoğlu, *Turkish Foreign Policy*, 46; Mango, "Reflections," 9–10; Robins, *Suits*.

17. Robins, "Foreign Policy," 319.

18. Hale, *Turkish Foreign Policy*, 332–33, traces the breakdown in the foreign policy consensus earlier, to the 1960s, but admits that the only real challenge—the attempt to define Turkey as more of a Third World state—was not particularly effective and disappeared until the late 1980s, when views on Turkish foreign policy became more diverse than ever.

19. Robins, "Confusion at Home," 155.

20. Özkeçeci-Taner, "Impact," 260; for a discussion of competing conceptions of national identity across political parties in the 1990s and the relationship to foreign policies toward Central Asia, the EU, and the Middle East, see see Bozdağlıoğlu, *Turkish Foreign Policy*. Özcan, *Harmonizing*, also discusses various Turkish identities.

21. Robins, *Suits*, 145.
22. See Çuhadar-Gürkaynak and Özkeçeci-Taner, "Decisionmaking Process Matters"; Tayfur and Göymen, "Decision Making"; Rubin and Kirişci, *Turkey;* Çarkoğlu and Rubin, *Turkey.*
23. Robins, *Suits*, 3; Çuhadar-Gürkaynak and Özkeçeci-Taner, "Decisionmaking Process Matters," 43.
24. Robins, *Suits*, 380; see also Çalış, "Turkish State's Identity."
25. Çalış, "Turkish State's Identity," 154.
26. Tayfur and Göymen, "Decision Making," 101; see also Çuhadar-Gürkaynak and Özkeçeci-Taner, "Decisionmaking Process Matters," 43; Özkeçeci-Taner, *Role.* Exceptions include Tayfur and Göymen, "Decision Making"; Çuhadar-Gürkaynak and Özkeçeci-Taner, "Decisionmaking Process Matters"; Efegil, "Foreign Policy-Making."
27. Hale, *Turkish Foreign Policy*, 205.
28. Makovsky and Sayarı, "Introduction," 4; Özcan, *Harmonizing*, 83; Çalış, "Turkish State's Identity."
29. Robins, *Suits.*
30. Makovsky and Sayarı, "Introduction," 4; also see Özcan, "Military"; Cizre Sakallıoğlu, "Anatomy"; Cizre and Çınar, "Turkey 2002."
31. Yalim Eralp, "Insider's View."
32. Makovsky, "New Activism," 106.
33. For a review of the constitutional changes and the expected impact, see Özcan, *Harmonizing*, 98–100. All of the cases in this chapter occurred before these changes took place.
34. Efegil, "Foreign Policy-Making," 149; see also Çalış, "Turkish Foreign Policy"; Özcan, "Military"; Yalim Eralp, "Insider's View."
35. Robins, *Suits*, 76; see also Efegil, "Foreign Policy-Making"; Yalim Eralp, "Insider's View."
36. Robins, *Suits*, 77; Makovsky and Sayarı, "Introduction," 4.
37. Larrabee and Lesser, *Turkish Foreign Policy*, 31.
38. Robins, *Suits*, 77. However, Cizre, "Problems," argues that the military broadened the definition of security issues through the end of the 1990s.
39. Robins, "Foreign Policy," 321.
40. Larrabee and Lesser, *Turkish Foreign Policy*, 29, 31; for the argument that the role of the military in foreign and security policy increased in the 1990s, see Özcan, "Military," 13.
41. Efegil, "Foreign Policy-Making," 158.
42. Robins, *Suits*, 72–74; see also Makovsky and Sayarı, "Introduction," 4; Robins, *Suits*, 71–74; Çalış, "Turkish State's Identity," 146–54. Others are more critical of the foreign ministry, citing a lack of coordination and creative thinking and an overload of work, especially since the end of the Cold War. See Yalim Eralp, "Insider's View."
43. Robins, *Suits*, 68.
44. Makovsky and Sayarı, "Introduction," 4.
45. Efegil, "Foreign Policy-Making," 149.

46. Makovsky and Sayarı, "Introduction," 4.
47. Makovsky and Sayarı, "Introduction," 4.
48. Özcan, *Harmonizing*, 83; Aydın, "Twenty Years"; Çalış, "Turkish State's Identity."
49. The Turkish president was elected by Parliament during all of the four cases in this chapter. Recent changes mean that the next president will be the first to be directly elected.
50. Çuhadar-Gürkaynak and Özkeçeci-Taner, "Decisionmaking Process Matters," 57–58. The president does have the power to declare war when Parliament is in recess and in the case of a military attack on Turkish soil (Efegil, "Foreign Policy-Making").
51. Makovsky and Sayarı, "Introduction," 5; see also Özcan, "Military," 14–15.
52. Çalış, "Turkish State's Identity."
53. Çalış, "Turkish State's Identity," 143.
54. Makovsky and Sayarı, "Introduction," 5; Hale, *Turkish Foreign Policy*, 205.
55. Özcan, *Harmonizing*.
56. Yalim Eralp, "Insider's View."
57. Makovsky and Sayarı, "Introduction," 5; Robins, *Suits*, 79.
58. Çalış, "Turkish State's Identity," 138.
59. Kesgin and Kaarbo, "When and How."
60. Robins, *Suits*, 90.
61. Makovsky and Sayarı, "Introduction," 6; Larrabee and Lesser, *Turkish Foreign Policy*, 34–35; Robins, "Foreign Policy," 323–24.
62. Larrabee and Lesser, *Turkish Foreign Policy*, 33.
63. Larrabee and Lesser, *Turkish Foreign Policy*, 34.
64. Winrow, "Turkey," 202; see also Özcan, *Harmonizing*, 101.
65. Makovsky and Sayarı, "Introduction," 7; see also Efegil, "Foreign Policy-Making," 158.
66. Robins, "Foreign Policy," 323. Yalim Eralp, "Insider's View," agrees that the role of the media may be increasing and argues that political and military elites pay close attention to media criticism.
67. The sole exception is Sezer (2000–2007), who was the chair of the Constitutional Court before becoming president.
68. Özkeçeci-Taner, "Impact," 263.
69. Özcan, "Military," 13.
70. This statistic excludes caretaker governments, such as Prime Minister Ecevit's minority government before the 1999 elections. For a history of Turkish governments, see Akşin, *Turkey*; Zürcher, *Turkey*; see also the website of the Turkish Grand National Assembly, http://www.tbmm.gov.tr/hukumetler/hukumetler.htm.
71. Çuhadar-Gürkaynak and Özkeçeci-Taner, "Decisionmaking Process Matters," 44. Özkeçeci-Taner, "Impact," and Özkeçeci-Taner, *Role*, are significant exceptions.
72. Aydın, "Determinants," 118.

73. Bahcheli, "Turkish Policy," 147.
74. Atila Eralp, "Turkey and the European Union," 81.
75. Hale, *Turkish Foreign Policy*, 195–96.
76. Hale, *Turkish Foreign Policy*, 331.
77. Robins, "Foreign Policy," 320. According to Keridis, "The election of the Justice and Development (AK) Party to power [in 2002] with a strong parliamentary majority was greeted by many of Turkey's friends abroad as a boost for Turkish democracy and a fresh start away from the corrupt and ineffective squabblings of the fragmented coalition governments of the past" ("Foreign Strategies," 321).
78. Dodd, *Politics*, 203.
79. Özkeçeci-Taner, *Role*.
80. Appearing both here and in Özkeçeci-Taner's research are the cases on the customs union, the Islamic opening, and the Helsinki Declaration.
81. Akçapar, *Turkey's New European Era*, 35.
82. For an analysis of the underlying dynamics in the ups and downs in Turkish-EU relations, see Öniş, "Luxembourg."
83. Atila Eralp, "Turkey and the European Union in the Post–Cold War Era," 180.
84. For a review of issues between the EU and Turkey over the customs union agreement, see Kramer, "EU-Turkey Customs Union."
85. Özkeçeci-Taner, "Impact."
86. Atila Eralp, "Turkey and the European Union in the Post–Cold War Era," 177.
87. Atila Eralp, "Turkey and the European Union in the Post–Cold War Era," 177.
88. Atila Eralp, "Turkey and the European Union in the Post–Cold War Era," 181.
89. Park, "Turkey's European Candidacy," 34; Atila Eralp, "Turkey and European Union in the Aftermath of the Cold War," 44.
90. Atila Eralp, "Turkey and the European Union in the Post–Cold War Era," 181.
91. Müftüler-Baç and Güney, "European Union," 287; Theophanous, "Cyprus," 223.
92. Atila Eralp, "Turkey and the European Union in the Post–Cold War Era," 181.
93. Öniş, "Luxembourg," 482.
94. The Republican People's Party had merged with the Social Democratic People's Party (SHP) but can be identified as the Republican People's Party for convenience; see Özkeçeci-Taner, "Role," 132 n. 76.
95. *Role*.
96. Özkeçeci-Taner, "Role," 186.
97. Kramer, "EU-Turkey Customs Union," 61.
98. Uslu, "Cyprus Question," 225.

99. The coalition briefly broke up in the fall of 1995 but formed again within twenty-five days. See Akşin, *Turkey*.
100. Özkeçeci-Taner, "Role," 135.
101. Özkeçeci-Taner, "Role," 139.
102. Özkeçeci-Taner, *Role*.
103. Quoted in Özkeçeci-Taner, "Role," 140.
104. Özkeçeci-Taner, *Role*.
105. Atila Eralp, "Turkey and the European Union in the Post–Cold War Era," 179.
106. Özkeçeci-Taner, *Role*.
107. Özkeçeci-Taner, *Role*.
108. Özkeçeci-Taner, *Role*.
109. Özkeçeci-Taner, "Role," 190.
110. Özkeçeci-Taner, "Role," 111–18, 191.
111. Özkeçeci-Taner, *Role*.
112. Özkeçeci-Taner, "Role," 194.
113. Özkeçeci-Taner, "Role," 192.
114. Özkeçeci-Taner, *Role*.
115. Ministry of Foreign Affairs, quoted in Özkeçeci-Taner, "Role," 198.
116. Özkeçeci-Taner, *Role*.
117. Özkeçeci-Taner, *Role*.
118. Özkeçeci-Taner, "Role," 193.
119. Özkeçeci-Taner, "Role," 200.
120. Özkeçeci-Taner, "Role," 200.
121. Özkeçeci-Taner, *Role*.
122. Özkeçeci-Taner, "Role," 204.
123. On the Goldstein-WEIS conflict-cooperation scale, this behavior is consistent with a +6.5 score, as it makes a "substantive agreement."
124. Kaarbo, "Power and Influence."
125. Cizre, "Tansu Çiller," 206.
126. Özkeçeci-Taner, "Role," 203.
127. Özkeçeci-Taner, "Role," 191.
128. Özkeçeci-Taner, "Role."
129. Çelik, *Contemporary Turkish Foreign Policy*, 90; see also Kirişci, "Turkey," 41–42; Ayata, "Changes."
130. Müftüler-Baç, "Never-Ending Story," 254.
131. Bozdağlıoğlu, *Turkish Foreign Policy*, 134.
132. Yavuz, "Political Islam," 63.
133. Çelik, *Contemporary Turkish Foreign Policy*, 90; Yavuz, "Political Islam," 72–73.
134. Kramer, *Changing Turkey*, 56.
135. Yavuz, "Political Islam," 80; see also Larrabee and Lesser, *Turkish Foreign Policy*, 41; Kramer, *Changing Turkey*, 56.
136. Cornell, *Turkey*, 34, 41.

137. Sayarı, "Changing Party System," 20; see also Ayata, "Changes."
138. Çelik, *Contemporary Turkish Foreign Policy*, 22.
139. Sayarı, "Changing Party System," 21
140. Cornell, *Turkey*, 46.
141. Çelik, *Contemporary Turkish Foreign Policy*, 83
142. Özdalga, "Necmettin Erbakan," 127.
143. Özdalga, "Necmettin Erbakan," 134–38.
144. Robins, *Suits*, 146. For a discussion of Erbakan's political career and the Welfare Party's connections to Islamic states and groups before assuming power, see Robins, *Suits*, 149–54.
145. Robins, *Suits*, 145.
146. Bozdağlıoğlu, *Turkish Foreign Policy*, 133.
147. Robins, "Turkish Foreign Policy," 86.
148. Robins, "Turkish Foreign Policy," 86; see also Robins, *Suits*, 146–49.
149. Hale, *Turkish Foreign Policy*, 238–39; see also Gunduz, "Turkey's Approach," 13.
150. Quoted in Robins, *Suits*, 148.
151. Cizre, "Tansu Çiller," 199.
152. Cizre, "Tansu Çiller," 200–202.
153. Cizre, "Tansu Çiller," 206–10.
154. Cizre, "Tansu Çiller," 202.
155. Hale, *Turkish Foreign Policy*, 197.
156. Hale, *Turkish Foreign Policy*, 239.
157. Bozdağlıoğlu, *Turkish Foreign Policy*, 135; see also Robins, "Turkish Foreign Policy," 88–90.
158. Bozdağlıoğlu, *Turkish Foreign Policy*, 133.
159. Quoted in Çelik, *Contemporary Turkish Foreign Policy*, 83.
160. Hale, *Turkish Foreign Policy*, 298.
161. Çelik, *Contemporary Turkish Foreign Policy*, 84. For a summary of the domestic reaction to this trip, see Robins, *Suits*, 156–57.
162. Bozdağlıoğlu, *Turkish Foreign Policy*, 134.
163. Çelik, *Contemporary Turkish Foreign Policy*, 84.
164. Çelik, *Contemporary Turkish Foreign Policy*, 84–85.
165. Robins, *Suits*, 158.
166. Robins, *Suits*, 158.
167. Bozdağlıoğlu, *Turkish Foreign Policy*, 135.
168. Hale, *Turkish Foreign Policy*, 226; see also Robins, "Turkish Foreign Policy," 85.
169. Hale, *Turkish Foreign Policy*, 226; see also Kirişci, "Turkey," 42–43.
170. Bozdağlıoğlu, *Turkish Foreign Policy*, 134; Kramer, *Changing Turkey*, 71; Robins, "Turkish Foreign Policy," 89–90.
171. Robins, "Turkish Foreign Policy," 90.
172. Hale, *Turkish Foreign Policy*, 298.
173. According to Goldstein-WEIS codes, most of these behaviors would be

moderate, falling into categories such as "denounce," (-3.4) "criticize" (-2.2), "visit" (+1.9) and "reassure" (+2.8). Only the "substantive agreement" with Iran would be considered somewhat extreme.

174. Hale, *Turkish Foreign Policy*, 238.
175. Robins, *Suits*, 156.
176. Robins, *Suits*, 156.
177. White, "Pragmatists or Ideologues?," 27.
178. Robins, "Turkish Foreign Policy."
179. Mufti, "Daring and Caution."
180. Robins, "Turkish Foreign Policy."
181. Robins, "Turkish Foreign Policy"; Robins, *Suits;* for the military's reactions to Erbakan's policies, see Özcan, "Foreign."
182. Bozdağlıoğlu, *Turkish Foreign Policy*, 135.
183. Hale, *Turkish Foreign Policy*, 298.
184. Kramer, *Changing Turkey*, 72.
185. Hale, *Turkish Foreign Policy*, 299.
186. Bozdağlıoğlu, *Turkish Foreign Policy*, 137; see also Ayata, "Changes."
187. Hale, *Turkish Foreign Policy*, 299; see also Çelik, *Contemporary Turkish Foreign Policy*, 86, Özdalga, "Necmettin Erbakan"; Cornell, *Turkey*, 47.
188. Robins, "Foreign Policy," 322.
189. Çelik, *Contemporary Turkish Foreign Policy*, 86.
190. Cizre, "Tansu Çiller," 204; see also Hale, *Turkish Foreign Policy*, 226; Robins, "Foreign Policy," 322.
191. Robins, "Turkish Foreign Policy," 96.
192. Özkeçeci-Taner, "Impact," 274.
193. Kramer, *Changing Turkey*, 71; see also Robins, "Turkish Foreign Policy"; Çelik, *Contemporary Turkish Foreign Policy.*
194. Özkeçeci-Taner, "Impact," 274.
195. Hale, *Turkish Foreign Policy*, 239.
196. Hale, *Turkish Foreign Policy*, 206.
197. Yavuz, "Political Islam," 63.
198. Atila Eralp, "Turkey and the European Union," 71–72; see also Bahcheli, "Turkish Policy," 140.
199. Özkeçeci-Taner, "Role," 342; Park, "Turkey's European Candidacy," 36.
200. Atila Eralp, "Turkey and the European Union in the Post–Cold War Era," 184; for a discussion of the factors that led to the EU approach at the Helsinki Summit, see Atila Eralp, "Turkey and the European Union," 75–79.
201. Bahcheli, "Turkish Policy," 140.
202. Çuhadar-Gürkaynak and Özkeçeci-Taner, "Decisionmaking Process Matters," 57; "Turkey: Justice Minister"; "Cem." For background on the Cyprus issue in EU-Turkish relations, see Müftüler-Baç and Güney, "European Union"; Süvarierol, "Cyprus Obstacle."
203. Çuhadar-Gürkaynak and Özkeçeci-Taner, "Decisionmaking Process Matters," 56.

204. Özkeçeci-Taner, "Role," 347. Öniş, "Domestic Politics," refers to the acceptance of the Helsinki Declaration as a "turning point."
205. Atila Eralp, "Turkey and the European Union," 75–79.
206. "Turkey's Long March." At this time, German, French, and U.S. leaders also contacted Turkey to urge the government to accept the offer (Park, "Turkey's European Candidacy," 38).
207. Çuhadar-Gürkaynak and Özkeçeci-Taner, "Decisionmaking Process Matters," 59.
208. Çuhadar-Gürkaynak and Özkeçeci-Taner, "Decisionmaking Process Matters," 59; "Turkish Cabinet."
209. Çuhadar-Gürkaynak and Özkeçeci-Taner, "Decisionmaking Process Matters," 59–60.
210. Çuhadar-Gürkaynak and Özkeçeci-Taner, "Decisionmaking Process Matters," 77 n. 50.
211. Çuhadar-Gürkaynak and Özkeçeci-Taner, "Decisionmaking Process Matters," 63.
212. Özkeçeci-Taner, *Role;* Çuhadar-Gürkaynak and Özkeçeci-Taner, "Decisionmaking Process Matters."
213. Hale, *Turkish Foreign Policy,* 241, argues that the leaders of these parties were more nationalistic on the question of Cyprus and less so toward the EU in general; see also Özkeçeci-Taner, *Role.*
214. Özkeçeci-Taner, "Role," 326.
215. Özkeçeci-Taner, "Role," 335–38.
216. Özkeçeci-Taner, "Role," 337.
217. Özkeçeci-Taner, "Role," 336–37.
218. Özkeçeci-Taner, "Role," 349.
219. Özkeçeci-Taner, "Role," 341–42.
220. Özkeçeci-Taner, "Role," 350.
221. Dunér and Deverell, "Country Cousin"; Tachau, "Bülent Ecevit."
222. Özkeçeci-Taner, *Role;* see also Arıkan, "Programme"; Özcan, *Harmonizing,* 88–89.
223. Özkeçeci-Taner, "Role," 349; see also Dunér and Deverell, "Country Cousin," 6–7.
224. Çuhadar-Gürkaynak and Özkeçeci-Taner, "Decisionmaking Process Matters," 60–61.
225. Özkeçeci-Taner, "Role," 348.
226. Özkeçeci-Taner, "Role," 352; see also Dunér and Deverell, "Country Cousin," 6.
227. Özkeçeci-Taner, "Role," 353.
228. Black, "Turkey"; Özkeçeci-Taner, "Role," 346; Park, "Turkey's European Candidacy," 38.
229. Çuhadar-Gürkaynak and Özkeçeci-Taner, "Decisionmaking Process Matters," 62; for specific articles of the Helsinki Declaration that were source of friction in the coalition, see Özkeçeci-Taner, "Role," 345.

230. Özkeçeci-Taner, "Role," 345.
231. Özkeçeci-Taner, "Role," 348; for a supporting quotation from the MHP's leader, see 349.
232. Özkeçeci-Taner, "Role," 353.
233. Robins, *Suits*, 111.
234. Özkeçeci-Taner, "Role," 342, 350.
235. Özkeçeci-Taner, *Role*, 175.
236. Çuhadar-Gürkaynak and Özkeçeci-Taner, "Decisionmaking Process Matters," 63.
237. Robins, *Suits*, 111.
238. Çuhadar-Gürkaynak and Özkeçeci-Taner, "Decisionmaking Process Matters," 62; see also Yalim Eralp, "Insider's View."
239. Robins, *Suits*, 111.
240. Çuhadar-Gürkaynak and Özkeçeci-Taner, "Decisionmaking Process Matters," 63.
241. Özkeçeci-Taner, *Roles*, 176.
242. Özkeçeci-Taner, "Role," 354.
243. "Ecevit Assures"; "'Out of the Question.'"
244. Çuhadar-Gürkaynak and Özkeçeci-Taner, "Decisionmaking Process Matters," 64, 77.
245. Özkeçeci-Taner, "Impact," 267.
246. In terms of the Goldstein-WEIS classification, the acceptance would be coded as +3.0 (agree to future action and to negotiate) and the separate memo as −3.4 (denounce, denigrate).
247. Özkeçeci-Taner, *Role*, 194.
248. Özkeçeci-Taner, "Role," 393.
249. Çuhadar-Gürkaynak and Özkeçeci-Taner, "Decisionmaking Process Matters," 61.
250. Dunér and Deverell, "Country Cousin," 10.
251. Özkeçeci-Taner, "Role," 355 n. 333.
252. Özkeçeci-Taner, "Role," 393.
253. For a history of human rights in Turkish foreign relations, see Robins, *Suits*, 34–42.
254. Atila Eralp, "Turkey and the European Union," 80.
255. Hale, "Human Rights," 118–19.
256. "Turkey Death Penalty."
257. "Turkey Won't Abolish Death Penalty."
258. "Turkey Death Penalty."
259. Frantz, "Turkey's Choice."
260. Dunér and Deverell, "Country Cousin," 2, 13; see also Yalim Eralp, "Insider's View," 2003.
261. "EU Says Turkey Can't Execute Ocalan."
262. Dogar and Dennis, "Turkey vs. Europe."
263. Robins, *Suits*, 30.

264. Rumford, "Failing," 51.
265. Hale, *Turkish Foreign Policy*, 351.
266. Hale, *Turkish Foreign Policy*, 352–53.
267. Hale, *Turkish Foreign Policy*, 340.
268. Hale, "Human Rights," 107.
269. Atila Eralp, "Turkey and the European Union," 80.
270. Öniş, "Domestic Politics," 13–14.
271. McLaren and Müftüler-Bac, "Turkish Parliamentarians' Perspectives."
272. Hale, "Human Rights," 122.
273. Although the only opposition party, the True Path Party supported EU accession and the abolition of the death penalty. Hale, "Human Rights," 109, argues that the party "could not be expected to help the government unless a pledge for early elections was part of the deal."
274. Hale, *Turkish Foreign Policy*, 350.
275. Hale, "Human Rights," 107.
276. Avcı, "Turkey's Slow EU Candidacy," 164.
277. "General Speaks."
278. Avcı, "Turkey's Slow EU Candidacy," 164.
279. Avcı, "Turkey's Slow EU Candidacy," 164. Yalim Eralp reports that the government "waited for the military to state that the execution or nonexecution of the PKK leader Öcalan—a matter in fact of deep interest to the military and to millions of Turks—did not concern them and that this was a decision for the parliament" ("Insider's," 121–22).
280. Yalim Eralp, "Insider's View," 80; see also Dunér and Deverell, "Country Cousin," 3.
281. "Turkey Death Penalty."
282. Hale, "Human Rights," 109.
283. Hale, *Turkish Foreign Policy*, 350; Özkeçeci-Taner, "Role," 334.
284. Avcı, "Turkey's Slow EU Candidacy," 160.
285. Dunér and Deverell, "Country Cousin," 3.
286. Hale, *Turkish Foreign Policy*, 109.
287. Özkeçeci-Taner, "Role," 352–53.
288. Ecevit, quoted in Dunn. "Move."
289. "Turkish Premier Signals."
290. "Turkish Justice Minister."
291. "Turkey's First Step."
292. Öniş, "Domestic Politics," 18. Although the Motherland Party generally supported EU reforms and the abolition of the death penalty, a few members dissented. See "Turkey: ANAP Official" (via FBIS Translated Excerpt); "Akbulut, Speaker of Parliament."
293. Tinc, "On Death Penalty," translated in FBIS, December 20, 1999; "Hang Öcalan."
294. Tinc, "On Death Penalty"; "Hang Öcalan."
295. "Hang Öcalan."

296. "Turkish PM."
297. "Justice Minister Turk."
298. Sisler, "EU's Death-Penalty Objection Divides Turkey"; "Turks Consider Lifting Death Penalty."
299. "Turks Consider Lifting Death Penalty."
300. "Deputy PM."
301. Avcı, "Turkey's Slow EU Candidacy," 160–61.
302. "Deputy PM."
303. Avcı, "Turkey's Slow EU Candidacy," 163.
304. "Turkey: Reforms."
305. Özcan, *Harmonizing*, 89, 153.
306. In terms of the Goldstein-WEIS scale, this foreign policy behavior would be coded as "yield position, retreat" (+0.6).
307. Kurşat Eser of Nationalist Action Party, reported in Tinc, "On Death Penalty."
308. Başkan, "At the Crossroads," 65.
309. "Turkey: Party Leaders."
310. "Turkey: Party Leaders."
311. Avcı, "Turkey's Slow EU Candidacy," 197.
312. Atila Eralp, "Turkey and the European Union," 80; Öniş, "Domestic Politics," 13–14.
313. Robins, *Suits*, 11.

## Chapter 7

1. Özkeçeci-Taner, *Role*.
2. The average number of parties in the extreme cases was 3.75. It was 3.3 in the cooperation cases and 2.75 in the cases of neutral and both conflictual and cooperative behavior.
3. The average number of parties in the conflict cases was 2.5. It was 3.3 in the cooperation cases and 2.75 in the cases of neutral and both conflictual and cooperative behavior.
4. The average number of parties in the cases with constraints in the direction of peace was 3.4; it was 2.4 in the cases without peace constraints. The average number of parties in cases where constraints were not successful was 3.4 and was 2.4 in the cases with successful constraints. The average number of parties in cases with no compromises was 3.25; it was 2.5 in the cases with compromises.
5. The average percentage of seats controlled in the cases of cooperation was 60.2; it was 58.5 in the cases of neutral and both conflictual and cooperative behavior and 51.5 in the conflict cases.
6. There were no rightist junior parties in conflict cases; half of the cases of cooperation and half of the cases of neutral and both cooperation and conflict had rightist junior parties.

7. There were rightist junior parties in 50 percent of the extreme cases and 38 percent of the moderate cases. There were no rightist junior parties in the cases with constraints in the direction of peace and there were rightist junior parties in 71 percent of the cases with constraints not in the direction of peace. There were rightist junior parties in 20 percent of the cases with successful constraints and in 57 percent of the cases with unsuccessful constraints. There were rightist parties in 25 percent of the cases with compromises and in 50 percent of the cases with no compromises.

8. In the Islamic Opening case, the result was both conflictual and cooperative policy.

9. For research on the boomerang effect and minority influence, see Maass and Clark, "Conversion Theory"; Gaffié, "Processes"; Wood et al., "Self-Definition."

10. Hudson, "Foreign Policy Analysis."

11. Nousiainen and Blondel, "Conclusion," 306; see also Frognier, "Single Party/Coalition Distinction."

12. Wood et al., "Processes"; Kaarbo and Beasley, "Political Perspective."

13. Massie, "Britain's Coalition of Pain."

14. Schafer and Crichlow, *Groupthink*.

# Bibliography

"53% Support Permanent Seat for Japan in UNSC, Says Poll." *Daily Yomiuri*, June 5, 1994.
Achen, Christopher H., and Duncan Snidal. "Rational Deterrence Theory and Comparative Case Studies." *World Politics* 41 (1989): 143–69.
Adamson, Fiona B. "Democratization and Domestic Sources of Foreign Policy: Turkey in the 1974 Cyprus Crisis." *Political Science Quarterly* 116 (2001): 277–303.
Adler, Emmanuel. *The Power of Ideology: The Quest for Technological Autonomy in Argentina and Brazil*. Berkeley: University of California Press, 1987.
"Afghanistan Is Netherlands' Most Disastrous Overseas Mission." *Xinhua News Agency*, November 4, 2005.
Ahmad, Ahmad. *The Turkish Experiment in Democracy, 1950–1975*. Boulder, Colo.: Westview, 1977.
Ahmad, Feroz. "The Historical Background of Turkey's Foreign Policy." In *The Future of Turkish Foreign Policy*, edited by Lenore G. Martin and Dimitris Keridis, 9–33. Cambridge: MIT Press, 2004.
Ahmad, Feroz. *The Turkish Experiment in Democracy, 1950–1975*. Boulder, Colo.: Westview, 1977.
Ahn, C. S. "Government-Party Coordination in Japan's Foreign Policy-Making: The Issue of Permanent Membership in the UNSC." *Asian Survey* 37 (1997): 368–82.
Ahn, C. S. "Interministry Coordination in Japan's Foreign Policy Making." *Pacific Affairs* 71 (1998): 41–60.
"Akbulut, Speaker of Parliament—'Regarding Terrorist Attacks in Turkey, Death Penalty Is Legal and Necessary.'" *Anadolu Agency*, June 7, 1999.
Akçapar, Burak. *Turkey's New European Era: Foreign Policy on the Road to EU Membership*. Lanham, Md.: Rowman and Littlefield, 2007.
Akihiko, Tanaka. "Domestic Politics and Foreign Policy." In *Japanese Foreign Policy Today: A Reader*, edited by Inoguchi Takashi and Turnendra Jain, 111–28. New York: Palgrave, 2000.
Akihiko, Tanaka. "UN Peace Operations and Japan-U.S. Relations." In *United*

*States-Japan Relations and International Institutions after the Cold War,* edited by Peter Gourevitch, Takashi Inoguchi, and Courtney Purrington, 59–83. La Jolla, Calif.: Graduate School of International Relations and Pacific Studies, 1995.

Akşin, Sina. *Turkey: From Empire to Revolutionary Republic.* New York: New York University Press, 2007.

Alvaro, Eusebio M., and William D. Crano. "Indirect Minority Influence: Evidence for Leniency in Source Evaluation and Counterargumentation." *Journal of Personality and Social Psychology* 72 (1997): 949–64.

Ames, Paul. "NATO Chief Urges the Netherlands to Quickly Agree on Sending Troops to Afghanistan." *Associated Press,* January 9, 2006.

Anderson, Karen, and Michael Kaeding. "Belgium, the Netherlands, and Luxembourg: Increasingly Cautious Europeans." In *The European Union and the Member States,* edited by E. E. Zeff and E. B. Pirro, 107–26. Boulder, Colo.: Rienner, 2006.

Andeweg, Rudy B. "Centrifugal Forces and Collective Decision-Making: The Case of the Dutch Cabinet." *European Journal of Political Research* 16 (1988): 125–51.

Andeweg, Rudy B., and Galen A. Irwin. *Governance and Politics of the Netherlands.* New York: Palgrave, 2002.

Andeweg, Rudy B., and Galen A. Irwin. *Governance and Politics of the Netherlands.* 2nd ed. New York: Palgrave, 2005.

Aoi, Chiyuki. "Asserting Civilian Power or Risking Irrelevance?: Japan's Post–Cold War Policy Concerning the Use of Force." In *Global Governance: Germany and Japan in the International System,* edited by S. N. Katada, H. W. Maull, and T. Inoguchi, 111–28. Aldershot: Ashgate, 2004.

Aoki, Naoko. "Aoki Favors Lifting Limit on Japan's Peacekeeping Role." *Japan Economic Newswire,* October 15, 1999.

Aoki, Naoko. "Obuchi Willing to Remove Ban on Japan's Peacekeepers." *Japan Economic Newswire,* September 17, 1999.

Apple, R. W., Jr. "U.S. Missiles and the Dutch: News Analysis." *New York Times,* May 28, 1981.

Arıkan, E. Burak. "The Programme of the Nationalist Action Party: An Iron Hand in a Velvet Glove?" *Middle Eastern Studies* 34 (1998): 120–34.

Asch, Solomon. "Opinions and Social Pressure." *Scientific American* 193 (1955): 31–35.

Asch, Solomon. "Studies of Independence and Conformity: A Minority of One against a Unanimous Majority." *Psychological Monographs* 70 (1956): 1–70.

Asmus, Ronald D. *The Politics of Modernizing Short-Range Nuclear Forces in West Germany.* Santa Monica, Calif.: Rand, 1989.

Auerswald, David P. "Inward Bound: Domestic Institutions and Military Conflicts." *International Organization* 53 (1999): 469–504.

Avcı, Gamze. "Turkey's Slow EU Candidacy: Insurmountable Hurdles to Membership or Simple Euro-Skepticism?" *Turkish Studies* 4 (2003): 149–70.

Axelrod, Robert. *Conflict of Interest.* Chicago: Markham, 1970.
Ayata, Sencer. "Changes in Domestic Politics and the Foreign Policy Orientation of the AK Party." In *The Future of Turkish Foreign Policy,* edited by Lenore G. Martin and Dimitris Keridis, 243–76. Cambridge: MIT Press, 2004.
Aydın, Mustafa. "Determinants of Turkish Foreign Policy: Changing Patterns and Conjunctures during the Cold War." *Middle Eastern Studies* 36 (2000): 103–39.
Aydın, Mustafa. "Twenty Years Before, Twenty Years After: Turkish Foreign Policy at the Threshold of the 21st Century." In *Turkey's Foreign Policy in the 21st Century,* edited by Tareq Ismael and Mustafa Aydın, 3–24. Aldershot: Ashgate, 2003.
Bäck, Hanna, and Patrick Dumont. "Combining Large-*n* and Small-*n* Strategies: The Way Forward in Coalition Research." *West European Politics* 30 (2007): 467–501.
Baehr, Peter R. "The Foreign Policy of the Netherlands." In *The Foreign Policy of the Netherlands,* edited by J. H. Leurdijk, 3–28. Alphen aan den Rijn: Sijthoff and Noordhoff, 1978.
Bahcheli, Tozun. "Turkish Policy toward Greece." In *Turkey's New World: Changing Dynamics in Turkish Foreign Policy,* edited by Alan Makovsky and Sabri Sayarı, 131–52. Washington, D.C.: Washington Institute for Near East Policy, 2000.
Barnett, Michael N., ed. *Israel in Comparative Perspective: Challenging the Conventional Wisdom.* Albany: State University of New York Press, 1996.
Barr, Cameron W. "Japan Plots a Less Pacifist Role." *Christian Science Monitor,* January 15, 1999.
Barton, David. "Nuclear Message from the Dutch." *Christian Science Monitor,* August 28, 1981.
Başkan, Filiz. "At the Crossroads of Ideological Divides: Cooperation between Leftists and Ultranationalists in Turkey." *Turkish Studies* 6 (2005): 53–69.
"Battle over Rice Imports Will Test Coalition; Hosokawa Faces a Tough Time Selling Japan's Concession on Farm Trade." *Financial Times,* October 20, 1993.
Bawn, Kathleen, and Frances Rosenbluth. "Short versus Long Coalitions: Electoral Accountability and the Size of the Public Sector." *American Journal of Political Science* 50 (2006): 251–65.
Baylis, Thomas. *Governing by Committee.* Albany: State University of New York Press, 1989.
Bazerman, Max H., Jared R. Curhan, Don A. Moore, and Kathleen L. Valley. "Negotiation." *Annual Review of Psychology* 51 (2003): 279–314.
Beasley, Ryan K. "Collective Interpretations: How Problem Representations Aggregate in Foreign Policy Groups." In *Problem Representation in Foreign Policy Decision Making,* edited by Donald Sylvan and James Voss, 80–115. Cambridge: Cambridge University Press, 1998.
Beasley, Ryan K., Juliet Kaarbo, Charles F. Hermann, and Margaret G. Hermann.

"People and Processes in Foreign Policymaking: Insights from Comparative Case Studies." *International Studies Review* 3 (2001): 217–50.

Beeston, Richard. "Dutch Think Again about Sending Forces to Afghanistan." *Times* of London, November 29, 2005.

Bennett, Andrew, and Colin Elman. "Complex Causal Relations and Case Study Methods: The Example of Path Dependence." *Political Analysis* 14 (2006): 250–67.

Berger, Thomas U. "Alliance Politics and Japan's Postwar Culture of Antimilitarism." In *The U.S.-Japan Alliance: Past, Present, and Future*, edited by Michael J. Green and Patrick M. Cronin, 189–207. New York: Council on Foreign Relations Press, 1999.

Berger, Thomas U. "The Construction of Antagonism: The History Problem in Japan's Foreign Relations." In *Reinventing the Alliance: U.S.-Japan Security Partnership in an Era of Change*, edited by G. John Ikenberry and Takashi Inoguchi, 63–90. New York: Palgrave Macmillan, 2003.

Berger, Thomas U. *Cultures of Antimilitarism: National Security in Germany and Japan*. Baltimore: Johns Hopkins University Press, 2003.

Berger, Thomas U. "Japan's International Relations: The Political and Security Dimensions." In *The International Relations of Northeast Asia*, edited by Samuel S. Kim, 135–70. Lanham, Md.: Rowman and Littlefield, 2003.

Berger, Thomas U. "The Pragmatic Liberalism of an Adaptive State." In *Japan in International Politics: The Foreign Policies of an Adaptive State*, edited by Thomas U. Berger, Mike M. Mochizuki, and Jitsuo Tsuchiyama, 259–300. Boulder, Colo.: Rienner, 2007.

Beunderman, Mark. "Crisis in Dutch Cabinet Formation over Iraq." *EUObserver.com*, March 19, 2003.

Bickerton, Ian. "Dutch Delay Peacekeeping Decision Again." *Financial Times*, December 20, 2005.

Bickerton, Ian, and Daniel Dombey. "Afghan Mission Doubts Threaten Dutch Coalition." *Financial Times*, January 13, 2006.

Bickerton, Ian, and Daniel Dombey. "Dutch Edge Closer to NATO Deployment as Opposition Chief Set to Come on Side." *Financial Times*, February 1, 2006.

Bickerton, Ian, Daniel Dombey, and Rachel Morarjee. "Dutch Decision to Send Troops to Afghanistan Eases NATO Concerns." *Financial Times*, February 4, 2006.

Bickerton, Ian, Daniel Dombey, and Rachel Morarjee. "Dutch MPs Back Sending Troops to Afghanistan." *Financial Times*, February 3, 2006.

Billings, Robert S., and Charles F. Hermann. "Problem Identification in Sequential Policy Decision Making: The Re-Representation of Problems." In *Problem Representation in Foreign Policy Decision Making*, edited by D. Sylvan and J. Voss, 53–79. Cambridge: Cambridge University Press.

Bjereld, Ulfand, and Ann-Marie Ekengren. "Foreign Policy Dimensions: A Comparison between the United States and Sweden." *International Studies Quarterly* 43 (1999): 503–18.

Black, Ian. "Turkey Embroiled in EU Membership Crisis." *Guardian*, December 11, 1999.

Blaker, Michael. "Negotiating on Rice: 'No, No, a Thousand Times, No.'" In *International Comparative Studies of Negotiating Behavior*, edited by Hiroshi Kimura, 211–40. Kyoto: International Research Center for Japanese Studies, 1998.

Blondel, Jean. "Introduction: Western European Cabinets in Comparative Perspective." In *Cabinets in Western Europe*, edited by Jean Blondel and Ferdinand Müller-Rommel, 1–16. New York: St. Martin's, 1997.

Blondel, Jean, and Ferdinand Müller-Rommel. "Introduction." In *Governing Together: The Extent and Limits of Joint Decision Making*, edited by Jean Blondel and Ferdinand Müller-Rommel, 1–19. New York: St. Martin's, 1993.

Bolkestein, Frits. Interview by author. March 2006.

Bolleyer, Nicole. "Small Parties: From Party Pledges to Government Policy." *West European Politics* 30 (2007): 121–47.

Bozdağlıoğlu, Yücel. *Turkish Foreign Policy and Turkish Identity: A Constructivist Approach*. New York: Routledge, 2003.

Brauer, Markus, and Charles M. Judd. "Group Polarization and Repeated Attitude Expressions: A New Take on an Old Topic." In *European Review of Social Psychology*, edited by Wolfgang Stroebe and Miles Hewstone, 7:173–208. Chichester: Wiley, 1996.

Breuning, Marijke. "Foreign Policy in America's Backyard: Dutch and American Responses to the December 8th Murders in Suriname." *Acta Politica* 32 (1997): 302–26.

Breuning, Marijke. "Words and Deeds: Foreign Assistance Rhetoric and Policy Behavior in the Netherlands, Belgium, and the United Kingdom." *International Studies Quarterly* 39 (1995): 235–54.

Brockner, Joel, and Jeffrey Z. Rubin. *Entrapment in Escalating Conflicts: A Social Psychological Analysis*. New York: Springer-Verlag, 1985.

Brown, Rupert. *Group Processes*. Oxford: Blackwell, 2000.

Browne, Eric C. "Considerations on the Construction of a Theory of Cabinet Coalition Behavior." In *Governmental Coalitions in Western Democracies*, edited by Eric C. Browne and J. Dreijmanis, 335–57. New York: Longman, 1982.

Bueno de Mesquita, Bruce, James D. Morrow, Randolph M. Siverson, and Alastair Smith. "An Institutional Explanation of the Democratic Peace." *American Political Science Review* 93 (1999): 791–807.

Bullock, Robert W. "Market Opening in Japan: Deregulation, Reregulation, and Cross-Sectoral Variation." In *New Perspectives on U.S.-Japan Relations*, edited by Gerald L. Curtis, 39–81. Tokyo: Japan Center for International Exchange, 2000.

Burnstein, E., and M. L. Berbaum. "Stages in Group Decision Making: The Decomposition of Historical Narratives." *Political Psychology* 4 (1983): 531–61.

Butera, Fabrizzio, and Gabriel Mugny. "Conflicts and Social Influences in Hypothesis Testing." In *Group Consensus and Minority Influence: Implications for*

*Innovation*, edited by Carsten K. W. De Dreu and Nanne K. De Vries, 160–82. Oxford: Blackwell, 2001.

Calder, Kent E. "The Institutions of Japanese Foreign Policy." In *The Process of Japanese Foreign Policy: Focus on Asia*, edited by Richard L. Grant, 1–24. London: Royal Institute of International Affairs, 1997.

Calder, Kent E. "Review: Japanese Foreign Economic Policy Formation: Explaining the Reactive State." *World Politics* 40 (1988): 517–41.

Çalış, Şaban. "The Turkish State's Identity and Foreign Policy Decision-Making Process." *Mediterranean Quarterly* 6 (1995): 135–50.

Çarkoğlu, Ali, and Barry Rubin, eds. *Turkey and the European Union: Domestic Politics, Economic Integration, and International Dynamics*. London: Cass, 2003.

Castle, Stephen. "Dutch Government Could Fall over Afghanistan." *Independent*, January 14, 2006.

Castle, Stephen. "Why an Expansion of NATO's Role Has Divided the Dutch." *Belfast Telegraph*, January 17, 2006.

Çelik, Yasemin. *Contemporary Turkish Foreign Policy*. Westport, Conn.: Praeger, 1999.

"Cem: Turkey's EU Bid Is Not an Obsession." *Turkish Daily News*. December 1, 1999.

Charlton, Sue Ellen M. *Comparing Asian Politics: India, China, and Japan*. Boulder, Colo.: Westview, 2004.

"Chief Cabinet Secretary Vows to Keep Japan PKO Principles Unchanged." *Jiji Press Ticker Service*, October 15, 1999.

Christensen, Ray. *Ending the LDP Hegemony: Party Cooperation in Japan*. Honolulu: University of Hawai'i Press, 2000.

Cizre, Ümit. "Problems of Democratic Governance of Civil-Military Relations in Turkey and the European Union Enlargement Zone." *European Journal of Political Research* 43 (2004): 107–25.

Cizre, Ümit. "Tansu Çiller: Lusting for Power and Undermining Democracy." In *Political Leaders and Democracy in Turkey*, edited by Metin Heper and Sabri Sayarı, 199–216. Lanham, Md.: Lexington, 2002.

Cizre, Ümit, and Menderes Çınar. "Turkey 2002: Kemalism, Islamism, and Politics in the Light of the February 28 Process." *South Atlantic Quarterly* 102 (2003): 309–32.

Clare, Joe. "Ideological Fractionalization and the International Conflict Behavior of Parliamentary Democracies." *International Studies Quarterly* 54 (2010): 965–87.

Clark, Russell D. "A Few Parallels between Group Polarization and Minority Influence." In *Minority Influence*, edited by Serge Moscovici, A. Mucchi-Faina, and A. Maass, 47–66. Chicago: Nelson-Hall, 1994.

Clark, Russell D., and Anne Maass. "Social Categorization and Minority Influence: The Case of Homosexuality." *European Journal of Social Psychology* 18 (1988): 347–64.

Close, David H. *Greece since 1945*. Harlow: Pearson Education Limited, 2002.

"Coalition Agrees on Basis of Japan's UNSC Bid." *Jiji Press Ticker Service*, September 9, 1994.

Cohen, Bernard C. *Democracies and Foreign Policy: Public Participation in the United States and the Netherlands*. Madison: University of Wisconsin Press, 1995.

Cooney, Kevin J. *Japan's Foreign Policy Maturation: A Quest for Normalcy*. New York: Routledge, 2002.

Cooper, Michael. "Iraq War Threat Splits Dutch Political Parties." *Het Financieele Dagblad*, March 19, 2003.

Cornell, Erik. *Turkey in the 21st Century: Opportunities, Challenges, Threats*. Richmond: Curzon, 2001.

Cortell, Andrew P., and James W. Davis. "When Norms Clash: International Norms, Domestic Practices, and Japan's Internationalization of the GATT/WTO." *Review of International Studies* 31 (2005): 3–25.

Couch, Gregory. "Dutch Help U.S. Men and Arms to the Gulf." *New York Times*, February 19, 2003.

Crano, William D. "Social Influence, Social Identity, and Ingroup Leniency." In *Group Consensus and Minority Influence: Implications for Innovation*, edited by Carsten K. W. De Dreu and Nanne K. De Vries, 160–82. Oxford: Blackwell, 2001.

Crano, William D., and Xin Chen. "The Leniency Contract and Persistence of Majority and Minority Influence." *Journal of Personality and Social Psychology* 74 (1998): 1437–50.

Crano, William D., and Radmila Prislin. "Attitudes and Persuasion." *Annual Review of Psychology* 57 (2006): 345–74.

Crano, William D., and Viviane Seyranian. "Majority and Minority Influence." *Social and Personality Psychology Compass* 1 (2007): 572–89.

Çuhadar-Gürkaynak, Esra, and Binnur Özkeçeci-Taner. "Decisionmaking Process Matters: Lesson Learned from Two Turkish Foreign Policy Cases." *Turkish Studies* 5 (2004): 43–78.

Curtis, Gerald L. *The Logic of Japanese Politics: Leaders, Institutions, and the Limits of Change*. New York: Columbia University Press, 1999.

Daalder, Hans, and Ruud Koole. "Liberal Parties in the Netherlands." In *Liberal Parties in Western Europe*, edited by Emil J. Kirchner, 151–77. Cambridge: Cambridge University Press, 1988.

Dalpino, Catharin. "The Role of Human Rights: The Case of Burma." In *Japan in International Politics: The Foreign Policies of an Adaptive State*, edited by Thomas U. Berger, Mike M. Mochizuki, and Jitsuo Tsushiyama, 213–28. Boulder, Colo.: Rienner, 2007.

Damgaard, Erik. "Cabinet Termination." In *Cabinets and Coalition Bargaining: The Democratic Life Cycle in Western Europe*, edited by Kaare Strøm, Wolfgang C. Müller, and Torbjørn Bergman, 301–26. Oxford: Oxford University Press, 2008.

Dawkins, William. "Japan Scales Down Ambitions at UN: Campaign for Seat May Divide Coalition." *Financial Times*, September 21, 1993.

Deboutte, Jan, and Alfred van Staden. "High Politics in the Low Countries." In *Foreign Policy Making in Western Europe*, edited by William Wallace, 56–82. Farnborough: Saxon House, 1978.

De Dreu, Carsten K. W., and Bianca Beersma. "Minority Influence in Organizations." In *Group Consensus and Minority Influence: Implications for Innovation*, edited by Carsten K. W. De Dreu and Nanne K. De Vries, 258–83. Oxford: Blackwell.

De Dreu, Carsten K. W., and Nanne K. De Vries, eds. *Group Consensus and Minority Influence: Implications for Innovation*. Oxford: Blackwell, 2001.

De Dreu, Carsten K. W., and Nanne K. De Vries. "Numerical Support, Information Processing, and Attitude Change." *European Journal of Social Psychology* 23 (1993): 647–62.

De Dreu, Carsten K. W., Nanne K. De Vries, Ernestine H. Gordjin, and Mieke S. Schuurman. "Convergent and Divergent Processing of Majority and Minority Arguments: Effects on Focal and Related Attitudes." *European Journal of Social Psychology* 29 (1999): 329–48.

Dempsey, Judy. "Dutch Down to the Wire on NATO Afghan Mission." *International Herald Tribune*, February 3, 2006.

Dempsey, Judy. "Dutch Future in Afghan Force Uncertain: NATO Awaits Final Decision by the Netherlands on Sending Troops." *International Herald Tribune*, December 24, 2005.

"Deployment of Dutch Troops in Iraq to Be Extended by Six Months." *Agence France Presse*, November 29, 2003.

"Deputy PM: Turkey Can't Join EU for a Decade, No Hurry for Reforms." *Associated Press*, June 11, 2002.

Derbyshire, J. Denis, and Ian Derbyshire. *Encyclopedia of World Political Systems*. Armonk, N.Y.: Sharpe, 2000.

Destler, I. M. "Comment: Multiple Advocacy: Some 'Limits and Costs.'" *American Political Science Review* 66 (1972): 786–90.

de Swann, Abram. *Coalition Theories and Government Formation*. Amsterdam: Elsevier, 1973.

Deutsch, Anthony. "Dutch Premier Says Cabinet Approves Troops to Afghanistan but Parliament Must Endorse." *Associated Press*, December 22, 2005.

Deutsch, Morton, and Shula Shichman. "Conflict: A Social Psychological Perspective." In *Political Psychology*, edited by Margaret G. Hermann, 219–50. San Francisco: Jossey-Bass, 1986.

Di Cicco, Michael. "Japan's PM Eases Socialist Stance." *United Press International*, July 18, 1994.

Dobson, Hugo. *Japan and United Nations Peacekeeping: New Pressures, New Responses*. London: RoutledgeCurzon, 2003.

Dodd, Clement H. *The Crisis of Turkish Democracy*. North Humberside: Eothen, 1983.

Dodd, Clement H. *Politics and Government in Turkey*. Manchester: Manchester University Press, 1969.

Dodd, Clement H. "Turkey and the Cyprus Question." In *Turkey's New World: Changing Dynamics in Turkish Foreign Policy*, edited by Alan Makovsky and Sabri Sayarı, 153–72. Washington, D.C.: Washington Institute for Near East Policy, 2000.

Dogar, Rana, and Mark Dennis. "Turkey vs. Europe." *Newsweek*, November 30, 1998.

Donnet, Pierre Antoine. "Japan Makes a Low-Key Pitch for Permanent Seat on UN Security Council." *Agence France Presse*, September 12, 1994.

Dooley, Robert S., and Gerald E. Fryxell. "Attaining Decision Quality and Commitment from Dissent: The Moderating Effects of Loyalty and Competence in Strategic Decision-Making Teams." *Academy of Management Journal* 42 (1999): 389–402.

Douma, Pyt. *The Netherlands and Rwanda: A Case Study on Dutch Foreign Policies and Interventions in the Contemporary Conflict History of Rwanda*. The Hague: Netherlands Institute of International Relations, 2000.

Drifte, Reinhard. *Japan's Foreign Policy in the 1990s: From Economic Superpower to What Power?* New York: St. Martin's, 1996.

Drifte, Reinhard. *Japan's Quest for a Permanent Security Council Seat: A Matter of Pride or Justice?* London: Macmillan, 2000.

Druckman, James N., and Paul V. Warwick. "The Missing Piece: Measuring Portfolio Salience in Western European Parliamentary Democracies." *European Journal of Political Research* 44 (2005): 17–42.

Dunér, Betril, and Edward Deverell. "Country Cousin: Turkey, the European Union, and Human Rights." *Turkish Studies* 2 (2001): 1–24.

Dunn, Ross. "Move to Scrap Death Penalty; Turkey." *Sydney Morning Herald*, July 3, 1999.

"Dutch Cabinet Formation Goes Ahead as Parties Compromise on Iraq Position." *AFX European Focus*, March 25, 2003.

"Dutch Cabinet Formation under Pressure as Parties Divided over Iraq." *AFX European Focus*, March 19, 2003.

"Dutch Cabinet for Sending Troops to Afghanistan, but No Decision." *Deutsche Presse-Agentur*, December 22, 2005.

"Dutch Discord Fuels Doubts over Afghan Mission." *Financial Times Information*, January 29, 2006.

"Dutch FM Admits That Looking Back Invasion of Iraq Was 'Not Wise.'" *Agence France Presse*, October 5, 2005

"Dutch Government Voices Only Political Support for War against Iraq." *Agence France Presse*, March 18, 2003.

"Dutch Join Pro-Bush Lobby." *Het Financieele Dagblad*, September 25, 2002.

"Dutch Opposition MPs Want Emergency Debate on Iraq Issue." *Radio Netherlands*, August 30, 2002.

"Dutch Parliament Appears Set to Approve Afghanistan Mission." *Agence France Presse*, February 1, 2006.

"Dutch Parliament Approves Afghanistan Mission." *Dutch News Digest*, February 3, 2006.

"Dutch Parliament Will Not Block Patriot Missile Shipment to Turkey." *Agence France Presse,* February 11, 2003.

"Dutch PM Firmly Backs Controversial Military Mission to Afghanistan." *Deutsche Presse-Agentur,* January 11, 2006.

"Dutch Population Supports War against Terrorism [Nederlandse Volk Ondersteunt Strijd Tegen Terrorisme]." *Global News Wire's Abstract,* December 5, 2001.

"Dutch Premier Says Whole Cabinet Now behind Afghan Mission." *Deutsche Presse-Agentur,* January 13, 2006.

"Dutch Prime Minister Cautious over Troops for Afghanistan's Hostile South." *Agence France Presse,* November 29, 2005.

"Dutch Troops Planned for Afghanistan Force." *Deutsche Presse-Agentur,* January 13, 2006.

"Dutch Troops to Leave Iraq in Mar 2005, after Eight-Month Extension." *Agence France Presse,* June 11, 2004.

"Dutch Would Back War in Iraq." *Het Financieele Dagblad,* December 7, 2002.

East, Maurice. "Size and Foreign Policy Behavior: A Test of Two Models." *World Politics* 25 (1973): 556–76.

"Ecevit Assures Turkey Will Not Back Down on Cyprus." *Agence France Presse,* December 12, 1999.

Efegil, Ertan. "Foreign Policy-Making in Turkey: A Legal Perspective." *Turkish Studies* 2 (2001): 147–60.

Eichenberg, Richard C. *Public Opinion and National Security in Western Europe.* Ithaca: Cornell University Press, 1989.

"Eighty Percent of Dutch against War on Iraq without the UN." *Agence France Presse,* February 20, 2003.

Elman, Miriam Fendius. "Unpacking Democracy: Presidentialism, Parliamentarism, and Theories of Democratic Peace." *Security Studies* 9 (2000): 91–126.

Emiko, Torazono. "Japan to Offer Rice Compromise." *Financial Times,* November 25, 1993.

Eralp, Atila. "Turkey and European Union in the Aftermath of the Cold War." In *The Political Economy of Turkey in the Post-Soviet Era: Going West and Looking East?,* edited by Libby Rittenberg, 37–50. Westport, Conn.: Praeger, 1998.

Eralp, Atila. "Turkey and the European Union." In *The Future of Turkish Foreign Policy,* edited by Lenore G. Martin and Dimitris Keridis, 63–82. Cambridge: MIT Press, 2004.

Eralp, Atila. "Turkey and the European Union in the Post–Cold War Era." In *Turkey's New World: Changing Dynamics in Turkish Foreign Policy,* edited by Alan Makovsky and Sabri Sayarı, 173–88. Washington, D.C.: Washington Institute for Near East Policy, 2000.

Eralp, Yalim. "An Insider's View of Turkey's Foreign Policy and Its American Connection." In *The United States and Turkey: Allies in Need,* edited by Morton Abramowitz, 109–43. New York: Century Foundation, 2003.

"EU Says Turkey Can't Execute Ocalan." *Associated Press,* December 12, 1999.

Everts, Philip, ed. *Controversies at Home: Domestic Factors in the Foreign Policy of the Netherlands*. Dordrecht: Nijhoff, 1985.
Everts, Philip. *Democracy and Military Force*. New York: Palgrave, 2002.
Everts, Philip. "Innocence Lost: The Netherlands and the Yugoslav Conflict." In *International Public Opinion and the Bosnia Crisis*, edited by Richard Sobel and Eric Shraev, 219–48. Lanham, Md.: Lexington, 2003.
Everts, Philip. *Public Opinion, the Churches, and Foreign Policy*. Leiden: Institute for International Studies, 1983.
Everts, Philip, and Guido Walraven, eds. *The Politics of Persuasion: Implementation of Foreign Policy by the Netherlands*. Aldershot: Avebury, 1989.
Finnemore, Martha. *National Interests in International Society*. Ithaca: Cornell University Press, 1996.
Fisher, Ronald. *The Social Psychology of Intergroup and International Conflict Resolution*. New York: Springer-Verlag, 1990.
Frantz, Douglas. "Turkey's Choice: European Union or the Death Penalty." *New York Times*, May 30, 2001.
Frognier, Andre-Paul. "The Single Party/Coalition Distinction and Cabinet Decision-Making." In *Governing Together: The Extent and Limits of Joint Decision-Making in Western European Cabinets*, edited by Jean Blondel and Ferdinand Müller-Rommel, 43–73. New York: St. Martin's, 1993.
Fukushima, Akiko. *Japanese Foreign Policy: The Emerging Logic of Multilateralism*. New York: St. Martin's, 1999.
Fukushima, Kiyohiko. "The Revival of 'Big Politics' in Japan." *International Affairs* 72 (1996): 53–72.
Gaenslen, Fritz. "Democracy vs. Efficiency: Some Arguments from the Small Group." *Political Psychology* 2 (1980): 15–29.
Gaffié, B. "The Processes of Minority Influence in an Ideological Confrontation." *Political Psychology* 13 (1992): 407–28.
Gallagher, Michael, Michael Laver, and Peter Mair. *Representative Government in Modern Europe*. 3rd ed. Boston: McGraw-Hill, 2001.
Gallagher, Michael, Michael Laver, and Peter Mair. *Representative Government in Modern Europe: Institutions, Parties, and Governments*. 4th ed. Boston: McGraw-Hill, 2006.
Gallhofer, Irmtraud N., Willem E. Sairs, and Robert Voogt. "From Individual Preference to Group Decisions in Foreign Policy Decision Making: The Dutch Council of Ministers." *European Journal of Political Research* 25 (1994): 151–70.
Gamson, William. "A Theory of Coalition Formation." *American Sociological Review* 26 (1961): 373–82.
Garrison, Jean. *Games Advisors Play: Foreign Policy Advisors in the Influence Process*. College Station: Texas A&M University Press, 1999.
"GATT Chief Urges Japan to Reach Early Decision on Rice." *Japan Economic Newswire*, December 13, 1993.
"A General Speaks His Mind: Growing Turkish Doubts about Joining the EU." *Economist*, March 16, 2002.

George, Alexander. "Case Studies and Theory Development: The Method of Structured, Focused Comparisons." In *Diplomatic History: New Approaches*, edited by Paul G. Lauren, 43–68. New York: Free Press, 1979.

George, Alexander. "The Causal Nexus between Cognitive Beliefs and Decision-Making Behavior." In *Psychological Models in International Politics*, ed. Lawrence S. Falkowski, 95–124. Boulder, Colo.: Westview, 1979.

George, Alexander, and Andrew Bennett. *Case Studies and Theory Development in the Social Sciences*. Cambridge: MIT Press, 2004.

George, Alexander, and Timothy McKeown. "Case Studies and Theories of Organizational Decision-Making." In *Advances in Information Processing in Organizations*, edited by Robert F. Coulam and Richard A. Smith, 21–58. Greenwich, Conn.: JAI, 1985.

Gladdish, Ken. *Governing from the Center: Politics and Policy-Making in the Netherlands*. DeKalb: Northern Illinois University Press, 1991.

Goldstein, Joshua S. "A Conflict-Cooperation Scale for WEIS Events Data." *Journal of Conflict Resolution* 36 (1992): 369–85.

Goldstein, Judith, and Robert Keohane, eds. *Ideas and Foreign Policy*. Ithaca: Cornell University Press, 1993.

Gould, Harold A., and Sumit Ganguly. *India Votes: Alliance Politics and Minority Governments in the Ninth and Tenth General Elections*. Boulder, Colo.: Westview, 1993.

Gözen, Ramazon. "Turkish Foreign Policy in Turbulence of the Post Cold War Era: Impact of External and Domestic Constraints." In *Turkish Foreign Policy in Post Cold War Era*, edited by Idris Bal, 27–52. Boca Raton, Fla.: Brown Walker, 2004.

Grant, R. L., ed. *The Process of Japanese Foreign Policy: Focus on Asia*. London: Royal Institute of International Affairs, 1997.

Green, Michael Jonathan. *Japan's Reluctant Realism: Foreign Policy Challenges in an Era of Uncertain Power*. New York: Palgrave, 2001.

Grimes, William W. "Institutionalized Inertia: Japanese Foreign Policy in the Post–Cold War World." In *International Relations Theory and the Asia-Pacific*, edited by G. John Ikenberry and Michael Mastanduno, 353–86. New York: Columbia University Press, 2003.

Gruenfeld, Deborah H. "Status, Ideology, and Integrative Complexity on the U.S. Supreme Court: Rethinking the Politics of Political Decision Making." *Journal of Personality and Social Psychology* 68 (1995): 5–20.

Gruenfeld, Deborah H., Melissa C. Thomas-Hunt, and Peter H. Kim. "Cognitive Flexibility, Communication Strategy, and Integrative Complexity in Groups: Public versus Private Reactions to Majority and Minority Status." *Journal of Experimental Social Psychology* 34 (1998): 202–26.

Gunduz, Zuhal Yesilyurt. "Turkey's Approach toward the EU: Views from Within." *Perceptions: Journal of International Affairs* 8 (2003): 1–19.

Haar, Roberta N. *Nation States as Schizophrenics: Germany and Japan as Post–Cold War Actors*. Westport, Conn.: Praeger, 2001.

Haas, Ernst B. *When Knowledge Is Power.* Berkeley: University of California Press, 1990.
Hagan, Joe D. "Does Decision Making Matter?: Systemic Assumptions vs. Historical Reality in International Relations Theory." *International Studies Review* 3 (2001): 5–46.
Hagan, Joe D. *Political Opposition and Foreign Policy in Comparative Perspective.* Boulder, Colo.: Rienner, 1993.
Hagan, Joe D., Philip P. Everts, Haruhiro Fukui, and John D. Stempel. "Foreign Policy by Coalition: Deadlock, Compromise, and Anarchy." *International Studies Review* 3 (2001): 169–216.
Hale, William. "Economic Issues in Turkish Foreign Policy." In *Turkey's New World: Changing Dynamics in Turkish Foreign Policy,* edited by Alan Makovsky and Sabri Sayarı, 20–38. Washington, D.C.: Washington Institute for Near East Policy, 2000.
Hale, William. "Human Rights, the European Union, and the Turkish Accession Process." *Turkish Studies* 4 (2003): 107–26.
Hale, William. *Turkey, the U.S., and Iraq.* London: Saqi, 2007.
Hale, William. *Turkish Foreign Policy, 1774–2000.* London: Cass, 2002.
Hallerberg, Mark, and Jurgen Von Hagen. "Electoral Institutions, Cabinet Negotiations, and Budget Deficits within the European Union." In *Fiscal Institutions and Fiscal Performance,* edited by James Poterba and Jurgen Von Hagen, 209–32. Chicago: University of Chicago Press, 1997.
"Hang Öcalan and Then Lift Death Penalty: Turkey-EU Commission Head." *Agence France Presse,* December 20, 1999.
Hanrieder, Wolfram F. *Germany, America, Europe: Forty Years of German Foreign Policy.* New Haven: Yale University Press, 1989.
Hanreider, Wolfram F., and Graeme P. Auton. *The Foreign Policies of West Germany, France, Britain.* Englewood Cliffs, N.J.: Prentice-Hall, 1980.
Harding, Gareth. "Analysis: Dutch Divided over Afghan Mission." *United Press International,* February 1, 2006.
Harding, Gareth. "Interview: Labor Party Leader Wouter Bos." *United Press International,* January 4, 2006.
"Hata Pushes Japan UNSC Bid." *Daily Yomiuri,* May 14, 1994.
Hayes, Louis D. *Introduction to Japanese Politics.* 5th ed. Armonk, N.Y.: Sharpe, 2009.
Heginbotham, Eric, and Richard J. Samuels. "Mercantile Realism and Japanese Foreign Policy." *International Security* 22 (1998): 171–203.
Heinrich, William, Jr., Akiho Shibata, and Yoshihide Soeya. *United Nations Peace-Keeping Operations: A Guide to Japanese Politics.* Tokyo: United Nations University Press, 1999.
Hellema, Duco A. *Dutch Foreign Policy: The Role of the Netherlands in World Politics.* Dordrecht: Republic of Letters, 2009.
Hellema, Duco A., Cees Wiebes, and Toby Witte. *The Netherlands and the Oil Crisis: Business as Usual.* Amsterdam: Amsterdam University Press, 2004.

Hennink, Susanna Contini. "Dutch Cabinet Now Says: 'Give Inspectors Time.'" *Het Financieele Dagblad*, February 17, 2003.
Herek, Gregory, Irving Janis, and Paul Huth. "Decisionmaking during International Crises: Is Quality of Process Related to Outcome?" *Journal of Conflict Resolution* 31 (1987): 203–26.
Hermann, Charles F. "Avoiding Pathologies in Foreign Policy Decision Groups." In *Force Diplomacy and Leadership: Essays in Honor of Alexander George*, edited by D. Caldwell and T. G. J. McKeown, 179–207. Boulder, Colo.: Westview, 1993.
Hermann, Charles F. "International Crisis as a Situational Variable." In *International Politics and Foreign Policy: A Reader in Research and Theory*, edited by James N. Rosenau, 409–21. New York: Free Press, 1969.
Hermann, Margaret G. "How Decision Units Shape Foreign Policy: A Theoretical Framework." *International Studies Review* 3 (2001): 47–81.
Hermann, Margaret G., and Charles W. Kegley Jr. "Rethinking Democracy and International Peace: Perspectives from Political Psychology." *International Studies Quarterly* 39 (1995): 511–33.
Hideo, Otake. "Political Realignment and Policy Conflict." In *Power Shuffles and Policy Processes: Coalition Government in Japan in the 1990s*, edited by Otake Hideo, 125–51. New York: Japan Center for International Exchange, 2000.
Hideo, Otake, ed. *Power Shuffles and Policy Processes: Coalition Government in Japan in the 1990s*. New York: Japan Center for International Exchange, 2000.
Hillebrand, Ron, and Galen A. Irwin. "Changing Strategies: The Dilemma of the Dutch Labour Party." In *Policy, Office, or Votes?: How Political Parties in Western Europe Make Hard Decisions*, edited by Wolfgang C. Müller and Kaare Strøm, 112–40. Cambridge: Cambridge University Press, 1999.
Hiroshi, Fujita. "UN Reform and Japan's Permanent Security Council Seat." *Japan Quarterly* 42 (1995): 436–42.
Hoekema, Jan. Interview by author. March 2006.
Hoekema, Jan. "Srebrenica, Dutchbat, and the Role of the Netherlands' Parliament." In *The 'Double Democratic Deficit': Parliamentary Accountability and the Use of Force under International Auspices*, edited by H. Born and H. Hanggi, 73–90. Aldershot: Ashgate, 2004.
Hofferbert, Richard, and Hans-Dieter Klingemann. "The Policy Impact of Party Programmes and Government Declarations in the Federal Republic of Germany." *European Journal of Political Research* 18 (1990): 277–304.
"Holland: Dutch Dilemma." *Economist*, December 15, 1979.
"Holland: Island Mentality." *Economist*, July 5, 1980.
"Holland: The Queen's Men Try Again." *Economist*, August 8, 1981.
Holsti, Ole. "Public Opinion and Foreign Policy: Challenges to the Almond-Lippmann Consensus." *International Studies Quarterly* 36 (1992): 439–66.
"Hosokawa Rules Out Opening Japan's Rice Market." *United Press International*, October 4, 1993.

"Hosokawa Says Japan Will Not Open Rice Market." *Agence France Presse*, September 26, 1993.
Hoyt, Paul. "The Political Manipulation of Group Composition." *Political Psychology* 18 (1997): 771–90.
Hrebenar, Ronald J., ed. *Japan's New Party System*. Boulder, Colo.: Westview.
Huber, John, and Ronald Inglehart. "Expert Interpretations of Party Space and Party Locations in 42 Societies." *Party Politics* 1 (1995): 73–111.
Hudson, Valerie. "Foreign Policy Analysis: Actor-Specific Theory and the Ground of International Relations." *Foreign Policy Analysis* 1 (2005): 1–30.
Hughes, Christopher W. *Japan's Re-Emergence as a "Normal" Military Power*. Adelphi Paper 368-9. Oxford: Oxford University Press for International Institute for Strategic Studies, 2004.
Hughes, Christopher W. *Japan's Remilitarization*. New York: Routledge for International Institute for Strategic Studies, 2009.
Hunsberger, Warren S., ed. *Japan's Quest: The Search for International Role, Recognition, and Respect*. Armonk, N.Y.: Sharpe, 1996.
Iitake, Koichi. "Japan: Battlelines Drawn over Future Peacekeeping Roles." *Asahi Shimbun*, September 24, 1999.
Ikuo, Kabashima. "An Ideological Survey of Japan's National Legislators." *Japan Echo* 26 (1999): 9–16.
"In About-Face, Dutch FM Now Says US Was Right to Invade Iraq." *Agence France Presse* (via FBIS Transcribed Text), October 6, 2005.
Inoguchi, Takashi. "Japan's United Nations Peacekeeping and Other Operations." *International Journal* 50 (1995): 325–42.
Inoguchi, Takashi, and Purnendra Jain. "Introduction: Beyond Karaoke Diplomacy?" In *Japanese Foreign Policy Today*, edited by Takashi Inoguchi and Purnendra Jain, xi–xix. New York: Palgrave, 2000.
Inoguchi, Takashi, and Purnendra Jain, eds. *Japanese Foreign Policy Today*. New York: Palgrave, 2000.
Ireland, Michael J., and Scott Sigmund Gartner. "Time to Fight: Government Type and Conflict Initiation in Parliamentary Systems." *Journal of Conflict Resolution* 45 (2001): 547–68.
Ishizuka, Katsumi. "Japan's Policy towards UN Peacekeeping Operations." *International Peacekeeping* 12 (2005): 67–86.
Ishizuka, Masahiko. "Security Council Issue Cuts to Heart of Japan's Global Role." *Nikkei Weekly*, July 11, 1994.
Iversen, Torben, and David Soskice. "Electoral Institutions and the Politics of Coalitions: Why Some Democracies Redistribute More Than Others." *American Political Science Review* 100 (2006): 165–81.
Jain, Purnendra. "Emerging Foreign Policy Actors: Subnational Governments and Nongovernmental Organizations." In *Japanese Foreign Policy Today: A Reader*, edited by Inoguchi Takashi and Purnendra Jain, 18–42. New York: Palgrave, 2000.
Janis, Irving. *Victims of Groupthink*. Boston: Houghton Mifflin, 1972.

"Japan Adopting Wait-and-See Stand on Opening Up Its Rice Market." *Straits Times,* November 7, 1993.
"Japan and the UN; Big Ambitions." *Economist,* September 17, 1994.
"Japan Backs Its Wider Role in UN Peacekeeping." *Agence France Presse,* January 7, 1999.
"Japan Bound to Bow on Rice." *Asahi News Service,* December 7, 1993.
"Japan Delays Decision on Rice Imports as Opposition Continues." *Agence France Presse,* December 9, 1993.
"Japan: Foreign Minister Views Lifting Freeze on UN Peacekeeping Role." *Kyodo News Service,* September 23, 1999.
"Japan's Fragile Coalition Bites the Bullet on Rice." *Agence France Presse,* December 13, 1993.
"Japan Gives Up Lifting Peacekeeping Freeze This Year: Reports." *Agence France Presse,* November 21, 1999.
"Japan: Government May Consider Lifting Ban on Defense Force Peacekeeping Role." *Kyodo News Service,* December 2, 1998.
"Japan Has Already Agreed to Open Rice Mart, Kantor Says." *Japan Economic Newswire,* December 11, 1993.
"Japan LDP Confirms Agreement on Three-Way Coalition." *AFX News Limited,* October 4, 1999.
"Japan May Partially Lift Rice Ban—Compromise Offer before GATT Deadline." *Financial Times,* November 30, 1993.
"Japan Opposition Urges Hokosawa's Cabinet to Resign If It Opens Rice Market." *United Press International,* November 29, 1993.
"Japan: Parties to End Restrictions on Military Participation in UN Peacekeeping." *Kyodo News Service,* August 23, 1999.
"Japan Peacekeepers Get OK for Golan." *United Press International,* August 29, 1995.
"Japan Renews Opposition to Tariffs for Rice." *Jiji Press Ticker Service,* October 15, 1993.
"Japan: Ruling Coalition Delays Plan to Lift Peacekeeping Freeze." *Kyodo News Service,* November 20, 1999.
"Japan: Ruling Party Official Calls for Review of Japan's Peacekeeping Policy." *Kyodo News Service,* September 16, 1999.
"Japan to Decide on Opening Rice Market to Imports Today." *Japan Economic Newswire,* December 13, 1993.
"Japan Says Rice Imports Do Not Represent Shift in Policy." *BBC Summary of World Broadcasts.* September 27, 1993.
"Japan Should Fully Join U.N. Peace Operations: Ozawa." *Jiji Press Ticker Service,* March 5, 1999.
"Japan Split on Importing Rice, but Worried about Safety." *Asahi News Service,* November 10, 1993.
"Japan to Make Final Decision on Rice Market in 'A Few Days.'" *BBC Summary of World Broadcasts,* December 11, 1993.

"Japan to Revise Law, Allow Troops to Join E. Timor Force: Obuchi." *AFX News Limited*, September 17, 1999.
"Japan Unlikely to Send Troops to Golan Heights in Nov." *Japan Economic Newswire*, May 31, 1995.
"Japan UNSC Membership Studied." *Daily Yomiuri*. August 6, 1994.
"Japan's Decision on Rice Trade Put Off beyond Saturday." *Japan Economic Newswire*, December 9, 1993.
"Japan's Socialists Again Threaten to Leave Coalition over Rice Issue." *Agence France Presse*, December 6, 1993.
"Japan's Stance on UNSC Membership Likely to Change." *Japan Economic Newswire*, July 6, 2004.
"Japan's Stance on UNSC Seat Unchanged, Saito Says." *Japan Economic Newswire*, August 29, 1994.
Jervis, Robert. "Deterrence and Perception." *International Security* 7 (1982–83): 3–30.
Jonas, Susanne. "The Denial of Grandeur: The Dutch Context." In *The Foreign Policy of the Netherlands*, edited by J. H. Leurdijk, 3–28. Alphen aan den Rijn: Sijthoff and Noordhoff, 1978.
"Justice Minister Turk—'Death Penalty Emerges as an Obstacle in Relations of Turkey with EU Countries.'" *Anadolu Agency*, August 8, 2000.
Kaarbo, Juliet. "Coalition Cabinet Decision Making: Institutional and Psychological Factors." *International Studies Review* 10 (2008): 57–86.
Kaarbo, Juliet. "Influencing Peace: Junior Partners in Israeli Coalition Cabinets." *Cooperation and Conflict* 31 (1996): 243–84.
Kaarbo, Juliet. "Power and Influence in Foreign Policy Decision Making: The Role of Junior Coalition Partners in German and Israeli Foreign Policy." *International Studies Quarterly* 40 (1996): 501–30.
Kaarbo, Juliet, and Ryan K. Beasley. "A Political Perspective on Minority Influence and Strategic Group Composition." In *Research on Groups and Teams*, edited by Margaret A. Neale, Elizabeth A. Mannix, and Deborah H. Gruenfeld, 1:125–47. Stamford, Conn.: JAI, 1998.
Kaarbo, Juliet, and Ryan K. Beasley. "Taking It to the Extreme: The Effect of Coalition Cabinets on Foreign Policy." *Foreign Policy Analysis* 4 (2008): 67–81.
Kaarbo, Juliet, Ryan Beasley, and Cristian Cantir. "Explaining Extreme Foreign Policy: The Effects of Coalition Cabinet Characteristics on Event Behavior." Paper presented at the annual meeting of the International Studies Association, San Francisco, March 26–30, 2008.
Kaarbo, Juliet, and Jeffrey S. Lantis. "The 'Greening' of German Foreign Policy in the Iraq Case: Conditions of Junior Party Influence in Governing Coalitions." *Acta Politica* 38 (2003): 201–30.
Kakuchi, Suvendrini. "Trade—Japan: Hosokawa Bears the Brunt of Anger over Rice." *Inter-Press Service*, December 10, 1993.
Kalaycioglu, Ersin. "Elections and Party Preferences in Turkey." *Comparative Political Studies* 27 (994): 402–24.

Kameda, Tatsuya, and Shinkichi Sugimori. "Psychological Entrapment in Group Decision Making: An Assigned Decision Rule and a Groupthink Phenomenon." *Journal of Personality and Social Psychology* 65 (1993): 282–92.

Katada, Saori N. "Why Did Japan Suspend Foreign Aid to China?: Japan's Foreign Aid Decision-Making and Sources of Aid Sanction." *Social Science Japan Journal* 4 (2001): 39–58.

Katzenstein, Peter J. *Cultural Norms and National Security: Police and Military in Postwar Japan.* Ithaca: Cornell University Press, 1996.

Katzenstein, Peter J., ed. *The Culture of National Security* (New York.: Columbia University Press, 1993).

Katzenstein, Peter J., and Nobuo Okawara. "Japanese Security Issues." In *Japan: A New Kind of Superpower?*, edited by Craig Garby and Mary Brown Bullock, 53–76. Washington, D.C.: Woodrow Wilson Center Press.

Kawasaki, Tsuyoshi. "Postclassical Realism and Japanese Security Policy." *Pacific Review* 14 (2001): 221–40.

Kawashima, Yutaka. *Japanese Foreign Policy at the Crossroads: Challenges and Options for the Twenty-First Century.* Washington, D.C.: Brookings Institution Press, 2003.

Keohane, Robert O., and Helen V. Milner. *Internationalization and Domestic Politics.* New York: Cambridge University Press, 1996.

Keridis, Dimitris. "Foreign Strategies and Domestic Choices: Balancing between Power Politics and Interdependence." In *The Future of Turkish Foreign Policy*, edited by Lenore G. Martin and Dimitris Keridis, 321–34. Cambridge: MIT Press, 2004.

Kerr, Norbert L. "Is It What One Says or How One Says It?: Style vs. Substance from an SDS Perspective." In *Group Consensus and Minority Influence: Implications for Innovation*, edited by Carsten K. W. De Dreu and Nanne K. De Vries, 201–28. Oxford: Blackwell, 2001.

Kerr, Norbert L., and Robert J. MacCoun. "The Effects of Jury Size and Polling Method on the Process and Product of Jury Deliberations." *Journal of Personality and Social Psychology* 48 (1985): 349–63.

Kesgin, Barış, and Juliet Kaarbo. "When and How Parliaments Influence Foreign Policy." *International Studies Perspectives* 11 (2010): 19–36.

Kin, Kwan Weng. "Japan Set for Golan Peacekeeping Role." *Straits Times,* August 26, 1995.

Kin, Kwan Weng. "Japan's Socialists Divided on Opening of Rice Market." *Straits Times,* December 14, 1993.

Kirişci, Kemal. "Turkey and the Muslim Middle East." In *Turkey's New World: Changing Dynamics in Turkish Foreign Policy,* edited by Alan Makovsky and Sabri Sayarı, 39–58. Washington, D.C.: Washington Institute for Near East Policy, 2000.

Klingemann, Hans-Dieter, Richard I. Hofferbert, and Ian Budge. *Parties, Policies, and Democracy.* Boulder, Colo.: Westview, 1994.

Kohno, Masaru. "The Domestic Foundations of Japan's International Contribu-

tion." In *Japan in International Politics: The Foreign Policies of an Adaptive State*, edited by Thomas U. Berger, Mike M. Mochizuki, and Jitsuo Tsushiyama, 23–46. Boulder, Colo.: Rienner, 2007.
"Kono Not Opposed to Japan's UNSC Seat." *Jiji Press Ticker Service*, September 2, 1994.
"Kono Sees Some Time before Japan Wins UNSC Permanent Seat." *Japan Economic Newswire*, August 29, 1994.
"Kono to State Japan Cannot Play Combat Role in UNSC." *Japan Economic Newswire*, September 19, 1994.
"Kono to Voice Japan's Wish for Permanent UNSC Seat." *Japan Economic Newswire*, September 13, 1994.
Kramer, Heinz. *A Changing Turkey: The Challenge to Europe and the United States*. Washington, D.C.: Brookings Institution Press, 2000.
Kramer, Heinz. "The EU-Turkey Customs Union: Economic Integration amidst Political Turmoil." *Mediterranean Politics* 1 (1996): 60–75.
Kremer, F., and A. E. Pijpers. "South Africa and European Sanctions Policy." In *The Politics of Persuasion: Implementation of Foreign Policy by the Netherlands*, edited by Philip Everts and Guido Walraven, 310–22. Aldershot: Gower. 1989.
Kulish, Nicholas. "Dutch Pull-Out from War Expected after Government Collapse." *New York Times*, February 22, 2010.
Kut, Sule. "The Contours of Turkish Foreign Policy in the 1990s." In *Turkey in World Politics*, edited by Barry Rubin and Kemal Kirişci, 5–12. Boulder, Colo.: Rienner, 2001.
Laderyet, Guy. "The Problem with PR." In *Electoral Systems and Democracy*, edited by Larry Diamond and Marc F. Plattner, 86–91. Baltimore: Johns Hopkins University Press, 2006.
Landers, Peter. "Japan Moves toward Rice Imports, but Ruling Coalition Divided." *Associated Press*, December 6, 1993.
Larrabee, F. Stephen, and Ian O. Lesser. *Turkish Foreign Policy in an Age of Uncertainty*. Santa Monica, Calif.: Rand, 2003.
Laver, Michael, and Ian Budge. *Party Policy and Government Coalitions*. New York: St. Martin's, 1992.
Laver, Michael, and Ben W. Hunt. *Policy and Party Competition*. New York: Routledge, 1992.
Laver, Michael, and Peter Mair. "Party Policy and Cabinet 1990 Portfolios in the Netherlands, 1998: Results from an Expert Survey." *Acta Politica* 34 (1999): 49–66.
Laver, Michael, and Norman Schofield. *Multiparty Government: The Politics of Coalition in Europe*. Oxford: Oxford University Press, 1998.
Laver, Michael, and Kenneth A. Shepsle. *Making and Breaking Governments*. Cambridge: Cambridge University Press, 1996.
"LDP, New Komeito to Work on Lifting Peacekeeping Ban." *Asahi Shimbun*, August 24, 1999.

Leblang, David, and Steve Chan. "Explaining Wars Fought by Established Democracies: Do Institutional Constraints Matter?" *Political Research Quarterly* 56 (2003): 385–400.

Leitenberg, Milton. "The Participation of Japanese Military Forces in United Nations Peacekeeping Operations." *Asian Perspective* 20 (1996): 5–50.

Lesser, Ian O. "Beyond 'Bridge or Barrier': Turkey's Evolving Security Relations with the West." In *Turkey's New World: Changing Dynamics in Turkish Foreign Policy*, edited by Alan Makovsky and Sabri Sayarı, 203–21. Washington, D.C.: Washington Institute for Near East Policy, 2000.

Leurdijk, J. H. *The Foreign Policy of the Netherlands*. Alphen aan den Rijn: Sijthoff and Noordhoff, 1978.

Levine, John L., and Juliet Kaarbo. "Minority Influence in Political Decision Making Groups." In *Group Consensus and Minority Influence: Implications for Innovation*, edited by Carsten K. W. De Dreu and Nanne K. De Vries, 229–257. Oxford: Blackwell, 2001.

Levy, Jack S. "The Diversionary Theory of War: A Critique." In *Handbook of War Studies*, edited by M. I. Midlarsky, 259–88. New York: Unwin-Hyman, 1989.

Levy, Jack S. "Qualitative Methods in International Relations." In *Millennial Reflections on International Studies*, edited by Michael Brecher and Frank P. Harvey, 432–54. Ann Arbor: University of Michigan Press, 2002.

Lieberman, Evan S. "Nested Analysis as a Mixed-Method Strategy for Comparative Research." *American Political Science Review* 99 (2005): 435–52.

Lijphart, Arend. *The Politics of Accommodation: Pluralism and Democracy in the Netherlands*. 2nd ed. Berkeley: University of California Press, 1975.

Lind, Jennifer M. "Pacifism or Passing the Buck?: Testing Theories of Japanese Security Policy." *International Security* 29 (2004): 92–121.

Lindell, Ulf, and Stefan Persson. "The Paradox of Weak State Power: A Research and Literature Overview." *Cooperation and Conflict* 21 (1986): 79–97.

Linz, Juan J. "The Virtues of Parliamentarism." *Journal of Democracy* 1 (1990): 51–69.

Long, William J. "Nonproliferation as a Goal of Japanese Foreign Assistance." *Asian Survey* 39 (1999): 328–47.

Lupia, Arthur, and Kaare Strøm. "Coalition Termination and the Strategic Timing of Parliamentary Elections." *American Political Science Review* 89 (1995): 648–65.

Maass, Anne, and Russell D. Clark III. "Conversion Theory and Simultaneous Majority/Minority Influence: Can Reactance Offer an Alternative Explanation?" *European Journal of Social Psychology* 16 (1986): 305–9.

Maass, Anne, and Russell D. Clark III. "Hidden Impact of Minorities: Fifteen Years of Minority Influence Research." *Psychological Bulletin* 95 (1984): 428–50.

Makovsky, Alan. "The New Activism in Turkish Foreign Policy." *SAIS Review* 19 (1999): 92–113.

Makovsky, Alan, and Sabri Sayarı. "Introduction." In *Turkey's New World: Chang-*

*ing Dynamics in Turkish Foreign Policy,* edited by Alan Makovsky and Sabri Sayarı, 1–8. Washington, D.C.: Washington Institute for Near East Policy, 2000.

Makovsky, Alan, and Sabri Sayarı, eds. *Turkey's New World: Changing Dynamics in Turkish Foreign Policy.* Washington, D.C.: Washington Institute for Near East Policy, 2000.

Mango, Andrew. "Reflections on the Atatürkist Origins of Turkish Foreign Policy and Domestic Linkages." In *Turkey's New World: Changing Dynamics in Turkish Foreign Policy,* edited by Alan Makovsky and Sabri Sayarı, 9–19. Washington, D.C.: Washington Institute for Near East Policy, 2000.

Maoz, Zeev. "Framing the National Interest: The Manipulation of Foreign Policy Decisions in Group Settings." *World Politics* 43 (1990): 77–110.

Maoz, Zeev, and Bruce Russett. "Normative and Structural Causes of Democratic Peace." *American Political Science Review* 87 (1993): 624–38.

Martin, Lanny W. "The Government Agenda in Parliamentary Democracies." *American Journal of Political Science* 48 (2004): 445–61.

Martin, Lanny W., and Randolph T. Stevenson. "Government Formation in Parliamentary Democracies." *American Journal of Political Science* 45 (2001): 33–50.

Martin, Lanny W., and Georg Vanberg. "Coalition Policymaking and Legislative Review." *American Political Science Review* 99 (2005): 93–106.

Martin, Lenore G. "Turkey's Middle East Foreign Policy." In *The Future of Turkish Foreign Policy,* edited by Lenore G. Martin and Dimitris Keridis, 157–89. Cambridge: MIT Press, 2004.

Martin, Lenore G., and Dimitris Keridi, eds. *The Future of Turkish Foreign Policy.* Cambridge: MIT Press, 2004.

Martin, Robin, and Miles Hewstone. "Afterthoughts on Afterimages: A Review of the Afterimage Paradigm in Majority and Minority Influence Research." In *Group Consensus and Minority Influence: Implications for Innovation,* edited by Carsten K. W. De Dreu and Nanne K. De Vries, 15–39. Oxford: Blackwell.

Massie, Alex. "Britain's Coalition of Pain." *New York Times,* May 11, 2010.

Maswood, S. Javed. "Japanese Foreign Policy and Regionalism." In *Japan and East Asian Regionalism,* edited by S. Javed Maswood, 6–25. London: Routledge, 2001.

Max, Arthur. "Military Ambition vs. Caution, as Dutch Buy Missiles and Weigh Afghan Deployment." *Associated Press,* December 9, 2005.

McLaren, Lauren M., and Meltem Müftüler-Bac. "Turkish Parliamentarians' Perspectives on Turkey's Relations with the European Union." *Turkish Studies* 4 (2003): 195–218.

Mershon, Carol. *The Costs of Coalition.* Stanford: Stanford University Press, 2002.

Metselaar, Max V., and Bertjan Verbeek. "Beyond Decision Making in Formal and Informal Groups: The Dutch Cabinet and the West New Guinea Conflict." In *Beyond Groupthink,* edited by Paul 't Hart, Eric Stern, and Bengt Sundelius, 95–122. Ann Arbor: University of Michigan Press, 1997.

Midford, Paul. "The Logic of Reassurance and Japan's Grand Strategy." *Security Studies* 11 (2002): 1–43.
Milgram, Stanley. "Behavioral Study of Obedience." *Journal of Abnormal and Social Psychology* 67 (1963): 371–78.
Milgram, Stanley. "Some Conditions of Obedience and Disobedience to Authority." *Human Relations* 18 (1965): 53–75.
Mitchell, Paul, and Benjamin Nyblade. "Government Formation and Cabinet Type." In *Cabinets and Coalition Bargaining: The Democratic Life Cycle in Western Europe*, edited Kaare Strøm, Wolfgang C. Müller, and Torbjørn Bergman, 201–36. Oxford: Oxford University Press, 2008.
Miyashita, Akitoshi. "Gaiatsu and Japan's Foreign Aid: Rethinking the Reactive-Proactive Debate." *International Studies Quarterly* 43 (1999): 695–731.
Miyashita, Akitoshi. "Japanese Foreign Policy: The Domestic-International Nexus." In *Foreign Policy in Comparative Perspective: Domestic and International Influences on State Behavior*, edited by Ryan K. Beasley, Juliet Kaarbo, Jeffrey S. Lantis, and Michael T. Snarr, 144–69. Washington, D.C.: CQ Press, 2002.
Miyashita, Akitoshi. "Where Do Norms Come From?: Foundations of Japan's Postwar Pacifism." In *Norms, Interests, and Power in Japanese Foreign Policy*, edited by Yoichiro Sato and Keiko Hirata, 21–45. New York: Palgrave Macmillan, 2008.
Mochizuki, Mike M. *Japan: Domestic Change and Foreign Policy*. Santa Monica, Calif.: Rand/National Defense Research Institute, 1995.
Mochizuki, Mike M. "Japan's Changing International Role." In *Japan in International Politics: The Foreign Policies of an Adaptive State*, edited by Thomas U. Berger, Mike M. Mochizuki, and Jitsuo Tsuchiyama, 1–22. Boulder, Colo.: Rienner, 2007.
Moon, Jeremy, and Campbell Sharmon, eds. *Australian Politics and Government*. Cambridge: Cambridge University Press, 2003.
Moore, Molly. "After Long Debate, Dutch Agree to Send Force to Afghanistan." *Washington Post Foreign Service*, February 3, 2006.
Moore, Molly. "Dutch Debate on Afghan Force Is Test for NATO." *Washington Post Foreign Service*, February 2, 2006.
Moore, Will H., and Bumba Mukherjee. "Coalition Government Formation and Foreign Exchange Markets: Theory and Evidence from Europe." *International Studies Quarterly* 50 (2006): 93–118.
Moscovici, Serge. *Social Influence and Social Change*. London: Academic, 1976.
Moskowitz, Gordon B., and Shelly Chaiken. "Mediators of Minority Social Influence." In *Group Consensus and Minority Influence: Implications for Innovation*, edited by Carsten K. W. De Dreu and Nanne K. De Vries, 60–90. Oxford: Blackwell, 2001.
Mufti, Malik. "Daring and Caution in Turkish Foreign Policy." *Middle East Journal* 52 (1998): 32–50.
Müftüler-Baç, Meltem. "The Never-Ending Story: Turkey and the European

Union." In *Turkey before and after Atatürk: Internal and External Affairs*, edited by Sylvia Kedourie, 240–58. London: Cass, 1998.

Müftüler-Baç, Meltem, and Aylin Güney. "The European Union and the Cyprus Problem." *Middle Eastern Studies* 41 (2005): 275–87.

Mulgan, Aurelia George. "International Peacekeeping and Japan's Role: Catalyst or Cautionary Tale?" *Asian Survey* 35 (1995): 1102–17.

Müller, Wolfgang C., Torbjørn Bergman, and Kaare Strøm. "Coalition Theory and Cabinet Governance: An Introduction." In *Cabinets and Coalition Bargaining: The Democratic Life Cycle in Western Europe*, edited by Kaare Strøm, Wolfgang C. Müller, and Torbjørn Bergman, 1–50. Oxford: Oxford University Press, 2008.

Müller, Wolfgang C., and Kaare Strøm. "Coalition Agreements and Cabinet Governance." In *Cabinets and Coalition Bargaining: The Democratic Life Cycle in Western Europe*, edited by Kaare Strøm, Wolfgang C. Müller, and Torbjørn Bergman, 159–99. Oxford: Oxford University Press, 2008.

Müller, Wolfgang C., and Kaare Strøm. "Coalition Governance in Western Europe: An Introduction." In *Coalition Governments in Western Europe*, edited by Wolfgang Müller and Kaare Strøm, 1–31. Oxford: Oxford University Press, 2000.

Müller, Wolfgang C., and Kaare Strom, eds. *Coalition Governments in Western Europe*. Oxford: Oxford University Press, 2000.

"Murayama Sounds Strong Support for Japan UNSC Bid." *Japan Economic Newswire*, September 16, 1994.

"Murayama Turns Positive about Japan's UNSC Bid." *Japan Economic Newswire*, September 6, 1994.

Myers, David G., and Helmut Lamm. "The Group Polarization Phenomenon." *Psychological Bulletin* 83 (1976): 602–27.

Nakano, Minoru. "The Changing Legislative Process in the Transitional Period." In *Japanese Politics Today: Beyond Karaoke Democracy?*, edited by Purnedra Jain and Takashi Inoguchi, 45–74. New York: St. Martin's, 1997.

Naoto, Nonako. "Characteristics of the Decision-Making Structure of Coalitions." In *Power Shuffles and Policy Processes: Coalition Government in Japan in the 1990s*, edited by Otake Hideo, 102–24. New York: Japan Center for International Exchange, 2000.

"NATO Approves Plan to Expand Afghan Force." *Agence France Presse*, December 8, 2005.

Neary, Ian. "Japanese Foreign Policy and Human Rights." In *Japanese Foreign Policy Today: A Reader*, edited by Inoguchi Takashi and Purnendra Jain, 83–95. New York: Palgrave, 2000.

Nemeth, Charlan, and Cynthia Chiles. "Modeling Courage: The Role of Dissent in Fostering Independence." *European Journal of Social Psychology* 18 (1988): 275–80.

Nemeth, Charlan, and Julianne Kwan. "Minority Influence, Divergent Thinking, and Detection of Correct Solutions." *Journal of Applied Social Psychology* 17 (1987): 786–97.

"Netherlands Again Puts Off Decision on Afghanistan Deployment." *Agence France Presse*, December 22, 2005.
"Netherlands Christian Democrats, VVD Agree to Coalition Government." *Agence France Presse*, May 14, 2003.
"Netherlands Expected to Decide in a Week on Afghanistan Deployment." *Agence France Presse*, December 2, 2005.
"Netherlands Hesitant about New Mission in Afghanistan." *Xinhua General News Service*, November 29, 2005.
"Netherlands Postpones Decision on Afghanistan Deployment." *Agence France Presse*, December 9, 2005.
"Netherlands Prime Minister Reaffirms Government Support for War against Iraq." *Agence France Presse*, March 20, 2003.
"Netherlands to Send 1,100 Troops to Iraq." *Agence France Presse*, June 6, 2003.
"Netherlands to Send More Troops to Afghanistan." *Agence France Presse*, February 2, 2006.
Newman, Edward. "Japan and International Organizations." In *Japanese Foreign Policy Today: A Reader*, edited by Inoguchi Takashi and Purnendra Jain, 43–64. New York: Palgrave, 2000.
Newman, Edward. "Japan's Multilateral Politics." In *Global Governance: Germany and Japan in the International System*, edited by Saori N. Katada, Hanns W. Maull, and Takashi Inogucki, 219–33. Aldershot: Ashgate, 2004.
"No Change in Japan's Rice Policy, Hokosawa Says." *Japan Economic Newswire*, November 19, 1993.
Nousiainen, Jaako, and Jean Blondel. "Conclusion." In *Governing Together: The Extent and Limits of Joint Decision-Making in Western European Cabinet*, edited by Jean Blondel and Ferdinand Müller-Rommel, 301–7. New York: St. Martin's, 1993.
Ogata, Sadako. "Japan's Policy towards the United Nations." In *The United Nations System: The Policies of Member States*, edited by Chadwick F. Alger, Gene M. Lyons, and John E. Trent, 231–70. Tokyo: United Nations University Press, 1995.
Öniş, Ziya. "Domestic Politics, International Norms, and Challenges to the State: Turkey-EU Relations in the Post-Helsinki Era." In *Turkey and the European Union*, edited by Ali Çarkoğlu and Barry Rubin, 8–31. London: Cass, 2003.
Öniş, Ziya. "Luxembourg, Helsinki, and Beyond: Towards an Interpretation of Recent Turkey-EU Relations." *Government and Opposition* 35 (2000): 463–83.
"Opening of Rice Market Sparks Fierce Protests in Japan." *Agence France Presse*, December 7, 1993.
"Opening Rice Market Could Split Japan's Ruling Coalition." *United Press International*, December 12, 1993.
Otake, Hideo, ed. *Power Shuffles and Policy Processes: Coalition Government in Japan in the 1990s*. Tokyo: JCIE, 2000.
"'Out of the Question' for Turkey to Renounce Its Stand on Cyprus." *BBC Summary of World Broadcasts*, December 13, 1999.

Owen, John M. *Liberal Peace, Liberal War: American Politics and International Security.* Ithaca: Cornell University Press, 1997.
Özcan, Gencer. "The Military and the Making of Foreign Policy in Turkey." In *Turkey in World Politics,* edited by Barry Rubin and Kemal Kirişci, 13–30. Boulder, Colo.: Rienner, 2001.
Özcan, Mesut. *Harmonizing Foreign Policy: Turkey, the EU, and the Middle East* Aldershot: Ashgate, 2008.
Özdalga, Elizabeth. "Necmettin Erbakan: Democracy for the Sake of Power." In *Political Leaders and Democracy in Turkey,* edited by Metin Heper and Sabri Sayarı, 127–46. Lanham, Md.: Lexington, 2002.
Özkeçeci-Taner, Binnur. "The Impact of Institutionalized Ideas in Coalition Foreign Policy Making: Turkey as an Example, 1991–2002." *Foreign Policy Analysis* 1 (2005): 249–78.
Özkeçeci-Taner, Binnur. "The Role of Ideas in Coalition Foreign Policymaking: Turkey as an Example, 1991–2002." Ph.D. diss., Syracuse University, 2004.
Özkeçeci-Taner, Binnur. *The Role of Ideas in Coalition Government Foreign Policymaking: The Case of Turkey between 1991 and 2002.* Dordrecht: Republic of Letters, 2009.
Palmer, Glenn, Tamar London, and Patrick Regan. "What's Stopping You?: The Sources of Political Constraints on International Conflict Behavior in Parliamentary Democracies." *International Interactions* 30 (2004): 1–24.
Palmer, John. "Holland at the Hustings." *Manchester Guardian Weekly,* March 22, 1981.
Park, William. "Turkey's European Candidacy: From Luxembourg to Helsinki—to Ankara?" *Mediterranean Politics* 5 (2000): 31–53.
Park, William. *Turkey's Policy towards Northern Iraq: Problems and Perspectives.* London: Routledge, 2005.
"Parliament Agrees to F16s, Troops." *Het Financieele Dagblad,* December 24, 2001.
Pascoe, Robin. "Dutch Back War but Won't Send Military Help." *Het Financieele Dagblad,* March 21, 2003.
Pekkanen, Robert, and Ellis S. Krauss. "Japan's 'Coalition of the Willing' on Security Policies." *Orbis* 49 (2005): 429–44.
Pérez, Juan A., and Gabriel Mugny. "Paradoxical Effects of Categorization in Minority Influence: When Being an Outgroup Is an Advantage." *European Journal of Social Psychology* 17 (1987): 157–69.
Perkovich, George. *India's Nuclear Bomb: The Impact on Global Proliferation.* Berkeley: University of California Press, 1999.
Peterson, Randall. "A Directive Leadership Style in Group Decision Making Can Be Both Virtue and Vice: Evidence from Elite and Experimental Groups." *Journal of Personality and Social Psychology* 72 (1997): 1107–21.
Peterson, Randall, P. D. Owens, Philip E. Tetlock, E. T. Fan, and P. Martorana. "Group Dynamics in Top Management Teams: Groupthink, Vigilance, and Alternative Models of Organizational Failure and Success." *Organizational Behavior and Human Decision Processes* 73 (1998): 272–305.

Peterson, Susan. "How Democracies Differ: Public Opinion, State Structure, and the Lessons of the Fashoda Crisis." *Security Studies* 5 (1995): 3–37.

Piggot, Garry. "Dutch Navy Submarine in Middle East." *Het Financieele Dagblad*, April 5, 2003.

Pijpers, Alfred. "The Netherlands: The Weakening Pull of Atlanticism." In *The Actors in Europe's Foreign Policy*, edited by Christopher Hill, 247–67. London: Routledge, 1996.

Powell, G. Bingham. *Elections as Instruments of Democracy: Majoritarian and Proportional Visions*. New Haven: Yale University Press, 2000.

"Pressure Mounts on the Netherlands to Send Troops to Afghanistan." *Agence France Presse*, January 30, 2006.

"Prime Minister Delays Decision on Opening Japan's Rice Market." *United Press International*, December 9, 1993.

Prins, Brandon C., and Christopher Sprecher. "Institutional Constraints, Political Opposition, and Interstate Dispute Escalation: Evidence from Parliamentary Systems, 1946–1989." *Journal of Peace Research* 36 (1999): 271–87.

Przeworski, Adam, and Henry Teune. *The Logic of Comparative Social Inquiry*. New York: Wiley-Interscience, 1970.

Putnam, Robert. "Diplomacy and Domestic Politics: The Logic of Two-Level Games." *International Organization* 42 (1988): 427–60.

Quade, Quentin L. "PR and Democratic Statecraft." In *Electoral Systems and Democracy*, edited by Larry Diamond and Marc F. Plattner, 92–97. Baltimore: Johns Hopkins University Press, 2006.

Ragin, Charles. *The Comparative Method: Moving beyond Qualitative and Quantitative Strategies*. Berkeley: University of California Press, 1987.

Rahat, Gideon. "Determinants of Party Cohesion: Evidence from the Case of the Israeli Parliament." *Parliamentary Affairs* 60 (2007): 279–96.

Rapkin, David P., and Aurelia George. "Rice Liberalization and Japan's Role in the Uruguay Round: A Two-Level Game Approach." In *World Agriculture and the GATT*, edited by William P. Aver, 55–94. Boulder, Colo.: Rienner, 1993.

Rathbun, Brian C. *Partisan Interventions*. Ithaca: Cornell University Press, 2004.

Rees, G. Wyn. "The Netherlands: Reorienting Its Defence Priorities." *Contemporary Security Policy* 17 (1996): 174–76.

Reiter, Dan, and Erik R. Tillman. "Public, Legislative, and Executive Constraints on the Democratic Initiation of Conflict." *Journal of Politics* 64 (2002): 810–26.

"Return to the Centre: Dutch Voters Have Punished the Populists." *Financial Times*, January 24, 2003.

Riker, William. *The Theory of Political Coalitions*. New Haven: Yale University Press, 1962.

Ripsman, Norrin M. *Peacemaking by Democracies: The Effect of State Autonomy on the Post–World War Settlements*. University Park: Pennsylvania State University Press, 2002.

Risse-Kappen, Thomas. "Public Opinion, Domestic Structure, and Foreign Policy in Liberal Democracies." *World Politics* 43 (1991): 479–512.

Robins, Philip. "Confusion at Home, Confusion Abroad: Turkey between Copenhagen and Iraq." *International Affairs* 79 (2003): 547–66.
Robins, Philip. "The Foreign Policy of Turkey." In *The Foreign Policies of Middle East States*, edited by Raymond Hinnebusch and Anoushiravan Ehteshami, 311–34. Boulder, Colo.: Rienner, 2002.
Robins, Philip. *Suits and Uniforms: Turkish Foreign Policy since the Cold War*. London: Hurst, 2003.
Robins, Philip. "Turkish Foreign Policy under Erbakan." *Survival* 39 (1997): 82–100.
Rochon, Thomas R. *The Netherlands: Negotiating Sovereignty in an Interdependent World*. Boulder, Colo.: Westview, 1999.
Roozendaal, Peter Van. *Cabinets in Multi-Party Democracies*. Amsterdam: Thesis, 1992.
Rosato, Sebastian. "The Flawed Logic of Democratic Peace Theory." *American Political Science Review* 97 (2003): 595–602.
Rose, Caroline. "Japanese Role in PKO and Humanitarian Assistance." In *Japanese Foreign Policy Today: A Reader*, edited by Inoguchi Takashi and Purnendra Jain, 122–35. New York: Palgrave, 2000.
Rubin, Barry, and Kemal Kirişci. *Turkey in World Politics: An Emerging Multiregional Power*. Boulder, Colo.: Rienner, 2001.
Rumford, Chris. "Failing the EU Test?: Turkey's National Programme, EU Candidature, and the Complexities of Democratic Reform." *Mediterranean Politics* 7 (2002): 51–68.
Russett, Bruce M. *Controlling the Sword*. Cambridge: Harvard University Press, 1990.
Saafeld, Thomas. "Institutions, Chance, and Choices: The Dynamics of Cabinet Survival." In *Cabinets and Coalition Bargaining: The Democratic Life Cycle in Western Europe*, edited by Kaare Strøm, Wolfgang C. Müller, and Torbjørn Bergman, 327–68. Oxford: Oxford University Press, 2008.
Saafeld, Thomas. "The West German Bundestag after 40 Years: The Role of Parliament in a 'Party Democracy.'" *West European Politics* 13 (1990): 68–89.
Sakallıoğlu, Cizre Ümit. "The Anatomy of the Turkish Military's Political Autonomy." *Comparative Politics* 29 (1997): 151–66.
Sakurai, Joji. "Japan Governing Party, Opposition Reach Compromise on Coalition." *Associated Press*, January 13, 1999.
Sathe, Vasant. "For a Directly Elected President." In *The Presidential System: The Indian Debate*, edited by A. G. Noorani, 187–90. New Delhi: Sage, 1989.
Sato, Yoichiro, and Keiko Hirata. "Introduction: Constructivism, Rationalism, and the Study of Norms in Japanese Foreign Policy." In *Norms, Interests, and Power in Japanese Foreign Policy*, edited by Yoichiro Sato and Keiko Horata, 3–17. New York: Palgrave Macmillan, 2008.
Sayarı, Sabri. "The Changing Party System." In *Politics, Parties, and Elections in Turkey*, edited by Sabri Sayarı and Yilmaz Esmer, 9–32. Boulder, Colo.: Rienner, 2002.
Schafer, Mark, and Scott Crichlow. *Groupthink vs. High-Quality Decision Making in International Relations*. New York: Columbia University Press, 2010.

Schafer, Mark, and Scott Crichlow. "The Process-Outcome Connection in Foreign Policy Decision Making: A Quantitative Study Building on Groupthink." *International Studies Quarterly* 46 (2002): 45–68.
Schie, Patrick Van. Interview by author. March 2006.
Schlaghecke, Hans. "Dutch Join Pro-Bush Lobby," *Het Financieele Dagblad*, September 25, 2002.
Schrodt, Philip A., and Deborah J. Gerner. "An Event Data Analysis of Third-Party Mediation." *Journal of Conflict Resolution* 48 (2004): 310–30.
Schultz, Kenneth A. *Democracy and Coercive Diplomacy*. New York: Cambridge University Press, 2001.
Schuster, Jürgen, and Herbert Maier. "The Rift: Explaining Europe's Divergent Iraq Policies in the Run-Up of the American-Led War on Iraq." *Foreign Policy Analysis* 2 (2006): 223–44.
Schwartz, Frank J. *Advice and Consent: The Politics of Consultation in Japan*. Cambridge: Cambridge University Press, 1998.
Schweiger, D. M., W. R. Sandberg, and J. W. Ragan. "Group Approaches for Improving Strategic Decision Making: A Comparative Analysis of Dialectical Inquiry, Devil's Advocacy, and Consensus." *Academy of Management Journal* 29 (1986): 51–71.
Schwenk, C. R. "Effects of Devil's Advocacy and Dialectical Inquiry on Decision Making: A Meta-Analysis." *Organizational Behavior and Human Decision Processes* 47 (1990): 161–76.
Shinoda, Tomohito. *Leading Japan: The Role of the Prime Minister*. Westport, Conn.: Greenwood, 2000.
Shinoda, Tomohito. "Japan's Decision Making under the Coalition Governments."*Asian Survey* 38 (1998): 703–23.
Shively, W. Philips. "Case Selection: Insights from *Rethinking Social Inquiry*." *Political Analysis* 14 (2006): 344–47.
Siccama, Jan G. "The Netherlands Depillarized: Security Policy in a New Domestic Context." In *NATO's Northern Allies: The National Security Policies of Belgium, Denmark, the Netherlands, and Norway*, edited by Gregory Flynn, 113–70. Totowa, N.J.: Rowman and Allanheld, 1985.
Sisler, Peter. "EU's Death-Penalty Objection Divides Turkey." *Washington Times*, February 19, 2002.
Smith, Christine M., R. Scott Tindale, and Elizabeth M. Anderson. "The Impact of Shared Representations on Minority Influence in Freely Interacting Groups." In *Group Consensus and Minority Influence: Implications for Innovation*, edited by Carsten K. W. De Dreu and Nanne K. De Vries, 183–200. Oxford: Blackwell, 2001.
Smith, James F. "Dutch Put Off NATO Missile Decision." *Associated Press*, November 16, 1981.
Smith, James F. "Three Parties Agree on Coalition." *Associated Press*, September 10, 1981.
Smith, Michael. "Afghan Posting 'Too Dangerous' for Dutch Army." *Sunday Times* (London), November 20, 2005.

Smyth, Jamie. "1,400 Dutch Troops Set for Afghanistan." *Irish Times*, February 4, 2006.
Smyth, Jamie. "Dutch Poised to Vote on Afghanistan NATO Mission." *Irish Times*, February 3, 2006.
Snyder, Jack. *Myths of Empire: Domestic Politics and International Ambition.* Ithaca: Cornell University Press, 1991.
Soetendorp, Ben. "The NATO 'Double Track' Decision." In *The Politics of Persuasion: Implementation of Foreign Policy by the Netherlands*, edited by Philip Everts and Guido Walraven, 149–60. Aldershot: Avebury, 1989.
Soetendorp, Ben, and Kenneth Hanf. "The Netherlands: Growing Doubts of a Loyal Member." In *Adapting to European Integration: Small States and the European Union*, edited by Kenneth Hanf and Ben Soetendorp, 36–51. London: Addison Wesley Longman, 1998.
Song, Young-Sun. "Japanese Peacekeeping Operations: Yesterday, Today, and Tomorrow." *Asian Perspective* 20 (1996): 51–69.
Soysal, Mümtaz. "The Future of Turkish Foreign Policy." In *The Future of Turkish Foreign Policy*, edited by Lenore G. Martin and Dimitris Keridis, 37–46. Cambridge: MIT Press, 2004.
Spector, Bertram I. "Negotiation as a Psychological Process." *Journal of Conflict Resolution* 21 (1977): 607–18.
Stinnett, Douglas M. "International Uncertainty, Foreign Policy Flexibility, and Surplus Majority Coalitions in Israel." *Journal of Conflict Resolution* 51 (2007): 470–95.
Stockwin, J. A. A. *Governing Japan.* Oxford: Blackwell, 1999.
Stockwin, J. A. A. *Governing Japan.* 4th ed. Oxford: Blackwell, 2008.
Stockwin, J. A. A. "The Social Democratic Party (Formerly Japan Socialist Party): A Turbulent Odyssey." In *Japan's New Party System*, edited by Ronald J. Hrebenar, 3rd ed., 209–51. Boulder, Colo.: Westview, 2000.
Strøm, Kaare. "A Behavioral Theory of Competitive Political Parties." *American Journal of Political Science* 34 (1990): 565–98.
Strøm, Kaare. *Minority Government and Majority Rule.* Cambridge: Cambridge University Press, 1990.
Strøm, Kaare, Ian Budge, and Michael Laver. "Constraints on Cabinet Formation in Parliamentary Democracies." *American Journal of Political Science* 38 (1994): 303–35.
Strøm, Kaare, and Wolfgang C. Müller. "The Keys to Togetherness: Coalition Agreements in Parliamentary Democracies." *Journal of Legislative Studies* 5 (1999): 255–82.
Strøm, Kaare, Wolfgang C. Müller, and Torbjørn Bergman, eds. *Cabinets and Coalition Bargaining: The Democratic Life Cycle in Western Europe.* Oxford: Oxford University Press, 2008.
Strøm, Kaare, and Stephen Swindle. "Strategic Parliamentary Dissolution." *American Political Science Review* 96 (2002): 575–91.
Struck, Doug. "Japan Forms a New Government; Premier Gets Large, but Unwieldy, Parliamentary Majority." *Washington Post*, October 6, 1999.

Süvarierol, Semin. "The Cyprus Obstacle on Turkey's Road to Membership in the European Union." *Turkish Studies* 4 (2003): 55–78.
Sylvan, Donald, and Stuart Thorson. "Ontologies, Problem Representation, and the Cuban Missile Crisis." *Journal of Conflict Resolution* 36 (1992): 709–32.
Tachau, Frank. "Bülent Ecevit: From Idealist to Pragmatist." In *Political Leaders and Democracy in Turkey*, edited by Metin Heper and Sabri Sayarı, 107–25. Lanham, Md.: Lexington, 2002.
Tadokoro, Masayuki. "The End of Japan's 'Non-Decision' Politics." *Asian Survey* 34 (1994): 1002–15.
Takahara, Takao. "Japan." In *Challenges for the New Peacekeepers*, edited by Trevor Findlay, 52–66. SIPRI Research Report No. 12. Oxford: Oxford University Press.
Talmadge, Eric. "In Major Concession, Japan Decides to Drop Ban on Imported Rice." *Associated Press*, December 13, 1993.
Tarrow, Sidney. "Bridging the Quantitative-Qualitative Divide." In *Rethinking Social Inquiry: Diverse Tools, Shared Standards*, edited by Henry E. Brady and David Collier, 171–79. Lanham, Md.: Rowman and Littlefield, 2004.
Tashakkori, Abbas, and Charles Teddie. *Handbook of Mixed Methods in Social and Behavioral Research*. Thousand Oaks, Calif.: Sage, 2003.
Tashakkori, Abbas, and Charles Teddie. *Mixed Methodology: Combining Qualitative and Quantitative Approaches*. Thousand Oaks, Calif.: Sage, 1998.
Tavits, Margit. "The Role of Parties' Past Behavior in Coalition Formation." *American Political Science Review* 102 (2004): 495–507.
Tayfur, M. Fatih, and Korel Göymen. "Decision Making in Turkish Foreign Policy: The Caspian Oil Pipeline Issue." *Middle Eastern Studies* 38 (2002): 101–22.
Tazaki, Makiko. "Japan's Socialist Premier Vows Dovish Foreign Policies." *Agence France Press*, July 18, 1994.
ten Napel, Hans-Martien. "The Development of Dutch Christian Democracy." In *Christian Democracy in the EU, 1945–1995*, edited E. Lamberts, 51–64. Leuven: Leuven University Press, 1997.
't Hart, Paul. "From Analysis to Reform of Policy-Making Groups." In *Beyond Groupthink*, edited by Paul 't Hart, Eric Stern, and Bengt Sundelius, 311–36. Ann Arbor: University of Michigan Press, 1997.
't Hart, Paul, Eric Stern, and Bengt Sundelius. "Foreign Policymaking at the Top: Political Group Dynamics." In *Beyond Groupthink*, edited by Paul 't Hart, Eric Stern, and Bengt Sundelius, 3–34. Ann Arbor: University of Michigan Press, 1997.
Theophanous, Andreas. "Cyprus, the European Union, and the Search for a New Constitution." *Journal of Southern Europe and the Balkans* 2 (2000): 213–33.
Therien, Jean-Philippe, and Alain Noel. "Political Parties and Foreign Aid." *American Political Science Review* 94 (2000): 151–62.
Timmermans, Arco. "Conflicts, Agreements, and Coalition Governance" *Acta Politica* 33 (1998): 409–32.

Timmermans, Arco. *High Politics in the Low Countries*. Aldershot: Ashgate, 2003.
Timmermans, Arco, and W. E. Bakema. "Conflicten in Nederlandse kabinetten." In *Ministers en Ministerraad*, edited by R. B. Andeweg, 175–92. The Hague: SDU Utigeverij, 1999.
Tinc, Ferai. "On Death Penalty with MHP Member Close to Europe." *Hurriyet Daily*, December 20, 1999.
Tindale, R. Scott, S. Sheffey, and L. A. Scott. "Framing and Group Decision Making: Do Cognitive Changes Parallel Preference Changes?" *Organizational Behavior and Human Decision Processes* 55 (1993): 470–85.
Tindale, R. Scott, Christine M. Smith, L. S. Thomas, J. Filkins, and S. Sheffey. "Shared Representations and Asymmetric Social Influence Processes in Small Groups." In *Understanding Group Behavior: Consensual Action by Small Groups*, edited by E. Witte and J. Davis, 1:81–104. Mahwah, N.J.: Erlbaum, 1996.
Tonra, Ben, ed. *The Europeanisation of National Foreign Policy: Dutch, Danish, and Irish Foreign Policy in the European Union*. Aldershot: Ashgate, 2001.
Traynor, Ian. "Netherlands Votes on Troops for Afghanistan." *Guardian*, February 2, 2006.
Tsuchiyama, Jitsuo. "War Renunciation, Article 9, and Security Policy." In *Japan in International Politics: The Foreign Policies of an Adaptive State*, edited by Thomas U. Berger, Mike M. Mochizuki, and Jitsuo Tsushiyama, 47–74. Boulder, Colo.: Rienner, 2007.
"Turkey: ANAP Official Favors Execution of Ocalan." *Anadolu Agency*, December 31, 1999.
"Turkey Death Penalty." *Associated Press*, November 25, 1998.
"Turkey: Justice Minister Assesses EU, Cyprus, Inflation." *World News Connection*, December 20, 1999.
"Turkey: Party Leaders Agree to Postpone Ocalan's Execution." *Radio Free Europe*, January 13, 2000.
"Turkey: Reforms Raise Hopes for EU Membership, but Brussels Remains Cautious." *Radio Free Europe*, August 6, 2002.
"Turkey Won't Abolish Death Penalty." *Associated Press*, December 26, 1998.
"Turkey's First Step to EU Membership a 'Landmark': Ecevit." *Agence France Presse*, December 11, 1999.
"Turkey's Long March towards European Membership." *Agence France Presse*, December 10, 1999.
"Turkish Cabinet Meets to Discuss Helsinki Outcome." *World News Connection*, December 10, 1999.
"Turkish Justice Minister on Cakici Case, Ocalan Sentence." *Anadolu Agency*, December 28, 1999.
"Turkish PM: Abolition of Death Penalty Would Be a 'Good Thing.'" *Agence France Presse*, June 11, 2000.
"Turkish Premier Signals Lifting Capital Punishment for EU Membership." *Associated Press*, December 4, 1999.
"Turks Consider Lifting Death Penalty." *Associated Press*, February 17, 2002.

Twomey, Christopher P. "Japan, the Circumscribed Balancer: Building on Defensive Realism to Make Predictions about East Asian Security." *Security Studies* 9 (2000): 178–219.

Uslu, Nasuh. "The Cyprus Question between 1974 and 2004 and Its Relations to Turkish Foreign Policy." In *Turkish Foreign Policy in the Post Cold War Era*, edited by Idris Bal, 211–52. Boca Raton, Fla.: Brown Walker, 2004.

Van den Berg, Stephanie. "Iraq War Threatens Dutch Moves to Form New Government." *Agence France Presse*, March 24, 2003.

Van den Berg, Stephanie. "New Dutch Government Can Be Formed after Agreement on Iraq." *Agence France Presse*, March 24, 2003.

Van den Berg, Stephanie. "Talks on New Dutch Center-Left Government Collapse." *Agence France Presse*, April 11, 2003.

Van Holsteyn, J. J. M. "The Dutch Parliamentary Elections of 2006." *West European Politics* 30 (2007): 1139–47.

Van Holsteyn, J. J. M., and Galen A. Irwin. "The Dutch Parliamentary Elections of 2003." *West European Politics* 27 (2004): 157–64.

Van Holsteyn, J. J. M., and Galen A. Irwin. "Never a Dull Moment: Pim Fortuyn and the Dutch Parliamentary Election of 2002." *West European Politics* 26 (2003): 41–66.

Van Praag, Philip, Jr. "Conflict and Cohesion in the Dutch Labour Party." In *Conflict and Cohesion in Western European Social Democratic Parties*, edited by David S. Bell and Eric Shaw, 133–50. London: Pinter, 1994.

Van Staden, Alfred. "The Changing Role of the Netherlands in NATO." *West European Politics* 12 (1989): 99–111.

Verbeek, Bertjan. *Decision-Making in Great Britain during the Suez Crisis*. Aldershot: Ashgate, 2003.

Verbeek, Bertjan, and Philip Quarles van Ufford. "Non-State Actors in Foreign Policy Making: A Policy Subsystem Approach." In *Non-State Actors in International Relations*, ed. Bas Arts, Math Noortmann, and Bob Reinalda, 127–44. Aldershot: Ashgate, 2001.

Verbeek, Bertjan, and Anna van der Vleuten. "The Domesticization of the Foreign Policy of the Netherlands (1989–2007): The Paradoxical Result of Europeanization and Internationalization." *Acta Politica* 43 (2008): 357–77.

Vertzberger, Yaacov Y. "Collective Risk Taking: The Decision-Making Group." In *Beyond Groupthink*, edited by Paul 't Hart, Eric Stern, and Bengt Sundelius, 275–308. Ann Arbor: University of Michigan Press, 1997.

Vertzberger, Yaacov Y. *The World in Their Minds*. Stanford: Stanford University Press, 1990.

Verzichelli, Luca. "Portfolio Allocation." In *Cabinets and Coalition Bargaining: The Democratic Life Cycle in Western Europe*, edited by Kaare Strøm, Wolfgang C. Müller, and Torbjørn Bergman, 237–67. Oxford: Oxford University Press, 2008.

Voorhoeve, Joris J. C. *Peace, Profits, and Principles*. The Hague: Nijhoff, 1979.

Wallfish, Asher, and Mark Segal. "Cabinet Approves Treaty, with Only Sharon, Landau Opposing." *Jerusalem Post*, March 20, 1979.

Warwick, Paul V. "Coalition Policy in Parliamentary Democracies: Who Gets How Much and Why." *Comparative Political Studies* 34 (2001): 1212–36.

Warwick, Paul V. *Government Survival in Parliamentary Democracies.* Cambridge: Cambridge University Press, 1994.

Warwick, Paul V., and James N. Druckman. "Portfolio Salience and the Proportionality of Payoffs in Coalition Governments." *British Journal of Political Science* 31 (2001): 627–49.

Watt, Nicholas. "'Shades of Srebrenica' Overshadow NATO's Mission in Afghanistan." *Guardian,* December 9, 2005.

Wendt, Alexander. *Social Theory of International Politics.* Cambridge: Cambridge University Press, 1999.

White, Jenny B. "Pragmatists or Ideologues?: Turkey's Welfare Party in Power." *Current History* 96 (1997): 25–30.

Williams, K. Y., and C. A. O'Reilly. "Demography and Diversity in Organizations: A Review of 40 Years of Research." *Research in Organizational Behavior* 20 (1998): 77–140.

Winrow, Gareth. "Turkey: Recalcitrant Ally." In *The Iraq War: Causes and Consequences,* edited by Rick Fawn and Raymond Hinnebusch, 197–208. Boulder, Colo.: Rienner, 2006.

Woldendorp, Jaap, Hans Keman, and Ian Budge. *Party Government in 48 Democracies (1945–1998).* Dordrecht: Kluwer Academic, 2000.

Wolinetz, Steven B. "The Netherlands: Continuity and Change in a Fragmented Party System." In *Parties and Party Systems in Liberal Democracies,* edited by Steven B. Wolinetz, 130–58. London: Routledge, 1988.

Wood, Wendy. "Attitude Change: Persuasion and Social Influence." *Annual Review of Psychology* 51 (2000): 539–70.

Wood, Wendy, Sharon Lundgren, Judith A. Ouellette, Shelly Busceme, and Tamela Black-Stone. "Processes of Minority Influence: Influence Effectiveness and Source Perceptions." *Psychological Bulletin* 115 (1994): 323–45.

Wood, Wendy, Gregory J. Pool, Kira Leck, and Daniel Purvis. "Self-Definition, Defensive Processing, and Influence: The Normative Impact of Majority and Minority Groups." *Journal of Personality and Social Psychology* 71 (1996): 1181–93.

"Yamasaki Eyes Removal of Ban on Japan's Peacekeepers." *Japan Economic Newswire,* September 8, 1999.

Yanık, Lerna K. "The Metamorphosis of Metaphors of Vision: 'Bridging' Turkey's Location, Role, and Identity after the End of the Cold War." *Geopolitics* 14 (2009): 531–49.

Yavuz, M. Hakan. "Political Islam and the Welfare (Refah) Party in Turkey." *Comparative Politics* 30 (1997): 63–82.

Zaller, John. "Information, Values, and Opinion." *American Political Science Review* 85 (1991): 1215–37.

Zisk, Kimberly Marten. "Japan's United Nations Peacekeeping Dilemma." *Asia-Pacific Review* 8 (2001): 21–39.

Zürcher, Erik J. *Turkey: A Modern History.* 3rd ed. London: Tauris, 2004.

# Index

*Note:* Page numbers in italics indicate tables.

Achen, Christopher H., 60
Afghanistan troop deployment case
 (Dutch), *62*
 coalition parties in, *83*
 coalition politics' role in, 118–19
 decision making in, 81–82, 109–19, 121, 269n304, 270n331, 270n335, 270n338, 271n371, 271n377
 in Dutch foreign policy, 1–2, 65, 108–9
 in images of coalition politics, *120*
 players and positions in, 110–11, *110*
 *See also* Christian Democratic Appeal party (Dutch); Democrats '66 Party (Dutch); Liberal Party (Dutch)
aggressive policies and behaviors
 in comparative case study analyses, 61, 64–66
 and diversion, 19–20, 25, *25*, 52, 55, 66, 148, 170, 196, 207, 233–34, 238, 239, 241
 and ideology, 23, 57–58, 234, 239
 in images of coalition politics, 8–9, 17–22, 24, 232, 234
 in Japanese foreign policy, 127, 153–54, 161, 177
 and junior parties, 20–21, 41, 57–58
 and number of parties, 23, 24, 56
 in quantitative studies, 22–24, 41–42, 234
 in Turkish foreign policy, 195, 207
 *See also* extreme policies and behaviors; peaceful policies and behaviors
Ahn, C. S., 131, 132–33, 134, 161–62

Akihiko, Tanaka, 126, 128, 131
Anderson, Karen, 81
Andeweg, Rudy B., 15, 35–36, 67, 72, 73, 79–80, 81–82, 94, 100, 114
Annan, Kofi, 1, 108–9, 126
Asch, Solomon, 27–28
Atatürk, Mustafa Kemal, 182. *See also* Kemalism
Auerswald, David, 18–19
Avci, Gamze, 226–27
Aydin, Mustafa, 188–89

Baehr, Peter R., 73, 77
Bahceli, Devlet, 189, 212, *214*, 215, 218, 219, 223, 224–25, 226–27, 228
Bakema, W. E., 80
Balkenende, Jan Pieter, *83*, 101, 103–4, *103*, 106, 111, *112*, 113, 114, 116
Bawn, Kathleen, 16–17
Baylis, Thomas, 14
Beasley, Ryan, 250n31
Bennett, Andrew, 60
Berger, Thomas U., 122, 125, 132, 133–35, 166
Bergman, Torbjørn, 15–16
Blondel, Jean, 13–14, 16, 35, 242
Bos, Wouter, 101, 105, 106, 110–11, 115, 117
Bot, Ben, *83*, 111, *112*, 113
Bremer, Paul, 1, 108, 116, 243
Brown, Rupert, 26, 27, 28
Bush, George H. W., 137

329

Bush, George W., 1, 106, 109, 113
Butera, Fabrizzio, 37

cabinet characteristics
  and commitment, 53, *53*, 54
  and conflict-cooperation, 49, 53, *53*, 54–55, *54*, 239
  and decision-making process, 239–40, 292nn2–6
  and extremity, 19–20, 25, 49–59, *53*, *54*, 55–56, *57*, 148, 170, 196, 233–34, 238, 239, 258n37, 292n2
  and patterns in coalition politics, 239–40
cabinet strength
  and case study outcomes, 237
  and commitment, 53, 54, *54*, 55–56, *55*, 258n37
  extremity and, 9, 19–20, 25, 42–48, 51–52, 53, *53*, 55, 66, 148, 170, 196, 233–34, 238, 239, 241, 258n37
  and inherent coalition weakness, 18, 19–20, 26, 99
  in Turkish foreign policy, 189, 207, 220, 222–23, 227, 228
cabinet type, 32–33, 42–48, *43*, *46*, *47*, *48*, 239, 257n22
Calder, Kent, 126, 133
Çalış, Şaban, 183, 186
case studies
  evidence for, 64, 260n61
  selection of, 61–63, 259n56
  significance of, 59–61
  structure and focus of, 63–66
  *See also individual cases by name*
Cem, Ismael, *190*, *194*, 212, *214*, 217, 218, 219
Chan, Steve, 22
China, 123, 159, 164, 205
Christian Democratic Appeal party (Dutch)
  in Afghanistan troop deployment case, 2, *83*, 109–10, 111, 114, 118
  in Balkenende cabinets, *103*, *112*
  in Dutch elections, *85*, *94*, *102*, *110*
  formation of, 265n141
  in Iraq War case, *83*, 100, 101–3, 104, 105–6, 107–8
  in NATO cruise missiles case, *83*, 93–97, 98–99
  in sanctions against apartheid South Africa case, *83*, 84–86, 87–90, 91, 92
  in van Agt cabinets, *86*, *95*
Çiller, Tansu, *190*, *194*, 198–99, 200–202, *202*, 204, 206–7, 209–11
CINC (Composite Indicator of National Capability), 45, 257n24
Cizre, Ümit, 283n38
Clare, Joe, 22, 23, 51
coalition cabinets, twenty-first century, 5
coalition cabinets in comparative politics, 13–17, 250n7, 251n8, 251n22, 256n4
coalition formation, 98, 105, 215, 254n102, 265n141
coalition politics and foreign policy patterns, 236, 238–39, 240
Cohen, Bernard C., 75
commitment
  and cabinet characteristics, 53, *53*, *54*, 55–56, *55*, 258n37
  and cabinet type, *46*, *47*, *48*
  in Dutch foreign policy, 67–68, 82, 92
  extremity and, 10–11, 44, 58, 257n17, 257n22
  and high-commitment behaviors, 44, *46*, 55–56, 58, 206
  and junior parties, 29, 58
  and parliamentary support, 10–11, 54, 55, 234, 239
  in quantitative analyses, 49, *53*, 54–55, *55*, 259n38
  in single-party government, 45, 55–56
  in Turkish foreign policy, 204, 206–7, 209, 218, 219, 224, 228, 231, *230*
comparative politics, coalition politics in, 13–17, 250n7, 251n8, 251n22, 256n4
Composite Indicator of National Capability (CINC), 45, 257n23
conflict-cooperation
  and cabinet characteristics, 49, 53, *53*, 54–55, *54*, 239
  and cabinet type, 32–33, 45, *46*, *46*, 47–48, *48*, 257n22
  and constraints, 59, 197, 239, 292n4
  in Dutch foreign policy, 78–79, 80–81, 82, *120*
  and ideology, *54*, 55, 56, *57*–58, 234, 239, 258n30, 292n6
  in images of coalition politics, 234–36, *235*
  in Japanese foreign policy, *178*

INDEX 331

and number of parties, 10, 54, *54*, *55*, 56, 234, 292n2, 292n3
  in quantitative studies, 41–42, *43*, 44, *46*, *48*, 49, *53*, *54*, *55*, 57, 59, 257n14, 257nn21–22
  in single-party government, 10, 16, 33, 46, 47, 233
  in Turkish foreign policy, 190–91, 207, 209, 229, *230*, 293n8
consistency, 29, *120*, *178*, 179, 190, 198, 210, 221, 229–31, *230*, 236, *237*, 237–38, 241, 243
constraint
  and behavioral expectations, 23–24, 41, 44, 107, 233, 235
  and conflict-cooperation, 59, 197, 235–36, 239, 292n4
  domestic and international, 5–6, 7, 17–19, 121, 137–38, 183, 199
  in Dutch foreign policy, 71–73, 79, 80, 81, 91, 99, 101, 105, 107, 118, 119, *120*, 121, *235*, 267n225
  as inherent in coalition cabinets, 2, 17–18, 41, 44, 91, 107, 232
  in images of coalition politics, 8–9, 17–18, 23, 233, 235–36, *235*, 239–40
  in Japanese foreign policy, 124–25, 127, 129–32, 134, 137–38, 148–49, 161, 170, 176, 177, *178*
  and peacefulness, 2, 8–9, 17–19, 23, 41, 44, 59, 119, 170, 235–36, 239, 241
  in Turkish foreign policy, 197–98, 207–8, 209, 210–11, 227, 229, *230*, 231, *235*, 282n6
  *See also* democratic peace theory
Correlates of War data set, 41, 45
Cortell, Andrew P., 127
Crichlow, Scott, 244
critical junior parties, 49, 51, 52, 57, 58, 227, 258n37. *See also* junior parties
critical parties (defined), 49
Çuhadar-Gürkaynak, Esra, 188, 213
customs union agreement case (Turkey), *62*
  coalition parties in, *190*, 286n99
  coalition politics' role in, 197–99
  decision making in, 195–97, 198–99, 286n123
  in images of coalition politics, 229, *230*, 231
  inconsistency in, 230, 231
  players and positions in, 193–95
  in Turkish foreign policy, 191–93
  *See also* Republican People's Party (Turkey); True Path Party (Turkey)
Cyprus, 289n213
  in customs union agreement case, 192–93, 194–97
  in Helsinki Summit offer case, 211–12, 214–15, 216–19, 229
  in Turkish foreign policy, 180, 182, 185, 187, 191–92, 207
  and Turkish nationalism, 213–14, 215

Davis, James W., 127
death penalty abolition case (Turkey), *62*
  coalition parties in, *190*
  coalition politics' role in, 227–28
  commitment in, 231
  decision making in, 225–28, *235*, 291n279, 291n292, 292n306
  in images of coalition politics, *230*
  players and positions in, 223–25
  in Turkish foreign policy, 220–23
  *See also* Democratic Left Party (Turkey); Motherland Party (Turkey); Nationalist Action Party (Turkey)
decision-making outcomes, explanations for, *120*, *178*, *230*, 236–41, *237*. *See also* decision-making process
decision-making process
  assessing quality of, 31–39, 254nn101–2
  and cabinet characteristics, 239–40, 292nn2–6
  in comparative case studies, 59–66, 234
  consistency in, 29, *120*, *178*, 179, 190, 198, 210, 221, 229–30, *230*, 236, *237*, 238, 241, 243
  disagreement in, 2, 4–8, 15, 22–23, 78–79, 80, 91, 93, 129, 179, 194, 232, 234, 237, 242–44
  in images of coalition politics, 232, 234–36, *235*
  in international relations, 242–45
  issue divisibility in, *230*, 236, *237*, *237*, 238
  leadership style in, 131, 149, 179, 198, 230–31, *237*
  locus of authority in, 92, 121, 228, 236, *237*, *237*, 238
  negotiation in, 15, 16, 17, 179, 240, 245, *248*

decision-making process (*continued*)
party unity in, 8, 91–92, *120*, 121, *178*, *230*, 236–37, *237*, 238, 241, 243
political calculation in, *120*, 149, 177, *178*, 179, 236, 237–38, *237*, 241
research on, 24–31, 36–39, 254n90
rigidity in, *178*, 179, *237*
theoretical implications of, 241–45
*See also* decision-making outcomes, explanations for
de Hoop Scheffer, Jaap, 1, *83*, 101, 102, 103, *103*, 105, 108, 109
de Koning, Jan, 85, *86*, 95
Demirel, Süleyman, 186, 203, 204, 213, 217, 220
Democratic Left Party (Turkey)
in death penalty abolition case, *190*, 221–22, 223, 224, 225, 226, 227–28
in 57th cabinet, 214, *214*
in Helsinki Summit offer case, *190*, 212–20
nationalism of, 214–15, 289n213
in Turkish elections, *193*, *201*, 213
democratic peace theory
and constraint, 17, 41, 58–59, 118, 119, 148, 170, 177, 197, 229
in images of coalition politics, 8–9, 17–18, 23, 235, 236
Democratic Socialist Party (Japan), *135*, *138*, *139*, 140, 141–42, 143–44, *155*
Democratic Socialist '70 party (Dutch), 85
Democrats '66 Party (Dutch), 270n338
in Afghanistan troop deployment case, 2, *83*, 109–10, 111, 113–14, 116, 117–18, 119, 270n338, 271n377
in Balkenende III cabinet, *112*
in Dutch elections, *85*, *110*
in Iraq War case, 106
in NATO cruise missiles case, *83*, 96–97, 98
depillarization, 72–73
diffusion of accountability, 9, 25, *25*, 34, 48, 52, 56–57, 59, 233–34
dissent
and extremity, 41–42
and groupthink, 26, 36, 244
in Japanese foreign policy, 162
minority parties and, 37–38
in Turkish foreign policy, 204, 219–20, 291n292

divergent thinking effect, 36–37, 91, *120*, *121*, 219, 236
diversionary theory, 19–20, 25, *25*, 52, 55, 170, 196, 197, 207, 233–34, 238, 239, 241
division of labor, 209–10, *230*, 231
Dobson, Hugo, 132
Dodd, Clement H., 35, 189
Drifte, Reinhard, 132, 151
D66 Party. *See* Democrats '66 Party (Dutch)
"dual-process" model of social influence, 28–29
Dutch cases. *See* Afghanistan troop deployment case (Dutch); Iraq War case (Dutch); NATO cruise missiles deployment case (Dutch); sanctions against apartheid South Africa case (Dutch)
Dutch foreign policy
actors in, 74–79, 262n63, 263n85
Atlanticism in, 67–68, 70, 72, 82
cabinet as primary decision-making unit in, 77–79, 81–82, 95
challenges and factors in, 67–74, 261n44
coalition formation in, 85, 265n142
commitment in, 67–68, 82, 92
conflict-cooperation in, 78–79, 80–81, 82, *120*
constraints in, 71–73, 79, 80, 81, 91, 99, 101, 105, 107, 118, 119, *120*, *235*, 267n225
and EU relations, 78, 81, 263n85
extremity in, 91, 107, 118, 119, *120*, 271n371
images of coalition politics in, 79–82, *83*, 91–92, 93–97, 99–100, 100–103, 107–8, 108–11, 118–19, *120*, 121
nationalism in, 203, 213–16, 220–21, 223, 231, 240
negotiation in, 81–82, 92, 96, 97, 98, 101–2, 105
partisanship in, 76–77, 79–80
in post–Cold War era, 69–71, 73–74, 78, 84
and Srebrenica,Yugoslavia, incident, 69–70, 72, 101, 110, 112, 113, 116, 119, 261n42
and U.S. relations, 67–69, 72, 93
*See also* Afghanistan troop deployment

case (Dutch); Iraq War case (Dutch); NATO cruise missiles deployment case (Dutch); sanctions against apartheid South Africa case (Dutch)
Dutch national elections, 85–86, *85*, 93–95, *94*, 101, *102*, 109, *110*, 265n141

East, Maurice, 44
Ecevit, Bülent, 284n70
  in death penalty abolition case, *190*, 222, 223–24, 225, 226, 228
  and 57th cabinet, *214*
  in Helsinki Summit offer case, *190*, 212, 216–17, 218, 219
  nationalism of, 215
  in Turkish foreign policy, 185–86
Economist, 93, 160, 266n179
Elman, Colin, 60
Elman, Miriam Fendius, 19, 20, 23, 33, 60
Eralp, Atila, 189, 222–23
Eralp, Yalim, 284n66, 291n279
Erbakan, Necmettin, *190*, 199–200, 200–206, *202*, 207–8, 209–11
EU
  and Dutch foreign policy, 78, 81, 263n85
  and Turkish relations, 184, 185, 191, 194–95, 198, 199, 219–20, 226, 289n213
  *See also* customs union agreement case (Turkey); death penalty abolition case (Turkey); Helsinki Summit offer case (Turkey)
European Union. *See* EU
Everts, Philip, 74, 81, 87, 93, 97, 98, 99
extreme policies and behaviors
  cabinet characteristics and, 19–20, 25, 49–59, *53, 54, 55*, 55–56, *57*, 148, 170, 196, 238, 239, 258n37, 292n2
  and cabinet type, 42–48, *46, 48*, 233–34, 257n22
  and commitment, 10–11, 44, 58, 257n17, 257n22
  in comparative case study analysis, 64–66
  diffusion of accountability in, 9, 34, 48, 52, 56–57, 59, 233–34
  and diversion, 19–20, 25, *25*, 52, 55, 66, 148, 170, 196, 207, 238, 239, 241
  and economic policies, 16–17, 242
  explanations for, 49–59

and ideology, 50–51, 239, 293n7
and images of coalition politics, 234–35, *235*
and junior parties, 10–11, 41, 44, 48, 51–52, *53, 54, 55*, 58, 233–34
and number of parties, 44–45, 54, *55*, 56–57, 233–34, 258n37, 292n2
in quantitative studies, 41, 42–48, *43, 46, 48*, 49–59, 233–34, 256n11, 257n14, 257nn17–18, 257nn22–24, 258n30

Farmers Party (Dutch), *85*
France, 4, *5*, 18–19, 20, 34, 164–65, 244
Frognier, Andre-Paul, 14

Gaenslen, Fritz, 33
*gaiatsu* thesis, 124–25, 126, 150
Gallagher, Michael, 16
Gallhofer, Irmtraud N., 34
Gartner, Scott Sigmund, 22
GATT, 89, 127, 136–37, 143–47, 148, 240. *See also* liberalization of rice imports case (Japan)
George, Alexander, 63
Germany, 4, *5*, 43, 45, 47, 49, 231, 244, 257n22
Gerner, Deborah, 44
Golan Heights peacekeeping case (Japan), 62
  coalition parties in, *135*
  coalition politics' role in, 170–71
  decision making in, 168–69, 179, 280n300
  in images of coalition politics, *178*
  in Japanese foreign policy, 163–66
  players and positions in, 166–68
  *See also* Japan Socialist Party; Liberal Democratic Party (Japan); Sakigake Party (Japan)
Goldstein, Joshua S., 43–44
Goldstein-WEIS conflict-cooperation scale, 247–48
  in case study analyses, 42–44, 49, 233
  in quantitative analyses, 64–65
Greece-Turkey relations, 180, 184, 187, 188, 192, 196, 197, 211–12, 214, 215, 216
Green, Michael J., 134, 151
Green Left Party (Dutch), *102, 110*
groupthink, 26, 36, 244

Gruenfeld, Deborah H., 37
Gulf War (1990–91), 81, 123–24, 164, 180, 186
Gürel, Şükrü Sina, 212, *214*, 217, 218, 219

Hagan, Joe, 19–20, 100
Hale, William, 181–82, 183, 189, 208, 224, 282n18, 291n273
Hata, T., *135*, *139*, 144, 145, 147, 150–51, 153–54
Helsinki Declaration. *See* Helsinki Summit offer case (Turkey)
Helsinki Summit offer case (Turkey), 62
  coalition parties in, *190*
  coalition politics' role in, 218–20
  Cyprus issue in, 211–12, 214–15, 216–19, 229
  decision making in, 216–18, 231, 290n246
  players and positions in, 212–16
  in Turkish foreign policy, 191, 211–12, 289n204, 289n206
  *See also* Democratic Left Party (Turkey); Motherland Party (Turkey); Nationalist Action Party (Turkey)
Hermann, Charles F., 33
Hewstone, Miles, 37
high-commitment behaviors, 44, 46, 55–56, *55*, 58, 206
hijacking, ideological
  in decision-making outcomes, *237*, 238
  in Dutch foreign policy, 118
  in images of coalition politics, 9, 19, 20–22, 233–34, 236
  in Japanese foreign policy, 161–62, *178*, 179
  and peacefulness, 23–24, 41
  in quantitative studies, 42, 44, 48, 51, 57–58
  in Turkish foreign policy, 63, 188–89
  *See also* junior party influence
Hirata, Keiko, 124, 128–29
Hiroshi, Fujita, 153
Hoekema, Jan, 270n335
Hofferbert, Richard, 17, 49
Hosokawa, Morihiro
  cabinet of, 138–39, *139*, 140, 141–42
  in liberalization of rice imports case, *135*, 142, 143–51
  and UNSC membership for Japan, 153, 154–55

ideology
  in case studies, 239–40
  and conflict-cooperation, *55*, *56*, 57–58, 234, 239, 258n30, 292n6
  and extremity, 50–51, 239, 293n7
  and junior parties, 9, 20, 49–50, 51, 57, 233–34, 239–40
  in quantitative analyses, 49–51, *53*, *54*, *55*, 57–58
  and senior parties, 20, 57, 58
  *See also* hijacking, ideological
India, 4, *5*, 34–35, *43*, *47*, 123
internationalism, 69, 71, 135–36, 182
international relations
  coalition foreign policy in, 241–45
  coalition politics' importance in, 1–12
  images of coalition politics in study of, 8, 13–17, 232–33
international relations theory, 7–8
Iraq
  and Dutch foreign policy, 1–2, 109, 110–11
  and Japanese foreign policy, 123, 124, 153
  and Turkish foreign policy, 180, 182, 184, 185, 186, 187, 199, 206, 208
  *See also* Iraq War case (Dutch)
Iraq War case (Dutch), 62
  coalition parties in, *83*
  coalition politics' role in, 107–8
  decision making in, 81, 82, 104–7, *235*, *237*, 238, 269n291
  in Dutch foreign policy, 100–102
  governing coalition in, *83*
  in images of coalition politics, *120*
  players and positions in, 102–3
  *See also* Christian Democratic Appeal party (Dutch); Labour Party (Dutch); List Pim Fortuyn Party (Dutch)
Ireland, Michael, 22
Irwin, Galen A., 67, 72, 79, 81–82, 94, 100
Islamic Opening case (Turkey), 62
  coalition parties in, *190*
  coalition politics' role in, 206–11
  decision making in, 204–6, 209–11, 287n173, 293n8
  extremity in, 229, 231
  in images of coalition politics, *230*
  players and positions in, 200–204
  in Turkish foreign policy, 199–200

INDEX 335

*See also* True Path Party (Turkey); Welfare Party (Turkey)
Israel
   coalition politics in, 4, *5,* 19, 21, 35, *43, 50, 56, 57,* 238, 253n76
   in quantitative case study analyses, 45, *47*
   in Turkish foreign policy, 207–8
issue divisibility, *230,* 236, 237, *237,* 238
Iversen, Torben, 17

Janis, Irving, 26, 36, 254n101
Japan Communist Party, *138, 155, 173*
Japanese cases. *See* Golan Heights peacekeeping case (Japan); liberalization of rice imports case (Japan); peacekeeping law revision case (Japan); UNSC membership case (Japan)
Japanese constitution, Article 9 of, 129–30, 152–53, 155, 157, 159, 164
Japanese foreign policy
   actors in, 127–33
   Article 9 of Japan constitution in, 129–30, 152–53, 155, 157, 159, 164
   bureaucratic influence in, 131–33, 136, 162, 165
   challenges and factors in, 122–27
   during Cold War, 122–23, 126, 129, 130, 152, 164
   constraints in, 124–25, 127, 129–32, 134, 137–38, 148–49, 161, 170, 176, 177
   decision making in, 133–34, 143–48, 150, 157–63, 168–69, 171, 175–76, *178,* 179
   explanations for case study outcomes in, *237*
   extremity in, 134, 161, 148, 170, 177, *178*
   images of coalition politics in, 133–36, 179
   nationalism in, 126–27, 128, 170
   negotiation in, 136–38, 139, 143, 146, 148–50, 166, 176, 179
   and passivity, 34, 122, 124–25, 157–58, 160, 161–62, 169, 170
   peacefulness in, 125, 157, 167–68, 176, 177
   political culture and constructivist norms in, 125–27, 127–28, 179
   in post–Cold War era, 123–26, 128–29, 130, 136, 151–52, 155, 163–64
   and U.S. relations, 122–25, 130, 160, 165, 167, 175
   *See also* Golan Heights peacekeeping case (Japan); liberalization of rice imports case (Japan); peacekeeping law revision case (Japan); UNSC membership case (Japan)
Japan New Party, *135,* 138, 140, 142, 145, *155*
Japan Renewal Party, *135,* 138–40, *138,* 141–42, 144, *155*
Japan Socialist Party, 275n95
   and Golan Heights case, *135,* 166, 167–69, 170–71
   in Hosokawa cabinet, *139*
   in Japanese elections, 126, *138, 155*
   in Japanese foreign policy, 129, 130, 134
   in liberalization of rice imports case, *135,* 138–42, 177, 179
   in peacekeeping law revision case, 163–64
   and UNSC membership case, *135,* 154–56, 157, 159, 161
Jonas, Susanne, 70–71
Jones, James, 1, 108, 116
junior parties
   and commitment, 29, 52, 58
   and consistency, 198, 229, 231, 236, 237–38, 243
   and constraint, 177, 235–36
   and cooperation, 10–11, 38, *55, 57,* 234, 258n37
   and extremity, 9, 10–11, 20–21, 23, 41, 49–50, 51–52, *53, 54,* 57–58, 233–34, 240
   and ideology, 9, 20, 27, 49–50, 51, 57, 58, 233–34, 239–40
   and negotiation, 21, 30–31
   *See also* hijacking, ideological; junior party influence
junior party influence, 19, 20–22, 24, 27, 29, 36, 41, 49–51, 58, 238, 243
Justice and Development (AK) Party (Turkey), 285n77

Kaeding, Michael, 81
Kameda, Tatsuya, 36, 38–39
Kamp, Henk, *83,* 102, 103, *103,* 104, 106, 108, 111, *112,* 117, 270n331
Kawasaki, Tsuyoshi, 125

Kemalism, 181–82, 183, 192, 195, 208, 209, 216
Klingemann, Hans-Dieter, 17, 49
Kohno, Masaru, 126
Komeito Party (Japan), *135*, 138, 139–40, *139*, 141–42, 143, 145, *155*, 172. *See also* New Komeito Party (Japan)
Kono Yohei, *135*, 154, *156*, 156–57, 158, 160–63, *174*
Kramer, Heinz, 193
Krause, Ellis S., 134
Kurdistan Worker's Party (PKK). *See* PKK
Kwan, Julianne, 36–37

Labour Party (Dutch)
  in Afghanistan troop deployment case, 109–10, 114–15, 116–18, 271n366
  in Dutch elections, 85, 94, *102*, *110*
  in Iraq War case, 83, 101–2, 103, 104, 105–6, 107–8
  in NATO cruise missiles case, 83, 93–96, 98–99
  in sanctions against apartheid South Africa case, 85, 87–88, 90
  in van Agt II cabinet, 95
Laqueur, Walter, 68–69, 99
Larrabee, F. Stephen, 180, 187
Laver, Michael, 16
leadership style, 131, 149, 179, 198, 230–31, *237*
Leblang, David, 22
Lesser, Ian O., 180, 187
Levy, Jack S., 40, 60, 61
Liberal Democratic Party (Japan)
  and Golan Heights peacekeeping case, *135*, 166, 167, 168–69, 171
  in Japanese elections, 138, *138*, *155*, *173*
  in Japanese foreign policy, 129–30
  in Japanese political system, 126, 127, 137, 140
  in liberalization of rice imports case, 142–43, 145
  in Obuchi cabinet, *174*
  in peacekeeping law revision case, *135*, 172–77
  and UNSC membership case, *135*, 152, 154, 155–58
liberalization of rice imports case (Japan), 62
  coalition parties in, *135*
  coalition politics' role in, 148–51
  decision making in, 143–48, 179, 277n168
  in images of coalition politics, *178*
  in Japanese foreign policy, 136–38
  players and positions in, 138–43
  *See also* Democratic Socialist Party (Japan); Japan New Party; Japan Renewal Party; Japan Socialist Party; Komeito Party (Japan); Sakigake Party (Japan); Shaminren Party (Japan)
Liberal Party (Dutch)
  in Afghanistan troop deployment case, 2, 83, 84, 109–11, 114, 116, 117, 270n331
  in Balkenende cabinets, *103*, *112*
  in Dutch elections, 85, 94, *102*, *110*
  in Iraq War case, 83, 100, 101–2, 103, 104–7, 108
  in sanctions against apartheid South Africa case, 83, 84–87, 88–89, 90, 91–92
  in van Agt I cabinet, 86
Liberal Party (Japan), *135*, 172–76, *173*, *174*
List Pim Fortuyn Party (Dutch), 83, 100, *102*, 103, 105, *110*, 117
locus of authority, 92, 121, 228, 236, 237, *237*, 238
London, Tamar, 22, 51, 55–56

Mair, Peter, 7, 16
Maoz, Zeev, 18, 21
Martin, Lanny W., 4, 16
Martin, Robin, 37
Metselaar, Max, 26
Milgram, Stanley, 27
minority influence, 25, 27–30, 36–38, 43, 66, 148, 198, 249n11, 252n55, 253n80
mixed-method research, 40
Miyashita, Akitoshi, 125
Mochizuki, Mike M., 123, 125–26, 132, 134
Moscovici, Serge, 28–29, 36, 253n80
Motherland Party (Turkey)
  and death penalty abolition case, *190*, 221–22, 224, 225, 227–28, 291n292
  in 57th cabinet, 214, *214*, 221
  in Helsinki Summit offer case, *190*, 212–20, 229
  True Path party coalition with, 201–2
  in Turkish elections, *193*, *201*, *213*
Mufti, Malik, 208
Mugny, Gabriel, 37

Mulgan, Aurelia George, 165–66, 169, 170, 171
Müller-Rommel, Ferdinand, 13–14, 15–16, 35
Murayama, Tomiichi
  cabinet of, *156*
  in Golan Heights peacekeeping case, *135*
  and liberalization of rice imports case, 147, 148, 150–51
  in UNSC membership case, *135*, 154, 157–60, 161, 162–63, 166, 167, 169

nationalism, 126–27, 128, 170, 182, 203, 214–15
Nationalist Action Party (Turkey)
  and death penalty abolition case, *190*, 221–22, 223–28, 229, 231, 239–40
  in 57th cabinet, 214, *214*
  in Helsinki Summit offer case, *190*, 212–20
  nationalism of, 213, 214–15, 289n213
  in Turkish elections, *201*, 213, 225
National Security Council (NSC), Turkey, 184, 186, 208, 223–24
NATO
  and Afghanistan troop deployment case, 1–2, 65, 108–19
  in Dutch foreign policy, 68–69, 70, 86–87
  and Turkish foreign policy, 180, 185, 191, 205, 207–8
  See also NATO cruise missiles deployment case (Dutch)
NATO cruise missiles deployment case (Dutch), *62*
  coalition parties in, *83*
  coalition politics' role in, 99–100
  decision making in, 98–100, 267nn224–25
  in Dutch foreign policy, 68–69, 75, 82, 92–93
  in images of coalition politics, *120*
  players and positions in, 93–97
  See also Christian Democratic Appeal party (Dutch); Democrats '66 Party (Dutch); Labour Party (Dutch)
negotiation
  in decision making, 15, 16, 17, 179, 240, 242, 245, *248*

  in Dutch foreign policy, 81–82, 92, 96, 97, 98, 101–2, 105
  in international relations, 78, 245
  in Japanese foreign policy, 136–38, 139, 143, 146, 148–50, 166, 176, 179
  and junior parties, 21, 30–31
  research on, 30–31, 254n90
  in Turkish foreign policy, 187–88, 191–96, 198, 201–2, 206, 217–18, 220, 228, 290n246
Nemeth, Charlan, 36–37
Netherlands. *See* Afghanistan troop deployment case (Dutch); Dutch foreign policy; Iraq War case (Dutch), NATO cruise missiles deployment case (Dutch); sanctions against apartheid South Africa case (Dutch)
Netherlands Communist Party, *85*, *94*
New Komeito Party (Japan), *135*, 172–73, *173*, *174*, 175–77
New Turkey Party, 223
*New York Times*, 123, 244
Nousiainen, Jaako, 242
number of parties, 23–24, 44–45, 54, *55*, 56–57, 58–59, 233–34, 239, 258n37, 259n42, 292nn2–4

Obuchi, Keizo, *135*, 172, *174*, *175*
Öcalan, Abdullah, 191, 221–22, 223, 224–26, 227, 228, 291n279. *See also* death penalty abolition case (Turkey)
Öniş, Ziya, 192, 225
Özal, Turgut, 185, 186
Ozawa, Ichiro, 127, 138–39, 140, 142, 144, 145, *156*, 172, *173*–75
Özcan, Gencer, 188
Özkeçeci-Taner, Binnur, 7–8, 187–88, *190*, 195, 196–97, 213, 214–15, 238, 285n80

Pacifist Socialist Party (Dutch), *85*, *94*
Pakistan, 123, 172, 205
Palmer, Glenn, 22, 51, 55–56
party unity, 8, 91–92, *120*, 121, *178*, 230, 236–37, *237*, 238, 241, 243
patterns in coalition politics and foreign policy, 236, 238–39, 240
peaceful policies and behaviors
  in case study analysis, 12, 58–59, 61, 64–66, 177, 235–36, *235*

peaceful policies and
  behaviors (*continued*)
  constraints and, 2, 8–9, 17–19, 23, 41,
    44, 59, 119, 170, 235–36, 239, 241,
    292n4
  and expectations, 12, 23–24, 50, 233, 236
  and ideology, 50–51
  in images of coalition politics, 17–19,
    24, 233, 236
  in Japanese foreign policy, 125, 157,
    167–68, 176, 177
  in quantitative research, 22–24, 41–42,
    44, 50–51, 65, 233
  in Turkish foreign policy, 207, 229
  *See also* democratic peace theory
peacekeeping law revision case (Japan),
    62, 259n55
  coalition parties in, *135*
  coalition politics' role in, 176–77
  decision making in, 175–76, 177, 179,
    281n334
  in Japanese foreign policy, 171–72
  players and positions in, 172–75
  *See also* Liberal Democratic Party
    (Japan); Liberal Party (Japan); New
    Komeito Party (Japan)
Peacekeeping Operations Cooperation
  Law, 164. *See also* peacekeeping law
  revision case (Japan)
Pekkanen, Robert, 134
Peterson, Susan, 20
Pijpers, Alfred, 68, 70
PKK, 181, 182, 184, 208, 221, 224, 226,
  228, 291n279. *See also* death penalty
  abolition case
  (Turkey); Öcalan, Abdullah
PKO Law. *See* peacekeeping law revision
  case (Japan)
polarization, 24–27, *25*, 76–77, 134, 201
political calculation, *120*, 149, 177, *178*,
  179, 236, 237–38, *237*, 241
political heterogeneity, 35–36, 79, 81, 134
Political Reformed Party (Dutch), *85*, *94*,
  *102*, *110*
Prins, Brandon, 19, 22, 33
procedural manipulation, 21–22, 58, 243
process tracing, 40, 60
Putnam, Robert, 6, 81

Radical Political Party (Dutch), *85*, *94*
Rathbun, Brian C., 6, 7, 250n18

rational decision-making perspective, 32,
  91
Reformed Political Union party (Dutch),
  *85*, *94*
Regan, Patrick, 22, 51, 55–56
Reiter, Dan, 22
Republican People's Party (Turkey),
  285n94
  in customs union agreement case, *190*,
    192–93, 193–97, 229
  in 50th cabinet (1993–95), 193, *194*
  in Turkish elections, *193*, *201*, *213*
rigidity, *178*, 179, *237*
Ripsman, Norrin, 18, 34
risk taking, 18, 20, 25–26, 30, 48, 55,
  56–57, 203, 234, 253n69
Robins, Philip, 182, 183, 184, 185, 187, 189,
  203, 207, 208, 217, 221, 231, 282n13
Rochon, Thomas R., 67, 71, 78, 80, 81, 96,
  264n116
Rosenbluth, Frances, 16–17
Russett, Bruce, 18

Sakigake Party (Japan)
  in Golan Heights peacekeeping case,
    *135*, 163–64, 166, 168, 169
  in Hosokawa cabinet, 138–40, *139*
  in liberalization of rice imports case,
    *135*, 139–40, 143–44
  in 1993 election, *138*, 155
  in UNSC membership case, *135*, 153–54,
    155, 157–58, 159, 160–61, 163, 177
sanctions against apartheid South Africa
  case (Dutch), 62
  coalition parties in, *83*
  coalition politics' role in, 91–92
  decision making in, 88–90, 91,
    266nn178–79
  in Dutch foreign policy, 83–85
  players and positions in, 85–88
  *See also* Christian Democratic Appeal
    party (Dutch); Liberal Party (Dutch)
Sato, Yoichiro, 124, 128–29
Schafer, Mark, 244
Scholten, Willem, *83*, *85*, *86*, 89–90
Schrodt, Philip, 44
Schuster, Jürgen, 7
Scott, L. A., 30
SDF (Self-Defense Forces), Japan, 164,
  165–66, 167–68, 169, 170, 171, 172,
  175

"Sèvres syndrome," 181
Shaminren Party (Japan), *135*, *138*, 139, *139*, 141–42, *155*
shared conceptual system, 29–30
Sheffey, S., 30
Shinoda, Tomohito, 130–31, 132, 149
Shively, W. Philips, 60
single-party government, 249n11
  in comparative politics, 13–17
  conflict-cooperation in, 10, 16, 33, 46, 47, 233
  in foreign policy behavior, 22, 23–24, 40, 41, 42–47, 55–57, 242–43
  in images of coalition politics, 233–34
  in Japanese foreign policy, 126, 134–35, 152, 162, 165
  in Turkish foreign policy, 189, 197
  *See also* cabinet type
sleeper effect, 38, 66
Snidal, Duncan, 60
Snyder, Jack, 56
Social Democratic Party of Japan. *See* Japan Socialist Party
Socialist Party (Dutch), *102*, 104, 105, 110, *110*, 115
social psychological research on coalition government, 24–31, 36–39, 198, 254n90
Solana, Javier, 212, 217, 221
Soskice, David, 17
South Korea, 123, 159, 164
Sprecher, Christopher, 19, 22, 33
Stinnett, Douglas, 19, 55
Strøm, Kaare, 8, 15–16
Sugimori, Shinkichi, 36, 38–39

Takemura, Masayoshi, 139–40, *139*, 142, 143–44, 145, 146, *156*, 158, 168
Tanaka, Shusei, 153–54, 154–55, *156*, 158, 159, 160–61, 163
Tarrow, Sidney, 40
theoretical implications, coalition foreign policy and, 241–45
Tillman, Erik, 22
Timmermans, Arco, 80
Tindale, R. Scott, 30
Tonra, Ben, 70
True Path Party (Turkey)
  in customs union agreement case, *190*, 192–99
  and death penalty abolition case, 291n273
  in Islamic Opening case, *190*, 199–200, 201–2, 204–7, 210–11, 229
  in Turkish cabinets, 193, *194*, 202, *202*
  in Turkish elections, 193, *193*, *201*, 213, 291n273
Tsuchiyama, Jitsuo, 127
Turkish cases. *See* customs union agreement case (Turkey); death penalty abolition case (Turkey); Helsinki Summit offer case (Turkey); Islamic Opening case (Turkey)
Turkish foreign policy
  actors in, 183–88, 283n42, 284n50, 284nn66–67, 284n70
  challenges and factors in, 180–82, 282n13, 282n18
  commitment level in, 204, 206–7, 209, 218, 219, 224, 228, 231
  conflict-cooperation in, 190–91, 195, 207, 209, 229, 293n8
  consistency in, 230–31, *230*
  constraints in, 197–98, 207–8, 209, 210–11, 227, 229, 231, *235*, 282n6
  decision making in, 183, 188, 190–91, 198–99, 209–10, 227–28, 229, *235*
  dissent in, 204, 219–20, 291n292
  and EU relations, 184, 185, 191, 194–95, 198, 199, 219–20, 226, 289n213
  explanations for outcomes in, *237*, *238*
  extremity in, 188, 197, 205, 207, 210–11, 219, 227, 229, *230*, 287–88n173
  images of coalition politics in, 188–91, 229, *230*, 231
  Islamism in, 65, 180, 182, 191, 199–201, 203, 206–8, 209, 210–11
  and Kemalism, 181–82, 183, 192, 195, 208, 209, 216
  military in, 184–85, 186, 208, 209, 223, 283n38, 283n40
  nationalism in, 182, 203, 213–15, 289n213
  negotiation in, 187–88, 191–96, 198, 201–2, 206, 217–18, 220, 228, 290n246
  in post–Cold War era, 180, 182, 199
  in Turkish history, 181
  U.S. relations and, 180, 184–85, 186, 187, 194, 204, 205

Turkish foreign policy (*continued*)
  *See also* customs union agreement case (Turkey); death penalty abolition case (Turkey); Helsinki Summit offer case (Turkey); Islamic Opening case (Turkey)
Turkish Grand National Assembly (TGNA), 186, 223
Turkish national elections, 193, *193*, 201, *201*, 212, *213*, 284n49, 285n77, 291n273
Tweede Kamer (Dutch), 75, 76, 85, 115–16

UN. *See* United Nations (UN)
unanimity, 21–22, 26, 33, 38–39, 58, 66, 130–31
UN Disengagement Force (UNDOF), 166, 168–69, 170, 280n300
United Kingdom, 5, 43, 45, 47, *47*, 257n22
United Nations (UN)
  and Dutch foreign policy, 1, 69–70, 84, 87, 101, 102, 106, 108, 109, 114
  in Turkish foreign policy, 185, 205, 206
  *See also* Golan Heights peacekeeping case (Japan); peacekeeping law revision case (Japan); UNSC membership case (Japan)
United Nations Security Council (UNSC). *See* UNSC membership case (Japan)
United States
  Dutch relations with, 67–69, 72, 93
  Japanese relations with, 122–25, 130, 160, 165, 167, 175
  Turkish relations with, 180, 184–85, 186, 187, 194, 204, 205
  *See also* Iraq War case (Dutch)
UNSC membership case (Japan), 62
  coalition parties in, *135*
  coalition politics' role in, 161–63
  decision making in, 157–61, 179
  in images of coalition politics, *178*
  in Japanese foreign policy, 151–54
  players and positions in, 154–57, *155*
  *See also* Japan Socialist Party; Liberal Democratic Party (Japan); Sakigake Party (Japan)
Uruzgan, Afghanistan. *See* Afghanistan troop deployment case (Dutch)
Uslu, Nasuh, 193

van Agt, Dries, *83*, 85, *86*, 88, 90, 94, *95*, 96
Vanberg, Georg, 4
van der Klaauw, Chris, *83*, 85, *86*, 89
van der Stoel, Max, *83*, 94, *95*
van der Vleuten, Anna, 71, 73, 76–77
van Mierlo, Hans, *83*, 94, *95*, 98
van Staden, Alfred, 72, 73
Verbeek, Bertjan, 26, 71, 73, 76–77, 261n42, 262n63
Vertzberger, Yaacov Y., 25–26, 253n69
Voorhoeve, Joris, 67, 73, 75–76

Warwick, Paul V., 15
Welfare Party (Turkey)
  in 54th cabinet, *202*
  hawkish ideology of, 239–40
  and Islamic Opening case, *190*, 199, 203–5, 206–11, 239–40
  rise of, 200–201, 202–3
  in Turkish elections, *193*, 201–2, *201*
West Germany, 4, 7, 17, 21, 34, 43, 45, *47*, 50, 52, 56, *57*, 97

Yavuz, M. Hakan, 200, 210
Yılmaz, Mesut, 213, *214*, 216, 221, 223, 224
Yoshida Doctrine, 122–23, 129–30